TEXAS

GUIDE

OPEN ROAD TRAVEL GUIDES SHOW YOU
HOW TO BE A TRAVELER – NOT A TOURIST!

*Whether you're going abroad or planning a trip in the United States, take Open Road along on your journey. Our books have been praised by **Travel & Leisure, The Los Angeles Times, Newsday, Booklist, US News & World Report, Endless Vacation, American Bookseller, Coast to Coast,** and many other magazines and newspapers!*

Don't just see the world – experience it with Open Road!

ABOUT THE AUTHOR

Judy Moore is a professional travel writer who makes her home in Austin, Texas. She is the co-author of *Teach Central Europe*, an educational directory for those interested in teaching opportunities in Eastern and Central Europe. She is also the author of Open Road's *Vietnam Guide*.

BE A TRAVELER, NOT A TOURIST - WITH OPEN ROAD TRAVEL GUIDES!

Open Road Publishing has guide books to exciting, fun destinations on four continents. As veteran travelers, our goal is to bring you the best travel guides available anywhere!

No small task, but here's what we offer:

• All Open Road travel guides are written by authors with a distinct, opinionated point of view – not some sterile committee or team of writers. Our authors are experts in the areas covered and are polished writers.

• Our guides are geared to people who want to make their own travel choices. We'll show you how to discover the real destination – not just see some place from a tour bus window.

• We're strong on the basics, but we also provide terrific choices for those looking to get off the beaten path and *experience* the country or city – not just *see* it or pass through it.

• We give you the best, but we also tell you about the worst and what to avoid. Nobody should waste their time and money on their hard-earned vacation because of bad or inadequate travel advice.

• Our guides assume nothing. We tell you everything you need to know to have the trip of a lifetime – presented in a fun, literate, no-nonsense style.

• And, above all, we welcome your input, ideas, and suggestions to help us put out the best travel guides possible.

TEXAS

GUIDE

BE A TRAVELER - NOT A TOURIST!

Judy Moore

OPEN ROAD PUBLISHING

OPEN ROAD PUBLISHING

We offer travel guides to American and foreign locales. Our books tell it like it is, often with an opinionated edge, and our experienced authors always give you all the information you need to have the trip of a lifetime. Write for your free catalog of all our titles, including our golf and restaurant guides.

Catalog Department, Open Road Publishing
P.O. Box 284, Cold Spring Harbor, NY 11724

E-mail:
Jopenroad@aol.com

Dedicated to Ms. Janet Peterson

1st Edition

Cover photos copyright Paris Permenter and John Bigley. Maps by Rob Perry. The author has made every effort to be as accurate as possible, but neither she nor the publisher assumes responsibility for the services provided by any business listed in this guide; for any errors or omissions; or any loss, damage, or disruptions in your travels for any reason.

I'd like to extend a big Texas thanks to: Dean Barrera, Brenda Baylor, Francis Blatt, Marci Buck, Dr. Christopher Champion, Dr. and Mrs. Minuth of El Paso, Mike Minuth, Mr. and Mrs. Michael of Houston, Susan Michael of Austin, Mr. and Mrs. Moore and Tess, Dr. Pringle of St. Edward's University in Austin, Daniel Springer, Tony Yardley, Cynthia Wilberts, Mr. and Mrs. Wright of Dallas.

TABLE OF CONTENTS

1. INTRODUCTION   13

2. EXCITING TEXAS! - OVERVIEW   14

3. SUGGESTED ITINERARIES   21

4. LAND & PEOPLE   27
Land   27
People   30

5. A SHORT HISTORY   35

6. PLANNING YOUR TRIP   50
Before You Go   50
    When to Go – Climate & Weather   50
    What to Pack   51
    Travel Specialists   51
    Foreign Consulates   52
Getting to Texas   53
    Major Airlines Serving Texas   53
Getting Around Texas   54
    By Air   54
    By Train   54
    By Boat   54
    By Bus   54
    By Car   54
    By Ferry   57
    Traveling to Mexico   58
Accommodations   59
    Hotels & Motels   59
    Bed & Breakfast   60

CONTENTS

Guest Ranches   61
Youth Hostels   61
Park Systems   61

7. BASIC INFORMATION   63

Banking & Money   63
Cost of Living & Travel   63
Holidays   64
Health Concerns   64
Retiting in Texas   64
Staying Out of Trouble   65
Taxes   65
Telegrams   65
Time   65

8. SPORTS & RECREATION   66

Biking   66
Birdwatching   67
Horseback Riding   67
Hiking   68
Hunting & Fishing   68
Running   69
Water Sports   70
Spectator Sports   70

9. TAKING THE KIDS   71

10. MAJOR EVENTS   74

Calendar of Monthly Events   74
Outdoor Musicals   75
Food Festivals   76
Cooking Festivals   76

11. FOOD & DRINK   78

Southern Cooking, Texas Style   78
Barbecue   79
Tex-Mex   80
Chain Restaurants   81
Mail Order Food From Texas   82
Home Grown   82
Produce   83

CONTENTS

Hard Liquor   83
Beer   84
Wine   84

12. TEXAS' BEST PLACES TO STAY   85

13. CENTRAL TEXAS   88
Austin   88
   Arrivals & Departures   90
   Orientation   90
   Getting Around Town   90
   Where to Stay   91
   Where to Eat   95
   Seeing the Sights   104
   Nightlife & Entertainment   106
   Sports & Recreation   110
   Excursions & Day Trips   110
   Practical Information   111
Waco   111
San Marcos   114
Wimberly   118
New Braunfels   121
Johnson City   127
Fredericksburg   130
   Luckenbach   135
Comfort   136
   Sisterdale   139
Kerrville   139
Bandera   142

14. NORTH TEXAS   145
Dallas   145
   Arrivals & Departures   145
   Orientation   146
   Getting Around Town   148
   Where to Stay   149
   Where to Eat   152
   Seeing the Sights   159
   Nightlife & Entertainment   163
   Sports & Recreation   164
   Shopping   165
   Excursions & Day Trips   165
   Practical Information   166

CONTENTS

Fort Worth   166
Abilene   174
Lubbock   177
Amarillo   180

15. EAST TEXAS   184

Houston   184
   Arrivals & Departures   186
   Orientation   188
   Getting Around Town   188
   Where to Stay   190
   Where to Eat   196
   Seeing the Sights   201
   Nightlife & Entertainment   206
   Sports & Recreation   209
   Shopping   211
   Excursions & Day Trips   212
      Liberty   212
   Practical Information   213
Galveston   214
Columbus   218
La Grange   220
Brenham   222
Burton   226
Independence   227
Chappel Hill   228
Bryan/College Station   229
Caldwell   231
Palestine   233
Rusk   237
Athens   238
Tyler   238
San Augustine   241
Jefferson   243

16. SOUTH TEXAS   246

San Antonio   246
   Arrivals & Departures   247
   Orientation   248
   Getting Around Town   248
   Where to Stay   249
   Where to Eat   254
   Seeing the Sights   258

CONTENTS

Nightlife & Entertainment   265
Sports & Recreation   267
Shopping   267
Excursions & Day Trips   268
Practical Information   268
Castroville   268
Seguin   272
Corpus Christi   275
Kingsville   284
Brownsville   286
    Matamoros, Mexico   289
    Port Isabel   290
South Padre Island   290
Mc Allen   294
    Reynosa, Mexico   296
    West of McAllen   297
    East of McAllen   298
Laredo   299
    Nuevo Laredo, Mexico   302
    San Ygnacio   303

17. WEST TEXAS   304

San Angelo   304
Junction   307
    Rocksprings   309
Del Rio   310
    Acuna, Mexico   315
    Brackettville   315
    Uvalde & Langtry   316
Midland/Odessa   317
Fort Stockton   321
Fort Davis   323
Alpine   327
    Marfa   330
Big Bend National Park   330
El Paso   335
    Arrivals & Departures   336
    Orientation   337
    Getting Around Town   337
    Where to Stay   338
    Where to Eat   340
    Seeing the Sights   343
    Nightlife & Entertainment   350

CONTENTS

Sports & Recreation   351
Shopping   352
Excursions & Day Trips   354
Practical Information   354
Juarez, Mexico   355

INDEX   358

MAPS

Texas   15
Downtown Austin   89
Dallas Area   147
Downtown Dallas   161
Houston   185
Downtown San Antonio   259
El Paso   345

CONTENTS

SIDEBARS

The Largest Texas Cities   14
Coastal Wildlife Refuge Areas   30
Native American Sites in Texas   31
Texas, The Mother of all Capitals!   34
Driving El Camino Real Today   37
Famous Texans from Tennessee   38
How Did Texas Join the Union?   40
Texas History Timeline   41
Majestic Courthouses of Texas   43
The Scandalous State   45
Trace Your Own Texas Genealogy   49
Texas Highway Abbreviations   56
Major Hotel Chains in Texas   60
The Best Barbecue in Texas   79
Hotter Than Hot   80
Central Texas in the Spring   87
The Bats   107
Volksmarsch   126
The Easter Fires of Fredericksburg   130
Barbecue Road Trip!   133
Spend Your Holidays in Comfort   137
Festivals in Kerrville   140
Helpful Numbers for DFW Airport   146
The Common Names of Dallas Highways   148
Dallas' Intimate, Historic Hotels   150
How Barbed Wire Changed the West   183
Sam Houston   186
Houston Highways & Their Changing Names   188
Resorts in the Houston Area   193
Transco Tower   202
The Jung Center in Houston   204
The Houston International Festival   209
Liberty's Bell   213
Texas' Only Native American Earth Mounds   236
Christmas Celebrations in East Texas & Louisiana   243
St. Louis Day Celebration   271
South Texas Golf   282
It's Never Too Late To Learn Something!   285
Eco-Educational Tourism   314
Ranger Stations in Big Bend   331
El Paso's Scenic Drives   344

1. INTRODUCTION

The Lone Star State, truly a land of diversity, opens its rich heritage to visitors. On a trip to Texas, you can experience many vacations in one. The rugged frontier past stands proudly next to futuristic modern cities. Not only does each region have its own demeanor, each city reveals a unique personality. You could spend a lifetime discovering the many aspects of Texas, but you only need a short visit to fall in love with it.

Texas is so large that many natives have never ventured to its far corners. El Paso is closer to Los Angeles than to Houston. And each city offers so much, you do not have to travel far for entertainment. Two of the nation's largest metropolitan areas, Dallas and Houston, give Texas famous skylines. The urban centers are alive with arts, music and entertainment.

Nature lovers find their own paradise in Texas. The rugged hills of Central Texas have excellent routes for bicycle touring. The sweeping coastline of the Gulf of Mexico boasts year-round fishing. An easy hike near Lake Amistad leads to ancient cave paintings of Native Americans. Getting off the beaten track will bring you face-to-face with living art. Texas' own slice of Route 66 leads to the quirky "Cadillac Ranch." Something akin to monumental art, the Ranch consists of ten vintage Cadillacs buried askew in the Panhandle plains.

Part of the excitement of Texas is its mystery. The "Marfa Lights," unexplained luminous globes that hover in the night sky, haunt the small west Texas town of Marfa. Venture to the home of the "Law West of the Pecos" to find the truth behind the legend of Judge Roy Bean. In Dallas, you can visit the Conspiracy Museum, which covers far more than theories about the assassination of President Kennedy.

Whether you desire excitement or solitude, the many cultures and landscapes of Texas will enchant all tastes. From the New West in Luckenbach or the Old West in Amarillo, Texas is unlike any other place in the world.

2. EXCITING TEXAS! - OVERVIEW

The legendary land of cowboys and oil barons lives on next to some of the most cosmopolitan cities in the world. On a trip to Texas you will find breathtaking landscapes, rich history and entertainment for every taste. From glorious beaches to mountainous desert, over one-quarter of a million square miles lie at your disposal.

One of the most striking aspects of Texas is how new things are. The Native Americans of the region, for the most part, did not change the face of the landscape, but were content to live off the land, which was not developed until hundreds of years after its discovery by Europeans. The buildings which are oldest in the state probably date from the early nineteenth century.

Texas is the second largest state in area, behind Alaska, and the second largest in population, behind California. Only within the last four years did Texas surpass New York in population. Today over 18.4 million people call Texas home. One hundred years ago, over 80 percent of Texans lived in rural areas. That has completely reversed today, with over 80 percent living in cities. You will be astonished at how distinctive each city is in Texas.

THE LARGEST TEXAS CITIES
Dallas: 1,047,000
San Antonio: 1,035,000
Houston: 1,700,00
El Paso: 554,000
Austin: 501,000
Fort Worth: 465,000

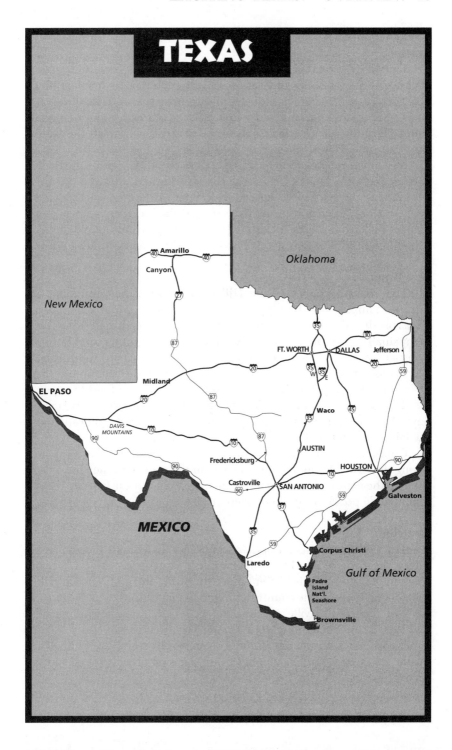

CENTRAL TEXAS

Austin

The state capital, Austin, is the largest city in central Texas. One of the fastest growing areas in the nation, it is a center of higher learning, government and high-tech industry. The **University of Texas**, with its large reserve holdings and active arts offerings, breathes international culture into Austin. The diverse theater and art scene reflects the avant-garde attitude of Austinites.

Live music can be found in coffee houses, trendy jazz clubs and in the rhythm and blues bars for which the city is renowned. Austin is the only city in the country to have its own television station devoted to area music. Many extraordinary musicians have started their careers with performances on Austin stages, including Janis Joplin and Stevie Ray Vaughn. Along famous 6th Street, stately historic buildings hum with live music.

New Braunfels

The charming cities of the **Hill Country** owe their founding to European immigrants. In this part of the state, the rugged frontier life in Texas produced modest structures made from local wood and stone. The many small homes and churches built by settlers emigrating from Europe bring a distinct character to the hills of central Texas. At one time central Texas was actually the western frontier. The isolated communities that thrived here retained much of the charm and heritage of old Europe.

This is paradise for nature lovers. Along the cool rivers you can enjoy days of kayaking, fishing or scuba diving. In the evenings you can enjoy the fabulous Southwestern cuisine of charming restaurants.

Country music is one way that the old European traditions remain strong. In **Gruene**, the oldest dance hall in the state, Gruene Hall, hosts some of the nation's foremost musicians. And you can still listen to bands that include polka in their repertoire, mixed in with country or rock.

Kerrville

The Hill country is a popular retreat for Texans. In the southern region the towns of **Bandera** and **Kerrville** have made ranching a form of tourism. Vacation ranches offer horseback riding and golf. The Kerrville folk festival is one of the country's foremost celebrations of native music.

Just north of Kerrville is an amazing section of dramatic, winding hills and vast lakes. **Enchanted Rock**, a spot regarded as sacred by Native Americans, is a giant granite dome surrounded by stone faced hills. The beauty and serenity of Enchanted Rock attracts nature lovers and sportsmen.

NORTH TEXAS

The old west thrived in north Texas, where rolling plains and steep canyons provided a backdrop for cattle drives and outlaws. Apache and Commanche once dominated the dry praries, and their legacy colors local history. Immense ranches stretched across the horizon, seemingly to the end of the land itself, and changed the face of Texas forever.

Amarillo

Only in Texas can you visit the **XIT**, the largest ranch on earth. The story of its founding sounds like a tale spun over a cowboy's campfire. Three million acres of land was given in payment for the construction of the state capital building, which stands in the center of Austin. Cowboys still test their skills at the XIT Rodeo.

Amarillo is in the northern region of the panhandle. It is a dream destination for a road trip. Not only does it sit right on the old Route 66, but is near the nation's second largest canyon.

The stark Texas plains dramatically give way to the red rock-face of **Palo Duro Canyon** in the northernmost lands. You can hike along the burnt orange canyon and stay in a cabin at one of the largest state parks. Here buffalo still roam the range, only today they are a protected species.

Forth Worth

In the saloons of **Hell's Half-acre** in Fort Worth the most menacing and notorious mingled. Bonnie and Clyde are said to have passed through, trying to evade lawmen. Doc Holliday practiced the art of dentistry in nearby Dallas.

Rugged settlers, hungry for the opportunities of a new frontier, braved sparse vegetation, fierce weather and hostility to carve out cities against all odds. Desolate army forts still stand as a tribute to those who chose this life. The settlers would be proud to see the modern ranges tamed by irrigation, producing grain, different crops and some of the state's finest wine.

Lubbock

Buddy Holly, whose rock and roll music changed our culture, hailed from Lubbock, which still keeps the music traditions of the south alive in its vibrant nightlife and active live music scene.

The richness of Texas' ancient history also is evident in Lubbock. The **Lubbock Lake Archaeological Site** has yielded evidence of Native American culture that is over 12,000 years old. The park has hiking trails that lead to archaeology excavations and a museum that explains the finds.

Dallas

Dallas stands on the borderlands of east and north Texas, overlooking both. Dallas is a new breed of city, offering the pleasure of both urban and suburban lifestyles. The monumental architecture of downtown Dallas fills the eye and boggles the mind.

For a city of its great size, Dallas is easy to visit as a tourist. **Dealy Plaza** is a short walk from the colorful **West End** area. You can take the light rail into downtown. **Deep Ellum** offers magical nightlife. Renowned music, dance and theater can satisfy the most sophisticated taste.

Dallas and Houston, illuminated masterpieces of modern development, are tributes to all Texans have become. Fine stores, extraordinary restaurants and vibrant clubs compare to the world's best. Houston, the second largest metropolitan area in the state, is the heart of east Texas.

EAST TEXAS

Houston

Nowhere is the contrast between old and new more apparent than in Houston. The city erupted with the gush of Texas crude oil and grew into an immense international city. In Houston you will never run out of diversions. The city offers a thriving cultural scene and a large museum district. You will discover new worlds in Houston, like exciting amusement parks and NASA's Visitors Center. An exciting nightlife, world class hotels and shopping are all found within proximity of the beautiful coast.

Galveston

The beautiful Victorian homes of Galveston testify to the grandeur of the city. At the turn of the century it was the largest port on the Texas Gulf Coast, with an affluent social scene to match. Today when you visit, the Strand, Galveston's main street, is a magical renovated Victorian city. The mansions of the elite families are now open for public tours.

A devastating hurricane whipped through the city and left it frozen in time. Only the most magnificent of the buildings remained, and the city never regained its port. Now it is a resort town.

Brenham & Washington

Thick woodlands characterize the region, which has a great deal in common with its eastern neighbor, Louisiana. Both French and Spanish colonists coveted beautiful east Texas. But neither could hold on to this crossroads of culture. In the dense wooded acres along the **Brazos River**, the small towns where the birth of the Texas independence movement took shape. The great frontiersmen of Texas legend — Davy Crockett, Stephen F. Austin, Sam Houston — were drawn to this land. They embarked on the creation of an independent state. Later in this area, European immigrants transformed the dense woods into pristine farms. The once dense woodland around Brenham is now a landscape of green rolling hills with cattle ranches, stables and dairies.

You can visit the unique cultural heritage left by the Native Americans of the eastern region. One such group were the **Caddo**, a tribe of the Mississippian culture who settled near the Big Thicket. The earth mounds built by the Caddo survive. Although they left the region long before colonization, the name *Tejas*, from which Texas is derived, is a Caddo word which means "friendship."

SOUTH TEXAS

South Texas is proud to be a land where two nations, cultures and histories meet. No symbol better represents Texas than the **Alamo**, which remains defiantly in the center of the modern city. The city is surrounded by history, from the jazz age buildings downtown to the ancient Spanish Missions.

San Antonio

The gorgeous **River Walk**, in the heart of downtown, has terrific dining, music and entertainment. An amazing array of culture and history awaits you in San Antonio. From ancient missions to modern art, the city proudly celebrates the past and future. This is probably the most Texan of any city, simply because the Alamo makes it so. You can spend an entire day at the Alamo, and in the beautiful downtown area.

In the evening, you can enjoy shows on the outdoor stage at the **River Center**, then take a cruise down the river before or after dinner. During any time of the year, you will find cultural activities galore. The warm people of San Antonio may be the friendliest in Texas, in a state known for hospitality.

Corpus Christi

The sparkling water of the Gulf of Mexico graces Texas' long coastline. Along the warm waters here, life seems to move at a slower, tropical pace. The riches of nature are eerily within your grasp. Deep sea fishing, surfing and swimming are but a few ways to spend your time here. You can also enjoy exceptional sailing easily in Corpus Christi Bay. Migratory birds inhabit the area's wetlands, making it a birdwatcher's paradise. Fresh seafood, miles of coastal nature preserves and tropical foliage attract visitors from around the world. And the city is just a few hours drive from the exciting border towns.

Kingsville

When you visit south Texas, you can see where real cowboys origi-nated. The land of the first ranches in North America has unique traditions dating back centuries. The **King Ranch** introduced longhorn cattle to the state. The tradition of Mexican vaqueros took on a new form: the Texas cowboy. Borrowing from the dress and gear used further south, Texans began to blaze new trails across their own land.

South Padre Island

South Texas shines from the vibrant cultural mix of Mexico and Texas, and it is most apparent in the resort town of **South Padre Island**. Spectacular dune-filled beaches are the backdrop to a host of resort hotels on the tip of Padre Island. Here the seafood is freshest, water sports most exciting, the atmosphere most inviting. Just a few miles away is the city of **Brownsville**, and the neighboring town of **Matamoros, Mexico**. Filled with history and awash in natural beauty, this part of the state attracts thousands of winter sun worshippers.

WEST TEXAS

Big Bend & Beyond

The **Chihuahuan Desert** is awash in flowering cactus and rocky ledges. The amazing desert landscape was once Commanche territory. The epic struggles of settlement — war, railroads, outlaws — are the life story of west Texas. Tickle your imagination by walking through the real frontier forts and small settlement houses.

To the north, the majestic **Davis Mountains** rise through the desert to one of the clearest horizons on earth. You can venture into the galaxy at the **McDonald Observatory**, which regularly lets the public view the heavens with giant telescopes.

El Paso

The enchantment of west Texas is characterized by the rich sunsets on the wide horizon. In **El Paso** you have four hundred years of history within your gaze. The **missions** of west Texas are state's oldest structures, dating from the Spanish empire. At the same time, the modern arts and culture of El Paso blossom.

A truly international city, El Paso is the gateway to the west for Texas. Its twin city in Mexico, **Juarez**, is the largest border town in Texas. From El Paso, you can embark on a journey to the magnificent Guadalupe mountains and New Mexico, the spectacular Copper Canyon and Mexi-can Pacific coast, or the Texas desert.

3. SUGGESTED ITINERARIES

There is so much to do and see in Texas, that you could easily spend a few weeks just getting to the basics. Most visitors — and natives — get around the state by driving. The following area itineraries have at least two weeks of options packed into one week. They are designed for a person arriving at the major urban center of one of the areas in the state. The basics are covered, then a "weekend" extension is offered. These weekend extensions take you to the most popular and representative spot within a day's drive. If you have the time, extend the weekends for travel at a slower pace or to cover more territory.

If you plan to travel between cities by plane, you can easily mix and match pieces of the itineraries to suit your timetable and schedule.

CENTRAL TEXAS TOUR

Day One: Arrive in Austin. Take a leisurely stroll down Congress Avenue and the historic 6th Street. Dine in the downtown area.

Day Two: Tour the State Capital Complex. Begin at the visitors center building, then the Capitol itself, and finish with the Governor's Mansion. Take in some live music on 6th Street in the evening.

Day Three: Enjoy the outdoors at Zilker Park and the Austin Nature Center. Walk along Town Lake. Drive to the Wildlife Research Center in the afternoon.

Day Four: Visit the University of Texas campus and the LBJ Library and Museum. Spend some time on Guadalupe Street, the Drag. Attend a cultural performance at the university.

Day Five: Enjoy the arts; Visit Laguna Gloria Art Museum and the Austin Art Museum. Dine and enjoy the nightlife in the Warehouse District.

Extended Tour

Day Six: Drive through the Hill Country to Fredericksburg. Stop at the LBJ State and National Park. Spend the night in Fredericksburg.

Day Seven: Visit Enchanted Rock. Bring a picnic lunch and spend the day at this serene park.

EAST TEXAS TOUR

Day One: Arrive in Houston. Drive through or go shopping in the Galleria and Post Area. Dine at one of the many restaurants there.

Day Two: Go to Allen's Landing Park. visit the historic beginnings of the city. Walk throughout the pedestrian tunnel system to visit the monumental buildings downtown. Dine in the theater area and take in a play.

Day Three: Visit NASA and Clear Lake. If you have time, drive to the Astrodome and take a tour. Watch a sports event in the evening.

Day Four: Visit Hermann Park; choose from the museums and gardens or zoo. In the evening, go out in the downtown area.

Day Five: Visit the Houston Musuem of Fine Arts and the Menil Collection.

Extended Tour

Day Six: Drive to Galveston. Walk along the sea-wall and along the historic Strand. Have dinner on the Strand.

Day Seven: Enjoy the beach, engage in some water sports or bird watching.

NORTH TEXAS TOUR

Day One: Arrive in Dallas. Visit the West End or Deep Ellum area and dine there.

Day Two: Visit the Dallas Museum of Art. Walk downtown and visit the Water Gardens Building and Neiman Marcus. In the evening, go to Greenville Avenue for food and fun,

Day Three: Visit Fort Worth. Check out the Kimball Museum and the cultural district. Go to the Stockyards in the evening. If possible, spend the night.

Day Four: Spend the day in Dallas visiting the Kennedy Memorial, the Sixth Floor Museum and the Conspiracy Museum. Take the trolley to McKinney Avenue for dinner.

Day Five: Spend the day at Fair Park, visiting the museums and grounds.

Day Six: Fly to Amarillo. Tour the city and Texas' own slice of Route 66.

Day Seven: Spend the day at Palo Duro Canyon. Hike along the nature trails and enjoy the breathtaking sunset.

SOUTH TEXAS TOUR

Day One: Arrive in San Antonio. Take a boat tour of the San Antonio River. Stroll along the River Walk and spend the evening dining and enjoying the festive atmosphere.

Day Two: Visit the Alamo. Return to the River Walk and visit River Center for shopping and dining. In the evening watch a show at the outdoor theater or at the IMAX.

Day Three: Take a tour of the Spanish Missions. If you have extra time, visit the Institute of Texan Cultures to see what life inside the missions looked like. In the evening, enjoy a cultural performance downtown.

Day Four: Make a day trip to Castroville to see the many historic buildings preserved in this Hill Country town.

Day Five: Spend the day at the Brackenridge Park, the museums and botanical gardens. Visit the San Antonio Art Museum.

Extended Tour

Day Six: Drive to Laredo to visit the Texas-Mexico border. Eat dinner at Victoria's in Nuevo Laredo.

Day Seven: Visit San Augustine Square in Laredo. Then cross the border for shopping and sight seeing in Mexico.

WEST TEXAS TOUR

Day One: Arrive in El Paso. Visit the downtown area and Chamizal National Monument. Dine in one of the popular restaurants along Cincinnati Street.

Day Two: Visit the Art Museum and the small galleries that display the work of regional artists. Treat yourself to a juicy steak at an area steakhouse.

Day Three: Take the trolley to Juarez, Mexico. Spend the day exploring areas of interest on the trolley route. Wind up with a shopping spree in the market area. Have dinner and drinks as Carlos n' Charlies.

Day Four: Take a tour of the Spanish Missions and then the Tigua Reservation. Have dinner at the Tigua Casino.

Day Five: Drive to Franklin Mountains State Park. Take in the fresh air and amazing view from the nature trails. Visit the Wilderness museum. In the evening, take advantage of the many cultural events held in El Paso.

Extended Tour

Day Six: Drive to Fort Davis, making a stop at either Hueco Tanks State Park for some light hiking, or at Balmorhea State Park, for a swim in the warm spring waters.

Day Seven: Make an early trip to the preserved Fort Davis complex and museum. The drive through the mountains to the McDonald Observatory for the tour of the telescopes. Participate in the solar observation held in the afternoon. Return to El Paso along the scenic mountain highway.

THE OLD WEST TOUR

Day One: Arrive in Fort Worth, visit the Stockyards during the day. Get suited up in your finest cowboy hat and boots to go to Billy Bob's in the evening.

Day Two: Visit the downtown arts district. After touring the Kimball Musuem, visit the museums that house art that depicts the old west.

Day Three: Drive (or fly) to Abilene. Along the drive, stop at historic Fort Griffin, north of Abilene.

Day Four: Visit Abilene and Fort Phantom Hill.

Day Five: Continue south to San Angelo, making a stop at Buffalo Gap.

Day Six: Visit San Angelo and Fort Concho, a major stop for stagecoach routes. Go to Miss Hattie's museum, an old west saloon.

Day Seven: Return along the open Texas highway to Fort Worth. Make a stop in Dublin to see the old Dr. Pepper bottling plant and museum.

THE REPUBLIC OF TEXAS TOUR

Day One: Arrive in Houston. Visit Allen's landing and the downtown historic area.

Day Two: Drive along Highway 290 to Brenham, enjoy the quaint small town atmosphere. Visit the Blue Bell creamery.

Day Three: Spend the day at Washington-on-the-Brazos State Park. Take day a trip to Independence and Chappel Hill.

Day Four: Continue along Highway 290 to Austin. Tour the State Capital, State Archives building and Governor's mansion.

Day Five: Enjoy Austin.

Day Six: Continue to San Antonio via Interstate Highway 35. Visit the Alamo. Spend the evening on the River Walk.

Day Seven: Tour the Missions or visit the Institute of Texan Cultures.

Day Eight: Spend the day doing what you skipped yesterday.

Day Nine: Drive to Columbus via Interstate Highway 10.

Day Ten: Continue onto Houston via Interstate Highway 10.

THE COASTAL BEND TOUR

Day One: Arrive in Corpus Christi. Visit the port of Corpus Christi and museum complex. Stroll along the waterfront, then dine at a seafood restaurant.

Day Two: Take a sailing tour of the Bay of Corpus Christi. Enjoy the laid-back nightlife of downtown Corpus Christi.

Day Three: Drive to Port Aransas; enjoy the best surf in the coastal bend and stay at a beach-front hotel or condo.

Day Four: Go deep sea fishing, diving or just relax on the beach. Drive down the island to visit the National Seashore. Spend the night in Port Aransas.

Day Five: Take Highway 37 to Highway 77, and head south to Kingsville. Visit the King Ranch or enjoy Baffin Bay. Spend the night in Kingsville.

Day Six: Have lunch at the King's Inn, then continue south to South Padre Island.

Day Seven and on: Enjoy the best beaches in Texas, and take the time to visit Brownsville and Matamoros, Mexico. Return by car, or fly from the Brownsville Airport.

TEXAS WINE & BEER TOUR

Day One: Arrive in Austin. Visit the modern Celis Brewery and in the evening dine at the Bitter End and Waterloo Brewpubs.

Day Two: Take Highway 290 west to Fredericksburg, with a stop at Sister Creek Vineyards in Sisterdale. Dine and drink at Fredericksburg's Brewery.

Days Three and Four: Head south, taking Highways 16 to 39, then Highway 83 to Uvalde. Get on Highway 90 west to Del Rio. In Del Rio visit the oldest winery in the state, Val Verde Winery. Take an extra day to visit Acuna, Mexico, or Lake Amistad.

Days Five and Six: Take Highway 90 east, all the way to San Antonio. In San Antonio, visit the large Lone Star Brewery; have dinner at the Laboratory brew pub.

Day Seven: Take Highway 90 east to Shiner, which is on Alternate Highway 90. Visit the Spoetzl Brewery, which is the second oldest brewery in the state. Rejoin Highway 90/Interstate Highway 10 and continue east. Make a stop at the Kreische Brewery State Historic Park, 17 miles west of Weimar on Farm Road 155. The Brewery, now in ruins, was founded by an immigrant from Saxony in the first half of the nineteenth century. Arrive in Houston.

Day Eight: Tour Houston and the Budweiser Brewery.

Day Nine: Fly back to Austin, or return via the scenic Highway 290.

TOWNS FAMOUS FOR THEIR NAMES TOUR

Texas is full of interesting roadside attractions. But sometimes the attraction is all in the name. Texas is so big, you can travel the world and never leave the state. You can make a brand new start of it in **New York, Texas** on Farm Road 607, about 13 miles from Lake Palestine.

Dublin, Texas has Dr. Pepper's oldest bottling plant. The town is 90 miles southeast of the birthplace of the Dr. Pepper soft drink, Waco.

Dallas could be in Europe judging from the towns around it. **Italy, Texas** is just east of Interstate Highway 35, about 45 miles south of Dallas. **Paris, Texas** made famous by the movie of the same name, is in the northeaster corner of the state, about 75 miles from Dallas. **Athens, Texas**, one of the oldest settlements in the state, is a small east Texas town about 70 miles south of Dallas on Highway 175

Just 65 miles west of Houston, off Interstate Highway 10, is the hamlet of **Weimar, Texas**. You can visit one of the state's oldest breweries. Nearby, **Egypt, Texas** is about 60 miles southwest of Houston, on Farm Road 102.

There is neither pomp nor circumstance in **London, Texas**, on Highway 377, about 130 miles northwest of San Antonio. Oddly enough, the replica of Stonehenge is not in London, but in nearby Ingram.

Of course, the only place anyone should want to go is **Utopia, Texas**, which is in the Hill Country. If nothing is to your liking, then visit **Nada, Texas**. Nada is the Spanish work for "nothing." The town is on State Highway 71, about 100 miles southwest of Austin.

4. LAND & PEOPLE

The varied and beautiful landscape of Texas holds diverse habitats, from the western desert to the southern tropical palm groves. The native animals, including some 600 species of birds and roughly 5000 species of plants, compose a natural kaleidoscope.

The vast lands of Texas have a variety of natural habitats that support diverse ecosystems. The state is really a number of smaller regions, each with defining characteristics and wildlife. When you drive thorough the regions of the state, you will notice a dramatic change of flora and landscape. Take your pick — desert, mountains, coastal plains, woodland — or visit a number of different areas.

Often portrayed as a dry land, Texas actually has 15 major rivers and over 1 million acres of lakes. Most of the rivers fall on diagonal lines which run from northwest to southeast on a map, and are staggered through the eastern half of the state. The Rio Grande, immortalized by songs and legends, is the best known river in the state. The Red River has the longest run through Texas. However, the Colorado River, which feeds the lakes of central Texas, is the largest.

THE WOODLANDS

As the eastern area begins, almost instantly pine trees appear. The rich soil that supports the piney woodlands of east Texas allows this dramatic transition from the surrounding arid landscapes. Four national forests, covering a total of over 600,000 acres, are found in east Texas. In these natural wonderlands, you can visit ancient Native American mounds, and enjoy canoeing, hiking and fishing.

Dense piney woodlands characterize a lot of east Texas. Much of the eastern land supports timber farms, and a number of forests are preserved as state and national parks. Both oak and pine trees flourish throughout most of the area, with willows and mesquite appearing toward the coast. The swampland and cypress trees that characterize the **Big Thicket Preserve** are so dense that the land lay untouched until modern times.

East Texas has the most rainfall in the state, with yearly averages as high as 50 inches. This rainfall combined with the mineral rich red clay topsoil supports a great deal of agriculture, including cotton and rice farming.

THE HILL COUNTRY

Central Texas is characterized by rocky hills with steep river canyons. During the age of dinosaurs, much of Texas was covered by shallow sea; central Texas was probably a coastal region. Today fossil hunters can find a variety of small fossils of sea life in dry creek beds and hills.

The **Hill Country** offers subterranean evidence of its colorful past. Beautiful caves, brimming with crystal formations, are found in **Sonora** and **New Braunfels**, as well as other cities. These wonderlands are open to the public for easy treks into the prehistoric past.

The rough hills, capped with beautiful stone ledges, are a peaceful retreat. The many rivers offer cool escapes from the hot days, and provided settlers with idyllic settings for their early hamlets. In the evenings, the land cools off quickly from the heat of the day, and a bright canopy of stars hangs overhead.

THE PANHANDLE

The northern region, or **panhandle**, has vast plains. The northernmost grasslands become sparse as the terrain transforms itself into canyons and rock formations of west Texas. The **Llano Estacado plain** covers most of the western part of the Texas panhandle. The rich soils of the blackland prairie support livestock, cotton and grapes for wine.

This region is the very southern tip of the nation's **Great Plains**. It is a point of divergence, where not only the landscape changes, but so does the culture. Just south of the panhandle, in former cow-towns such as **Fort Worth** and **Abilene**, the old West and Texas frontier met.

The landscape is hardly uniform in the panhandle. The nation's second largest canyon, **Palo Duro Canyon**, cuts through the center of this area. The most dramatic portion of the canyon is located near Abilene. Over 100 miles to the south, the canyon smoothes somewhat into more rounded hills of **Cap Rock Canyon**.

THE DESERT

The richly colored sunsets of west Texas fade into starry, desert nights. West Texas contains the state's only true desert, the **Chihuahuan Desert**. Cactus covers land stretches for miles. Beautiful flowering trees and shrubs such as the redbuds, make remarkable spring landscapes.

And this is the mountain region of the state, also. The **Davis Mountains** run through the center of the area. Some towns on the desert plateaus are at heights of over 3000 feet above sea-level.

In **Big Bend**, the desert meets the **Rio Grande** in an eruption of canyons. The mountains of Big Bend have extraordinary granite-faced peaks. In the higher elevations pine forests thrive. The Rio Grande snakes along the state's southern border. Dramatic canyons in the Big Bend area blend into the Rio Grande Valley in the south.

El Paso is the westernmost city in the state, over 800 miles from both Houston and Los Angeles. In the desert region just south of New Mexico, the Spanish established their first mission outposts in the state.

THE GULF COAST

The coastal plains of south Texas blend into the wetlands habitat that stretches along the Gulf of Mexico. **Padre Island**, a long barrier island, sits just off the Texas coast and offers hundreds of miles of untamed beach. A good deal of the land resembles simple grassland, so you would never guess that this area has the most diverse animal population in the state. Parts of south Texas are rather dry and receive as little as 16 inches of rain during the year. Closer to the coast, rainfall and humidity increase.

The southern tip of the state, the **Rio Grande Valley**, has eco-systems unique to the United States. A few of the last remaining sub-tropical forests on the continent are protected areas. The palm groves and wild olive trees characterize the region.

WILDLIFE

The most common wildlife in Texas would be considered exotic most anywhere else. The state mammal, the **armadillo**, has a series of protective plates that cover its body. The famous **longhorn steer**, which is the mascot of the University of Texas but not the state, was imported from Spain as a cash crop for the dry ranch-land of south Texas.

Coyotes prefer south Texas and **black bears** live in Big Bend and east Texas. **Mountain lions** are protected and live in the west Texas mountains. **Bobcats** still roam the east Texas forests.

Roadrunners do zip through west Texas, and love to scoot along the pavement. Far harder to spot are the elusive coyotes which roam during the evening. **Rattlesnakes** are found throughout the dry central and western regions as are **scorpions** and **tarantulas**. The **opossum** (or simply "possum" to Texans) live throughout the state.

Central Texas is part of the migratory route of **Mexican Freetail bats**. They pass through the state from March to November; and in August you will see the greatest numbers. They live and breed in caves and also under the Congress Street Bridge in Austin, where they attract nightly crowds who watch their emergence. **Monarch butterflies** and **whooping cranes** make annual journeys through the state.

Texas makes a great effort to protect endangered animals. As mentioned above, in the west Texas mountains of Big Bend, mountain lions roam the rocky peaks. They have a protected breeding ground in the park. The **bison** (buffalo) now roam the river basins in the panhandle. Once there were huge herds of these majestic creatures. Today they survive in small herds on nature preserves.

COASTAL WILDLIFE REFUGE AREAS

*The **Brazoria National Wildlife Refuge**, 1212 North Velasco Street, Angleton, Tel. 409/849-6062, has one of the nation's largest populations of snow geese during winter migration. In south Texas, efforts are being made to preserve the unique tropical habitat of the region. **Padre Island National Seashore** covers 130,000 acres. The Audobon Society has a 45,000 acre tropical sanctuary, the **Laguna Atacosta National Wildlife Refuge**, Farm Road 1847, Rio Hondo, Tel. 956/748-3608, which has hiking trails that lead through the preserved land. Also in South Texas, the **Santa Ana National Wildlife Refuge**, Farm Road 907, Alamo, Tel. 956/787-3079, preserves a rare palm tree grove. Thousands of acres of sub-tropical forest are the home to many animals not seen elsewhere in the state.*

PEOPLE

NATIVE AMERICANS

The true native Texans are the Native Americans who called Texas home long before the Spanish traversed the land in search of gold. The most famous of these are the **Commanche**, who became the antagonists of many popular Western movies and novels. They were fierce warriors, but were far from characteristic of most of the Native Americans of Texas. Texas was inhabited by many diverse tribes throughout its history.

The **Apache** dominated the Great Plains of the United States, a region which includes the northernmost area of the Texas panhandle. Eventually the Commanche pushed the Apache out of this area. The Lipan Apache lived in the central Texas region and had contact with the Spanish who colonized the state. They were both strong adversaries, and in fewer cases, allies of the Spanish. The Lipan Apache and Commanche were allies of Stephen F. Austin in the fight for independence.

The northern plains and woodlands borders was the home of the **Tonkawa**. They were preceded by the **Caddo**, who lived prosperously in the woodlands of east Texas. The Caddo are part of the Mississippi peoples of the southeastern part of North America. They enjoyed a peaceful, agriculture-based and highly developed culture. The ceremonial mounds and artifacts in east Texas indicate the area was occupied as early as 1000 BC. For mysterious reasons the civilization appears to have moved in the twelfth century, although there are no signs of hostility, disaster or evidence of where they went.

In south Texas, the history is more mysterious. The **Karankawa** were said to be tall and fierce. They inhabited the southern coastal regions, but left virtually no material history.

The Spanish were the first Europeans to move into Texas. The character of the state is shaped by the missions and settlements that they brought into this land. The development of a major route through Texas, connecting eastern lands to the interior of Mexico, played a major part in

NATIVE AMERICAN SITES IN TEXAS

In the north Texas plains, where herds of buffalo still graze, the remains of a 10,000 year old buffalo kill can be visited.

The Macular Apaches left a legacy of cave paintings at what is now **Hueco Tanks State Park**. *The rugged territory of* **Seminole Canyon** *in the southwestern region of Texas, near the Rio Grande, holds over 300 cave paintings. One of the easiest areas to view is a panorama painting at a cave site that had probably 13,000 years of occupation.*

Archaeological excavations at the **Caddoan Mounds State Historical Park**, *Highway 21, Route 2 Box 85C, Alto, open daily 10am to 6pm, have yielded many artifacts including large ear spools that were worn similar to earrings and ceremonial spears.*

The ancient plains culture is preserved at the **Lubbock Lake Landmark State Historical Park**, *3600 Landmark Lane, Lubbock, Tel 806/765-0737, Tuesday to Saturday 9am to 5pm, Sunday 1pm to 5pm, which has a 20 acre excavation and a museum.*

population centers of the state. San Antonio was a meeting point along the **Camnio Real**, or Royal Way. The first settlements established by immigrants from the United States were placed in east Texas by the Spanish authority.

South Texas was an indistinguishable continuation of the lands of northern Mexico. The large ranches of this area gave birth to the tradition of the **cowboy**. This area was the starting point of the cattle drives that pushed the growth of cities along the western frontier.

The **Latino culture** is an important part of Texas today. More that just the food and architecture, Latinos contribute the deep roots of their collective identity. The rich and varied history of the state is composed to a large extent of Latino heritage. The vast majority of Latinos in Texas are **Chicano**, tracing their heritage to Mexico. In Texas, the national holidays of Mexico are celebrated. The Sixteenth of September, the commemoration of Mexico's independence from Spain, is celebrated throughout the state. Festivities take place the preceding night. **Cinco de Mayo**, May fifth, marks Mexico's liberation from French rule, when the emperor Maiximillian was ousted. This event is celebrated with festivals and parades during the day. Another cultural celebration is the **Dia de los Muertos**, or the Day of the Dead, which is concurrent with Halloween. This is a time to commemorate ancestors and loved ones no longer with us. A parade marks the occasion, which has blended with All Soul's Day.

The sounds of the culture resonate with **Tejano music** played in the clubs and bars of Texas. But the essence of Tejano music is the merging of German polka and Spanish guitars. Small bands that play dance music, or **conjunto music**, are popular throughout central and south Texas. Freddy Fender popularized Tejano music nationwide in the 1970s. This is a different breed of melodies than those played by Mariachi bands, which have strong vocals and traditional, strumming guitars.

THE EUROPEAN IMMIGRATION

The mid-nineteenth century saw a wave of immigrants enter the state directly from Europe. The largest number of families hailed from Germany and settled in central and east Texas. To a lesser extent Poles, French, and Scandinavians came to the new lands. The legacy of the various groups lives in celebrations and museums which play active roles in many communities.

One example of the strength and determination of the European settlers is **Castroville**, a small town just outside of San Antonio. This is the state's own piece of Alsace. The Alsace region of Europe is rich in the culture and tradition of Germany and France. Likewise, the Alsatian settlers who founded Castroville transplanted that Old World charm to

Texas. Many of the historic buildings have the architecture of Germany blended with the style of old Texas. This unique combination of heritage remains a vibrant accent to this small community. Every year the town of Castroville remembers its founding and shares its traditions with the Saint Louis Day Celebration, held on the third Sunday of August. Music, food, and dancing demonstrate the Alsatian culture, and you can also learn about the area's rich history.

For decades the inhabitants of many central Texas towns spoke and published newspapers in such languages as German and Czech. Now it is less common to find these foreign languages in use. But the culture remains solid. You can find strudel or German sausage more easily than a hamburger in towns like Fredericksburg.

THE IMAGE OF TEXAS

On the surface, it is easy to overlook the great diversity of the Texas persona. To a great extent, the world's image of Texas is formed by the movies about Texans. While they cannot present a complete picture, many of the movies are a source of pride for those who call themselves Texan.

Probably the most lasting portrayal of Texas was the movie *Giant*, filmed in Marfa in 1955. James Dean and Elizabeth Taylor starred, and the rough-cut character Dean portrayed left an indelible mark on the image of the Texan.

John Wayne played Davy Crockett in *The Alamo*, shot in Texas in 1959. In real life, Crockett was probably quite different than Wayne's character in appearance and personality. Certainly he and the defenders of the Alamo were no less brave. The film version of the outlaw life and bloody death of *Bonnie and Clyde* was filmed outside Dallas in 1967, starring Warren Beatty and Faye Dunaway. The gangsters did actually run thorough Texas before meeting their demise under the blaze of Texas Ranger gunfire.

More recently, the border towns have captivated the imagination of movie makers. *El Mariachi*, the predecessor to *Desperado*, was shot in Acuna, Mexico (just across the border from Del Rio). El Mariachi propelled writer/director/Austinite Robert Rodriguez to fame. *Lonestar*, a 1994 release, may have had a fantastic storyline, but the setting and the characters were realistically plucked from the southwest Texas border.

Another great source of Texan influence on the world has been music. The music of Texas is a product of influences as diverse as the cultures of the state. Texas can claim one of the pioneers of rock music, Buddy Holly. Janis Joplin sang the blues in Austin before becoming an international celebrity. A native of Texas' gulf coast, Joplin attended the University of Texas.

Johnny Winter hails from the sweltering hot lands of south Texas. Willie Nelson and Waylon Jennings, who made Luckenbach famous in the annals of country music, both hail from Texas. George Jones brought the solemn song style from east Texas.

TEXAS, THE MOTHER OF ALL CAPITALS!

*Austin, the state capital is the seat of state government and also the home of the University of Texas. Many of the towns around the state have proclaimed themselves to be "capitals" in their own right. Austin modestly calls itself the **Live Music Capital of the World**.*

*In the Hill Country, you will find Bandera, the **Cowboy Capital of the World**. Stonewall, the birthplace of Lyndon Baines Johnson, is dubbed the **Peach Capital of the World**. East Texas also has food-related capitals. Jacksonville calls itself the **Tomato Capital of Texas**. Athens is proud to claim its right as **Black-eyed Pea Capital of the World**.*

*Temple, about 80 miles north of Austin, is the **Wildflower Capital of Texas**. Not to be outdone, Brenham, in east Texas, is known as the **Bluebonnet Capital of the World**.*

---

5. A SHORT HISTORY

PREHISTORY

At one time much of central Texas was submerged undersea. If we venture back about 100 million years, Texas would be a genuine Jurassic wonderland. From the late Triassic (about 200 million years ago) to the late Cretaceous (about 70 million years ago) dinosaurs roamed the lands of west, central and northern Texas.

Texas even has its own unique dinosaurs. Frolicking with the better-known Tyrannosaurus was the Alamosaurus, a plant-eater who weighed about 30 tons. Alamosaurus was found near San Antonio, and was named after the state's most treasured monument, the Alamo, also found in San Antonio. The Technosaurus was a tiny meat-eater which lived in north Texas. This dinosaur was found by researchers from Texas Tech University in Lubbock.

For much of the time, central Texas was a coastal land; a shallow sea covered the hills. West Texas probably was covered with thick vegetation, which is hard to imagine when looking at the cactus-covered desert. West Texas has the greatest variety of fossil remains, but central Texas has the largest abundance. In most of the dry creek beds and rock faces in the Hill Country, you can find the fossil remains of small sea creatures.

The first traces of human occupation date to sometime around the tenth millennium BC. It is believed that people may have entered the lands of what is now Texas while migrating to South America. Prehistoric civilizations carried on trade and lived as tribal communities as early as 8000 BC. For the most part, the culture of the early Texans is shrouded in mystery. Little archaeological evidence has been discovered about them. What is known opens up fascinating areas of history as yet basically unexplored.

The traces of the ancient history of Texas begin around the year 8000 BC, when skilled hunters dominated the vast plains of the north. The land offered an abundance of flora and fauna for the ancient tribesmen. Much of what is known about their lifestyle comes from the archaeological remains of a buffalo kill found in **Caprock Canyon**, near Lubbock. The site may date to 10,000 years ago.

Even in ancient times a variety of cultures lived in Texas. During the fourth millennium, cave dwellers, possibly distantly related to Mescalero Apaches, inhabited southwest Texas. The area was far more fertile and had better water supplies than today. The paintings they left on the walls of their communal dwellings show artistic representation unlike any in the world. Much of the cave art, which depicts shamans and animals, can be visited.

A dramatically different culture thrived later in east Texas. The **Caddo**, related to the Mississippian culture, occupied the east Texas woods as early as 1000 BC. They left a legacy in their ceremonial mounds that stand near Crockett, Texas. The Caddo were farmers, traders, and had a rich material culture. Their civilization left the area for unknown reasons around 1100 AD. The lives of Native Americans in Texas proceeded unhindered by Europeans until the Spanish conquest of Mexico in the seventeenth century.

EUROPEAN CONQUEST

In 1519, the Spanish explorer Alonso Alvarez de Pineda sailed along the Texas cost and made the first known map of the region. The first Spaniards to set foot on Texan soil did so by accident. In 1541, a shipwreck in the waters off Galveston left Cabeza de Vaca among the stranded crew. The men spent years as captives of the Karankawas of the Texas coast, a native tribe known for their strength and fierceness. In the end only four Spaniards survived. Cabeza de Vaca was among them and continued on through south and west Texas for years.

The Spanish, thirsty for gold and riches, pushed land exploration up through Mexico. **Francisco Coronado** traversed the Chihuahuan desert of west Texas seeking the fabled cities of gold. He did not find any riches.

When the English first began to colonize Virginia, the Spanish had spent nearly a century mapping and exploring Texas. Yet despite early enthusiasm about the possibility of wealth in the new world, the Spanish found it difficult to live in the Texas lands. They did not attempt to establish the first mission until 1619, 162 years after Hernan Cortez defeated the Aztecs in Mexico. After conquering Tenochitlan (Mexico City), the Spanish spread their influence and rule throughout Mexico, which at the time included Texas, Louisiana and the American west.

The Spanish explorers and merchants settled land grants in Mexico, leaving the northern territories, which included Texas, to the missionaries, who had different goals. The Spanish Missionaries worked in brutal environments, often in areas where the Native Americans were hostile toward outside influence. Mission life was extremely difficult; often missions had to be moved and reestablished in areas with better resources or population. There are at least fifty sites of missions in Texas, but far fewer structures remain.

One of the main roads used during the Spanish and early Mexican times was known as **El Camino Real para los Texas**, The Royal Road to Texas. From 1690 to the mid-nineteenth century, this road served as the main artery of commerce, communication and migration for the colonial people. The Spanish developed the route along established trails that Native Americans has used for generations.

The route stretched from Coahuila, Mexico to Louisiana, which was then Los Ades. The road passed through Saltillo, Mexico then broke into two branches — one going through Laredo, the other Guerero — which met in San Antonio and continued through present-day Houston and through east Texas. From the years 1691 to 1800, El Camino Real connected the **San Antonio Valero Mission (The Alamo)** to the small settlements in east Texas. By the time the Alamo was founded, the route from Mexico City to Louisiana was well traveled.

DRIVING EL CAMINO REAL TODAY

Much of the oldest part of El Camino Real can be driven along today. Interstate Highway 35 from San Antonio to Austin was part of the earliest trail. A route known as the Camino Arriba, or High Road, was used from 1795 to 1900. The modern highway system could not improve on the basic trail which cuts across the state diagonally, and you can drive along much the same road as the early travelers used. From San Antonio, take Interstate Highway 35 to San Marcos, then head east on Highway 21. Just past Caldwell you can take the OSR, Old San Antonio Road, which is a scenic loop back to Highway 21. The last Texas town on Highway 21 is San Augustine.

TEJAS, MEXICO; INDEPENDENT TEXAS; & TEXAS, USA

In 1821 Mexico won independence from Spain. The Mexican government continued to offer land grants, as the Spanish had done. That same year the father of **Stephen F. Austin**, Moses Austin, received a land grant from the Spanish government. Moses Austin died soon after receiving the grant, and left his son Stephen to take on the responsibility. Stephen F. Austin went to Mexico City where, with some difficulty, he renegotiated with the new Mexican government.

These settlers were the founders of the nation and later the state of Texas. They served the purpose of securing the land of Mexico's northern frontier for the capital, Mexico City. Austin's colony also was a strategic stronghold against the threat of French intervention in east Texas. And it placed Anglo newcomers in the territory settled by the Cherokee, which today is Van Zandt County.

Stephen F. Austin and brought the first Anglo settlers into Texas; most were from Tennessee. They are known as the Texas Original 300, and the families settled throughout east Texas. The first capital of the colony was called San Felipe de Austin and was established in 1837.

FAMOUS TEXANS FROM TENNESSEE

Many of the original Anglo settlers in Texas came from Tennessee. They contributed their lives and legacies to the founding of the state.

Sam Houston was a politician from Tennessee when he came to Texas in the early nineteenth century. Houston led Texas forces to independence at the battle of San Jacinto, then served two terms as President of the Republic of Texas. He became one of the first United States Senators from the state of Texas, then returned to serve as governor.

Jim Bowie was famous for the thick-bladed knife he carried which became known as the Bowie Knife. Bowie was a defender of the Alamo and died with William Barret Travis, the leader of the defending forces, and Davy Crockett.

Crockett, Texas is named for none other than legendary frontiersman Davy Crockett. Recently evidence turned up that indicates Crockett may have survived the siege of the Alamo and been held prisoner by General Santa Anna. Crockett would have possibly undergone torture and almost certainly been killed.

Hostility between settlers and Native Americans ran high as more land was taken over. However, Mexico did not provide enough protection for the settlers. So in 1822, Austin organized a band of men which would officially become the **Texas Rangers** in 1835.

Texas Rangers began as a defensive militia. Sam Houston requested frontier police from the capital, Mexico City, for the settlers. When insufficient action was taken, the locals took up arms to protect themselves against the hostile bandits that roamed the frontier lands. Once the Republic of Texas became a reality, the Rangers organized officially. The myth of the Texas Rangers as men who enforced their own brand of justice by any means they saw fit is well founded.

The Texas Rangers also did much to protect families, uphold laws and provide assistance to rural settlements. The Rangers also stepped in to fight the bad guys that local lawmen could not or would not confront. And there were plenty of outlaws to keep the Rangers busy. *The Lone Ranger* by Zane Grey is said to be based loosely on the Texas Rangers.

Other issues strained relations between the settlers from North America and Mexico, and when the Mexican government declared that no more land grants would be issued to North Americans, the leaders of Austin's colony were incensed.

Numerous small uprisings characterized the fiercely independent face of Texas. The revolution became an official armed rebellion in 1835 when the Mexican army requested the residents of Gonzales, in south-central Texas, to return a cannon which had been given to them by Mexico. The people of Gonzales refused and battle ensued.

The prominent men of the Austin Colony met to decide the fate of their homes and families. In a small wooden house on the banks of the Brazos River, the Declaration of Independence for the **Republic of Texas** was signed on March 2, 1836.

The forces of **General Santa Anna** were already moving toward Texas. On the march north from Mexico, they encountered armed resistance at the **Alamo**. Although the defenders of the Alamo knew they were outmatched ten-to-one, they valiantly decided to engage Santa Anna. The 13-day siege remains the most remembered battle of the war.

Those who fought for independence called themselves Texian. They vowed revenge for the massacre at the Alamo. When Sam Houston's militia engaged Santa Anna's army at **San Jacinto**, near Houston, the battle cry was "Remember the Alamo." Houston emerged victorious and the Republic of Texas was born.

Mexico never recognized the Republic of Texas as a nation, although the United States and European nations did. In the eyes of the Mexican government, the land of Texas was still part of the Mexican territory of Cohuila y Tejas. The frontier did not become quiet; fighting continued between Native Americans and settlers. And border disputes erupted with Mexico as well. One noteworthy attempt at statehood was made by a group of ranchers in the Laredo area. The **Republic of the Rio Grande** existed from 1839-1841 and declared its capital to be Laredo.

As a nation, and later as a state, Texas looked very different than its famous modern outline. Part of Colorado, New Mexico and Oklahoma stretched the north and western borders. These lands were given up eventually when Texas entered the United States as the 28th state in 1845. With the new state, the United States took on a new war with Mexico. With the strength of the United States military, Texas was able to secure its border with Mexico. The **Treaty of Guadalupe Hidalgo** ended the war

HOW DID TEXAS JOIN THE UNION?

Some Texans will tell you that they live in the only state that was not really annexed into the United States. The claim is based on a technicality. The Republic of Texas voted to join the United States before the annexation was official. Once Texas became a state, the United States military moved into the territory to quell the fighting.

According to the history of Mexico, the Republic of Texas never did exist. The lands of Texas were a cause of turmoil, but never recognized as independent. Texas was offered to the United States by Mexico as a condition to end the war between Mexico and the US.

Regardless of the legislative processes at play, ceremonies for the annexation of Texas took place in Austin, Texas in 1846, and the President of the Republic of Texas, Sam Houston, presided.

with Mexico and granted the United States new territory which included Texas. As westward expansion inflamed the imagination of Americans, Texas grew in population.

THE CIVIL WAR & AFTERMATH

During the mid-nineteenth century, as beef became an increasingly valuable commodity in the United States, new breeds of cattle were introduced to Texas. But before the state could begin serious integration into the national economic system, the state found itself deeply involved in yet another bloody conflict. The Civil War greatly disrupted the advancement of Texas. The trauma of the Civil War caused intense moral dilemmas in the new state.

The Governor of Texas, **Sam Houston**, was firmly against joining the Confederate States, and the German settlers throughout the state, many newly arrived, did not want to fight for principles with which they disagreed.

Many Texans had relocated from Tennessee and other southern states. However, others had no connection to the economic concerns of the deep south, nor the social institution of slavery. Under the government of Spain, slavery was not common. During Spanish rule many African-Americans lived in Texas as free men. They played a major role in the settlement of the lands and before the year 1800 constituted as much as one-fourth of the population. Mexico made slavery illegal, although Anglo settlers did not necessarily recognize the laws of the Mexico City government.

Still, the southern faction won out, and Texas joined the Confederacy. The governor at the time, Sam Houston, strictly opposed supporting the Confederate States and resigned from office.

Juneteenth celebrates the freedom of African-Americans in Texas, the last state to learn of the Union victory in the Civil War. Even after the Confederate Army surrendered in April 1865, Texans remained unaware of the end of the war. When Union soldiers finally arrived in Texas on June 19, 1865, the news of freedom began to spread. It was two years after the Emancipation Proclamation declared that all slaves became free citizens that the State of Texas began to obey the law of the land. Today June 19th, known as Juneteenth is an official holiday and is celebrated throughout the state.

Texas earned the dubious distinction of wagin the last battle of the Civil War. Near Brownsville, at Palmito Ranch, on May 12, 1865, Confederate forces emerged victorious, although the South had fallen one month earlier.

Union troops occupied Texas following the Civil War, although little fighting had occurred in the state.

After the close of the Civil War, the Texas frontier was without organized national protection. The United States military sent newly formed cavalry divisions to defend settlers and travelers against possible attacks by Native Americans. Many of the enlisted men were African-Americans; the Native Americans called them Buffalo Soldiers.

The Buffalo Soldiers endured some of the harshest conditions in the United States. The heat and arid climate made life at the Texas forts nearly unbearable. Officers attempted to exercise control through rigid daily routines and severe punishments for those who deviated from regulations.

TEXAS HISTORY TIMELINE

1519: The territory which will one day become Texas is claimed by the Spanish crown

1718: Construction of the first missions in San Antonio begins. Mexico wins independence from the Spanish crown.

1822: Stephen F. Austin enters Texas with North American settlers

1836: Texas declares independence from Mexico. Mexican forces enter Texas to crush the revolt.

1845: Texas becomes a state.

1846: Texas is annexed to the United States; US-Mexico War ensues

From 1867 to 1885, cavalry and infantry units of Buffalo Soldiers were stationed at Fort Davis (on Highway 17, north of Interstate Highway 10). the fort held 12 companies and was one of the largest of its kind. The troops of Fort Davis were foot-soldiers in the Indian Wars of the American frontier. Another of the larger forts at which Buffalo Soldiers were stationed is Fort Stockton.

The military played a major role in the development of the economy. Not only were many employed by the forts that sprang up in the harshest territory, but cities benefited from the security of having soldiers nearby. With the end of the Reconstruction, the rise of the cattle barons began.

FRONTIER LIFE

The famous **Chisholm Trail** was the cowboy's highway, and it ran from south Texas to Fort Worth and on to Kansas City. The great days of the cowboy were few in number, and after only 12 years rail transportation eclipsed cattle drives.

The west was conquered by the iron horse. In 1883 the final stake was laid that connected the **Southern Pacific Railroad** from El Paso to San Antonio. This changed the face of Texas forever. For the first time the remote desert regions were accessible to American settlers. Soon English replaced Spanish as the common tongue of the region.

Texas was neither rich nor cosmopolitan at the turn of the century. It was a land of opportunity—at least for the opportunistic. The rough and tumble country was a haven for those who wanted to flee justice, strike out solo or start anew. At the time, the dusty trails through the countryside offered little protection for residents or travelers. Outlaws took advantage of this.

Many wild men passed through Texas; most moved on to the boom towns of the west. Doc Holliday began his life of crime in Dallas, leaving his life as a dentist behind. **Wild Bill Hickock** frequented the cow-town of Abilene. Still others stayed in Texas permanently, not by choice but by the fire of a gun.

Both a family man and an outlaw, **John Wesley Hardin**, attempted to live a dual life. He moved between north and east Texas, and from time to time left the life of crime. His reputation as a ruthless killer and inability to steer clear of trouble caught up with him in west Texas, where he was killed in 1895.

Although a few different tales tell conflicting stories, Hico claims to be the last home and place where **Billy the Kid** died. Supposedly "the Kid" lived to the age of 90 and died of natural causes. The **Billy the Kid Museum**, *Pecan Street, Hico, Tel. 817/796-4244*, tells Hico's version of the outlaw's life.

The beginning of the twentieth century marked a difficult time for the state of Texas. The vast majority lived in the countryside and struggled as farmers. Still, Texans struggled to pull their societies into the cultural forefront. A wave of construction swept through the state. Many courthouses were built at this time.

Some of the buildings were monumental in their design and materials. The most popular styles of the time, patterned after European taste and style, were Renaissance Revival, Romanesque and French Second Empire. Often the finest granite, limestone and native wood was used. Towns grew up around the courthouse squares, which were the center of the social life in small towns.

Texas benefited greatly from the generosity of the Carnegie Foundation, which allocated funds to bring libraries to small communities. Thirty-four Carnegie Libraries were built around the turn of the century. Few of the Greek Revival buildings remain, and none are still used as libraries. But most of Texas was anything but a peaceful haven of culture.

The many changes brought about through technology meant further restructuring. Riverboats, initially a booming industry, disappeared as shipping and rail transportation gained a stronghold. Oil would fuel the new systems, and oil production began in Texas in the late nineteenth century. But it took nearly twenty years for the industry to take shape.

MAJESTIC COURTHOUSES OF TEXAS

Many courthouses in Texas are exemplary Victorian buildings. Lockhart, the seat of Caldwell County, has a beautiful courthouse built in 1894 in the French Second Empire style. Tall green-tiled towers and arched windows accent the limestone building.

The height of Victorian design in Texas is marked by the use of red brick and fanciful ornamental elements. The Gonzales County courthouse, built in 1894, has repetitive arches and columns of the Renaissance Revival architectural style. The courthouse is in the center of the town of Gonzales.

The Erath County courthouse, built in 1892, stands in Stephanville. Solid, square lines in heavy limestone blocks are offset by a red roof and red sandstone window frames. The large center clock tower dominates the city skyline.

OIL & BOOM TIMES

Then in the year 1901, the face of Texas changed forever, due to an unexpected discovery that history remembers as **Spindletop**. Oil exploded out of Spindletop and this was the first major oil discovery in

Texas. The gushing Texas crude would change the face of the state once again.

Enter the era of the **boomtown**. Overnight communities based on quick money and hard labor sprang up across the northeast of the state. Not only did workers flood the towns hoping to turn a quick dollar, but fortunes on a grand scale ensued. Many **wildcatters** made fortunes rise from the ground. A wildcatter was the name given to someone who would drill for oil based on the lay of the land and pure instinct.

The companies that would become Texas oil giants were born at this time. The father of Howard Hughes made his first million making parts for oil rigs. Those who made the big money eagerly spent it. Stores that would grow into some of the nation's leading retailers, Neiman-Marcus and Sakowitz, opened during this era.

The contrast of Texas was evident economically in the disparity between the wealthy and very poor, and also in great moral diversity. As debauchery characterized boomtowns, the foundations of the **Bible Belt** were being laid. Small towns had no use for decadence. Texans easily jumped into Prohibition. The legacy of Prohibition remains to this day, as "dry" counties that restrict the sale of alcohol still exist.

Galveston became one of the largest cities in the state of Texas, with a population of about 50,000. The wild reputation of the town which was once a haven for pirates lived on. Overshadowing its sister city, Houston, Galveston boasted the largest port on the Gulf of Mexico. In 1900, a fierce hurricane ripped through the town, destroying it almost entirely. Over 5000 people died and Galveston never regained its prominence.

Along with the soldiers and resources that Texas contributed to World War I was a battleship proudly bearing the state's name. **Battleship Texas**, which now is docked outside the city of Houston, is a tourist attraction. It is not the only warship to be named after Texas. More recently a nuclear submarine was named after the city of Corpus Christi, which is the home of a naval air station. The name had to be changed when complaints about the implications of its Latin meaning (Body of Christ) were voiced.

The oil industry helped buoy Texas through the Great Depression. While the nation struggled though economic despair, Texas became the largest producer of oil in the country. Although the general population suffered through hard times, Texas became known as the land of oil barons. A new facade was added to the Texas myth: the Oilman. And Texas could take credit for larger-than life figures who were not mythical.

The tycoon **Howard Hughes**, a native of Houston, was the son of a manufacturer of equipment for oil drilling; he began the fortune for which the more famous son would become known. Hobby Airport was named first Howard Hughes Airport, after he built the facility's first control tower in 1938. The name was changed because federal law denies government funds to an airport named for a living person.

The infamous gangsters **Bonnie and Clyde** briefly brought the wild west back to Texas when they spent over two years traversing the state as fugitives, with the Texas Rangers in hot pursuit. Bonnie Parker was born in Rowan, Texas and spent time in the Kemp, Texas jail. Their path went from Dallas to San Antonio, then through east Texas. Texas Rangers gunned them down in Louisiana in 1933.

THE SCANDALOUS STATE

Texas has had its share of infamy thorough tragedy and scandal. The most well known stories are often the darker tales. One of the most shocking events took place in August of 1966, when a lone gunman atop the University of Texas tower open fire on the campus. Seventeen people died and the shooter was killed by police.

The Branch Davidians put themselves and Waco on the map because of a nearly two month standoff with the United States Government. In August of 1993 the compound, which was the residence of the religious cult, burned to the ground. Ninety people died, including four government agents.

The Republic of Texas attempted to rise again when an obscure group claimed the right to this historic name and declared themselves an independent nation. In 1997, in the west Texas Davis Mountains, the trailer that was called an "embassy" was the scene of yet another standoff with government agents. In the end, the group was brought into custody.

20TH CENTURY TEXAS

One of Texas' major contributions to World War II was Admiral Chester Nimitz, who hailed from the small town of Fredericksburg. Today you can visit the boyhood home of Nimitz, and stroll through a museum which documents his life and monumental role in the War in the Pacific. Another was General Dwight D. Eisenhower, who was the first United States president to have been born in Texas.

After the end of World War II, Texas benefited from the various governmental agencies that constructed bridges, highways and parks. Many of the lakes which now are enjoyed by thousands annually were built as part of these programs.

Slowly, the Texas economy improved, and many small towns were born in the 1950s and 1960s. The basic squared-off store fronts are unmistakable. In some areas you will see entire main streets that were built in this time. Department stores and drug store sprang up, and curbed the rural atmosphere of the state. Now Texas was more of a system of small cities than rural farming communities. The Farm to Market and Ranch to Market Roads were being replaced with major highway systems, and the state was in many ways growing closer together.

Texas struggled through the turbulent years of the 1960s, riding waves of civil and political unrest. The atmosphere was tense at best, especially in the larger cities of Dallas and Houston. The political leaders who rose to power during this time brought Texas into the forefront of national politics. At no time before were Texans able to wield as much power and influence in Washington.

John Tower was the first Republican from Texas to be elected senator since the time of Reconstruction. John Connally, the Governor, would become well known as a passenger in the presidential motorcade in Dallas in November 1963.

The day President Kennedy was assassinated in downtown Dallas drew all eyes to the Lone Star State. The event epitomized the chaotic times in the nation, and in Texas. Although not as engulfed in civil unrest as some of the neighbors in the deep south, Texas fought turbulent currents of crisis.

The national leader who took over the office of the presidency, **Lyndon Baines Johnson**, was an example of Texan strength and determination. LBJ brought the image of the Texan to the stage of international politics. His no-nonsense style, smooth southern accent and obvious will once again defined the Texan persona. While governing the nation, LBJ remained prominent in the state political arena, offering opinions about local matters and frequently visiting the state. He stayed close to Texas, stopping often at his family ranch in central Texas.

Science and technology began to blossom in Texas. **Texas Instruments**, based in Dallas, was at the forefront of the development of semiconductors and silicon chips. **NASA** began operations in Houston. And the science and engineering departments of state universities gained prestige and endowments.

With the onslaught of quick and efficient transportation, and also the development of air-conditioning systems for the mass market, Texas was able to experience unprecedented population growth. The 1970's were a boom time for the Texas economy. The oil industry kept the crude flowing at higher and higher prices. High tech, although in its infancy, was an important part of the Texas scene.

In the early 1980s, in part to keep up with the many new residents and businesses in the state, and in part to keep pace with the economy, Texas experienced a building boom. Skyscrapers had been part of the Dallas and Houston skylines for years, but now the modern age was upon us. And with it amazing post-modern architectural marvels shot up, above the skylines. Even smaller towns, such as Fort Worth, Austin and El Paso now could boast concrete and steel high rises.

Unfortunately no one anticipated the bust. Texas slid from boom to bust seemingly overnight. Many jobs were lost and personal bankruptcies ensued. And like a house of cards the business economy tumbled. Savings and loans, entangled in their own scandals and teeming with defaulted loans, began to crumble. Real estate prices plummeted, and much of the striking modern downtowns stood vacant.

The economic rumblings that shook Texas slowly spread across the nation. As the national economy faced hard times, Texas has already begun a recovery. The 1990's saw the influx of business and industry. A number of major corporations chose Dallas for the relocation of their headquarters. The low cost and high standard of living in Texas cities easily appealed to workers around the nation. Central Texas began to be a center of the high tech industry, and is still surging ahead in that area.

Today Texas is truly a melting pot. The state has an abundance of big business and thriving small enterprises. With the second highest population in the United States, the state is home to people of all nationalities and backgrounds. The rich history is the fascinating collage of the foundations of this dynamic and ever changing state.

THE STATE SYMBOLS

Texas has many symbols which identify the uniqueness of the land and our heritage. These symbols are part of the pride for which Texans are famous.

The **Texas flag**, with horizontal fields of red and white and a vertical blue field with a single large star, served as the banner of the Republic of Texas before the state joined the union in 1845. Texans are deeply proud of their flag, and you will see it flown along highways, in front yards and just about anywhere there's a breeze.

Also of great importance are the Six Flags of Texas, which reflect the varied history of the state. Each stage of the state's leadership contributed aspects of the overall Texan culture. These flags are an important symbol to Texans, and you will see them flying side by side throughout the state.

The first to claim the land with a banner were the Spanish. The Spanish Flag flew over Texas from 1519 to 1685 and 1690 to 1821. As the first explorers in the New World, the Spanish preceded the Dutch who settled New England. Over 100 years passed before missionaries began to settle the area.

The French made a brief and ill-fated attempt to settle the Texas coast. The French Flag was the banner of Texas from 1685 to 1690. There was no need to wage war with the explorers and settlers; eventually the French claim simply faded.

Once Mexico gained its independence from Spain, the Mexican Flag flew over the state from 1821 to 1836. For years the Germans and settlers of other European origin set up their homes and shops under the rule of Mexico. The influence of Mexico is still pronounced in south Texas, which was a center of frontier trade.

The Flag of The Republic of Texas, which flew from 1836 to 1845, eventually developed into the present day design. Texas made its way as an independent nation, with its own legislature and presidents, for nearly a decade. The idea of a fiercely independent Texan persona survives in Texas heritage and identity.

During the Civil War, from 1861 to 1865, the Flag of the Confederacy was officially flown. This is not the red banner with an "x" of stars which were the war colors. Texas did not enter the Confederacy without turmoil. The State Governor at the time, Sam Houston, strictly opposed supporting the Confederate States and resigned from office for this stance.

The Flag of the United States, flown from 1845 to 1861 and 1865 to the present, often is unfurled next to the state flag.

Other Official Symbols

If you drive through central Texas in the spring, you will understand why the **bluebonnet** is the state flower. The countryside becomes covered with theses aromatic blue flowers.

The **pecan** is the state tree, and you will have no problem finding native pecan nuts to sample. East Texas has the greatest concentration of pecan trees in the state, and consequently the best pecan pie in the world. Many of the trees grow wild and reach heights of 100 feet.

Contrary to popular belief, fire ants are not the state insect. The legislature of the State of Texas chose the **monarch butterfly** as the state's official insect. Monarch butterflies have large gold and black wings. They are the only butterflies known to migrate. You may be lucky enough to see swarms of monarchs during the late fall in central and north Texas.

Since 1927, the State of Texas has claimed the **mockingbird** as the official state bird. The **Guadalupe Bass** is the official state fish and can be caught in the fast flowing rivers of central Texas. The official stone is **topaz**.

TRACE YOUR OWN TEXAS GENEALOGY

If you think you may be part of Texas history, you can easily find out more about your ancestry. Archives, museums and libraries throughout the state are at your disposal. With the assistance of historical societies, you can conduct your research. Many visitors come to Texas to rediscover their own roots. And many Texans find their family history far more exciting than they had imagined.

*One of the most important research centers is **The Alamo Library**, which is part of the grounds of the Alamo. The library has extensive holdings which deal with the founding of Texas and the battles for independence. The library is open to the public. For more information about the facilities or to begin research, contact **The Daughters of the Republic of Texas Library**, P.O. Box 1401, San Antonio, Texas 78295-1401, Tel. 210/225-1071, Fax 210/212-8514.*

*The **Dallas Genealogical Society** has a web page (http:// www.chrysalis.org/dgs/txgenweb.htm) which provides researchers information and links to other sites on the web. Data is accessible through an index of counties; you can e-mail contacts in Texas counties directly through the web page. Also links to government records offices are provided.*

***Fayette Heritage Museum and Archives**, 855 South Jefferson Street, La Grange, Tuesday to Friday 10am to 5pm; Saturday 10am to 1pm, Sunday 1pm to 5pm, has information about the founding families of the east Texas area. Many of the settlers in the area were part of Stephen F. Austin's Original 300 who came from Tennessee. The archives are open to the public.*

6. PLANNING YOUR TRIP

BEFORE YOU GO

Texas is a tourist-friendly destination. Texans love to show off their state. You can obtain a wealth of information from the **Texas Department of Transportation**, *Tel. 800/452-9292*.

WHEN TO GO - CLIMATE & WEATHER

In general, the best time to visit any region of Texas is either mid-Spring or mid-fall, when temperatures are moderate. However, because Texans rely so heavily on air conditioning, even the middle of summer can be comfortable for travel.

Summers are blazing hot, with the highest temperatures usually occurring in the Lower Rio Grande Valley and west Texas. Central and eastern Texas can be very humid, while the north and west is dry. Always pay close attention to the heat index, which is the temperature adjusted for other conditions, such as humidity and wind. When temperatures exceed 90 degrees Fahrenheit, the heat index can be substantially higher. A day with a temperature of 90 degrees can affect your body as though you were in 110 degree weather.

When you are outdoors in temperatures over 80, exercise extreme caution against sun exposure and dehydration. In temperatures over 90, beware of heat exhaustion and sunstroke.

Winter does sweep through Texas. In the Panhandle, the temperatures can dip below freezing and snow and ice are not uncommon. Most of the state experiences only a few weeks of cold temperatures in the middle of winter. When severe winter weather, such as ice or freezing rain, does occur businesses often close. Since Texans do not get a lot of practice driving on ice, the roads become very hazardous in cold weather.

The various regions each have unique weather phenomena. The gulf coast stands in the center of "hurricane alley," and tropical storms are a threat from May through September. Northern and part of central Texas have the right conditions for tornadoes. April to June are the months in which tornadoes are most likely. Funnel clouds often develop in severe thunder storms, and can occur in any month.

Thunder storms frequently develop and can bring flash floods, high winds and lightning. Spring and fall often bring dramatic changes in the temperature and, accompanying this, storms. While visiting coastal areas, be certain to check the weather advisories before entering the water. Coastal conditions can change rapidly and without warning.

Despite the frequent storms, it seems that there is always a drought in Texas. Even during years with intense flooding, droughts may develop during the long, hot summers. All regions of the state are subject to droughts, which can last years, making water conservation an ongoing concern to Texans. Increased chances of grass fires threaten the state during the summer.

WHAT TO PACK

Dallas and Houston are generally considered places where dressing counts. However, most parts of the state require casual attire only. A good deal of businesses are of the coat and tie variety, but even in the professional world you will encounter khaki and denim clad executives.

When traveling in the summer months, a hat and sunscreen are essential to comfort. Shoes that offer protection from the hot street pavement but are still lightweight will make your sightseeing easier. Most places are air conditioned, so you may want to carry a light sweater to protect against the chill of the indoors. Nights are generally cool and comfortable throughout the state.

In the spring and fall in most parts of the state bringing an umbrella or light raincoat is a good idea. Winter can be dramatic and unpredictable throughout the state. In the northern part of the state, including Dallas, and especially in the panhandle, the dead of winter can be very cold. Hat, gloves and coat are often required from December through March. West Texas, with its clear skies, desert climate and high altitudes also experience cold winters.

The majority of the state is best described as unpredictable. Temperatures may drop 20 degrees or more when a "blue northern," or real cold front, blows through. Even in December it is common to have very warm days. Then, seemingly without warning, a week or two of ice and freezing weather may appear.

TRAVEL SPECIALISTS

An easy way to plan a vacation is at **Travel Fest**, *West 6th Street, Austin, Tel. 512/469-7906* or *800/590-FEST, Open daily 9am to 9pm.* This is a travel superstore and travel agency in one. Since they are located in Texas, they can offer expert advice on traveling in the state.

Eco-tourism is a new field of interest in Texas. The state's vast natural reserves are accessible through the state and national park system. As more people with less time wish to experience the state's natural beauty, eco-tourism will take hold.

You can experience the best of each area of the state with **Texas Passport Adventures**. For a free catalog call: The Texas Parks and Wildlife Department, *Tel. 800/841-6547*. They work in cooperation with a number of tour companies to offer trips that respect and conserve nature. Some of the trips are educational, such as an artists workshop in Big Bend or a nature photography workshop. Others, like trail rides, rock climbing and mountain bike tours, are hands-on adventures.

The **Texas Back Roads Scholar**, *2802 Oak Park Drive, Austin 78704, Tel. 512/444-4550*, offers tours to those who wish to get off the well-trodden path and learn the history, nature and ecology of Texas. Texas Back Roads Scholar himself guides the tours. He has spent his life studying the state, its culture and scenery. The span of tour topics is vast, from brew pub tours to hiking and camping expeditions. Each tour is a unique experience and can include your special interests.

Although their headquarters is not in Texas, **Outpost Wilderness Adventures**, *P.O. Box 7, Lake George, Colorado 80827, Tel. 210/238-4788, Fax 210/238-4348*, specialize in mountain climbing adventure trips. Rock climbing, alpine climbing and mountain bike treks are scheduled throughout the summer in Texas. Destinations include Hueco Tanks and Enchanted Rock for rock climbing. This tour company also takes groups through Mexico's Copper Canyon in the northern state of Chihuahua.

FOREIGN CONSULATES

Mexico

If you plan to cross into a border town for a short visit, you need to present a valid **United States drivers license** at the customs points. For longer stays of up to 180 days or to visit the interior of the country, you will need a **tourist card**. The tourist card is actually just a paper form and can be obtained easily at the airport or through a travel agent. Once you have your tourist card, do not lose it while in Mexico. You may be detained at the airport or the border crossing and fined if you do not have the original tourist card.

When entering Mexico and returning, you will need to present a valid **passport**. In lieu of a passport, citizens of the United States may present a form of legal photo identification (such as a drivers license) plus one of the following: a birth certificate, notarized affidavit of citizenship, naturalization papers, permanent resident card or valid voter registration card.

Citizens of foreign countries should always carry their passport as identification. Over fifty countries have consulate offices in Texas; most are located in Houston, and to a lesser extent in Dallas. Mexico has consulates in 13 Texas cities.

Foreign Consulates in Texas
- **Canada**, *750 North St. Paul Street, Dallas. Tel. 214/922-9806*
- **France**, *2300 Interfirst Tower, Suite 974, Austin. Tel. 512/480-5605*
- **Germany**, *1330 Post Oak Boulevard, Houston. Tel. 713/627-7770*
- **Mexico**, *3015 Richmond Avenue, Houston. Tel. 713/524-3400*
- **United Kingdom**, *813 Stemmons Tower West, Dallas. Tel. 214/637-3600*

GETTING TO TEXAS

Part of the international character of the state of Texas is an abundance of air traffic. You can fly direct from Dallas or Houston to London, Paris, New York and Los Angeles. On the other end of the spectrum, Texas offers an extensive system of commuter air connections.

MAJOR AIRLINES SERVING TEXAS
- **Aeromexico**, *Tel. 800/AEROMEX*
- **American Airlines**, *Tel. 800/433-7300*
- **British Airways**, *Tel. 800/247-927*
- **Continental Airlines**, *Tel. 800/525-0280*
- **Delta Airlines**, *Tel. 800/221-1212*
- **Air France Group**, *Tel. 800/237-2747*
- **KLM Royal Dutch Airlines/Northwest**, *Tel. 800/374-7747*
- **Lufthansa German Airlines**, *Tel. 800/645-3880*
- **Southwest**, *Tel. 800/435-9792*
- **United Airlines**, *Tel. 800/241-6522*

Texas has one of the busiest airport systems in the United States. The largest airports in the state are **Dallas-Fort Worth International** and **George Bush Intercontinental** in Houston. All major cites handle air traffic. From their airports, you can easily find car rental agencies, shuttle services and taxi stands.

GETTING AROUND TEXAS

BY AIR

Southwest Airlines got its start operating out of Love Field in Dallas. The airline quickly became known as the most hassle-free way to get around the state. Southwest offers direct flights between cities and package trips to major tourist destinations in Texas. For more information, contact Southwest Airlines, *Tel. 800/435-9792*. The large airlines operate services to the far reaches of the state. American, Continental and Delta offer commuter service.

Conquest Airlines, *Tel. 800/722-0860*, serves some of the smaller metropolitan areas of Texas. With its home base in Austin, Conquest has direct flights between Austin and Abilene, San Angelo, Tyler, Beaumont, Corpus Christi and San Antonio. Laredo and McAllen are served through San Antonio. The best fares are offered for tickets purchased at least two weeks before travel.

BY TRAIN

One way to escape the monotony of the long deserted drive through west Texas is to travel by train. **Amtrak**, *Tel. 800/USA-RAIL (872-7245), http://www.amtrak.com*, has one major line that cuts across the state along much the same route as Interstate Highway 10. The Sunset Limited is a transcontinental route which runs between Los Angeles and Miami. The train has reserved coach seats, First Class sleepers , a dining car, a lounge and recreational activities such as movies. **Amtrak Vacations**, *Tel. 800/ 321-8684*, let passengers expand their itineraries with travel packages and add-on hotel options that include San Antonio. Texas cities on this route, from east to west, are Houston, San Antonio, Del Rio, Sanderson, Alpine and El Paso. In the small cities of Sanderson and Alpine, accommodations are within walking distance of the train station. In the large cities, the stations are downtown.

When traveling on the Amtrak Southwest Chief, which runs between Chicago and Los Angeles, you can connect to Amarillo via Albuquerque by **Greyhound Bus**. The Greyhound Station is one block from the Albuquerque Amtrak Station, Tel. 505/247-2581.

BY BOAT

Norwegian Cruise Lines, *Tel. 800/327-7030*, docks at the Port of Houston. From this point ships embark to the western Caribbean. The seven-day cruises include Mexico and Central America.

BY BUS

Both express buses and regular routes serve the state of Texas. **Greyhound Bus Service**, *Tel. 800/231-2222*, lets you sit back and enjoy the scenery of the state. The **Kerrville Greyline Bus Company**, *Tel. 210/227-5669, or 800/335-3722*, operates lines throughout the state. This company also runs a charter and tour service, *Tel. 800/256-4723*

The **Kerrville Bus Company**, *Tel. 800/256-4723*, is one of the largest charter bus companies in the state. The buses originate in Austin, Dallas, Fort Worth, Houston and San Antonio. The Kerrville Bus Company offers tours throughout the state, many include lodging and meals. The Southwestern Natural Wonders Tour lasts 13 days and includes Dallas, San Antonio and the Hill Country. Other tours include Mexico or the Smoky Mountains.

BY CAR

Not every Texan has a car, but it appears as though they do. Texas, with its winding country roads and long highways, seems to have been designed for a road trip. The best way to see most of the state is behind the wheel of a car. Since trade to Mexico has increased, so has the truck traffic on interstate highways.

If you plan to make a highway trip, rent a car large enough to allow you to feel comfortable and safe. Although convertibles are beautiful and romantic, during the summer months the air conditioning will be your best friend. Keep in mind that unless you already know precisely where you plan to go, you will probably want the rental rate for unlimited mileage. Even if you stay in one large city, you may put a few hundred miles on a car in just a few days.

These are some of the national rental chains that provide service in Texas. Often you will receive the best rates and availability through the toll-free desk. The representative can place your rental at the most convenient branch office. Local car rental agencies are listed in each chapter.

• **Advantage**, *Tel. 800/777-5500*
• **Alamo**, *Tel. 800/327-9633*
• **Avis**, *Tel. 800/831-2847*
• **Budget**, *Tel. 800/527-0700*
• **Dollar**, *Tel. 800/800-4000*
• **Enterprise**, *Tel. 800/325-8007*
• **Hertz**, *Tel. 800/654-3131*
• **National**, *Tel. 800-227-7368*
• **Thrifty**, *Tel. 800/367-2277*

Highway Travel

When you come to Texas you will find over 75,000 miles of highways at your disposal. All the state asks is that you observe the laws, which include mandatory auto insurance and wearing of front seat-belts.

The weather in Texas is known to change at the drop of a ten-gallon hat. Every region of the state has its own severe weather threats. The gulf coast receives hurricanes, north Texas has its share of tornadoes, central Texas is plagued by flooding and west Texas is known for wind storms.

There is a saying in Texas: if you don't like the weather, hang on, it's about to change. For the current highway conditions and latest information and travel advisories about highway construction, exit closings and weather, call the **State Department of Highways and Public Transportation,** *Tel. 800/ 452-9292,* or visit the **Texas Department of Public Transportation**'s website, *http://www.dot.state.tx.us.*

One of the most valuable resources for travelers is the system Information Centers found on major routes and by state borders. You can find free information about the entire state, including maps, tourist information and advice. Before your trip you can receive information by calling the **Texas Department of Transportation,** *Tel. 800/452-9292.*

Texas **Travel Information Centers** are found on the following highways:
• When arriving from the north on Interstate Highway 40, near Amarillo
• When arriving form the south, on Interstate Highway 35, near Laredo
• When arriving from the west on Interstate Highway 10, near Anthony
• When arriving from the east, on Interstate Highway 10, near Orange

Two major Interstate Highways cross Texas. **Interstate Highway 10** runs east/west, through Houston and San Antonio to El Paso. Jacksonville, Florida and Los Angeles, California are at either end of Interstate Highway 10. Both Oklahoma and Mexico are connected to Texas by **Interstate Highway 35.** Running north to south, Dallas, Austin, San Antonio and Laredo lie on Interstate Highway 35. In San Antonio Interstate Highway 37 branches off to Corpus Christi and the Gulf Coast. Texas uses the highway and warning signs that are standard throughout the United States.

TEXAS HIGHWAY ABBREVIATIONS
RR: Ranch Road
FM: Farm to Market Road
IH: Interstate Highway

Rest areas are found throughout the state. Many people stop for a picnic, to walk around or to take a short nap. Some of these areas have historical markers and small park areas. Along large highways rest areas and vending machines may be available.

U. S. Highways in Texas

• **US 281** goes from North Dakota through San Antonio to McAllen, Texas.
• **US 90** begins in Jacksonville, Florida and continues through San Antonio.
• **US 87** runs from Raton, New Mexico through San Antonio and south to Port Lavaca, Texas.
• **US 181** connects San Antonio to Corpus Christi.
• **US 81** runs south from San Antonio to Laredo and continues through Nuevo Laredo, Mexico.

Rural Roads

The older roads called **Farm-to-Market Roads** or **Ranch-to-Market Roads** connect small towns. Back roads often take you through the most scenic and interesting areas.

Since there are so many rural areas, the state has a few laws that apply to these settings specifically. When driving on a two lane highway, you must yield to a car that wants to pass. When you enter a free range area (marked by warning signs with animal icons) the animals have the right of way. At a livestock crossing, you must stop to let animals pass. Injuring or killing an animal in these protected areas carries a large fine.

Other driving habits are observed as courtesy. For example, when a car on a two lane road wants to pass, the lead driver will pull as far onto the shoulder as possible to give the passing driver plenty of room. The most important of the many unwritten rules that Texans observe is a friendly wave in the rear-view mirror which is the standard "thanks" gesture.

You will find emergency phones along the major highways and in rest areas. When driving in rural areas, the State Highway Patrol assists drivers in trouble. You can call the **State Highway Department Hotline**, *Tel. 800/525-5555*, for roadside assistance.

The **American Automobile Association**, *Tel. 800/765-0766*, has 15 offices in Texas and offers 24-hour road service, *Tel. 800/222-4357*, for members.

BY FERRY

Although you cannot take any major trips by ferry in Texas, if you have the opportunity to use a ferry, do it. The Island Port Aransas ferry crossing, just north of Corpus Christi, gives you the opportunity to see porpoises. You can ride a hand-pulled ferry across the Rio Grande.

TRAVELING TO MEXICO

When taking an extended trip to Texas, remember that easy access to Mexico is one of the best bargains the state offers. The adventurous can embark on a train trip from Laredo (Nuevo Laredo, Mexico) or El Paso (Juarez, Mexico) into the interior of Mexico.

You can find bargain-priced all-inclusive package trips from major Texas cities. The best time for low fares is during the summer (from May to September) when travel to resorts slows down. The trips are advertised in the Sunday editions of *The Dallas Morning News* and *The Houston Chronicle*. Most travel agents can assist with trips to Mexico,

The easiest way to go to Mexico is to just walk across the border. The largest border cities are **Laredo** and **El Paso**. Naturally bigger is not always preferable, and you may prefer the quaint atmosphere of the smaller border cities in the lower Rio Grande Valley or the villages in west Texas.

The only document you need to cross the border is a valid drivers license or government issued photo identification card. Citizens of the United States may remain in Mexico for 72 hours without a special permit.

Driving in Mexico

Mexico uses kilometers to measure speed. A rule of thumb is that 60 miles per hour equals 100 kilometers per hour. Citizens of the United States are permitted to drive across the international bridges that connect border towns. The main traffic route is through Laredo on Interstate Highway 35. Brownsville and Hidalgo (near McAllen) are other major highway routes. In order to have an extended stay or drive into the interior of the country, you must have a special travel permit. Contact the Mexican Consulate to obtain forms and documents for your trip. It is best to have all your documents in order before you reach the border.

You may drive across the border without presenting any special documentation about vehicle ownership and insurance. You may travel freely within a fifteen mile limit from the border crossing.

If you plan to go beyond the fifteen mile limit, you are required to obtain a permit. You must present proof of vehicle ownership and United States automobile insurance. Once you cross the border into Mexico, your United States insurance policy probably does not provide coverage for accidents in Mexico. You can purchase temporary policies for Mexico. Contact your insurance company for advice concerning your specific situation. One of the oldest and largest traveler's insurance companies in Mexico is **Sanborns U. S. Mexico Insurance Service**, *2212 Santa Ursula Street, Laredo, Tel. 210/722-0931.*

Customs Restrictions

Routine searches of vehicles and people are common at the border crossings. When driving to a border city in the United States, you may be required to stop at a vehicle inspection point to answer questions about your trip. These immigration check points are set up on most highways in Texas.

Tourists must obey certain restrictions on the items they bring back into the United States. Every 30 days, you may bring 100 cigars and 10 packages of cigarettes without paying a duty. Cuban cigars may not be brought back, and the minimum age to transport tobacco is 18 years.

Adults over the age of 21 years may bring one quart of alcohol, one case of beer (in 12 ounce bottles only), and three gallons of wine without paying a duty. Beyond this limit you must pay a per item duty. Up to $400 of goods is duty-free. And produce, plants, and animals are not permitted.

ACCOMMODATIONS

HOTELS & MOTELS

Texans enjoy luxury and style; this is apparent in the beautiful hotels gracing the state. Dallas and Houston undoubtedly offer the most opulent hotels. From the urban resort of the Houstonian to Dallas' extravagant 1000 room Anatole, you can find exclusivity in a wide range of tastes.

Perhaps the most charming are the many historic hotels in Texas. Built during the 1920s, the Adolphus in Dallas, the Menger in San Antonio and the Lancaster in Houston offered the highest standards in the travel industry in historic settings.

Many hotels (and motels) have business meeting rooms. Many hotels permit children to stay free with parents. Some offer playgrounds for children or areas for walking your pets. You can obtain further discounts by checking for specials, such as week-end packages. Hotels tend to be grouped at interchanges of major highways.

Best Western, *Tel. 800/528-1234*, has over 100 locations in Texas, in all large urban areas and many popular vacation spots. Many of the Best Westerns are new and some offer special amenities, such as health and recreational facilities. The rates are usually reasonable and the standard of the rooms and service is very good. Perks like complimentary morning coffee and courtesy vans to airports make the hotels comfortable places when taking long trips.

The **Marriott Hotels** group includes lower priced hotel chains. **Courtyard Inn**, *Tel. 800/321-2211*, offers well appointed motels, as does

Fairfield Inn, *Tel. 800/228-2800*. **Holiday Inn**, *Tel. 888/223-2323*, has four types of motels, ranging from resorts to the Holiday Inn Express, which are located on major highways. **Choice Hotels International**, T*el. 800/327-9155*, operates six hotel chains, including Clarion, Rodeway and Econo Lodge.

Other hotel chains that offer quality budget accommodations in Texas include:
- **Days Inn**, Tel., *800/329-7466 (DAYS-INN)*
- **Hampton Inn**, Tel. *800/426-7866 (HAM-PTON)*
- **La Quinta Inn**, *Tel. 800/531-5900*
- **Ramada**, *800/272-6232 (2-RAMADA)*

You can find hotels which are entire apartments or suites. These are excellent choices on long trips, when space and amenities such as a kitchen are desired. **Doubletree**, *Tel. 800/222 8733*, offers exceptional suites in luxuriously decorated buildings. **Embassy Suites**, *Tel. 800/362-2779*, also has large suites with kitchenettes or full kitchens. The **Marriott Residence Inn**, *Tel. 800/331-3131*, have apartment-style suites geared for long stays, as does **Homewood Suites**, *Tel. 800/225-5466*.

The highways of Texas have a multitude of **motel options**. A good deal of the motels are very new and have high standards of service, providing excellent rooms at low rates. Often you will find such amenities as complimentary continental breakfast, fitness facilities, an indoor or outdoor pool, small refrigerators in rooms and outdoor play areas for children. You should expect that all rooms will have standard amenities such as cable television, phones and non-smoking room options.

MAJOR HOTEL CHAINS IN TEXAS
Hilton, Tel. 800/916-2221
Hyatt, Tel. 800/532-1496
Sheraton, Tel. 800/325-3535
Wyndham, Tel. 800/822-4200

BED & BREAKFAST

In recent years a plethora of bed and breakfasts have opened in Texas. A great variety of homes operate as bed and breakfast, and experiences can vary greatly.

From small towns to large cities, most areas have some bed and breakfast (B&B) inns. Many are in historic homes, filled with antiques and luxurious surroundings. Others are simply run as guest rooms in modern homes. A few are in rural surroundings and offer the opportunity to hike, go horseback riding or swimming.

Most breakfasts are home-made and have a number of courses. Some inns offer elaborate weekend brunches, served on fine china. Often the proprietors are enthusiastic cooks, who can prepare dinner or picnic lunches for a fee.

It is important to discuss the arrangements with the proprietor when making reservations. Many inns impose rules such as no children, no smoking and so on. Minimum stays may be required at certain times of the year.

The bed and breakfast experience is always unique. Staying at a bed and breakfast generally allows you to learn about the town you are visiting through residents, the proprietors. For more information, contact **Bed and Breakfast Texas Style**, *Tel. 214/298-8586 or 800/899-4538, Fax 214/298-7118*

GUEST RANCHES

Another way to experience Texas is at a guest ranch. Generally the stay is based on an all-inclusive package price. Depending on the time of year in which you visit, nightly entertainment, cook-out or trip to local establishments for food and drink may be on the schedule. Some ranches offer golfing, swimming pools and other leisure activity that lets you leave the western theme behind.

You will even find genuine Texans at the guest ranches, vacationing in their own backyards. One town that is famous for operating cowboy theme ranches is **Bandera**, in central Texas.

YOUTH HOSTELS

Texas has two International Youth Hostels. They offer rates far below the market. You need not be a member to stay at the hostels, but members do get lower rates. You can buy an International Youth Hostel Card at either of the hostels. The **El Paso** location is in an historic hotel. The **Austin** hostel is on the lovely Town Lake, and offers exceptional budget accommodations.

PARK SYSTEMS

Texas has 125 state parks, many of which offer recreational facilities and camping areas. Some have screened shelters, cabins or inns for rent. Camping facilities range from primitive campsites without water or electricity to historic inns. Campsites begin at $4 per night, those with full hook-ups cost from $10 to $16 per night. Cabins run from $35 to $75 per night, depending on the size and amenities. Each person over the age of

13 years must pay a park entrance fee, from $1 to $5 per day. Some parks have special discounts and others waive the entrance fee.

You can call a central reservations number to check availability and reserve a spot at any of the state parks by calling the **Texas Parks and Wildlife Department**, *Tel. 800/792-1112.* They can provide information about facilities at each park.

Usually a deposit is required; parks may be booked-up weeks in advance, especially in the summer and over holiday weekends. Once you have made a reservation, a confirmation notice will be sent. The remainder of the total amount will be due upon arrival at the park.

Some state parks offer rustic cabins which can accommodate up to six people. Other sites operate **State Park Hotels**, which can be exceptional values located in beautiful surroundings. One example of this is the 39 room **Indian Lodge**, *Tel. 915/426-3254, $60 to $85, in the* dramatic desert setting of west Texas. The white adobe walls compliment the charming ranch-style interior. Breakfast is included for each room, and the on-site restaurant serves excellent meals. You can spend your days hiking the mountain trails or relaxing at the pool; during the evening enjoy the vast sky and peaceful surroundings.

In central Texas, the eight-room **Landmark Inn**, *Tel. 830/931-2133, $45 to $55*, is an historic building dating from the Republic of Texas. The park grounds have trails, and guests can go fishing or canoeing on the river. Breakfast is included.

7. BASIC INFORMATION

Part of the excitement of traveling through Texas is that even native Texans are often tourists in their own state. Texas is so vast, and the possibilities of recreation so exceptional, that you will meet Texans traveling through their own backyards for the first time – so you need never be embarrassed to ask what may seem to be an obvious question.

BANKING & MONEY

Automated Teller Machines (**ATMs**) are located in many convenience stores, in tourist areas and shopping centers. The machines usually charge an access fee, and a screen providing the option to cancel the transaction alerts you to the amount of the fee. The use of debit cards at restaurants and grocery stores is becoming increasingly popular in Texas.

Banks keep hours similar to those you'll find elsewhere in the US.

COST OF LIVING & TRAVEL

Texas can be very economical compared to other domestic destinations. Texans expect to get more than what they pay for, and they often do. Even if you choose to dine at the finest restaurants in Dallas or Houston, you will find prices significantly lower than in New York or San Francisco, and the quality of food and service can be just as high.

Since Texans rely on their automobiles for long and very long journeys, car rental and gas prices are reasonable. You will find that in west Texas gas may cost 15 percent more than in the more populated regions of the state.

Train travel, often overlooked as a mode of transportation, is slow and expensive compared to driving. Many train passengers make Texas a stop in their larger trips. Southwest Airlines made its start in Texas, moving people across the state for reasonable fares; they and other smaller commuter airlines can get you almost anywhere in the state.

HOLIDAYS

Texas observes all national holidays and certain state holidays. State government offices may be closed on state holidays, but most businesses operate as usual. **Texas Independence Day** is commemorated on March 2, the date that the Republic of Texas declared independence form Mexico. The battle in which the troops of Sam Houston defeated Santa Anna is **San Jacinto Day**, celebrated on April 21. **Junteenth**, or Emancipation Day, is June 19, and is the day that slaves were declared free. August 27 is the **birthday of Lyndon Baines Johnson**.

HEALTH CONCERNS

The greatest health threat in Texas is the heat. Whether you are in a humid or dry area, be careful about dehydration. When exerting yourself strenuously in the heat of summer, it can be necessary to drink up to one gallon of water per day, which is recommended for back-country hikers in west Texas.

Many are drawn to the promise of sunny days in Texas. While the sun is one of the state's greatest attractions, care should be used to avoid overexposure. Daily use of sunscreen is advised.

In larger cities, pollution is a risk. Watching the local television weather reports will alert you to days when the air is low-quality. This can help asthma and allergy sufferers to breathe more easily. Central Texas is the allergy belt of the state. In the spring flowering plants, trees and molds often irritate allergy suffers. The fall brings cedar. Air quality reports on the news include information about air-borne allergens.

When trekking into the countryside, first seek information about possible threats from wild animals. Snakes live throughout the state, not just in the desert regions. Rattlesnakes, copperheads and water moccasins can inflict serious injury. In east Texas and along the coast, mosquitoes can be an annoyance. However there are no threats from major mosquito-carried infectious diseases. Specific concerns can be addressed by the **Texas Department of Health**, *Tel. 888/484-8538*.

RETIRING IN TEXAS

South Texas, especially the Lower Rio Grande Valley, and west Texas are popular places for retirement and extended vacations. Every year the area becomes a temporary home to Winter Texans, retirees fleeing the harsh weather of northern climates. In some towns you may find more license plates from Canada than from Texas on recreational vehicles.

Many special offers are extended to Winter Texans, such as temporary country club memberships which may run as low as $33 per month with unlimited use of the club facilities.

STAYING OUT OF TROUBLE

For the most part, Texas shares the same laws and restrictions as the rest of the United States. The legal drinking age is 21 years. According to law, all automobile drivers must have valid liability insurance. Passengers in the front seats must wear seat belts. On most parts of Interstate Highways and many State Highways, the speed limit is 70 miles per hour. The speed limit is always posted. It is illegal to drink and drive in Texas. The legal blood alcohol level is below 0.1 percent. Texas does use breath tests to determine intoxication.

A few years ago, it became legal to carry a concealed weapon in Texas, provided that one has the proper permit. In anticipation of gun-toting patrons, establishments posted "no guns" symbols on the front doors of buildings and stores. However, very few Texans take advantage of the concealed weapon law. So just because you see the sign, for the most part there is no need to fear the presence of guns.

TAXES

Texas has the reputation as being a state with low, low tax rates. This is true if you live here — there is no state income tax. Visitors may find a different scenario. The state sales tax is 8.5 percent. Many cities charge hotel tax, which can add an extra three to five percent to a bill.

TELEGRAMS

You can find **Western Union** offices in most large grocery stores throughout the state.

TIME

Most of Texas is in the **Central Time Zone**, which is one hour earlier than Eastern Time Zone. The very western region of the state, west of Van Horn and including El Paso, is in the Mountain Time Zone, which is two hours earlier than the Eastern Time Zone.

8. SPORTS & RECREATION

The great outdoors is very accessible in Texas. Every city has a Parks and Recreation Department that operates public swimming pools, tennis courts, golf courses and park facilities. These are available at low cost and open during most of the year. The state park system has reserves and facilities all over the state. Many parks have cabins, hiking trails, lakes with boat launches and day use facilities, such as picnic areas. The state park system offers informative guided walks and nature courses at some facilities.

The national system is well represented as well. In west Texas and east Texas full park facilities are available. In the south, a number of national wildlife refuge areas can be visited during the day.

BIKING

The rolling terrain of central Texas is a favorite of cycling enthusiasts. The country roads and smaller highways run through spectacular scenery and offer challenging rides for even experienced cyclists.

Every year on the second weekend in May, bicycle enthusiasts can join the **Rolling Hills Challenge**, a ride through east Texas sponsored by the Columbus Lions Club. The longest route is 100 miles; many participants choose shorter rides. For information, contact the **Columbus Convention and Visitor's Bureau**, *Tel. 409/732-8385, Fax 409/732-5881.*

Mountain Biking

There could be no better place for mountain biking than Texas.

Some cities have their own velo-centers. The velo-way, an outdoor track near the Wildflower Research Center in Austin, is especially beautiful during the spring when wildflowers burst into bloom. This area is also popular for in-line skating. Houston has its own velodrome which is open for public use. Some of the state parks have trails designed specifically for mountain biking. **McKinney Falls State Park** near Austin offer easy and challenging trails. Although primarily used by horse riders, the **Hill Country State Natural Area** in Bandera, Texas, has 36 miles of trails, many of which can be used by mountain bikers.

In southwest Texas, **Seminole Canyon State Historical Park** on Highway 90 near Comstock has a six mile mountain bike trail which includes a scenic overlook of the canyon. And the Dallas area has 100 acres of moderate to advanced trails at **Cedar Hill State Park**. In the woodlands of east Texas, **Tyler State Park** has an 8.5 mile trail for mountain biking.

BIRDWATCHING

Birdwatching is a pastime in which most everyone who lives in the Coastal Bend can participate. The **Padre Island National Seashore**, with its miles of undisturbed beach, is a haven for water birds, most notably whooping cranes and kingfishers. The national park service offers bus tours of bird habitats and trails with observation areas are always open.

The coastal bend is full of spots which birds love to frequent.

Mustang Island near Port Aransas has acres of undisturbed beach which coastal birds inhabit. Near Rockport, **Goose Island State Park** is yet another sanctuary. Further south, **Baffin Bay**, near Kingsville, has trails and quiet shores for bird nesting.

Guided birdwatching tours are available from **Bird Song Natural History Adventures**, *3525 Bluebonnet, Corpus Christi, Tel. 512/882-7232*. Tours range from half-day to extended trips for groups or individuals.

Further north on the Texas coast, the **Aransas National Wildlife Refuge** is devoted to the preservation of birds and fauna. Near Galveston, the **Anahuac National Wildlife Refuge** has a number of areas that are sanctuaries for birds.

HORSEBACK RIDING

When people imagine Texas, the images of oil wells and horses come to mind. Western trail riding is the common pastime here, although you can find English riding clubs in Houston and Dallas. The place that Texans go to ride horses is the central Texas Hill Country. The terrain is both flat and rugged, so the riding trails are exciting yet not perilous. Many ranches in central Texas rent horses by the day or hour. You can also get riding lessons or guided trips. The town of Bandera has a number of guest ranches which will get you saddled up.

The camel cavalry did not prove to be a success in Texas, but **llama trekking** is here to stay. The climate of central and west Texas is just the right combination of dry and hot to keep llamas happy. So for a twist on a regular trail, ride a llama. **Texas Treks**, *8100 Baker Road, Weatherford. Tel. 817/596-7731, Fax 817/451-0979*, leads llama treks and can arrange short or long trips in the Dallas/Fort Worth area.

HIKING

The state and national parks have extensive hiking trails at all levels of difficulty. The most challenging part of the state is found in **Big Bend**, which has many backcountry and mountain trails for expert hikers.

A great way to get into the great outdoors while offering services to the community is to participate in a volunteer vacation. The **American Hiking Society**, *1422 Fenwick Lane, Silver Spring, Maryland 20910, Tel. 301/565-6704, Fax 301/565-6714*, has trips for those who want to volunteer to work on construction and maintenance of hiking trails. Participants usually work in a national park and must provide their own camping equipment. In the past Big Bend is one of the parks in which volunteers have been placed.

HUNTING & FISHING

Hunting

The great outdoors beckons hunters to every region of Texas. State regulations require permits for seasonal hunting. Fall is the season that Texans take to the hills to bag their game for the winter. For dove hunting, the season begins at the start of September in the southern coastal plains region. Quail are hunted from November to the end of February. Deer season begins in November. Exact dates of seasons vary by county, method of hunting and, of course, game.

In general, the year for sportsmen begins on September 1 – this is the beginning of the annual hunting and fishing seasons. Before you load the rifles and put on camouflage, the proper licenses and permits must be purchased. Also, all hunters 17 years of age or older must complete the mandatory Hunter Education Course.

The *Outdoor Annual* publication provides detailed information about hunting and fishing. It is available at no cost. You can write to the **Texas Parks and Wildlife Department**, *4200 Smith School Road, Austin, Texas 78744, or call them at Tel. 900/792-1112 (General Information) Monday to Friday 9am to 5pm; Tel. 800/895-4248 (Licenses and Permit information); and Tel. 800/792-1112 (Scientific and Education Permits).* You may also purchase hunting and fishing licenses at any of the 3000 locations where the permits are sold in Texas.

Hunting licenses vary in price from $6 to $250 depending on residence status of the applicant and the type of game hunted. Exotic game and fur animals are two examples of fauna requiring special permits. In addition to the general permit, certain game, such as turkey and migratory birds (including duck), require a special stamp. Those who hunt with archery equipment or muzzle-loading weapons need special stamps.

Once you are ready to go, you can hunt on your own or you can go on a real life safari. Texas has big game ranches that breed animals especially for hunters with exotic tastes. For more information about these opportunities, contact the **Exotic Wildlife Association**, *Ingram, Texas, Tel. 830/367-4997.*

Fishing

Fishing requires a general license and special tags for specific types of fish. All fish and shellfish are restricted by gear and area regulations.

The coastal waters of the Gulf of Mexico teem with shrimp, blue crab, and a variety of sport fish. During every day of the year, at least three or more fish are at peak season in the gulf. Redfish, black drum and croaker are some of the more popular varieties.

Freshwater offers excellent fishing year-round as well. Some varieties such as catfish, striped bass and crappie are plentiful nearly all year. Central Texas offers great rivers for fly fishing, especially on the **Guadalupe River**. Salt water fly fishing is less popular although more challenging. The coastal tides and larger equipment add to the challenge. The only day of the year when you do not need a special permit for sport fishing is June 1.

Fly fishing is also a popular pastime on the **Colorado River** in central Texas. Since 1933, **Pico Outdoor Company**, *Kerrville, Texas, Tel. 210/895-4348 or 800/256-5873*, has been the Hill Country experts on fly fishing. The company makes equipment, offers lessons and guides tours.

Poaching is a serious violation of law and seriously threatens the safety of sportsman and wildlife. The **Texas Parks and Wildlife Department** operates a 24-hour hotline to report poachers, *Tel. 800/792-GAME or 713/649-0708 (in Houston), or 512/389-4848 (in Austin).*

RUNNING

Just as nearly everywhere else, Texas is full of runners. Almost every city has parks with busy running trails. The cities that do not are so small that you will see running enthusiasts jogging down country roads. Some of the larger hotels offer indoor jogging tracks, so you can avoid the Texas heat.

In the Houston area, **Huntsville State Park**, *Park Road 40, Huntsville, Tel. 409/295-5644*, hosts a marathon that is anything but the usual long-distance run. The annual **Texas Trail Endurance Runs** is known as an ultra-marathon, and athletes from around the world participate. Runners must cross 20 miles of rough trails. A number of events lead up to the race and celebrate its completion.

WATER SPORTS

All along the Texas coast, water sports await you. In Galveston, Corpus Christi and South Padre Island, surf shops offer equipment rental for wind surfing and sailing. On the beach itself you will probably find sail boats for rent, either as equipment or as a tour.

The warm waters of the Gulf of Mexico offer excellent diving. You can take long shallow dives off the coast, or go deep into the bays to descend to the living communities of the oil rig platforms. Entire ecosystems full of fish, crabs, starfish and anemones take over the legs of the rig. You can see sharks and rays in the deeper gulf waters.

SPECTATOR SPORTS

Texas has world class sports events for spectators. The **Dallas Cowboys**, *Tel. 214/556-9900*, may be the most famous football team in the world. And since the Oilers left Houston, they are the only NFL team in the state.

Texas boasts two excellent baseball teams, the **Houston Astros**, *Tel. 713/799-9600*, who play in the Astrodome, and the **Texas Rangers**, *Tel. 817/273-5222*, based at The Ballpark in Arlington, near Dallas.

No town could be more proud of a basketball team than San Antonio is of its **Spurs**, *Tel. 210/554-7700*. The Alamodome in the center of the city is the Spurs' home. The **Dallas Mavericks**, *Tel. 214/748-1808*, play in Reunion Arena. The **Houston Rockets**, *Tel. 712/627-3865*, are based in the Summit.

Texas has universities with excellent athletic facilities and teams: the **University of Texas** in Austin, **Texas A&M** in College Station, **Texas Tech** in Lubbock are but a few schools that host a variety of the best collegiate athletics in the country. Football, basketball, baseball and volleyball fans will appreciate the quality and action of college sports in the state.

Ice Hockey — yes, that's right, *ice* — arrived in Texas a few years ago and is gaining popularity. The state has only one major league professional team. The **Dallas Stars**, *Tel. 214/868-2890*, play in Reunion Arena in Irving.

9. TAKING THE KIDS

Texas is an excellent place for family travel. Most hotels and motels have recreation areas with swimming pools and some have game rooms or outdoor play areas for kids. You may be able to rent a crib at the hotel. Some hotels offer babysitting services.

Traveling with kids can also be economical. You can easily find accommodations that allow children to stay in their parents room at no extra charge. Many casual restaurants have special children's menus. And a current trend in dining is to offer free dinners for children when they accompany parents.

You can find tours that focus on families and include destinations with kids-oriented activities. There are a few major theme parks in the state, which are always popular with kids. **Six Flags Over Texas** has parks in Dallas/Fort Worth, Houston and San Antonio, which also has a **Sea World Park**.

The main health concern for kids is the same as for adults: the sun. It is important to always wear sunscreen, a hat and to drink plenty of water. Watch your kids carefully for overexposure to the heat and overexertion. Give them enough "time outs" to keep them cool. The national and state parks offer special programs for kids. Also, the vast recreational opportunities, including beaches, lakes and hiking trails are fun for the entire family.

The Texas Department of Parks and Wildlife offers a variety of programs for all ages. For example, kids can learn about conservation and the challenges and rewards of the outdoors when they become park rangers for a day. **Junior Ranger Camps** are half-day programs for kids ages 6 to 12.

Visit the State of Texas website, *http://www.tpwd.state.tx.us*, for educational and fun activities as well as information about events just for kids.

The cities of Texas have extensive park and recreational areas that can be entertaining for kids and adults. **Hermann Park** in Houston is such a place. The large, green park has outdoor play areas, a lovely zoo and museums.

One of the most worthwhile museums in the state is the **Wilderness Museum**, *2000 Transmountain Road, El Paso, Tel. 915/755-4332, Tuesday to Sunday 9am to 5pm. Admission free.* The indoor/outdoor exhibits do not have much to do with wilderness. Instead the material culture of Native Americans is displayed in detail. You can walk around trails leading to displays of daily life before colonization. The nature trail stretches for one mile and has recreations of various houses, including a pithouse, a partially underground structure with a twig roof, a pueblo, and an early agricultural settlement. Archaeological sites of Mexico and the American southwest are brought into context with maps, artifacts and historic descriptions. Paintings depict the daily life of the tribes of west Texas. Visitors gain valuable insight to the petroglyphs and painted pottery and material culture of the area's first inhabitants.

Visitors to Brenham can take the short, scenic trip to see the seat of the independence movement of the Texas pioneers at **Washington-on-the-Brazos State Park**, *Box 305, Washington, Texas, Tel. 409/878-2214.* The park has an excellent museum and the scenic drive makes you feel as if you are stepping back through time. The 154-acre park has reconstructed homes of the pioneers of the state of Texas. A small wood cabin, Independence Hall, was the place where the Texas Declaration of Independence from Mexico was signed.

The **Star of the Republic Museum**, also in the park, provides a thorough overview of the road to independence and later statehood for Texas. This excellent collection has reproductions of photographs and portraits as well as artifacts from the period of the Republic of Texas. Many of the famous men for whom Texas counties are named are profiled here, as are the leaders of the Republic of Texas.

Your kids can trek into the future at the **Museum of Science and History**, *1501 Montgomery Street, Fort Worth, Tel. 817/732-1631, Monday to Friday 9am to 5pm, Saturday and Sunday 9am to 9pm, Admission adult $5, child $3.* Learning is fun in this high-tech center located in the city arts district. The hands-on exhibits allow children to dig like an archaeologist, experience the galaxy in the planetarium and take fun and educational workshops. The museum's **Omni Theater**, *Tel. 817/732-1631*, shows movies from 10:30am to 11:30pm; daily schedules vary.

In Austin, a city seemingly designed for children, you can spend entire days enjoying the great outdoors. Adults and kids alike fill Austin's largest playground, **Zilker Park**. There are over 400 acres of jogging trails from Town Lake through Zilker Park. Playing fields are used for soccer and frisbee games nearly all year long. The outdoor Zilker Hillside Theater offers free summer performances. The **Austin Area Garden Center** spotlights plants native to the region. **Barton Springs**, *Tel. 512/*

476-9044, a large, natural spring-fed pool is open year-round. The ice-cold water feels as good in the winter as the summer.

During the summer, Austin Circle of Theaters sponsors **Children's Playfest**, which includes local and touring groups. The festival runs for ten weeks and in the spring and summer months. Performances include puppet theater, artistic performances and theater productions.

10. MAJOR EVENTS

JANUARY

In the Rio Grande Valley, in the town of Mission, you can experience the **Texas Citrus Festival**. This celebration of fruit culminates in a parade which features entire floats made from all parts of the citrus fruit.

FEBRUARY

The year begins with rodeo season breaking into full swing. Rodeos are celebrated with parades and live music. They last over the course of two weekends.

The **El Paso Livestock Show and Rodeo** is a genuinely western event, drawing participants from Arizona and New Mexico.

The **Houston Rodeo**, at the end of February and beginning of March, is the largest in the state.

MARCH

Texas Cowboy Poetry Gathering takes place on the first weekend of March at Sul Ross University in Alpine.

The **Easter Fires Pageant** mixes tradition and modern fun over Easter weekend in Fredericksburg.

Austin's South-by-Southwest (SXSW) festival is held in mid-March. For one week, practically every live music venue all over town is packed with nightly performances by bands from all over the world.

APRIL

The arrival of Spanish colonists passing thorough west Texas four hundred years ago is celebrated with **The First Thanksgiving** in El Paso.

San Antonio celebrates its heritage with **Fiesta**, a celebration the includes everything from a gala ball to weekend musical performances.

For one long weekend in mid-April, **Main Street Arts Festival** takes over downtown Fort Worth.

The **Houston International Festival** celebrates world cultures during the last half of April. Food, dance, music and art fill twenty blocks of downtown Houston.

MAY

The beautiful grounds of Laguna Gloria Art Museum in Austin host **Fiesta**, a celebration of the arts in Texas. The event includes art and crafts, food and entertainment.

The **Kerrville Folk Festival**, on the last weekend of May, attracts the best folk musicians in the nation, and the biggest folk fans in the state.

JUNE

The **Annual Juneteenth Blues Festival** brings the best blues and jazz musicians to Houston. The evening performances take place on the first weekend of June.

The **Juneteenth Freedom Festival** is an all day celebration of music held on June 19 at the Miller Outdoor Theater in Houston.

JULY

Real Texans celebrate Independence Day at the big **Picnic** in Luckenbach. Of course, Willie Nelson is the featured act.

SEPTEMBER

The **Texas State Fair** is a giant carnival-style event held at Fair Park at the end of September and early October in Dallas.

OCTOBER

In Tyler, the **Rose Parade and Festival** concludes with a gala ball.

NOVEMBER

The German heritage of central Texas is the theme of **Wurstfest** in New Braunfels.

DECEMBER

In Kingsville and San Antonio, candlelight Christmas parades called **Las Posadas** are held in mid-December.

OUTDOOR MUSICALS

Texans love to celebrate their history in the great outdoors. Summer musicals bring the past to life while giving the audience a bit of culture and a bit of nature. Even during the hottest summer, the evenings are cool and comfortable.

Fort Griffin Fandangle, *Albany, Texas. Tel. 917/762-3642.* Do not miss the pre-performance barbecue dinner, served picnic-style on the front steps of the Albany Courthouse. The town of Albany participates in this amateur musical interpretation of the westward pulse of the American frontier. The show has been produced every year since 1938, except during World War II.

God's Country, *Rio Blanco Heritage Foundation, Blanco Canyon. Tel. 806/675-2906.* This amateur musical is performed in Blanco Canyon, about as close to God's country as you can get on earth. Thousands have seen the musical in the ten years that it has been presented. Blanco Canyon is 11 miles north of Crosbytown, off FM 651.

Keepers of the Legend, *Muleshoe Heritage Center, Muleshoe, Texas. Tel. 806/272-4405.* This production combines drama and music to tell the story of family life on the Texas frontier. The musical is performed for one week only in early July. All seven performances begin at 8:30pm and admission is $10.

Texas!, *Texas Palo Duro State Park, Amarillo, Texas.* For over 30 years the professional production of the musical Texas has drawn tens of thousands of visitors to the canyons of Palo Duro. The large amphitheater seats 1700 spectators under the clear night sky of north Texas. The musical is performed each night at 8:30pm from June through August. Tickets often sell out far in advance, so it's best to make plans well in advance of the performance day.

FOOD FESTIVALS

Every September on the second Saturday of the month, the culture and food of Czech immigrants is celebrated at the **Kolache Festival**. The state championship bake-off of kolaches is held in Caldwell, the Kolache Capital of Texas. If you are eligible to enter neither the amateur nor professional categories, consider taking a kolache baking class. Until you try one of the many varieties of kolache — poppy seed, apricot or sausage, for example — you are missing a culinary delight.

On Columbus Day the town of Columbus hosts **Columbus Day Fall Fest**. This has nothing to do with the discovery of the New World; actually it is a celebration of the Old World, Germany to be precise. The day is full of cooking contests for the best sausage, sauerkraut and strudel. Local music played with German rhythm continues into the evening. Columbus is on Highway 71, west of Austin.

COOKING FESTIVALS

Every November the winter heats up with the Terlingua Chili Cook-off. This small town near Big Bend ignites the tastebuds with standard recipes and new renditions of the Texas-bred cowboy food. The event claims to be the largest Chili competition in the world. Every Fourth of July the **Brisket Cook-off**, *2341 North Main, Junction, Tel. 800/397-3916*, brings out the best barbecue cooks and hungriest locals. The three-day event includes live music and picnic games on ten acres of beautiful Hill Country.

11. FOOD & DRINK

Meal time is always a chance for an exceptional adventure. The latest additions to Texas cuisine are innovative southwestern recipes. Our western neighbor, New Mexico, gives much of the flavor of this food. Chile and native ingredients from the southwest combine with rich Mexican cooking for enticing new creations. Blue corn, smoked sauces and fiery peppers are the stock overtones in these dishes. The more daring chefs borrow from Asian and Indonesian repertoires, using ginger, rice noodles and other variants as enhancing elements.

The cuisine of Texas is as varied as the peoples who formed the traditions of cooking. Central Texas was settled in great part by Germans and people of Slavic origin, primarily Poles and Czechs. The culinary traditions of Texas reflects this. Sausage-making is an art in Central Texas, where you can find German restaurants that grind their own. Pastries and bread that rival the European variety stock many small bakeries. Kolaches, Czech pastry filled with either sweet fruit or succulent meat, are as excellent as the German strudel.

The more recent immigrants who have relocated in Texas also bring their native cuisine to the state. You can indulge in authentic Moroccan, French and Vietnamese food, to name only a few.

SOUTHERN COOKING, TEXAS STYLE

Welcome to the land of the chicken fried steak. The pure variety, most easily found in west Texas, is a real cut of steak, breaded, deep fried and covered with thick cream gravy. Other versions use ground beef, chicken breast and very rarely, vegetarian patty.

We Texans like to start our days with a big bowl of grits. The white grainy cereal is hominy that has been hulled, stripped, bleached, ground and boiled. There is no rational explanation for why grits are great. Next to a couple of eggs and some biscuits and bacon, grits make a splendid meal.

Forget low-fat or even vaguely healthy southern cooking; it does not exist. And the evils of ingestion are balanced by the pleasures of the palate.

Although it could be a meal in itself, the favorite dessert, pecan pie, will stick to the roof of your mouth, your teeth, and your tastebuds.

BARBECUE

Barbecue, the word and the cooking method, may have originated from the long cooking method used by the indigenous people of the Americas. In Texas you can sink your teeth into two types of barbecue. The first is the style of the American south, which focuses on pork and rich, sweet sauce. The second style, more prevalent in Texas, is the dry smoked meat which relies on wood chips for flavor. Sauces are tangy and served on the side. The coup de grace of Texas barbecue is brisket, usually served in slices.

Cattle has been raised to a fine art in Texas, and native meat from the larger ranches is a delicacy. You can dine at internationally known restaurants such as Morton's of Chicago in San Antonio and Houston. For variety, you cannot beat the exotic flavors of game meat, which Texas chefs love to serve.

THE BEST BARBECUE IN TEXAS

No greater controversy can arise than who serves the best barbecue. And in most every city and town you can find the local heroes of the art of smoked meat. The following humble suggestions are guaranteed to at least please your palate and satiate your hunger. Restaurants like Bill Miller and Sonny Bryan's are the heavy hitters and can be found throughout the state. But there is no more authentically Texan experience than visiting an out-of-the way barbecue spot.

Two great places to try include:

COOPER'S OLD TIME PIT BAR-B-Q, *604 West Young Street. Llano. Tel. 915/247-5713. Credit cards accepted.*

In a state as big as Texas, it could take a lifetime to find the very best barbecue restaurant. Luckily, everyone has his or her own favorite spot, which is proclaimed the very best. And time and again Cooper's receives this honor. It is easy to see why. The small town of Llano practically survives on hunters who know their meat. Cooper's caters to this crowd, and they are loyal fans.

JOE COTTEN'S BARBECUE, *Highway 77 South, Robstown. Tel. 512/767-9973.*

The least pretentious and most famous barbecue restaurant in south Texas serves its food on butcher paper. The atmosphere is pure Texas. The waiters will bring you all the barbecue you can eat, then ask if you want more. This is the delectable mesquite-smoke variety of meat served with Cotten's own tangy sauce.

Texas game meat runs the gamut from the common sustenance of frontier life like squirrel or rabbit — a rarity nowadays — to ostrich and exotic game, which is imported from the far reaches of the globe. In southwestern Texas, a variety of game is raised on ranches catering to safari-style hunters. Lone star hunters usually bring home deer (venison), dove or quail.

TEX-MEX

Many visitors to Texas think that Tex-Mex food is all that Texans eat. Actually the cuisine in Texas is as diverse as the cultural foundations of the state; but by and large we do eat tons of Tex-Mex.

Tex-Mex is far removed from true Mexican food, which, in Texas, is about as difficult to find as French food. Some of the Tex-Mex staple items are the same as those used in Mexico, like corn meal, beans and hot peppers.

The most important element of any Tex-Mex meal is the tortilla. North of the border, flour tortillas are far more popular than the corn variety. And the role of the tortilla is simple — put any kind of food in it and eat — removing the necessity of a fork and knife.

In most restaurants you will see plates of sizzling fajitas brought right to the table. They come in a number of varieties: beef (skirt steak), chicken or shrimp and include mild green peppers and onions. An array of condiments is served, like guacamole, salsa, and tomatoes, which are wrapped up in a tortilla with the meat.

Salsas come in variety of strength, from mild to inferno. Salsa verde (green sauce), generally made with tart tomatillos (green Mexican tomatoes) is the mildest variety. Chipotle is a smoky-flavored pepper commonly used in southwestern cuisine. Friendly jalapeno peppers are on the mild side of the spectrum and the smaller bright green serrano peppers add real kick to salsa. The hottest sauces are made from habenero peppers. These almost always are served in bottles, like Tabasco sauce. Watch out; one drop can singe your taste buds off.

HOTTER THAN HOT

*It sounds crazy to have a chile festival in the middle of summer, but really it's quite logical. When you eat spicy food, the theory goes, the pores on your skin open, causing you to cool off. The **Texas Fiery Foods Show** is held at the end of August in Austin's Coliseum. The event draws chile lovers from all over, including chefs and growers eager to talk shop. Just as the show cools down, the **Austin Chronicle Hot Sauce Contest** takes place.*

The rather mild poblano peppers are stuffed with corn or cheese, breaded and deep fried to make chiles rellenos. Chile peppers are not to be confused with bowls of chili, which gets its flavor from ground red peppers. Real chili is made with meat (chile con carne), never beans. One sauce which tastes far better than it sounds is mole (mo-lay). The dark brown sauce used on chicken or pork has cocoa as one of its ingredients. The taste is anything but chocolate, and it is fantastic. The recipes come from deep inside Mexico.

Tamales are steamed masa (corn meal) cakes wrapped in corn husks. They may be filled with a tasty meat mixture, usually pork, which is traditional, or contain cheese, beans or chopped vegetables, which is a vegetarian twist. In Mexico tamales are food of the indigenous people and depending on the region can be wrapped in banana leaves or corn husks. Tamales are eaten especially at Christmas time; they take so long to make that "tamale season" is a big event. To eat a tamale, simply untie and peel the corn husk and eat the tamale with a fork. Another, less common way of preparing masa are gorditas, griddle fried cakes topped with beans and cheese.

Mexico sends fresh, exotic produce to Texas kitchens. Avocado, mango and chile peppers appear common next to the vast array of Mexican delicacies available in many supermarkets. Jicama is a root which resembles a large turnip and is eaten raw in salads and has a fresh, crisp taste. Nopal cactus leaves are pickled or stewed and said to have medicinal powers. The cactus fruit, tuna, can be eaten raw or made into preserves.

CHAIN RESTAURANTS

You are never far from a good meal in Texas. Some of the nation's most successful chain restaurants got their start in the Lone Star State. **Chili's** and **Fuddruckers** both originated in San Antonio, as did **Taco Cabana**. **Luby's** still has its corporate headquarters in the Alamo City.

Schlotzsky's has their flagship cafe in Austin, complete with a gourmet bakery. And at **U. R. Cooks**, you not only pick the steak you will eat but you can grill it yourself. **Zuzu**, a Dallas-based chain, is somewhere between a restaurant and fast food place. The three specialty salsas and the freshest produce are their trademarks.

Many the state's most loved restaurants are state-wide. The casual atmosphere of **Landry's** lets you imagine you are eating right at the docks. Landry's is best known for its shrimp specialties. Steak, chicken and pasta are also served.

There is hardly a Texas city untouched by the crazy waitstaff, party atmosphere and good, food at **Joe's Crabshack**. Every type of crab you can imagine is served at Joe's. The bucket in the center of your picnic table is for the crab shells, and you will get another bucket if you order bottled beer. You cannot miss the big "eat at Joe's" signs throughout the state. The **Papa Bros. Restaurants** maintain gourmet standards. **Papadeaux** specializes in Louisiana-style seafood, serving creamy crawfish etoufee, huge bows of gumbo and generous po'boy sandwiches. **Papasito's** offers upscale Tex-Mex food.

La Madeleine, the French bakery from Dallas, serves the same rich and delicious treats in the Austin location. Comfortable French county-style setting, good salads, rich individual quiches, breakfast sandwiches including authentic Croque monsieurs (grilled cheese and ham sand-wiches) and wine tasting are features of La Madeleine restaurants.

MAIL ORDER FOOD FROM TEXAS

You don't even have to visit Texas to taste the home grown flavors of great Texas cuisine. The miracle of mail order puts the food within your reach anytime.

The **El Paso Chile Company**, *909 Texas Avenue, El Paso, Texas, Tel. 915/544-3434*, sells salsa, sauces and just about anything else you can put a pepper in!

The name says it all: **Delicious Tamales**, *1330 Culebra Road, San Antonio 78201, Tel 210/735-0275 or 800/TAMALE-1*, will send you a dozen tamales for about $18 with shipping.

The **Salt Lick Barbecue**, *5446 Highway 290 West, Suite 103, Austin 78735, Tel. 800/690-1433, Fax 512/892-6237*, which made Driftwood famous, delivers Texas holiday meals to your door. Among the choices are Angus brisket ($44.95) or whole smoked turkeys ($34.95). Certain meat can be marinated in the signature Habanero pepper sauce. Naturally, you can get the famous Salt Lick Sauce with your feast.

HOME GROWN

Naturally not all the cattle in Texas is made into barbecue. A select few live on the state's dairies. The **Blue Bell Creamery**, *Farm Road 577, Brenham, Tel. 409/830-2197 or 800/327-8135*, is internationally famous for its delicious ice cream. The genuine Texas flavors, like the peach ice cream, are near and dear to the hearts and stomachs of all Texans.

In south Texas, the **Promised Land Dairy**, *Highway 181, Floresville, Tel. 210/393-7182*, churns out fresh, gourmet-quality dairy products. They package milk the old fashioned way — in bottles — and sell flavors like chocolate, mocha and cherry. Promised Land boasts the largest heard of Jersey cows in the state.

PRODUCE

Cooks love the sweet onions which are grown in south Texas. The rich flavor, devoid of bite, accents soups and steaks alike. The onions have been farmed in this region since the late 1800's. Over fifty years of breeding make the Texas sweet onions excellent quality.

Central Texas has a multitude of peach orchards, and the freshest are sold in roadside stands. Peach ice cream and preserves are often available.

The state tree is the pecan, which is native to the eastern region. Southeastern Texas produces an abundance of pecans. You will find front yards littered with pecans in the fall. Pralines, the sugary pecan candies from Louisiana, are a specialty of the region, and of course so is pecan pie. Seguin claims the title of the Home of the World's Largest Pecan.

The citrus of south Texas is unsurpassed in quality. The Rio Grande Valley grows sweet ruby red grapefruit and oranges. In the beginning of the year you will find a ton of Texas citrus in grocery stores, and produce stands throughout south Texas sell the freshest, most succulent citrus you will find.

Agriculture is a way of life for much of the state. Unique festivities have become annual celebrations of the harvest. In January in the Rio Grande Valley, in the town of Mission, is the site of the **Texas Citrus Festival**. This celebration of fruit culminates in a parade which features entire floats made from citrus — peel, leaves and seeds. Just south of San Antonio, the small town of Poteet welcomes the spring with the **April Strawberry Festival**. Every September the tomato harvest is celebrated at the **Jacksonville Tomatofest** which features the Miss Tomato Pageant.

A rather recent addition to the state's agriculture, herb farms are flourishing throughout the state. Fresh locally grown herbs can be found in many better supermarkets. And excellent restaurants in all regions of the state, in big cities and small towns alike, use these plants.

It seems ironic that in a state with recurring droughts, rice cultivation would flourish. Just south of Houston rice fields produce this grain year round. The most famous is Texmati rice.

HARD LIQUOR

Over 20 percent of the counties in Texas are "dry," meaning you cannot buy liquor within county lines. Restaurants get around the law by offering membership to their own "clubs." A membership card may cost a few dollars and allow you to drink liquor with your meal.

Texas has no local spirits that it can claim as its own. Tequila is as close to a native drink as you will find. The only real tequila is made in Mexico from the agave cactus. While you may not want to drink like a Texan, knowing the local rituals will add to your fun. Tequila is served in a small shot with coarse salt and lime on the side. The drinker licks the part of the hand between the first finger and thumb and makes a fist, then pushes it into the salt, so the salt sticks. Then the shot is consumed as quickly as possible. Lick the salt and bite the lime to kill the taste. It is so much trouble it makes you wonder why people drink the stuff at all.

BEER

Small Texas breweries produce some excellent beer. Connoisseurs will enjoy visiting Texas breweries, which perform their craft in the German tradition. The **Spoetzl Brewery** in south Texas is one of the oldest small breweries; **Celis**, in Austin, is rather new and produces exceptional beer.

Brew pubs became legal in the state only a few years ago. High quality house beer is produced at many of them. You will find brew pubs in all major cities, and many of the smaller towns popular with tourists.

WINE

The hot, arid lands of Texas are excellent ground for growing grapes. There are wineries all over the state, each with varying degrees of quality and craftsmanship. You will find select few wineries which produce their own grapes and follow traditional aging methods for all their vintages.

Texas vineyards make the art of wine-making into science at the state's largest winery at **Ste. Genevieve**, *Fort Stockton, Tel. 915/395-2417.* The winery works in cooperation with the University of Texas to research irrigation techniques, grape varieties and fermentation. Ste. Genivieve produces 1.5 million gallons of wine which is sold throughout the state and nation.

Some of the smaller wineries are even more interesting to visit. Many produce extremely small vintages and use the wine-making traditions of Europe. The attention to detail and care shines through in the end product at **Grape Creek Vineyards**, *Highway 290, Stonewall, Tel. 830/644-2710, Fax 210/644-2746.* The barrel-aged white wine is extraordinary. The modern winery and gift shop are on the small vineyard. The owners are often in the shop and offer personal insight to the making of their award-winning wine.

Other wineries overflow with history. **Val Verde Winery**, *100 Qualia Drive, Del Rio, Tel. 210/775-9714,* is such a place. The winery is still run by the family that came from Italy and founded it in the 1880's. You can see photos of the family and their wine-making operation. The gift shop and storage area are in an original stone building which stays surprisingly cool with little need of air conditioning. This is one of the few places that produced liquor during prohibition. (The wine was made for the Church). The winery produces only 5000 cases a year and does not sell the wine in any retail outlet. The excellent port wine should not be missed.

12. TEXAS' BEST PLACES TO STAY

THE HOUSTONIAN, *111 North Post Oak Lane, Houston. Tel. 713/ 680-2626 or 800/231-2759, Fax 713/680-2992. Rates: $180 to $359.*

Located in the center of urban Houston, the Houstonian is an extraordinary country retreat. The resort combines the finest accommodations with proximity to business and shopping centers of Houston. The gorgeously manicured eighteen acre grounds are a pleasure to behold. Each room is graciously furnished with elegant decor. The suites are large and comfortable enough to be a home away from home.

The cafe and restaurant serve gourmet meals in elegant settings. The tranquillity of the location and feeling of privacy add to the dining experience. The no-frills names of the dining facilities do not do justice to the posh atmosphere and impeccable service. The Cafe, which overlooks the hotel's eighteen fabulous manicured acres, could be a secluded lodge. The light food is perfect for lunch or a mid-day snack. The Manor House serves health-conscious American food and is exclusively for guests of the Houstonian.

HYATT REGENCY HILL COUNTRY RESORT, *9800 Resort Drive, San Antonio. Tel. 210/647 1234, Fax 210/681-9681. Rates: $190 to $425; Suites $485 to $1700. Credit cards accepted.*

The amazing land and recreational activities of the Texas Hill Country is at your disposal here. The splendid dining is the setting for a lavish breakfast every morning. This ranch-style resort is decorated in the most posh and comfortable modern style. The rolling hills west of San Antonio are the backdrop for the pool and eighteen hole golf course. You can float along a private stretch of river or stroll over the 200 acres of grounds. Designed in the style of a stately ranch house, the resort gives a majestic elegance to the serene hill country setting.

For those who want true rest, the day spa offers facials, massage and salon services such as manicures and hair cuts. The resort is an ideal retreat for families; special children's activities are held each day. And guests under the age of 18 years can stay free with their parents. Package prices are offered throughout the year.

INDIAN LODGE, *Indian Lodge State Park, Park Road 3, Fort Davis. Tel. 915/426-3254. Rates: Credit cards accepted.*

This adobe hideaway is the perfect retreat for nature lovers. Built with thick walls in a rambling Pueblo style, the hotel has outdoor patios with striking views of the mountains. Each room is charmingly furnished; many rooms have handmade rustic furniture which dates from the 1930s. The original section of the hotel was constructed at this time. And the feeling of the old west remains in the decoration throughout.

The secluded Davis Mountains offer miles of serene hiking trails. An outdoor pool and adjoining recreational room give the lodge areas for socializing. The 39 rooms have modern amenities such as telephones, televisions and central heat and air conditioning. The Black Bear Restaurant serves excellent breakfast, lunch and dinner meals.

LA MAISON DEL RIO BED AND BREAKFAST, *123 Hudson Drive, Del Rio, Tel. 210/768-1100. Singles/doubles $85 to $125. Credit cards accepted.*

The true charm and beauty of south Texas is found at La Maison. This elegant and artistic home is nestled in the city's oldest neighborhood. The design and interior epitomize the traditions of the early settlers. The house is built in the Mexican style with porches lining the exterior, stucco walls. The bright, tile floors were shipped from Italy, and the wide beamed ceiling is Mediterranean cypress wood. The interior is a beautiful blend of original antiques and modern renovation. A series of small murals line the main rooms; these were painted by the previous owner, Mrs. Foster. The house holds a treasure chest of such art, which the proprietor is happy to show.

The rooms are large and artfully decorated. The largest suite, the Judge's French Door Suite, has a large private bath and sun porch. The three upstairs rooms have queen size-beds. The Peacock room has a private balcony and separate sun porch and private bathroom.

You can spend hours of tranquillity relaxing under the large shade trees on the two acre yard. Allow ample time in your day to relax and savor the atmosphere of this historic house, which was built in 1887. Afternoon tea and breakfast features homemade bread and fresh juice.

MESSINA HOF WINE CELLARS, *4545 Old Reliance Road, Bryan. Tel. 409/778-9463, Fax 409/778-1729. Rates: $79.95. Credit cards accepted.*

One of the more unusual and private places to stay is the **Vintor's Loft** at Messina Hof Wineries. The country vineyard retreat gives you the best of the countryside, with the comfort of a modern home. The Messina Hof Winery began producing wine 15 years ago and has an annual bottling of

100,000 gallons. The winery sits on 45 acres of lush east Texas land. You are assured privacy, as you will occupy the only room open to visitors.

The single room is located over the visitor's center, and has a television but no telephone. A night here is for the true wine lover; breakfast features wine jelly and port wine chocolates. Since only one room is available, reservations are essential.

STAGE STOP RANCH, *Fischer. Tel. 830/935-4455 or 800/782-4378, Fax 830/935-4445. Rates: $75 to $225 per couple.*

You can get away to an area that still feels like the old frontier. The ranch was in existence even before stage coaches made it a rest stop. Stage Stop Ranch has a marvelous setting for water recreation. It is near both Canyon Lake and the Guadalupe River.

The interior offers lovely western furnishings. Three private rooms in the main house each have a private bath and are drenched in sunlight. The Wells Fargo Room is a perfect romantic getaway, with deeply colored wood paneling, a large fireplace and a door to the outdoor hot tub. The separate cabins have air conditioning and heating and modern western-style furnishings. The largest cabin, Live Oak Lodge, is large enough to hold a family and has a kitchenette. Enjoy the outdoors Texas-style, with horse riding, fishing or just strolling through the great outdoors.

CENTRAL TEXAS IN THE SPRING

*In the heart of Texas lies the rugged area known as the **Texas Hill Country**. The rolling terrain is rich in marble, granite and limestone. Prickly pear cactus, mesquite and cedar trees and brush add green color to the region. In the spring the countryside is blanketed with wildflowers, the most a distinctive being the state flower, the bluebonnet, which has a gentle scent.*

This is the romantic part of Texas, and an area bursting with old-fashioned bed-and-breakfast retreats and vacation ranches. You can even find little Luckenbach, Texas, made famous by a country song and Willie Nelson's annual Fourth of July picnic.

The Texas Hill Country has a rather dry climate marked by hearty spring rain. Late spring is marked by blossoms of wildflowers that cover the countryside in vivid colors. The summer can reach sweltering highs of over 100 degrees, and the heat index makes the temperature feel even hotter.

13. CENTRAL TEXAS

AUSTIN

Everyone seems to love **Austin**. The city consistently makes the top ten lists of the best places to live in the United States. Growth in the high tech industry, excellent institutions of higher education and the beautiful environment of the Hill Country contribute to the city's popularity.

This was not always the case. In the days when the Republic of Texas was a fledgling nation, some of the leaders wanted to move the capital to east Texas. Austin was chosen as the seat of government because it stood between the eastern settlements and the open ranges of west Texas. Yet the dingy town had dirt streets and few supporters outside the area. During a conflict with Mexico, word spread that the capital would be transferred east. A group of Austinites secretly hid the state archives so the government could not officially leave.

Today the city has the best of urban life and nature. The Austin Metropolitan Area (which includes five counties) has increased from a population of just over one-half million in 1980 to nearly one million in 1995. And Austin itself has half a million residents.

The true quality of life in Austin cannot be measured by statistics. The city's casual atmosphere, growing music scene and abundance of good food keep Austinites happy. The city has a well-deserved reputation as a haven of environmentalists, and consequently many parks grace the landscape.

Austin sees itself as "the live music capital of the world," and in keeping with this, hosts music festivals geared to attract the world's attention. The largest such event is the **South-by-Southwest** (SXSW) festival. For one week, practically every live music venue is packed with nightly performances by bands from all over the world. Producers and talent scouts fill the audience, and bands hope for the fabled "big break." SXSW is held in mid-March. A film festival and multi-media conference are part of the SXSW schedule.

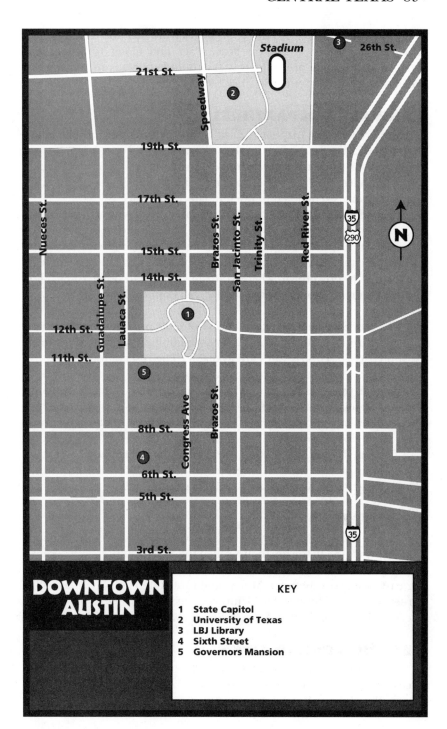

21st St.

Speedway

Stadium

26th St.

19th St.

17th St.

15th St.

14th St.

12th St.

11th St.

8th St.

6th St.

5th St.

3rd St.

Nueces St.

Guadalupe St.

Lauaca St.

Congress Ave

Brazos St.

San Jacinto St.

Trinity St.

Red River St.

Brazos St.

35

290

35

N

DOWNTOWN AUSTIN

KEY

1 State Capitol
2 University of Texas
3 LBJ Library
4 Sixth Street
5 Governors Mansion

Jazz blossoms in early June at the **Clarksville Jazz and Arts Festival**. The two day event is held at Pease Park and along with excellent performances, there are children's events and concessions. During the week preceding the festival local clubs host evening jazz performances.

ARRIVALS & DEPARTURES

Robert Mueller Airport is near central Austin, just off Interstate Highway 35; take the Airport Boulevard exit and head east. A new airport is under construction on the site of Bergstrom Air Force Base in Manor, about 15 miles from the current airport. The Austin Bergstrom International Airport is scheduled to open in late 1998.

From the Robert Mueller Airport, a taxi ride to downtown costs about $8, and to the Arboretum area about $20. The taxi pick-up is in front of the airport. **Capital Metro Buses** (Route 20/Manor Road) serve the airport, and the bus stop is just in front of the terminal. This bus connects the airport to downtown, where you can transfer to other routes. For more information about city bus service, call Capital Metro, *Tel. 512/474-1200*.

The **Star Shuttle Service**, *Tel. 512/479-8100*, provides shuttle service from the airport to Austin and nearby communities. A ride to downtown Austin costs $6. Hourly rates are available. The reservation desk at the airport is located near the baggage carousel.

Amtrak operates infrequent rail service through Austin. The route runs from San Antonio to Chicago and includes stops in Fort Worth and Dallas. The Amtrak Station, *215 North Lamar, Austin*, is about one mile west of the downtown area.

The **Greyhound Bus Station**, *916 East Koenig Lane, Austin, Tel. 512/458-4463*, is located near the intersection of Interstate Highway 35 and Ranch Road 2222 (Koenig Lane), near Highland Mall.

ORIENTATION

Mopac Expressway (Loop 1) runs between Highway 71 in the south and Highway 183 in the north. It's called the Mopac Expressway because it runs parallel to the Missouri-Pacific (Mopac) Railroad. The main roads for east-west access between Mopac and Interstate Highway 35 are 38th Street and Sixth Street. The University of Texas area is most easily accessed by Martin Luther King Jr. Street (MLK Street).

GETTING AROUND TOWN

The public transportation system in central Austin provides easy access to the central business district, the Capitol and the University of Texas. Regular city buses cover the areas, and green trolley-style buses called Dillos run special centralized routes. Regular adult fare is $1, and children under six years ride free. You can get information about the routes and schedules by calling **Capital Metro**, *Tel. 512/474-1200*. You can take a romantic horse-drawn carriage ride through central Austin with **Austin Carriage Service**, *Tel. 512/243-0044*. The carriages take walk-up rides and are stationed by the larger hotels downtown. Rides are given all day and through the night. Evening tours cost $20 per 20 minutes, and you can choose from standard routs such as Town Lake, The Capitol or Sixth Street. The last tour of the evening ends by 11pm.

Even better than riding around the lake is to take a boat ride on Town Lake. The **Lone Star River Boat**, *Tel. 512/327-1388*, offers one and one-half hour cruises from March through October. Boats leave for afternoon, sunset and evening cruises; times depend on the season. Adult fare, $9; children $6. The dock is located on the south side of the lake, on the trail between the Congress Street and South First Street Bridges.

WHERE TO STAY
Central

THE DRISKILL, *604 Brazos Street, Austin. Tel. 512/474-2214 or 800/ 252-9367, Fax 512/474-2214. Rates: $125 to $145. Credit cards accepted.*

The historic Driskill Hotel, built in the 1880's, is one of the most architecturally unique buildings in the state. Designed in the Texas Victorian tradition, the exterior has ornamentation such as cattle heads and other western motifs in the facade. The lobby bar is decorated in grandiose western fashion, with large paintings of the important Austinites from the turn-of-the century. The grand entrance has the original marble columns and large stairway leading to the ballrooms. The rooms are decorated with the charm of Victorian-style furnishings. The Driskill is located in the heart of downtown Austin, within walking distance from the State Capitol, the Warehouse District and Congress Avenue. An American Airlines office is located downstairs in the hotel. It's on the corner of Brazos and 6th Streets.

THE FOUR SEASONS, *98 San Jacinto Street, Austin. Tel. 512/478-4500 or 800/332-3232. Rates: $185 to $475. Credit cards accepted.*

The Four Seasons is Austin's premier hotel. The beautiful building stands on Town Lake, with the bar and dining room overlooking the lakeside patio. Each of the 292 rooms is elegantly appointed. The hotel is built in the style of a large villa, with an airy sandstone lobby decorated in a modern southwestern theme. The hotels offers large suites with king-size beds and two bathrooms. The Shoreline Grill Restaurant serves excellent seafood and steak. The Four Seasons is within walking distance to the Austin Convention Center and the Warehouse District and is on the ten mile jogging trail which encircles Town Lake.

THE OMNI, *700 San Jacinto Boulevard, Austin. Tel. 512/476-3000 or 800/843-6664, Fax 512/320-1450. Rates: $155 to $175. Credit cards accepted.*
The 300-room Omni is built around a ten-story atrium Glass elevators and all-glass exterior characterize the hotel that was built during the boom-economy of the early 1980s. The outdoor pool is located on the roof, and recreational facilities include a fitness room and spa. The hotel's premier restaurant, Ancho's, serves extraordinary southwestern and Mexican food. A second Omni Hotel is located in the south of the city.
CLUB HOTEL, *1617 Interstate Highway 35, Austin. Tel. 512/479-4000 or 888/444-CLUB. Rates: $109-$114. Credit cards accepted.*
This brand new Doubletree Hotel is located at the intersection of Interstate Highway 35 and MLK Boulevard. The hotel has an ideal location, near the University of Texas and the State Capitol. The 152 commodious rooms have coffee makers and phone lines with data ports for computer hook-up. The hotel offers business services, informal dining and a complete fitness center with outdoor pool. Doubletree operates a Guest Suites location in central Austin and a Doubletree Hotel on north Interstate Highway 35.
HABITAT SUITES, *500 Highland Mall Boulevard, Austin. Tel. 512/ 467-6000 or 800/535-4663. Rates: $145. Credit cards accepted.*
All rooms in this hotel are suites, with either one or two bedrooms. Some have fireplaces and kitchens. This is an ideal accommodation for a family or for those who want the feel of a home instead of a hotel. The central location of this apartment-style hotel is only five minutes from the University of Texas, ten minutes from downtown, and next to Interstate Highway 35 and U. S. Highway 290. Weekend breakfast and happy hour are included in the price of the rooms. A very healthy and delicious vegetarian macrobiotic lunch buffet is served Monday to Friday and Sunday 11:45am to 2pm, $7 including tax and tip, in the dining room.

South
THE HYATT REGENCY, *208 Barton Springs Road, Austin. Tel. 512/ 477-1234 or 800/233-1234. Rates: $155 to $180. Credit cards accepted.*
This seventeen-story high-rise hotel has spacious rooms, but the best part of a stay at the Hyatt are the recreational opportunities. The hotel has a pool, large indoor atrium and workout facilities. You can take full advantage of the Town Lake jogging trail with the hotel's mountain bikes for guest use. From the bar you have a romantic view of the sparkling Austin night-time skyline. The hotel is located just on the south side of the Congress Street Bridge.
AUSTIN MOTEL, *1220 South Congress Avenue. Tel. 512/441-1157. Rates: $39.95 to $99.22. Credit cards accepted.*
This funky relic of the 1950's has been renovated into one of the

favorite get-away spots for weekend tourists. The sign outside advertises "what a cool pool," and the emphasis on cool carries on throughout the hotel. The rooms are simple and comfortable. Austin Motel is an essential fixture of the artsy South Congress area. El Sol y La Luna, the restaurant in the front of the motel, serves excellent Mexican food in the laid-back style for which Austin is famous. Reserve your room well in advance, the hotel is often booked up. The hotel is located just south of Town Lake, a long walk or short taxi ride from the downtown hot-spots.

AUSTIN INTERNATIONAL YOUTH HOSTEL, *2200 South Lakeshore Drive, Austin, Tel. 512/444-2294. Rates: $8 per person.*

The Austin Youth Hostel is open to people of all ages. The large hostel is on Town Lake and has a complete kitchen and common area. Rooms have multiple beds, but are smaller than dormitory-style facilities. The friendly staff can offer information about experiencing the best of Austin. Plenty of free parking is available and you can purchase travel books or an international youth Hostel (IYH) membership at the front desk.

North

THE RENAISSANCE, *9721 Arboretum Boulevard, Austin. Tel. 512/343-2626 or 800/468-3571, Fax 512/346-7945. Rates: $167 to $187. Credit cards accepted.*

The 478 room Renaissance Hotel is located in Austin's best shopping area, the Arboretum. The overwhelming use of marble and brass make the atmosphere elegant. An emphasis is placed on service and attention to detail. The hotel has a full gym and indoor and outdoor pools. The Tratorria Grande specializes in the cuisine of northern Italy and is open for lunch and dinner. The hotel has its own nightclub, Tangerines.

HOMEWOOD SUITES HOTEL, *10,925 Stonelake Boulevard, Austin. Tel. 512/349-9966 or 800/CALL-HOM. Rates: $119 to $179.*

Spacious rooms, a large outdoor pool and plenty of parking make guests feel that they are staying in a home, not a hotel. Guests can enjoy breakfast, evening snacks and exercise facilities. The Homewood Suites is in the heart of Austin's suburban growth area, about 15 miles north of downtown. Many high-tech companies and a lot of shopping centers make this part of town popular for young professionals. From Mopac Expressway, exit Braker Lane. The hotel is on the west side of the expressway.

Bed & Breakfasts

THE BROOK HOUSE, *609 West 33rd Street, Austin. Tel. 512/459-0534. Rates: $69 to $89. Credit cards accepted.*

Located close to the University of Texas, the Brook House is a late Victorian home with five guest rooms. Antique furniture and stained glass windows add to the charm of this inn. The Loer Carriage Room has a private deck under shade trees; the Cottage is a secluded suite with a kitchen and its own yard. From Interstate Highway 35, take the 38 1/2 Street exit west. At Gudalupe Street, turn south to 33rd Street.

SOUTHARD HOUSE, *908 Blanco Street, Austin. Tel 512/474-4731. Rates: $69 to $159. Credit cards accepted.*

The Southard House is the largest of three restored homes that offer rooms for guests. Of the six beautiful rooms in the Southard House, the Treaty Oak Suite is the stateliest, with a fireplace and antique sink in the bathroom. The Lone Star Inn dates from the 1920s and has four rooms, each decorated with a theme from Texas history, like the Pancho Villa Room and Judge Roy Bean Room. The Republic house is a Victorian treasure, with five exquisite rooms and a large front porch. On weekends a full breakfast is served. During the week, continental breakfast is served buffet-style. From Interstate Highway 35, take 10th street west. Turn south on Blanco.

THE SUMMIT HOUSE, *1204 Summit Street, Austin. Tel. 512/445-5304. Rates: $69. Credit cards accepted.*

The tranquil Summit House sits on a hill amid large trees. A single guest room is available for up to two adults. Every day begins with a home-style breakfast. The location provides a true neighborhood feeling of Austin, far from the traffic congestion of downtown.

THE CHEQUERED SHADE, *2530 Pearce Road, Austin. Tel. 512/346-8318. Rates: $75 to $85. Credit cards accepted.*

This bed and breakfast is on Lake Austin, just a short distance from Emma Long Park. The two-story stone house offers one suite upstairs. To reach the house from Interstate Highway 35 or Mopac expressway, take Highway 290/Ranch Road 2222 west. After you pass Loop 360 take a left at City Park Road, which leads to Emma Long Park. Turn down Pearce Road.

DABNEY HOUSE, *701 Autumn Lane, Dripping Springs. Tel. 512/894-0161. Rates: $75.*

Two lovely rooms are available at the Dabney House; both have private bath. The homey decoration lets you feel as though you are visiting family. The Cottage Garden Suite is a second floor apartment behind the house. The suite has a kitchenette and patio. Dripping Springs is located about 25 miles from Austin. The rustic town has quaint shops. From Austin go west on Highway 71/290. Head south on County Road 190 for two miles, then east on County Road 220 for about three miles. Take a left on County Road 191 and look for the mailbox labeled Dabney. The Dabney House does not accept credit cards.

LAKE TRAVIS BED AND BREAKFAST, *4446 Eck Lane, Austin. Tel. 512/266-3386, or 800/484-9095, extension 5348. Rates: $125 to $155. Credit cards accepted.*
This comfortable modern home on Lake Travis has a lovely pool and hot tub on a deck overlooking the lake. The views of the lake are some of the finest from this cliff-side dwelling. Three guest suites have a bath and deck access. You are just minutes away from the lake. A minimum stay of two nights is required.

WHERE TO EAT
Central
BITTER END, *300 Colorado Street, Austin. Tel. 512/478-2337. Credit cards accepted.*
This was one of the first brew-pubs to open in Austin, and one of the first restaurants to bravely move into the warehouse district. The risks paid off, as Bitter End is one of the most popular night spots in the city. The bar, which overlooks the dining tables and is a smoking area, becomes crowded in the evening, although there is usually no wait for a table in the dining area.
The fried calamari is a platter large enough for three people to share. The grilled vegetables vary in quality from day to day; the polenta and portabello mushroom is usually very tasty. After 10:30pm you can still order appetizers and wood-fired oven pizza. The pasta dishes are generally good, and the salad Nicoise is a true version of the French, with a generous amount of olives and pickled vegetables. Order the tuna fillet on the well-done side. The lamb is generally good. Open Monday to Friday, 11:30am to 1am Saturday and Sunday, 5pm to 2am (full menu served until 10:30pm).
Bitter End is in the warehouse building at the corner of 3rd and Colorado. You can valet park across the street ($4). B Side Bar is connected to Bitter End, but may require you to pay a cover charge, even if you dined in the restaurant.
HUT'S HAMBURGERS, *807 West 6th Street, and 1000 Research Boulevard, Austin. Tel. 512/477-4795. Credit cards accepted.*
It would be hard to convince an Austinite that a better hamburger could be found anywhere other than Hut's. Even the vegetarian burgers are excellent. Weekly two-for-one specials. Once you step inside the campy little establishment, go all out and indulge in the giant onion rings. The Research Boulevard location is in the Arboretum Shopping Center.
HYDE PARK BAR AND GRILL, *4206 Duval Street, Austin. Tel. 512/458-3168. Credit cards accepted.*
A meal at Hyde Park is not complete without an order of the batter-dipped fries. One full serving is enough for four hungry folks. The cafe,

in a cozy, remodeled house, has the classic neighborhood feeling of Austin's Hyde Park. The salads are fresh and generous, hamburgers are served in numerous styles, including a very good vegetarian burger. The restaurant has daily soup specials and fresh, steamed seasonal vegetables. Sunday brunch features eggs benedict and french toast. Local art lines the walls, and is both an exhibit of talent and a gallery of works for sale. Monday to Sunday, 11am to midnight.

BIG BOWL NOODLE HOUSE, *2901 Guadalupe Street, Austin, Texas, Tel. 512/ 472-4754*

This is a favorite of the university crowd, who seek out good low-cost food. The menu at Big Bowl Noodle House is predominantly Japanese, with a few popular Thai and Chinese dishes on the menu. The fried green tea ice cream is a real treat. Daily lunch specials feature Japanese lo mein, Teriyaki beef or chicken and miso noodle soup, all under $5.

CASTLE HILL CAFE, *1101 West 5th Street, Austin, Tel. 512/476-7218..* Credit cards accepted.

Castle Hill Cafe is one of the best kept dining secrets in Austin. The restaurant's reputation is based on the marvelous sauces — from the very mild white sauce used on seafood pasta to the fiery habenero pepper sauce served on meat — which are original creations. The menu changes weekly and reflects an eclectic mix of world cuisine such as chutneys, oriental noodle dishes and middle eastern side dishes. The Tuscany-style lasagna made with cream and tomato sauces is a vegetarian feast. With only 30 tables, the warm atmosphere and artistic decoration is a pleasure for the senses. The upstairs room is used for private parties. The excellent wine is offered at reasonable prices. Top your meal off with the chocolate mousse — a chocolate fantasy. Expect at least an hour wait on weekends; reservations are not taken. Monday to Friday 11am to 2:30pm and 6pm to 10pm; Saturday 6pm to 10pm; closed Sunday.

COYOTE CAFE, *612 West 6th Street, Austin. Tel 512/476-0612. Credit cards accepted.*

Coyote Cafe, with its home in Santa Fe, New Mexico, lights up the array of southwestern fare available in Austin. Using a mix of unique Mexican ingredients, such as huitelacoche mushrooms, and North American flavors like New Mexican peppers, the food ignites the tastebuds. Often themes dominate the menu, such as unusual dishes prepared with corn. The rooftop bar features happy hour and is open from Wednesday to Saturday only. The restaurant is open Monday to Thursday, and Sunday 5:30pm to 10pm; Friday and Saturday, 5:30pm to 10:30pm.

GILLIGAN'S, *407 Colorado Street, Austin. Tel. 512/474-7474. Credit cards accepted.*

The amusing island decor is a prelude to the tangy southwestern touches on the menu. A large variety of fresh fish fillets prepared with sassy sauces is the trademark of Gilligan's. In the evening, live piano music rings through the restaurant. Monday to Thursday 11:15am to 10pm; Friday 11:15am to 11:30pm; Saturday, 5-11pm; Sunday 5:30 to 9:30pm. Gilligan's is near the corner of 4th and Colorado Streets.

IRONWORKS BAR-B-QUE, *100 Red River, Austin. Tel. 512/478-4855. Credit cards accepted.*

The shack that houses this barbecue restaurant was an old iron works in the days before Austin was much of a town. Fans of "the Works" will swear this is the best barbecue in the galaxy. The meat and chicken are mesquite smoked to perfection. The tangy sauce is excellent. You can sit at a picnic table inside or on the patio overlooking Waller Creek.

JEFFREY'S, *1204 West Lynn, Austin. Tel. 512/477-5584. Credit cards accepted.*

Many consider Jeffrey's the best restaurant in Austin. The menu changes daily, and is always full of exotic gourmet dishes. Appetizers such as crispy Oysters on Yucca Root Chips and Habanero Honey Aioli or Crab Cakes with Mango Relish and Yellow Pepper Sauce are but a prelude. The entrees include meat such as elk loin or veal ossobucco; duck and pheasant are regularly featured. Entrees run from $20 to $30. Monday to Thursday, 6pm to 10pm; Friday and Saturday, 6pm to 10:30pm. Reservations recommended.

LAS MANITAS AVENUE CAFE, *211 Congress Avenue, Austin. Tel. 512/472-9357. Credit cards accepted.*

Las Manitas serves simple dishes with the authentic flair of the food of interior Mexico. This may be the only place in Austin to find dishes like Huevos Motulenos, which are standard fare in Mexico. The sauces here have the punch of Mexican peppers, like ancho and chipotle. The aguas frescas, sweet fresh fruit drinks, are excellent. The art over the booths changes often and adds to the Mexican flavor of the restaurant. Las Manitas is a favorite informal spot and does get crowded, especially around noon on the weekend. There's never a wait if you sit at the bar. And if you're solo, you can take the opportunity to catch up on the news in the latest local periodicals (which are found on the shelves at the front of the restaurant). Or, if you prefer fresh air, walk straight through the kitchen to the back patio. Las Manitas is open for breakfast and lunch only. The weekday lunch specials are a favorite of the downtown business crowd. The outdoor patio is a favorite of the weekend brunch crowd.

MANGIA CHICAGO STUFFED PIZZA *3500 Guadalupe Street, and 2401 Lake Austin Boulevard, Austin. Tel. 512/469-7677. Credit cards accepted.*

Don't be put off by the dinosaur on wheels in the parking lot. That's just the Mangia signature delivery vehicle. You will get a true pizza pie at Mangia. The Chicago-style thin-crust slices are overstuffed with toppings, sauce and cheese. Lunch specials of lasagna or pizza with salad for around $5. One slice makes a meal.

MANUEL'S, *301 Congress Avenue, Austin. Tel. 512/472-7555.*

Manuel's brings the sophisticated taste of Mexico to Austin. The fresh, full spinach salad or Sopa de Elote, creamy corn soup begins the meal. Specialties of the house include Lomo de Puerco, grilled pork tenderloin medallions with sesame and pumpkin seed sauce, or Enchiladas de Jaiba, stuffed with fresh crab and tomatillo sauce. The drink list is eclectic as well, with drinks like the Tatooed Canary, a spicy mango and tequila shot, and the watermelon margarita. From 4pm to 7pm every day, half price appetizers and drinks are offered. On Sunday you can have brunch while listening to live Jazz music. Monday to Thursday and Sunday, 11am to 10:30pm; Saturday and Sunday, 11am to 11pm.

MEZZALUNA, *310 Colorado Street, Austin, Texas. (512) 472-6770. Credit cards accepted.*

Mezzaluna has been a favorite of Austinites since it first opened. Many of the regulars crowd the bar for a few hours before settling down to a late Saturday night dinner. The menu selection changes according to the season, with heavy cream pasta sauces featured in the winter and lighter vegetable sauces in the summer. The wood-fired oven in the middle of the dining room cranks out superb pizzas all night. Lunch specials are featured on weekdays. Monday to Thursday, 11:30am to 10:30pm; Friday 11:30am to 11pm. Saturday 5pm to 11pm; Sunday 6pm to 10pm.

STUBBS, *801 Red River Street, Austin. Tel. 512/480-8341. Credit cards accepted.*

The first barbecue joint opened by Stubbs was a small stand that sold home smoked meat and the sauce that won the reputation as Austin's best. Now the operation works on a grand scale. Stubb passed away some years ago, leaving his name and secret recipes behind. The barbecue is still excellent southern-style food, without the neighborhood atmosphere. Side dishes are good; try the onion rings which are heavy on the grease and light on the batter. The restaurant strives to be as much a music venue as a food establishment. On most nights a band will play the inside or outside stage, occasionally without a cover charge. The shows outside have the atmosphere of a party, while the inside is a less desirable venue because the space is simply too small to do justice to amplified music. The happy hour is a favorite of Austinites; free music shows and discounted beer are the highlights. If you want to take home some of Stubb's secret recipes, go ahead — the sauce and spices are sold under their own label.

SULLIVAN'S, *300 Colorado Street, Austin. Tel. 512/495-6504. Credit cards accepted.*

In Texas, the land of cattle, it is difficult to stand apart as a steakhouse. Sullivan's distinguishes itself both with its food and decor. The sophisticated piano bar attracts a full house on weekend nights. The restaurant has a warm, refined atmosphere and exemplary wait staff. The steaks here are the best you will find in central Texas. The 12 ounce Filet Mignon ($22.95) is cooked to perfection and the house specialty is the mammoth 20 ounce Kansas City Strip ($24.95). Every entree is served with a large wedge of iceberg lettuce covered in Sullivan's own creamy bleu cheese dressing. Side dishes are served family style, in generous portions. The creamed spinach and horseradish mashed potatoes stand out as the biggest crowd pleasers.

TRUDY'S TEXAS STAR, *409 West 30th Street, Austin. Tel. 512/477-2935.*

The patio at the West 30th Street location is a great spot for taking in a summer happy hour. Trudy's makes a great frozen margarita that can put out the fire of the red and green salsa that comes with the baskets of tortilla chips. Fresh, delicious non-greasy renditions of your favorite Tex-Mex dishes — including some vegetarian selections — are served. Entrees under $10. Monday to Thursday, 7am to midnight, Friday to Sunday, 8am to 2am. Credit cards accepted.

Z TEJAS, *1110 West 6th Street, Austin. Tel. 512/478-5355. Credit cards accepted.*

This is one of Austin's most enjoyable dining experiences. The airy atmosphere of Z Tejas resembles a large patio. The food integrates foreign flavors into the south's own taste. The Voodoo Tuna ($14.95) is a blackened Tuna fillet served with soy mustard sauce. The Grilled Ribeye ($16.95) is served with chipotle pepper sauce. Breakfast served every day, starting at 7:30am. Monday to Thursday, 7am to 10pm; Friday 7am to midnight; Saturday, 8am to midnight; Sunday 8am to 10pm.

North
FONDA SAN MIGUEL, *2330 West Loop Boulevard, Austin. Tel. 512/459-4121. Credit cards accepted.*

The lush garden atmosphere and rich colors replicate a Mexican hacienda. The finest food of interior Mexico is served at Fonda San Miguel. Quail and fresh seafood highlight the menu. The excellent sauces are true to genuine Mexican traditions. The quesidillas stuffed with flowers from squash should not be missed. Happy hour drink specials are offered in the patio bar. Every Sunday a large buffet brunch is served. Take Lamar Street North and turn west onto West Loop Boulevard. The restaurant is located in a residential area. Monday to Thursday, 5:30pm to 9:30pm; Saturday 5:30pm to 10pm; Sunday 11am to 2pm and 5:30pm to 9:30pm. Credit cards accepted.

HOUSTON'S, *2408 West Anderson Lane, Austin. Tel. 512/451-7333. Credit cards accepted.*

This is the original Houston's, and operated independently from the restaurants with the same name and theme in other cities. The food meets or surpasses the other locations. Large fresh salads, steaks and fish grilled to perfection and delicious sides such as couscous and creamed spinach are the mainstay of the short menu. The service is exceptional.

THREADGILLS, *6414 N. Lamar Street, Austin. Tel. 512/451-5440. Credit cards accepted.*

Threadgills has been around long enough to establish itself as an Austin legend. Janis Joplin sang on the Threadgills stage when she was an undergraduate at the University of Texas. Today most come for the decadent home cooking. The chicken-fried steak is a masterpiece of crunchy breading and thick gravy. The cornbread is moist and sweet. Although Threadgill's is known for the hearty vegetable side-dishes, these can be a bit of a disappointment. The corn and spinach taste as if they're fresh from a can. So skip the greens and head straight to Threadgill's homemade pies, which are a taste of true Texas home cooking. Threadgill's is on the west side of Lamar Street. Monday to Sunday 11am to 10pm.

WATERLOO ICE HOUSE, *600 North Lamar, Austin, Texas. Tel. 512/472-5400. Credit cards accepted.*

This is a wholesome alternative to fast food. Place your order at the counter and seat yourself. Good hamburgers, fresh salads and delicious creamy corn soup are the house specialties. On Friday and Saturday nights local bands provide music. Monday to Saturday 7am to 11pm. Sunday 8am to 10pm. Credit cards accepted.

South

EL GALLO, *2910 South Congress, Austin. Tel. 512/444-6696. Credit cards accepted.*

For over a generation, El Gallo has served home tasting Tex-Mex to south Austin and especially the students of Saint Edward's University, located across the street. The food here is authentic Tex-Mex, which means you should expect pinto beans, corn tortillas and specialties such as cabrito (goat meat) fajitas. The salsa has a bite to it, which makes the margaritas all the better. Prices are low and the atmosphere is great. Mariachis play on weekend nights

EL SOL Y LA LUNA, *1224 S. Congress Avenue, Austin. Tel. 512/444-7770. Credit cards accepted.*

This small restaurant attached to the Austin Motel reflects the eclectic nature of south Austin. The whimsical interior offers an insight to the food, which is Tex-Mex cooking with the flair of interior Mexican cuisine. El Sol y La Luna reproduces Mexican dishes, such as tacos al pastor, which is simply grilled meat in a soft corn tortilla. The caldo de pollo, Mexican chicken soup, is delicious and also a meal in itself. You can choose from a full array of breakfast at any time. The weekday lunch specials often feature vegetarian food.

GUERO'S TACO BAR, *1412 South Congress Avenue, Austin. Tel 512/ 447-7688. Credit cards accepted.*

Guero's is an informal and enjoyable dining experience. For nearly ten years this restaurant has been a favorite, for both food and drinks. Guero's is in an historical building which was once the Central Feed & Seed Store. Now Ausitnites come to feed themselves, instead of buying groceries or animal feed.

The restaurant is reminiscent of a border-town cafe. Reproductions of old photographs of the Mexican frontier (and those brave enough to live there) cover the walls. A guitar player makes the rounds, taking requests and tips from dinner guests. And, of course, a photographer, instant camera in hand, is eager to record your evening. As you sit under the tall, rough sandstone walls, senses are filled with the aromas of the open kitchen: fresh tortillas, sauces and sizzling meat.

Before you order a meal, turn to the best part of the menu — the very back — which lists the margaritas. The margaritas are made with fresh lime juice and hand-shaken at the bar. You can choose specifically which type of tequila (from Cuervo Gold to Patron Silver) best suits your taste. Guero's is on Congress Avenue, about one-half mile south of the Congress Avenue bridge that crosses Town Lake. Monday to Friday 7am to 10pm; Saturday to Sunday, 8am to 10pm.

MAGNOLIA CAFE, *1920 Congress Avenue, Austin, Texas, Tel. 512/ 445-0000. Credit cards accepted.*

You do not really know Austin until you have eaten at Magnolia Cafe, preferably in the wee hours of the morning. Slackers gravitate to weekend brunch; sometimes the wait is over an hour for a table. Late night study sessions are a great reason to indulge in the pancakes that are the trademark of Magnolia Cafe. If you can't decide what to eat, the menu features well-known locals espousing their favorite dishes. Monday to Sunday open 24 hours a day.

SKYLINE GRILL, *801 Lamar, Austin. Tel. 512/443-7300. Credit cards accepted.*

As you enter Skyline Grill, you will probably smell the mesquite smoke from the kitchen rising into the air. The grill is the trademark of this cozy restaurant. Simple yet delicious food made with daring ingredients make this one of the best informal restaurants in the city. Game Ravioli ($10.95) is stuffed with full-bodied meat filling and covered in tomato basil sauce. The Blue Corn Chile Relleno ($8.95) is stuffed with Texas-made goat's milk cream cheese and covered in smoked tomato sauce. Grilled fresh fish form the Gulf of Mexico is featured daily, and meat lovers will enjoy the Black Angus New York Strip ($14.95), rubbed with bourbon butter. Sunday to Thursday, 11am to 10:30pm; Friday and Saturday, 11am to 11pm.

West

CARLOS 'N CHARLIE'S, *5973 Hi Line Road, Austin, Texas. Tel. 512/ 266-1685.*

The famous party filled Carlos 'n Charlie's has made its way form the heart of Mexico to Austin's own Lake Travis. Somewhere along the way the great Mexican food became Tex-Mex, and the margaritas lost the fresh, tart lime. Still, sitting on the lake makes up in atmosphere for the food, which doesn't rate much better than average. Live music on weekend evenings is featured. The best way to reach Carlos 'n Charlie's is by boat. If you're confined to the road, take Loop 1 north, then Ranch Road 2222 west to Loop 620; turn left and follow Loop 620 past Mansfield Dam. Continue for two miles, then take a right onto Hudson Bend and follow the signs to Hi Line Road.

COUNTY LINE, *5204 Ranch Road 2222, Austin. Tel. 512/346-3664.*

The County Line is on an inlet of Lake Austin. From the patio you can have a beautiful view of the rolling hills surrounding Bull Creek. The restaurant is famous for the giant servings of family-style barbecue dishes. Steaks and seafood are available, but the ribs are reputed to be unbeatable. There's not much for vegetarians here, especially when the kitchen runs out of baked potatoes. Open daily 11:30am to 2pm and 5pm to 10pm.

THE OASIS, *6550 Commanche Trail, Austin. Tel. 512/266-2441. Credit cards accepted.*

The Oasis has 28 rambling decks that cover a hillside overlooking Lake Travis. This is a standard stop for a visitor to Austin. Drop by to catch the sunset over Lake Travis. On long summer evenings, you can spend a few hours out here waiting with a few hundred other patrons for the last rays of light. Particularly beautiful nights warrant a gentle round of applause.

The menu includes appetizers and sandwiches. This is not the place to have your evening meal—just the prelude to it. To get to the Oasis, from Mopac Expressway, take Ranch Road 2222 west. Continue past Loop 360 and the road becomes Bullick Hollow. Turn left onto Oasis Bluff and follow this to the Oasis. Monday to Thursday and Sunday 11am to midnight; Friday and Saturday 11am to midnight

Outside Austin
THE SALT LICK, *Ranch Road 1826, Driftwood. Tel. 512/858-4959.*
Sawdust floors, picnic tables, and the best barbecue around – the Salt Lick has the stuff that legends are made of. The barbecue served is the traditional southern style, heavy on the sauce and nice, juicy meat. On Sunday, the specialty is ribs. You can bring your own bottle of beer or wine. Wednesday to Sunday noon to 10pm; closed Monday to Tuesday. Take Loop One south. When the highway deadends at Ranch Road 1826, turn left.
BLUEBONNET CAFE, *211 Highway 281, Marble Falls. Tel 512/693-2444. Monday to Thursday, 6am to 8pm; Friday and Saturday 6am to 9pm; Sunday 6am to 1:45pm. Cash only.*
You will find the drive to Marble Falls is worthwhile, just to have breakfast at the Bluebonnet Cafe. While the crowds clamor into Austin restaurants for brunch, you can be in a genuine diner instead. For over 50 years, the Bluebonnet has served the best Texas breakfasts you can find. If you don't fill up on the pancakes, have a slice of homemade pie. From Austin, take Highway 71 east to Marble Falls. The Bluebonnet is at the intersection of Highways 71 and 281.

Round Rock
GUMBO'S, *14,735 Bratton Lane, Round Rock. Tel. 512/251-1606. Credit cards accepted.*
On a weekend night you may have to wait an hour for a table. Although the restaurant does not appear to be anything special from the outside – it's housed in a suburban shopping center – its worth the wait. This is real New Orleans Cajun-style cooking. The generous bowls of thick and spicy gumbo are practically a meal in themselves. The etoufee is the hearty tomato-based version, and one serving is enough to feed two people. You may want to sample the delicious bread pudding, but unless you are careful you may be too full to down another bite by the end of the meal. Even the coffee is served in a big, bowl-sized cup.
LA MARGARITA, *1402 North Interstate Highway 35, Round Rock. Tel. 512/388-1103. Credit cards accepted.*
Take a step back in time to the mid-1900's when you enter La Margarita. The Tex-Mex standards, like enchiladas and fajitas, are served with plenty of fresh vegetables. The margaritas are so good that an after-work crowd fills the restaurant nearly every night. Monday to Thursday and Sunday, 11am to 10pm; Friday and Saturday 11am to 11pm.

Cafes

CAFE MOZART, *3825 Lake Austin Boulevard, Austin. Tel. 512/477-2900.*

The atmosphere is the thing at Cafe Mozart, which sits right on the water of Lake Austin. A variety of coffee drinks, pastries and desserts are offered. Jazz bands are featured on weekend nights; during the summer the bands play on the outside deck. Monday to 7am to 11pm; Friday 7am to midnight; Saturday and Sunday 8am to midnight.

DOLCE VITA GELATO & ESPRESSO BAR, *4222 Duval Street, Austin. Tel. 512/323-2286. Credit cards accepted.*

This cafe is next to Hyde Park Bar and Grille. The gelato and sorbetto are made on the premises. Technical lingo aside, this is the best ice cream in the city. Coffee and an array of unusual spirits are offered. Other tempting and rich European-style desserts such as creme brulee are offered.

QUACK'S, *Guadalupe Street, Austin. Tel. 512/472-4477.*

Captain Quackenbush's Intergalactic Espresso Bar has been around so long that its known by its nickname, Quack's. This is the place to go for a reminder of the caffeine filled days and nights of college life. Healthy food including beans and rice, tabouli salad or hummus and pita bread are featured daily. The coffee drinks, which have fueled many all-night study sessions, have generous amounts of milk.

TEXPRESSO, *2700 West Anderson Lane #409, Austin, Texas, Tel. 512/467-9898. Credit cards accepted.*

Texpresso claims to have "the best coffee in the Lone Star State." Actually they should lay claim to the best cheesecake, which is flown in from Los Angeles. The owners fine-tuned their coffee serving skills on the glitzy Rodeo Drive in Beverly Hills, California. Their photo collection of celebrities smiling and sipping coffee lines the walls of the cafes. They still have the cheesecake shipped from California. Although it's hard for a Texan to admit a preference for anything Californian, the desserts at Texpresso are phenomenal.

The locations of the cafes do not have much charm; they are both housed in retail shopping centers. However, they do have a solid local clientele. The north location, on West Anderson Lane, is across from the Village Cinema, a theater that shows excellent films, both domestic and foreign.

SEEING THE SIGHTS

In the center of Austin stands the **State Capitol**, which is taller than the US Capitol Building in Washington, DC. The impressive pink granite structure took over four years to build and the job was done in exchange for the land that would become the 3 million acre XIT Ranch. You can tour the Senate and House Chambers from Monday to Friday 9am to 5pm and Saturday 10am to 5pm. Guided tours are free to the public; for information or special arrangements, call the Visitors Center, *Tel. 512/305-8400*. When the legislature is in session you can view the action during the morning hours.

Housed in the General Land Office built in 1856, The **Capitol Complex Visitors Center**, *112 East 11th Street, Tel. 512/305-8400*, is located on the southeast corner of the Capitol Grounds. The Center has a small display about the building and recent renovation of the Capitol, and a short movie which gives the historical account of the founding of the state capitol.

The **Governor's Mansion**, *1010 Colorado Street, Tel. 512/463-5518*, is a southern mansion dating from 1856. The part of the lower floor is open to the public on weekdays from 10am to 11:30am only. This is the official residence for the governor and family.

You will have no doubt that Texas was indeed a nation when you visit the only foreign diplomatic residence in the Republic of Texas. In 1839, the French king commissioned the **French Legation**, *802 San Marcos Street*. You can take a tour of the museum and house from Tuesday to Sunday, 1pm to 4:30pm. The home looks much as it may have when it stood overlooking vast empty land and a young capital. The landscaping reflects the southern charm of the architecture. To reach the French Legation, travel east on 7th street. Turn north on San Marcos Street, which east of Interstate Highway 35.

The **Republic of Texas Museum**, *510 Highway 183, Tel. 512/339-1997, Monday to Friday 10am to 4pm, admission $2 adults, $50 students*, is a pride-filled remembrance of the days of true independence on the frontier. The museum is operated by the Daughters of the Republic of Texas, an organization of descendants of the founding fathers of the Republic of Texas and their families. The exhibits include documents and memorabilia. From Interstate Highway 35, go west on Highway 183; the Museum is close to the intersection on the north side of the highway.

The University of Texas received the Lyndon Baines Johnson Presidential Library. The large oriental-style building stands on the main campus near the LBJ Graduate School o f Public Affairs. The **LBJ Library and Museum**, *2313 Red River Street, Tel. 512/916-5136, open daily 9am to 5pm*, provide extensive resources for the public to become acquainted with and research in depth Johnson's life and presidency. The Museum exhibits include memorabilia from his presidency and artistic interpretations of the national figures of prominence. Use of the museum and library are free to the public. From Interstate Highway 35, exit 26th Street and take the loop under the highway. Turn south onto Red River. Free visitor's parking is available in the university lots. The **Visitor's Center for the University of Texas** is located in the low rise building close to the parking lot. The main areas of the campus are quite far away, however. The **Austin Museum of Art**, *823 Congress Street, Tel. 512/458-8191, Tuesday to Saturday 10am to 9pm; Sunday 1pm to 5pm, admission $2 adults, children $1,* is housed in a temporary location. Exhibits featuring contemporary artists change frequently. The aim of the museum is to bring international art to the local audience. On Thursdays the museum remains open until 9pm and does not charge admission.

The **Laguna Gloria Museum**, *3809 West 35th Street, Tel. 512/458-8191,* highlights artists of prominence in the southwest. The museum grounds on the shore of Lake Austin, have modern sculpture and walking trails. During the first weekend of May the museum hosts Fiesta, a celebration of children and art.

Austin's largest playground, **Zilker Park**, covers 400 acres. Jogging trails from town lake run through Zilker Park, and the many fields are used for soccer and Frisbee games nearly all year. **Barton Springs**, *Tel. 512/476-9044,* a large, natural spring fed pool is open year-round.

Nearby, **Zilker Hillside Theater** hosts free summer performances. The **Austin Area Garden Center** spotlights plants native to the region. The **Botanical Gardens** include a tour of dinosaur tracks unearthed at the site. To get to Zilker Park, from central Austin take Mopac Expressway south, exit Zilker Park. The park entrances are located on west Barton Springs Road.

Austin has the one and only **National Wildflower Research Center**, *4801 La Crosse Avenue, Tel. 512/292-4100.* Most of the facility is devoted to cultivation and research of native plants. The main building has informative displays about local wildflowers, and you may walk around the seasonal growing beds. The facility sponsors classes throughout the year. Across the street, the veloway is an ideal track for in-line skating and bicycle riding. The National Wildlife Research Center is located off Mopac Expressway South.

NIGHTLIFE & ENTERTAINMENT

The **Austin Symphony**, *1101 Red River Street, Tel. 476-4626,* performs at the beautiful Symphony Square outdoor auditorium and at the University of Texas Fine Arts Complex. Guest musicians of international notoriety are featured during the season. The city receives its dose of opera from the **Austin Lyric Opera**, *200 East 6th Street, Tel 512/472-5927.* And the **Ballet Austin**, *3002 Guadalupe Street, Tel. 476-9051,* presents some of the best known ballets. The **University of Texas Performing Arts Center**, *Tel. 512/471-1444,* hosts these Austin companies and traveling shows throughout the year. The **University of Texas Frank Erwin Center**, *Interstate Highway 35 and Martin Luther King Boulevard, Tel. 512/477-6060,* hosts large concerts.

You can buy tickets to local theater productions, the Austin Ballet, Austin Symphony, and some touring performances at **Austix**, *The Box Office Inside BookPeople, 603 North Lamar, Tel. 512/454-TIXS, Wednesday to Saturday 11:30am to 6pm, Sunday to Tuesday closed; cash and checks only.* Half-price tickets are available for many performances. These tickets are offered at the discretion of the producers of each performance, so there are no advance schedules available for upcoming events. Availability of tickets for weekend performances is announced each Wednesday. You may purchase tickets on the day of performance only. Credit cards are not accepted.

Children's Playfest, *Dougherty Arts Center, 1110 Barton Springs Road, Tel. 512/454-TIXS,* is sponsored by the Austin Circle of Theaters and features local and touring groups. The festival runs for ten weeks and in the spring and summer months. Performances include puppet theater, artistic performances and theater productions. Tickets are $4.50 for all ages; most performances run from Tuesday-Saturday at 10am and 3pm on weekends.

THE BATS

*Most of the year at sunset you will see crowds lining the **Congress Street Bridge** over Town Lake waiting for the bats to appear. On summer nights, just after dark, hundreds of thousands of Mexican Freetail bats emerge in clouds. Austin is part of their migration, which in the Austin area begins in the spring and ends in November. During August you have the chance to see the greatest number of bats. You can watch the bats from the Town Lake aboard **Capital Cruises**, at the Hyatt Regency on Town Lake, Tel. 512/480-9264. The boat leaves 15 minutes before sunset; fare $8 adult, $5 child.*

Central Austin

THE TAVERN, *922 West 12th Street. Tel. 512/474-7494. Monday to Sunday, 11am to 2am. Credit cards accepted.*

Outside the neon sign reads "air conditioned." And its true. The tavern offers a taste of college life, with pitchers of cold beer, greasy burgers and fries. The university crowd has filled this bar for over 60 years. You will find yourself in a cheering section when the Longhorns play ball. Upstairs are the pool tables and smoking section.

TEXAS CHILI PARLOR, *1409 Lavaca Street. Tel. 512/472-2828. Credit cards accepted.*

The bravest souls who venture into the Texas Chili Parlor order a bowl of XXX Chili. The "X" designates the spice factor: one "X" is merely mild, which means you may need a very cold beer to cut the sting; "XX," or medium is strong stuff. The "XXX" will light a fire in your mouth. This is the real thing, filled with meat and no beans. Vegetarians should stick to the Tex-Mex dishes.

The Texas Chili Parlor is close to the state government offices and the University of Texas. It is a friendly saloon with good drinks and a smoking section. Happy hour specials draw a local clientele and offer a good excuse to avoid the rush hour traffic that clogs the streets downtown. Monday to Wednesday, 11am to midnight; Thursday to Saturday, 11am to 2am; Sunday, noon to midnight.

WATERLOO BREWING COMPANY, *401 Guadalupe Street. Tel. 512/ 477-1836. Credit cards accepted.*

The food is nothing exceptional at Waterloo Brewing Company; stick to the beer. The very casual crowd enjoys the home-brew while playing pool or lounging on the roof-top deck. O Henry's Porter is the stout signature beer. Monday to Sunday 11am to 2am.

6th Street

Sixth Street fancys itself a Bourbon Street in miniature. Most people who visit Austin believe that 6th Street is the center of Austin's nightlife. The blocks between Congress Avenue and Interstate Highway 35 are filled with bars, music and dancing. The historic buildings give the area character.

PARADISE CAFE, *401 6th Street. Tel. 512/476-5667. Credit cards accepted.*

The Paradise Cafe feels like a neighborhood hangout. The casual renovation of an historic building provides an excellent atmosphere for relaxed drinks or a simple meal. The young crowd at Paradise represents the mature side of college life. Generally a low-key and crowded bar on the weekends, this is a good spot to either begin or round off your evening. Light food such as sandwiches, salads and pasta is served from lunchtime (11:30am) until 1am.

WYLIE'S BAR AND GRILL, *400 East 6th Street. Tel. 512/472-3712. Credit cards accepted.*

Wylie's is a classic 6th Street bar — packed with college students on weekend nights. This bar still retains enough dignity to attract professionals as well. In an environment that is used to places coming and going almost overnight, Wylie's has stood the test of time. The space often fills to standing-room only, even on the patio. During the day food is served.

ESTHER'S POOL, *525 East 6th Street. Tel. 512/320-0553. Credit cards accepted.*

Some of the best and brightest actors and comedians perform at Esther's, which is painted to resemble a large swimming pool. Two shows on Friday and Saturday night poke political satire and slapstick comedy at local politicians. Even if you are not up on the latest local news, you will get a big laugh from the Ester's performers.

Warehouse District

B-SIDE, *300 Colorado Street. Tel. 512/478-2337. Credit cards accepted.*

Generally this small bar attached to Bitter End restaurant features local jazz musicians. Some nights, however, home-grown celebrities such as Will Sexton take the stage. The beer on tap are the same as those featured in Bitter End. Their trademark bitter beer has a strong aftertaste and full body; the softer EZ Wheat beer is complimented by a slice of lemon and is a very satisfying brew. A full selection from the bar is also available. This is a comfortably trendy bar which generally has a manageable crowd.

CEDAR STREET, *208A West Fourth Street. Tel. 512/708-8811. Credit cards accepted.*

Jazz music bounces off the stone walls surrounding Cedar Street's outdoor stage. The bar specializes in redefining the martini; the Cedar Street Martinis mixes tequila, cointreau and Cabernet Sauvignon — and the taste is extraordinary. The cigar room just inside the bar on the right sells only the best stogies.

SPEAKEASY, *412 Congress Avenue. Tel. 512/476-8017. Credit cards accepted.*

Indeed, the crowd is *tres chic*; and as long as cigars are in vogue, Speakeasy will lead the local bar scene. The entrance is through the alley behind the building on Congress Avenue. This bar has the dark wood paneling and crystal chandeliers which so compliment beautiful people drinking martinis. Lounge music featured on the weekends. Dance lessons are given on Tuesday nights at 8pm. If you can learn in a crowd of about 50 novices, you may have a shot of success with the jitterbug.

RUTA MAYA, *400 Lavaca. Tel. 512/472-9638 Credit cards accepted.*

The coffee house is named for the route that connects the ancient Maya cities of Central and Meso-America. Ruta Maya imports its coffee beans from the Maya region and roasts the beans in Austin. Ruta Maya has successfully done what few cafes can claim, merged an alcohol-free environment with the night scene. Bands play on weekend nights. If the music is too loud, you can hang out with the slackers on the sidewalk in front of Ruta Maya and watch the crowds shuffle by. Bulletin board monitors the latest website chatter about the revolutionary conflicts in

Mexico. The tobacco shop sells cigarettes and cigars. Monday to Thursday 7am to midnight; Friday, 7am to 2am Saturday 8am to 3am; Sunday 8am to midnight.

SPORTS & RECREATION

The best outdoor trails in the Austin area are the **Barton Creek Greenbelt**. Hikers, mountain bikers, cross-country runners and even leisurely walkers flock to the greenbelt. Do not despair if the serenity of the preserve is threatened by hoards of nature seekers; the crowds thin out by the time you hit the interior trails.

There are a number of access points for the greenbelt, and a variety of paths you can take once on it. You can pick up a map at most local bookstores or just go to one of the trial heads and follow the signs. The easiest access is from **Zilker Park** (you can park by Barton Springs Pool).

The young, mobile population of Austin is crazy about mountain biking. There are a number of excellent trails ranging in difficulty from beginner to very advanced. **Emma Long Park** lets bikers enjoy Lake Travis from atop two wheels. The short trail loop is entirely over difficult terrain. This is also a **motor-cross loop**. From Austin, take Farm Road 2222 west. Just past the intersection with Loop 360, take the first road north; a sign will point the way to the city road that leads to the park.

Sailing on Lake Travis is perhaps the best way to see the beauty of the Hill Country. You can charter or rent a sailboat from **Sail Aweigh Charters**, *Tel. 512/250-8141*. Hourly rates for a boat and captain range from $35 to $55 for up to six adults. Customized cruises and sailing lessons can be arranged.

Town Lake, in the center of Austin, is one of the few places in the southwest where you can go **sculling**. The **Texas Rowing Club**, *Tel. 512/328-7180*, located on Town Lake, offers lessons which begin at $55 per hour. The boats are located on the north side of the lake on the trail between the First Street and Lamar Street Bridges.

Spectator Sports

Get out your burnt orange sweatshirt and watch sports the action of the **University of Texas Longhorns**, *Tel. 512/471-3333 or 800/982-BEVO*. The football season runs September to December; the baseball season runs from February through May. And both women's and men's Longhorns basketball is exceptional.

EXCURSIONS & DAY TRIPS

Why not take a train to nowhere? The **Hill Country Flyer**, *Tel. 512/477-8468*, is a steam train which travels along rails laid in 1881. The train starts in the Austin suburb of Cedar Park. The 33 mile trip to Liberty Hill takes two and one-half hours; the train runs once per day on weekends. Departure from Cedar Park is at 10am, and departure from Liberty Hill is at 3pm. Occasionally the **Twilight Flyer** makes evening runs.

The **Vanishing Texas River Cruise**, *Tel. 512/756-6986*, is a good way to see the bio-diversity of the lakes of Central Texas. The cruise takes two and one-half hours and sails all year. You will see small waterfalls, lovely rock cliffs and the flora and fauna of the Hill Country. The cruises run Wednesday, Saturday and Sunday at 11am. From Austin, take Interstate Highway 35 south then turn east onto Ben White/Highway 71. At Marble Falls, go north on Highway 281. When you reach Burnet, take Highway 29 west for three miles, then head north on Ranch Road 2341 for 14 miles. Call ahead for current schedules and fares.

No matter how hot the weather gets, **Longhorn Cavern**, *Ranch Road 2 Box 23, Burnet, Tel. 512/756-4680 or 756-6976 (recorded tour information)*, remains a cool 64 degrees. Visiting the caves allows a look into the spectacular geology of central Texas. The guided tour leads through 1.25 miles of underground rock formations. On the outside you can walk along two miles of easy trails that cover but a fraction of the 600 acre park. Tours of the cavern begin daily at 10am. From Burnet, take Highway 281 west. The Longhorn Cavern State Park is on Park Road 4.

PRACTICAL INFORMATION

For roadside assistance and other help – if you're a member – contact the **American Automobile Association** (AAA), *3005 South Lamar Boulevard, Suite D113, Austin, Tel. 512/444-4757.*

The **Austin Visitor Center**, *201 East 2nd Street, Austin, Tel. 512/478-0098*, is located downtown, near the Convention Center.

The **Texas Back Roads Scholar**, *2802 Oak Park Drive, Austin, Tel. 512/444-4550*, arranges tours for individuals and groups. Ecology and history are the focus of the tours.

WACO

Waco is named for the Native Americans who lived in the area at the time of the Spanish Conquest. Agriculture has always played a major role in this city. The historic downtown area is the product of the cattle boom days, when the Chisholm Trail blazed through Waco. **Baylor University** is located in Waco. The Baylor mascot, a baby black bear, lives in a park at Baylor University. Actually there are three bears, each one year apart in age, which live together on the stream. The Baylor Bears are always cubs; when they reach adulthood they are given to wildlife preserves. A number of interesting museums add to the area's cultural heritage.

ARRIVALS & DEPARTURES

The **Waco municipal airport** is 10 miles from the center of the city. American Eagle and Continental Airlines serve Waco.

ORIENTATION

Downtown Waco is just west of Interstate Highway 35. Baylor University is located on the east side of Interstate Highway 35. Waco Transit Service operates the city buses, *Tel. 817/753-0113.*

WHERE TO STAY

DOWNTOWN COURTYARD, *101 Washington Avenue, Waco. Tel. 817/752-8686 or 800/321-2211. Rates: $79. Credit cards accepted.*

Staying in downtown Waco is a pleasant switch from the highway orientation of the most modern part of the city. The central business area has a number of turn-of-the-century high-rise office buildings that exemplify the boomtown. The inn has an outdoor pool. The hotel is at the corner of University Parks Drive and Washington Avenue.

HAMPTON INN, *4259 North Interstate Highway 35, Waco. Tel. 817/412-1999 or 800-HAMPTON. Rates: $74.95 to $84.95. Credit cards accepted.*

The 119 room Hampton Inn in Waco is new and offers amenities that appeal to business travelers. A hospitality room can be provided for groups of 18 or more and there is a business center with fax and copy machines. Rooms have microwave ovens, coffee makers and hair dryers. Some rooms have a spa bath. From Interstate Highway 35, exit Lakeshore Drive. The inn is on the west side of the highway.

FAIRFIELD INN, *5805 North Woodway Drive, Woodway. Tel./Fax 817/776-7821. Credit cards accepted.*

The Fairfield Inn is a comfortable and convenient place to stay while in the Waco area. Amenities include an indoor pool. All rooms receive continental breakfast. The inn is about five miles southwest of the city center. From Interstate Highway 35, take the Loop 340/Highway 6 exit. Travel north to Waco Drive, also called Highway 84. The inn is at the intersection of Highways 84 and 6.

WHERE TO EAT

THE ELITE CAFE, *2132 Valley Mills Drive, Waco. Tel. 817/754-4941. Credit cards accepted.*

For over 50 years, the Elite Cafe has been catering to the residents of Waco and those just passing though. This is a pleasant place to stop for a coffee break or a full meal. The Elite Cafe is just what its name says, an upscale diner that serves both healthy and downright decadent food. The cafe is known for its generous chicken fried steaks. And, naturally, the shakes are great. Soups and salads are among the lighter menu items.

SEEING THE SIGHTS

The first fort of the Texas Rangers was constructed in Waco. Today the **Texas Rangers Museum**, *University Parks Drive, Tel. 817/750-8631, open daily 9am to 5pm, admission $3.50 adult, $1.50 child,* documents the history of this notorious police force. Displays chronicle the history of the Texas Rangers and give insight to the dangerous life on the Texas frontier. The museum sits on 35 acres and wagon tours of the grounds are conducted daily.

On the west of Interstate Highway 35, at University Parks Drive and 4th Street, you will find a **suspension bridge** built in 1870. According to local lore this very bridge was used as a model for the much larger Brooklyn Bridge.

Waco is the birthplace of Dr. Pepper, and the **Dr. Pepper Museum**, *300 South 5th Street, Tel. 817/757-1024, Monday to Saturday 10am to 4pm and Sunday noon to 4pm, admission $3.50 adult, $1.50 students,* pays homage to the tasty soft drink. The drink was invented in 1885 at a local soda fountain which stood at Austin Avenue and 4th Street. Its popularity quickly grew, and by 1906 the drink was being bottled for distribution. Dr. Pepper has not been produced in Waco since 1922. The museum features memorabilia and an old-fashioned soda fountain that serves Dr. Pepper.

EXCURSIONS & DAY TRIPS

The oldest Dr. Pepper bottling plant, operating since 1891, is in Dublin, 94 miles west of Waco. The **Dr. Pepper Bottling Company**, *Highway 377, Dublin, Tel. 817/445-3466, Monday to Friday 8am to 5pm,* jumps into action every Tuesday, when the bottling is done. Visitors are welcome to tour the small factory and museum. You can buy the Dr. Pepper produced here, which is made according to the original specifications with pure cane sugar. From Waco, take Highway 6 west. Dublin and the Bottling Company are located at the intersection of Highways 6 and 377.

PRACTICAL INFORMATION

The **Waco Chamber of Commerce**, *University Parks Drive, Waco, Tel. 817/752-6551 or 800/WACO-FUN,* provides tourist information.

A **hotline** lists upcoming special events, *Tel. 817/752-9226.*

SAN MARCOS

The city of **San Marcos** is known for its quaint homes, old town square and **Southwest Texas State University**. The university has a student population of about 20,000, which gives this town of 35,000 much of its personality.

Before the area was colonized in the mid-nineteenth century, Native Americans had inhabited the fertile river banks as early as 12,000 years ago. The cool springs and river access made San Marcos a desirable retreat for settlers and travelers in the nineteenth century. Today the city is an escape for Austinites seeking a little fun. The San Marcos river stays a perfect 72 degrees, making it a year-round sports attraction. City parks line the river, offering beautiful spots for picnics and recreation.

On the first weekend of may you can get a rare glimpse into the historic homes of San Marcos when they are open to public tours for the **Tours of Distinction**. On the third weekend in April you can see the sky fill with color at the **Bluebonnet Kite Fest**. Just as the heat of summer is beginning to subside, the **Chilympiad** ignites taste buds. The chili cook-off is held on the third weekend of September and is one of the largest events of its kind.

ARRIVALS & DEPARTURES

San Marcos is on Interstate Highway 35, about 40 miles south of Austin. Highways 21, 80 and 123 from the east meet in San Marcos.

When departing, if you are heading south to **New Braunfels**, an alternative to the congested Interstate Highway 35 is Hunter Road (Farm Road 2439). This road follows the Union-Pacific Railroad tracks south through Gruene to New Braunfels.

ORIENTATION

San Marcos Transit (SMT), *Tel. 512/353-4768*, runs trolley-style buses that serve all the tourist destinations and the outlet malls, Southwest Texas State University and the parks along the river. The main transfer point is located across form the courthouse. Regular one-way adult fare is 50¢, children under five ride free.

For Greyhound information, call the **Greyhound Bus Station**, *Tel. 512/392-4649*.

WHERE TO STAY

CRYSTAL RIVER INN, *326 West Hopkins, San Marcos. Tel. 512/396-3739. Rates: $60 to $120. Credit cards accepted.*

This large two story Victorian home was built in 1883. The two-story columns and patio on the front of the house give it southern charm. The house has stately gardens and twelve rooms for guests, each exquisitely furnished. You can walk through the surrounding quiet streets and see the town pretty much as it may have been at the turn of the century. The beautiful rooms offer special touches such as fresh flowers.

FORGET-ME-NOT RIVER INN, *Main Street, Martindale. Tel. 512/ 357-6385. Rates: $60 to $100. Credit cards accepted.*

The Victorian house, built in 1899, has unique architecture. The center room is a round tower, which gives character to the style of the home. The grounds run right to the banks of the San Marcos River, and are surrounded by woods. Each of the three rooms is decorated in a theme, like the Russian Ivy room or the Irish Rose room. A separate three bedroom cottage can accommodate an entire family. For a romantic touch, you can request breakfast in bed instead of dining with other guests in the music room. The house is about five miles from San Marcos, in the center of Martindale, one of the towns where the movie *A Perfect World* was filmed. From San Marcos, take Highway 80 south to Martindale.

STAGE STOP RANCH, *1100 Old Mail Route, Fischer. Tel. 830/935- 4455 or 800/782-4378, Fax 830/935-4445. Rates: $75 to $225. Credit cards accepted.*

The ranch was in existence even before stage coaches made it a rest stop. The ranch is near both Canyon Lake and the Guadalupe River. Three private rooms in the main house each have a private bath and are drenched in sunlight. The Wells Fargo Room is a perfect romantic getaway, with deeply colored wood paneling, a large fireplace and a door to the outside hot tub. The separate cabins have air conditioning and heating and modern western-style furnishings. The largest cabin, Live Oak Lodge, is large enough to hold a family and has a kitchenette. Enjoy the outdoors Texas-style, horse riding, fishing or just strolling through the great outdoors. From San Marcos, take Ranch Road 12 west and to Ranch Road 32. Continue to the foot of Devil's Backbone scenic drive, where the ranch is located.

AQUARENA INN, *One Aquarena Springs Drive, San Marcos. Tel. 512/ 245-7500 or 800/893-9466. Rates: $69 to $79. Credit cards accepted.*

This motel has 24 rooms and caters to families and youngsters under the age of 15 years stay free. The on-site pool and golf course give guests recreational options other than the Aquarena park itself. The rooms are simple and of good standards. Continental breakfast is included.

HOLIDAY INN EXPRESS, *108 Interstate Highway 35, San Marcos. Tel. 512/754-6621, or 800/HOLIDAY. Credit cards accepted.*

The new Holiday Inn express includes a breakfast buffet and free local calls in all the rooms. Cable television and fax/modem phone lies are some of the perks. Recreational facilities include an outdoor pool and hot tub.

WHERE TO EAT

BALLOO'S BISTRO, *423 North LBJ Street, Suite H, San Marcos. Tel. 512/392-2639. Credit cards accepted.*

Balloo's brings New Orleans muffallettas to central Texas. The trademark sandwich is not only large, but topped with Balloo's own olive sauce ($3.99). The generous wraps are a bargain and feature handmade pita bread ($2.99). A variety of vegetarian sandwiches highlight the menu; fresh soup is featured daily. The cozy restaurant is located between the main square and the university.

PALMER'S, *216 West Moore Street, San Marcos. Tel. 512/353-3500. Credit cards accepted.*

This beautiful restaurant has a large outdoor courtyard, fully shaded by trees. As you walk in you will understand the motto "paradise found;" the lush garden fills the place, inside and out. The food comes in generous portions and is of the highest quality. The extensive menu includes grilled tuna ($10.95), Tenderloin Marsala ($13.45) and an array of sandwiches and vegetables. The southern corn fritters are a treat, served with honey. Palmer's is located south of the town square, at the corner of Hutchison and Moore Streets.

CENTERPOINT STATION, *3946 Interstate Highway 35, San Marcos. Tel. 512/392-1103, Fax 392-1108. Credit cards accepted.*

After a long day of shopping at the outlet mall, or to break up your highway drive, stop in at Centerpoint Station. The five-and-dime theme diner serves simple and inexpensive burgers and fries. The toys and gifts for sale are accented by the best collection of antique signs you will find.

SEEING THE SIGHTS

Southwest State University sits on a hill to the west of downtown. Just off the Town Square you will find the historic homes on **Blevins Street**, a lovely atmosphere for a stroll or Sunday drive.

Mix a dribbling of science with an amusement park and you come up with **Wonder World**, *Highway 80, Tel. 512/392-3760 or 800/782-7653, extension 228, open daily March to October 8am to 8pm.* The main attraction is Wonder Cave which has crystal rock formations and fossils. The cave is part of the Balcones Fault. Tours of the cave run every 15 minutes and last 45 minutes. On top of the ground you can climb the steps of the really tall (110 feet) observation tower which overlooks the petting zoo. The park is best appreciated by small children who will get a kick out of the "anti-gravity house" and mini-train ride. The Wonder Cave is interesting in itself, but pales in comparison to the Caverns of Sonora or Longhorn Caverns.

Formerly an amusement park, **Aquarena**, *Aquarena Springs Drive, Tel. 512/396-8900*, is an educational center which teaches guests about the rich flora and fauna native to the San Marcos River. The glass bottom boat tours of the river are the main attraction. You can see straight through the crystal clear water of the San Marcos River, and practically enter the underwater world. Students from Southwest Texas State University are guides through the botanical park. From Interstate Highway 35, take the Aquarena Springs exit and follow the signs about one-half mile to Aquarena.

NIGHTLIFE & ENTERTAINMENT

San Marcos has a lively collegiate nightlife all year round.
CAFE ON THE SQUARE & BREW PUB, *126 North LBJ Street. Tel. 512/353-9289.*

This lively brew pub serves the freshest beer in town. The cafe is popular with locals and the college crowd. Live music take the stage in the evenings. Open Tuesday to Saturday.
CHEATHAM STREET WAREHOUSE, *119 Cheatham Street. Tel. 512/396-7009.*

Students from Southwest Texas State University fill the place up on weekends. This casual venue has live music many nights; Thursday night features keg beer.

SPORTS & RECREATION

The truly adventuresome can jump out of a plane with **Skydive San Marcos**, *Tel. 512/488-2214.* They can plan dives for all skill levels, from advanced to novice.

To enjoy the fun of river sports, you can visit either of two canoe and rafting rental shops. Both the **T. G. Canoe Livery**, *Tel. 512/353-3946,* and **Spencer Canoes**, *Tel. 512-357-6113,* are located on Highway 80, just southeast of the Blanco River. From Interstate Highway 35, take exit 205.

SHOPPING

You can actually spend days shopping in San Marcos. The **San Marcos Factory Shops**, *3939 Interstate Highway 35 south, Tel. 800/628-9465 Monday to Saturday 10am to 9pm, Sunday 11am to 6pm,* is the largest outlet mall in Texas. Next door is the **Tanger Outlet Center**, *Tel. 512/396-7444 or 800/4-TANGER, Monday to Saturday 9am to 9pm, Sunday 11am to 6pm.* The outlet centers are on the east side of Interstate Highway 35; take exit 200.

EXCURSIONS & DAY TRIPS

One of the most scenic drives in the state is a stretch of curving country road called **Devil's Backbone**, just southwest of San Marcos.

From San Marcos, go west on Ranch Road 12, which turns into Ranch Road 32. The 25 mile drive offers striking views and the unique cliffs are part of the Balcones Faultline. During the afternoon or evening, stop by **Devil's Backbone Tavern**, *Ranch Road 12*, about five miles west of San Marcos. This old-time diner and watering-hole will give you a chance to meet the local folk.

Thirty miles west of San Marcos, on Highway 473 you will find a small, white Catholic Church built in 1889. The small house of worship does not have a name. The structure and interior were constructed from materials that had to be transported at least 30 miles over the unsettled Texas hills. The original interior remains intact, but the church is usually closed. It stands as a testimony of the resilience and determination of Texas settlers.

Visitors are welcome at the **Holy Archangel Greek Orthodox Monastery**, which is found at the end of a winding single lane country road off of Highway 473. The ranch-style buildings have a single bell tower in the Greek style. The countryside is beautiful and the quiet semi-manicured grounds provide a refuge for religious contemplation. Visiting hours are during daylight and religious services. The dress code should be respectfully observed. Women wear skirts that fall below the knee (pants and shorts are not permitted) and should wear a scarf or veil. Men should wear long pants and shirts with long sleeves.

PRACTICAL INFORMATION

The **Visitor's Center**, *Tel. 512/353-3435 or 888/200-5620*, is on the west side of Interstate Highway 35; take exit 206 and watch for the blue "Tourist Information" exit sign. At the office you can pick up a free brochure which explains a driving tour of the historic houses and buildings of the town.

WIMBERLY

Wimberly, settled in 1848, typifies the central Texas lifestyle. Surrounded by the beauty of nature, the town attracts tourists who yearn for a touch of simplicity. The **Blanco River** feeds the community water, the most precious resource in the dry Texas hills.

The residents of Wimberly, at home in the wilderness and striving to retain their history, have made the city one of the coziest tourist destinations in the state. Unlike the more crowded cities of Fredericksburg or Castroville, Wimberly still feels like home. The gloss of non-native influences has not yet stained the mesquite wood of Wimberly.

On the first week of each month, Wimberly holds **First Saturday Market Day** from April to December. You can find locally made crafts, antiques and a variety of collectibles.

ARRIVALS & DEPARTURES

Wimberly is on Ranch Road 12, between Austin and San Marcos. From Interstate Highway 35, exit Ranch Road 12 in San Marcos. Travel northwest to Wimberly, 15 miles from San Marcos.

WHERE TO STAY

There are well over 100 places to stay in the Blanco River area. The following accommodations services can place reservations specific to your needs:
- **Bed and Breakfast of Wimberly,** *Tel. 512/847-9666*
- **Country Innkeepers,** *Tel. 800/230-0805*
- **Guest Reservation Service,** *Tel. 800/230-0805*
- **Hill Country Accommodations,** *Tel. 512/847-7322 or 800/926-5028*
- **Wimberly Lodging and Reservation Service,** *Tel. 512/847-3909 or 800/ 460-3909*

BLAIR HOUSE, *100 Spoke Hill Road, Wimberly. Tel. 512/847-1111, Fax 847-8820. Rates: $135. Credit cards accepted.*

Blair House has seven spacious rooms each elegantly furnished in the traditional southern manner, in a commodious house on rural land about one mile from the center of town. A gourmet breakfast is served every morning, and in the evening your sweet tooth will be delighted at the dessert selection.

HEART HOUSE, *12,711 Ranch Road 12, Wimberly. Tel. 512/847-1414. Rates $75.*

You will have the cozy feeling of being an honored guest at the Heart House. The single guest room in Heart House includes continental breakfast. On Market Day weekends, the room is available for two nights minimum.

MOUNTAIN VIEW MOTEL, *Ranch Road 12, Wimberly. Tel. 512/847-2992. Rates: $65 to $70. Credit cards accepted.*

This simple, country hotel is a quaint no-frills alternative to staying in a local bed and breakfast. The solitude and beautiful vistas from the hotel make up for the lack of decorative flair on the interior. Continental breakfast is included. Take Ranch Road 12 south for three miles.

7-A RANCH, *River Road, Wimberly. Tel. 512/847-2517. Rates: $50.50 to $79.50 Credit cards accepted.*

Thirty cabins compose a virtual community of weekend outdoor enthusiasts at the 7-A ranch. You can rent an entire lodge which can hold up to 40 people. Contact the ranch for more information about large groups. Swimming in the creek or hiking along the nature trails is a good way to pass the time while here.

20

WHERE TO EAT

CYPRESS CREEK CAFE, *on the Village Square, Wimberly. Tel. 512/ 847-2515. Credit cards accepted.*

The cafe serves light fare including a healthy selection of vegetarian items. The bar in the back becomes lively on weekend nights. Tuesday to Thursday 7:30am to 9:30pm, Sunday 7:30am to 3pm.

JOHN HENRY'S RESTAURANT AND CLUB, *on the Village Square, Wimberly. 512/847-5467. Credit cards accepted.*

You can sit on the patio above Cypress Creek and indulge in the down-home flavors that make John Henry's one of the most loved restaurants in central Texas. If your taste buds are gentle, you may want to ask for the jalapenos on the side. Steaks and chicken as well as soup and salads make up the menu. A meal costs about $10.

SEEING THE SIGHTS

The reason most visitors spend time in Wimberly is to simply enjoy the beauty of the hill country and slow pace of a small town. The **town square**, located on Ranch Road 12 in the center of town, has antique shops and art galleries. A second center of small shops, the **Olde Town Square**, connects to the town square.

A mixing of craftsman and artist describes the resident glassblower at **Wimberly Glass Works**, *Spoke Hill Road, Tel. 512/847-9348, Friday, Saturday, Sunday and Monday noon to 5pm and by appointment.* Age old glass blowing techniques coupled with creative designs produce a show and a work of art. You can watch unique pieces blown while a guide tells about the history and technique of glass blowing. From Wimberly, take Ranch Road 12 south about one and one-half miles. The sign points the way to the Glass Works entrance, which is behind a church. During the summer Wimberly Glass Works opens at 10am.

The Wimberly locals hang out atop **Mount Alberta**, *Ranch Road 2325 at Woodcreek.* The limestone cliff stands 1200 feet high, but getting to the summit is easy. A path of steps leads you there with no mountain climbing gear necessary.

NIGHTLIFE & ENTERTAINMENT

CYPRESS CREEK CAFE, *on the Village Square, Wimberly. Tel. 512/ 847-2515. Credit cards accepted.*

After dinner at the Cyprus Creek Cafe, you can linger to take in some live music. The cafe serves coffee drinks to the tunes of local jazz musicians on Thursday, Friday and Saturday nights.

PRACTICAL INFORMATION

The **Chamber of Commerce**, *1400 Ranch Road 12, Wimberly, Tel. 512/ 847-2201*, offers information about recreational activities and accommodations along the Blanco River.

NEW BRAUNFELS

The city of **New Braunfels** was named for Prince Carl Solms of Germany, who purchased the land of New Braunfels for German settlers during the days of the Republic of Texas. The German heritage remains strong in the town; German food, language and architecture stand out as the most obvious signs of the past.

During the summer the area is flooded by Texans seeking the refreshing waters of the Comal and Guadalupe Rivers. Local industry (including mills on the Comal River), farming and ranching have sustained New Braunfels over the decades. Today tourists are one of the city's largest resources.

You can have the best time at **Wurstfest**. While that pun is hardly new, the German celebration provides unique family fun. You will see lots of sausage, accordions and a general carnival atmosphere. A ten kilometer run is part of the festivities that take place in the first week of November. The event is held at the Wursthalle, which is on Landa Park Drive, just north of the city square.

ARRIVALS & DEPARTURES

New Braunfels is on Interstate Highway 35, between Austin and San Antonio. The city is only 45 miles south of Austin and 30 miles north of San Antonio. National chain restaurants and hotels are located along the highway.

ORIENTATION

From Interstate Highway 35, take the Seguin Street, New Braunfels exit. Head west along Seguin Street to reach the town square.

WHERE TO STAY

HOTEL FAUST, *240 South Seguin Street, New Braunfels. Tel. 830/625-7791, Fax 620-1530. Rates: $59 to $89. Credit cards accepted.*

The Faust is by far the most historical, cozy and interesting hotel in the area. The legendary ghost sightings come to life when you look at the old pictures of the former owners hanging in the halls. The Faust was built in the late 1920's and must have been the largest hotel by far in the city. The interior is furnished in the period decor and an antique car stands in the entry foyer. The hotel has a modern renovation, but certain features, such as the tile bathrooms and large bathtubs, original fixtures, adding character to the rooms. Each room has a phone, television and ceiling fan. The hotel bar is frequented by travelers and locals alike.

KUEBLER-WALDIP HAUS, *1620 Hueco Springs Loop, New Braunfels. Tel. 830/625-8372 or 800/299-8372. Rates: $85 to $135. Credit cards accepted.*

You can wander around real frontier buildings on the 40-plus acres of grounds. The main house, built in 1847, is an extraordinary example of hand construction in the German style. And the 1863 schoolhouse was used by the area's children for years. Few structures dating from the period are in current use. The name Kuebler-Waldip does not hint about the origins of the land's first owners, who were French. The house has been lovingly maintained and restored over the years. The farm-style decorations are true to the central Texas lifestyle, which has the rugged flair of a ranch tempered by the grace of country decoration. Each of the nine rooms has a private bath and includes a large homemade southern brunch. Special amenities include spa baths and kitchens and business facilities.

PRINCE SOLMS INN, *295 East San Antonio Street, New Braunfels. Tel. 830-625-9169 or 800/625-9169. Rates: $95 to $150. Credit cards accepted.*

The beautiful two-story Prince Solms Inn is as historic as its namesake, the founder of New Braunfels. For over 145 years the hotel has given travelers a cushy haven in the city. The beautiful antique and modern furnishings reflect the elegant character of the German architecture of 1898, when the house was built. Each of the eight rooms and two suites have private baths. Behind the house a lush courtyard provides a garden setting for relaxation and reading. The inn has a top-notch restaurant, Wolfgang Keller's Restaurant, which serves some of the finest cuisine in the area. You can arrange special events here, including Mystery Weekends, where guest solve the mystery played out by actors. From the main plaza, take San Antonio Street east; the inn is on the corner of Market Street and San Antonio Street.

RIVERSIDE HAVEN, *1491 Edwards Boulevard, New Braunfels. Tel. 830/625-5823. Rates: $85 to $115. Credit cards accepted.*

The large white house, with two levels of porches, overlooks the Guadalupe River. The four guest rooms have river views and homey decor. The largest, The Room With a View, sleeps four. This is the perfect place to stay if you want to enjoy the fun of the Guadalupe River and return home to a lovely accommodation. The owners make every effort to ensure you have an enjoyable stay. Two canoes are available to guests, or you can launch your own tube and float down the river with the stream of summer sun-worshippers. Riverside Haven is only one-half mile from the restaurants and fun of Gruene. From Interstate Highway 35 north of New Braunfels, take Farm Road 306 west to Hunter Road. When the road stops at the Gruene Dance Hall, bear right onto Gruene Road. Take the first right after the bridge on Erveber Road and follow this to the end. Go right on Edwards Boulevard.

THE WHITE HOUSE, *217 Mittman Circle, New Braunfels. Tel. 830/ 629-9354. Rates: $40 to $70. Credit cards accepted.*

The White House gives you southern hospitality and personal service, with rates far lower than most inns and hotels. The White House is one of the first bed and breakfasts to be established in the area and has operated for over a decade. With only three guest rooms, you will be able to enjoy the peace and quiet of the hill country nights while relaxing on the outdoor patio. The house has a small pond and acreage for nature walks. The breakfast, which is included with each room, is a hearty assortment of fresh fruit and juice, homemade pancakes or waffles and sausage.

GRUENE MANSION, *1275 Gruene Road, New Braunfels. Tel. 830/ 620-0760, Fax 625-2442. Rates: $100 to $135. Credit cards accepted.*

The Gruene Mansion is a large, stately home which is a bed and breakfast and restaurant. The beautiful rooms provide a homelike place for repose when visiting Gruene. The Gruene Dance Hall is just a few steps away. The Restaurant at Gruene Mansion serves the finest food in the area. The food has a Cajun inspired French zest. Chicken Poivrade, a chicken breast in port sauce ($9.95), and blackened shrimp over fettucini Alfredo ($13.95) are examples of the light, inventive dishes. A complete selection of wine is available to accompany all tastes. A large deck overlooks the hill country. To get to Gruene, form Interstate Highway 35, exit Highway 337 and travel west. At Gruene Loop Road go north; this will lead you to Gruene.

RODEWAY INN, *1209 Interstate Highway 35 East, New Braunfels. Tel. 210/629-6991 or 800/967-1168, Fax 210/629-0754. Rates: $35.95 to $99.95. Credit cards accepted.*

The Rodeway Inn has 130 rooms. Continental breakfast is included and laundry facilities on the premises are available for guest use. The inn is located at the intersection of Interstate Highway 35 and Highway 46.

WHERE TO EAT

HUISACHE GRILL, *303 D East San Antonio Street, Hew Braunfels. Tel. 830/620-9001. Credit cards accepted.*

The Huisache (pronounced "wee-sach") Grill is a gem of a restaurant. The casual yet elegant atmosphere reflects the nature of the food — easy going and original. The menu items could be described as American or

German cuisine, but that would not give credit to the accents, such as cilantro sauce, jalapeno butter and mint salsa. The vegetarian feast is a plate of the season's freshest veggies grilled to perfection. For example, Chicken Del Rio has roasted red pepper sauce and comes with a side of garlic spinach. Lighter fare includes sandwiches and appetizers. The 3030 Salmon Salad is salade Nicoise with a twist, salmon instead of tuna. Entrees are reasonable, from $6.75 to $10.95. Wine and beer is served.

THE GRIST MILL, *1287 Gruene Road, New Braunfels. Tel. 830/ 625-0684. Credit cards accepted.*

This is one of the most unique places to eat. The restaurant is built in the ruins of a nineteenth century cotton gin. The outdoor seating is cooled by fans and breezes from the nearby river. The food and atmosphere is informal, making the Grist Mill a family tradition for vacationers after a long, hot day of tubing on the Guadalupe River. All the salsas are homemade; the best is the tomatillo sauce, made with avocados and green Mexican tomatoes and served with corn chips. Entrees range from $6.99 for the grilled chicken to $13.99 for the Texas T-bone steak. The hamburgers are a sure bet, and a good deal ($4.49). The fries are round-cut and a delicious indulgence.

WOLFGANG KELLER'S RESTAURANT, *295 East San Antonio Street, New Braunfels. Tel. 830/625-9169. Credit cards accepted.*

This restaurant offers the only opportunity for truly fine dining in the area. The elegant atmosphere sets a romantic mood for a long meal. On weekend nights piano performances are offered. The European food has a distinctively German influence. Wednesday to Saturday 5pm to 10pm, Sunday 11am to 3pm and 5pm to 9pm.

SEEING THE SIGHTS

The local historical societal preserves a small corner of the past at **Conservation Plaza**, *1300 Church Drive, Tel. 830/629-2943, Tuesday to Friday 10am to 3pm, Saturday and Sunday 2pm to 5pm.* The cluster of restored frontier buildings includes a barbershop, a cabinetry workshop and schoolhouse. Some of the historical homes were moved from the countryside. The earliest, the Baege House, dates from 1852.

To catch a glimpse of what may have gone into the old structures, visit the **Museum of Handmade Furniture**, *1370 Church Hill Drive, Tel. 830/ 629-6504, Tuesday to Saturday 10am to 4pm, Sunday 1pm to 4pm, Admission $3 adults.* The collection has elegant German-influenced American designs made from 1850 to 1870. You can walk into the cabinetmakers' workshop to see the tools and techniques used by the furniture craftsmen. From Interstate Highway 35, take exit 189 and travel north on Loop 337. Church Hill Drive intersects with Loop 337.

To complete your tour of German settlement history, venture to the **Sophienburg Museum**, *401 West Coll Street, Monday to Saturday 10am to 5pm, Sunday noon to 5pm.* The exhibits include the personal possessions of the German Prince Solms, who founded the town.

Fans of the cute little figurines based on designs of Sister M. I. Hummel of Germany will enjoy the private collection of the **Hummel Museum**, *199 Main Plaza, Tel 830/625-5636 or 800/456-4866, Fax 830/625-5966, Monday to Saturday 10am to 5pm, Sunday noon to 5pm.* This is the only museum dedicated to Hummel figurines in the world. The entire collection belongs to a European family and includes some of the original drawings and artwork that inspired the Hummel collector's figurines. Of course the museum has a fully-stocked shop.

The oldest landmark in the area is **Natural Bridge Caverns**, *26,495 Natural Bridge Caverns Road, Tel. 830/651-6101,* which is 140 million years old. Guided tours take you through the many "rooms" of crystal stalactites and stalagmites. It takes 120 minutes to make your way through these caverns. The caverns open at 9am and tours leave every 30 minutes. Credit cards are not accepted. From Interstate Highway 35, exit Farm Road 3009 and travel west.

Up on the surface of the earth you can visit **Natural Bridge Wildlife Ranch**, *Tel. 830/438-7400, open daily 9am to 5pm,* a 200 acre safari-style park. Drive along paved paths to see the ranch, which was turned into a wildlife park for endangered species. The petting zoo has llamas and goats.

NIGHTLIFE & ENTERTAINMENT

When in New Braunfels for the evening, head over to Gruene, a group of historic buildings. Even if you are not a country music fan, you will have a ball at the **Gruene Dance Hall**. The restored town of Gruene is actually part of New Braunfels. The old buildings and the famous Gruene Dance Hall stood vacant for decades. An artful renovation turned the city into a popular destination for vacationers. The many antique and crafts shops in Gruene are only a fraction of the attraction. In fact, you can do everything in Gruene that you can in New Braunfels.

To get to Gruene, from Interstate Highway 35 north of New Braunfels, take Farm Road 306 west to Hunter Road. When the road stops at the Gruene Dance Hall, bear right onto Gruene Road.

SPORTS & RECREATION

Tubing is the national sport of the **Guadalupe River**. Occasionally the river has real rapids for kayaking. Most of the summer the river is a highway of people floating along in giant inner tubes. You can rent an inner tube from the concessionaires on the river. Usually the tube rental is for the entire day, and you can take the company's shuttle bus back to the starting point. If you have a choice go ahead and get a tube with a bottom, the extra cost will be well worth it when you bottom-out on the rocky segments of the river.

For man-made water fun, try the giant German-theme water park, **Schiltterbahn**, *305 West Austin Street, Tel. 830/625-2351*, which stands on the banks of the Guadalupe River. Many giant curly waterslides, a wave pool and a small, contained segment of the river for tubing are parts of the attraction.

During the spring and fall parts of the river become rapids. You can rent canoes at **Whitewater Sports**, *11860 Farm Road 306, Tel 830/964-3800*. The points at which shuttles will pick up people floating down the river permit you to have a trip lasting from three to more than six hours. From Interstate Highway 35, take the Farm Road 306/Canyon Lake Exit. Go west to the store. Canoe rental costs $35 for two people.

The **Ole Mill Stream** claims to offer the longest segment for floating on the river. The charge for a tube is $5, admission is $2 if you bring your own tube. The picnic tables at the park must be rented, but most people snack on the river then head over to nearby Gruene for dinner. From Interstate Highway 35, exit New Braunfels (#187) and go west on South Seguin Street. Landa Street is a fork in the road that veers to the left.

VOLKSMARSCH

*If you happen to be in New Braunfels during the first week of January, you will find the water of the Guadalupe is far too cold for a swim. But you can still get into the local outdoors by participating in the annual **Volksmarsch Event**. This is an eleven kilometer walk through the scenic hill country to benefit charity. For more information about the walk, contact the New Braunfels Marsh-und Wandergruppe, P. O. Box 310778, New Braunfels, Texas 78131-0778.*

Right in the center of New Braunfels you will find one of the nicest public parks anywhere, **Landa Park**, *110 Golf Course Drive, Tel 830/608-2160*. There is a variety of outdoor activities for all interests. The park has an Olympic-size spring-fed swimming pool, 18 hole golf course (green fees $12 to $16), and an area for tubing. You can take a walking tour of the grounds with a park ranger, or rent a picnic table for the afternoon.

Golf enthusiasts will enjoy **Sundance Golf Course**, *2294 Common Street, Tel. 830/629-3817*. The eighteen hole par-58 course has a driving range and offers lessons. Greens fees range from $7 to $12; golf carts are available for $6 to $8. From Interstate Highway 35, take Exit 189 and go west on Loop 337. Common Street is about one mile from the highway. Texans who learn tennis often spend a few weeks at the **John Newcombe Tennis Ranch**, *Highway 46 (P. O. Box 310469), New Braunfels, Tel. 800/444-6204*. The training camp has taught children and adults for over 20 years. Adult packages are from two to five days. The children's and junior's programs run throughout the summer. Special arrangements can be made for visitors who want to use the courts during the day or arrange overnight stays without lessons.

SHOPPING

The **New Braunfels Factory Stores**, *651 Interstate Highway 35 North, Tel. 5830/620-6806 or 888/SHOP-333*, was one of the first outlet malls to be built in the state. You can avoid the mobs that clog the larger mall in San Marcos by stopping here instead. From Interstate Highway 35, take Exit 188; the mall is on the west side of the highway.

PRACTICAL INFORMATION

For tourist information, contact the **New Braunfels Chamber of Commerce**, *Tel 800/572-2626*.

JOHNSON CITY

The grandfather of the nation's 36th president, Lyndon Baines Johnson, founded **Johnson City**. Johnson was raised on the ranch in Johnson City, although he was born in nearby Stonewall. President Johnson so well represented the strength and stature of the Texan persona that to native Texans he is simply "LBJ."

ARRIVALS & DEPARTURES

Johnson City is on Highway 290, about 50 miles east of Austin. Highway 281 connects the city to the north and south.

WHERE TO STAY

CRIDER'S MOTEL, *Highways 290 and 281, Johnson City. Tel. 830/868-7163*.

A night at Criders takes you back to the 1950's. Every front door of the motel is painted a different color, as are the metal lawn chairs on the porches. Each room has a small kitchenette and homey furnishings. This is a cute and comfy place to bunk for the night.

Camping

The **Lyndon Baines Johnson State Park**, *Highway 290, Stonewall, Tel. 830/644-2252 or for reservations 512/389-8900*, has camp sites, recreational areas and nature trails. The park is 15 miles east of Johnson City on Highway 290.

Camp at the **Pedernales Falls State Park**, *Ranch Road 3232, Johnson City, Tel. 830/868-7304 or for reservations 512/389-8900*, to enjoy the natural beauty of the hill country. The park has 69 sites with hook-ups and primitive camping areas. The many underground springs near Pedernales Falls allows the lush trees and seasonal foliage to thrive.

WHERE TO EAT

THE FEED MILL CAFE, *103 West Main (Highway 290) Johnson City. Tel. 830/868-7771 or 830/868-7299.*

The funky Feed Mill is a big piece of "living art" in the center of Johnson City. Fried green tomatoes and chicken fried steaks are specialties. Sandwiches ($3.95 to $7.95) are Texas sized and will fill up the hungriest cowboy. For an unusual and delicious twist to a Texas classic, order the grilled cilantro catfish ($6.95). Do not pass up the chance to start your meal with a big plate of fried green tomatoes ($4.95). Beer, wine and margaritas accompany the food.

SEEING THE SIGHTS

There are two parks that keep alive the legacy of President Johnson. The modest childhood home of the nation's 36th president, Lyndon Baines Johnson, is part of the national park which includes two separate sites in central Texas. The museum complex is located in Stonewall on the **LBJ Ranch**, where Johnson was born. The LBJ Boyhood Home is in Johnson City. Both parks receive over 180,000 visitors annually.

The main entrance to the park and the museum complex is at the **Lyndon Baines Johnson State Historical Park**, *Tel. 830/644-2252*, in Stonewall. Stonewall is 15 miles east of Johnson City on Highway 290. From this point you can take a bus tour of the ranch (admission $2 adults, free for children under 12 years) and visit the Sauer-Beckman Living History Farm. Each year the park celebrates President Johnson's birthday by offering free tours of the ranch. A small ceremony is held in the morning and light refreshments are offered to guests all afternoon.

Lyndon Baines Johnson National Historic Park in Johnson City has a visitor center, the home in which Johnson grew up and an exhibit which describes the Johnson Settlement family life. The park is open daily from 8:45am to 5pm. There is no admission charge to walk through the exhibits. A shuttle bus runs from the National Park Visitor Center in

Stonewall to the park in Johnson City. The Visitor's Center is open daily from 8:45am to 5pm.

Just east of Johnson City is the **Pedernales Falls State Park**, *Ranch Road 3232, Tel. 830/868-7304 or for reservations 512/389-8900.* The waterfalls are really gentle cascades of the Pedernales River as it slopes through the Hill Country. The water ranges from a trickle to rushing rapids, depending on the rainfall of the season. The park has campsites, swimming and fishing areas and a 7.5 mile nature trail.

NIGHTLIFE & ENTERTAINMENT

Old Crofts Mill, which produced feed, cotton and flour was hand built over 115 years ago. Modern artistic vision transformed the mill into an eccentric shopping center. Now called the **Feed Mill**, *103 West Main (Highway 290), Tel. 830/868-7771 or 868-7299,* there is a theater here that occasionally holds plays or poetry readings. The Theater is located in the rough stone cellar of the Feed Mill Mall. You sit under cross-timbers in the cool cave-like atmosphere. The Feed Mill Cafe has live country music performances on the weekends. Out back you will find an antique carousel that really works and a petting zoo.

SHOPPING

Johnson City has a number of unique shops that sell gift items. You can stroll through the stores at the **Feed Mill**, like Enchanted Olive, which sells gourmet olive oil and food. Or walk along the old streets through shops brimming with kitschy memorabilia.

EXCURSIONS & DAY TRIPS

The sleepy hamlet of **Blanco** is a favorite spot for day trips from Austin or San Antonio. This town was usurped as the county seat by Johnson City in 1891. The town square used to be the seat of local government and is now virtually frozen in time. Today the antique shops on the town square and the beautiful courthouse are appreciated by the tourists that trickle through town on weekends.

If you are serious about finding unique antiques, try the **Olde Blanco Auction Company**, *318 4th Street, Blanco,* just a few blocks off the town square. The large, non-air conditioned warehouse is the best of a garage sale and antique mart, with seemingly acres of memorabilia, glassware and furniture. On the third Saturday of the month at 6pm, the Old Blanco Auction Company practices what it does best, auctions. This is in conjunction with **Olde Blanco Market Day**, when the town itself becomes a marketplace. Market Days are held from April to November, the third Saturday of each month.

After a long day of shopping, stop by the **Blanco Bowling Club Cafe** which serves diner food such as fries and burgers. But don't eat and run. In the back of the cafe is a small bowling ally. The German-style lanes have nine pins. **Pecan Street Bakery** on the town square attracts the weekend city escapees by serving brunch into the afternoon on weekends.

PRACTICAL INFORMATION

The **Chamber of Commerce**, *406 Highway 290, Johnson City, Tel. 830/ 868-7684*, offers general information and a map that shows historical buildings in the city.

FREDERICKSBURG

The town of **Fredericksburg** was an early frontier settlement in the rough Old West. Driving through the picturesque Hill Country today, you could hardly guess that the town was once a dangerous border land between settlers and Native Americans.

Weekend travelers now flood Fredericksburg and the surrounding areas, which have over 90 bed and breakfasts. You can catch a current flick at the historic Palace Movie Theater on Main Street. Outdoor enthusiasts cannot get enough of Enchanted Rock, a large granite dome which was a sacred spot for Native Americans and nearby Pedernales Falls.

You can also enjoy the specialized gift and antique shops Fredericksburg offers.Many of the merchants in Fredericksburg are true crafts-people. The handicrafts offered are the highest quality and represent a unique blend of interests. You can pick out a hand-crafted guitar, toiletries made from locally grown herbs or wine from the area.

ARRIVALS & DEPARTURES

Fredericksburg is on Highway 290.

THE EASTER FIRES OF FREDERICKSBURG

*One of the more unique celebrations in the area is the **Easter Fires**. Every Easter, hillside fires light up the horizon. The tradition has been part of the Easter holiday as long as locals can recall. A few different explanations for the ritual persist. The hillside fires may be a carry-over of the old European Easter fires. The fires are set to chase bad spirits away and are known as "witch burning." Another oral tradition asserts that when the pioneer children saw fires on distant hills, the adults told them that the Easter Bunny was boiling eggs (actually the fires were Cherokee camps!).*

ORIENTATION

Highway 290, which passes through Austin on the east, turns into Main Street in Fredericksburg. The central part of Main Street is a prosperous small town full of shops and restaurants. The streets that surround Main Street to the north and south have charming old houses and are pleasant for an afternoon stroll. The town square is on Main Street. just east of the merchant center. This is where you will find the visitor information center and town museum.

WHERE TO STAY

If you plan to visit on a holiday weekend you may find using a reservation service the easiest way to get room, since they have a variety of options and can save you the time and trouble of calling many inns:

• **Bed and Breakfast of Fredericksburg**, *240 East Main Street, Fredericksburg. Tel. 830/997-4712* . They have an office where you can walk in and make reservations or call.

• **Be My Guest**, *Tel. 830/972-7227*

• **Gasthaus Schmidt Reservation Service**, *Tel. 830/997-8282*

• **Hill Country Lodging Service**, *Tel. 830/990-8455*

GILES MANOR, *110 North Bowie, Fredericksburg. Tel. 830/990-8400. Rates: $70t o$100. Credit cards accepted.*

Giles Manor has two separate bed and breakfasts on the premises. Alfred's is a log cabin dating from the 1870's which has been made into a cozy hide-away. The Granary is the building which was once the smoke house for the manor. Both accommodations are inviting and have romantic accents, such as fireplaces. But they cannot help but pale in comparison to the elegant main house, which is a two-story limestone home built in the 1870's.

DELFORGE PLACE, *710 Ettie Street, Fredericksburg. Tel. 830/997-6212. Rates: $85 to $95. Credit cards accepted.*

At Delforge Place you can choose to stay in the country-style Weber guest house or in the more elegant main house. The Weber House was a log cabin which was renovated into a guest cottage in the 1880's. The main house has rooms with old fashioned furnishings. You can use the kitchen in the main house. Breakfast is included for each room.

FREDERICKSBURG BED & BREW, *243 East Main Street, Fredericksburg. Tel. 830/997-1646, Fax 997-8026. Rates: $79 to $89. Credit cards accepted.*

Upstairs at the brew pub you will find twelve rooms, pleasantly furnished. Part of the charm of staying here is the convenience of being on the main street, where the town's shops and restaurants are located.

If you do not wan to join the fun downstairs, you can receive a sampling of the beer, which is brewed on-site.

MAGNOLIA HOUSE, *101 East Hackberry Street, Fredericksburg. Tel. 830/997-0306 or 800/880-4374, Fax 830/997-0766. Rates $75 to $125. Credit cards accepted.*

Located on a quiet residential street, just a few blocks from Main Street, the Magnolia House is the classic architecture of small town Texas. The large front porch is a relaxing place for morning and evening alike. Each of the six rooms in the Magnolia House is lovingly furnished with antiques and a unique theme. The romantic Bluebonnet Rooms has a private entrance and a wood burning fireplace. The large bathroom has an antique tub. All rooms include a homemade breakfast buffet.

WHERE TO EAT

FREDERICKSBURG BREWING COMPANY, *245 East Main Street, Fredericksburg. Tel. 830/997-1646. Credit cards accepted.*

You cannot miss this brew pub; it is one of the largest storefronts on Main Street. Copper tanks line the walls of the dining room. You can ask for sample of the current brew, or buy a sample tray which gives a substantial taste of each. The beer is of excellent quality, and the bar is a good place to spend a few hours in the evening if you desire some social interaction.

The food here is good; grilled chicken, burgers and pasta dishes are made with enough flavor and spice to accompany the beer well. Rock climbers making the trek home from a long day at Enchanted Rock often fill the pub on Friday and Saturday nights. They usually head for the back room, which is filled with picnic tables.

NAVAJO GRILLE, *209 East Main Street, Fredericksburg. Tel 830/990-8289, Fax 997-5199. Credit cards accepted.*

Southwest flavors enliven the food of the Navajo grille. The sophisticated, modern atmosphere brings a new aspect to dining in the traditionally German Fredericksburg. The food comes alive with piquant spices and the taste of the grill. Grilled rack of lamb, fresh fish, steak with crawfish remoulade are examples of the always changing nightly specials. Dinner entrees run under $20.

Outside Fredericksburg

HILLTOP CAFE, *Highway 87, Fredericksburg. Tel. 830/997-8922.*

This former filling station now fuels stomachs, not gas tanks. The menu is an eclectic combination of Greek and Cajun fare. The place is packed on the weekends, especially in the summer. Take Highway 87 south from Fredericksburg for 10 miles to reach Hilltop Cafe.

BARBECUE ROAD TRIP!

COOPER'S OLD TIME PIT BAR-B-Q, 604 West Young Street. Llano. Tel. 915/247-5713. Credit cards accepted.

Eating barbecue is practically a hobby for many Texans. And driving one hundred miles to chow down at your favorite restaurant is not out of the question. The brisket is smoked for nearly a full day in giant barbecue pits. It comes out plain and simple – no fancy spices or oil – and perfect. The servings are generous and the meat has an unbeatable flavor. Probably the best in the state. Coopers is located just west of Llano on Highway 29, which is also called Young Street. From Fredericksburg, take Highway 16 north about 40 miles.

SEEING THE SIGHTS

Growing and using herbs is a tradition which has been raised to an art at the **Fredericksburg Herb Farm**, *402 Whitney Street, Tel. 830/997-8615.* Over fourteen acres are cultivated in lovely patterned gardens. Guests can tour the grounds and learn about growing and utilizing the small crops. The herbs are made into a variety of products from candles to toiletries to edible infusions. The selection of essential oils is extensive and of the highest quality. The shop offers a selection of books to turn the novice into a masterful herb gardener. The herb farm is on the western outskirts of Fredericksburg. From Main Street (Highway 290) head west out of town. Go south on Whitney Street. The Fredericksburg Herb Farm has a bed and breakfast and a tea room. The Tea Room is open for lunch and dinner seven days per week. Try the homemade soup, which proves that home-grown fresh herbs make the meal.

History buffs will enjoy the **Verins Kirche Museum**, *100 Main Street,* which is a replica of the city's first public building. The museum represents the melding of European and Texas cultures and shows the transition between tradition and innovation in its unusual design. The wooden, octagonal structure holds a small collection of personal artifacts from the pioneers who settled Fredericksburg. The museum stands on Market Square.

The famous admiral of World War II, Chester Nimitz, was born and raised in Fredericksburg. The **Admiral Nimitz Historical Center**, *304 East Main Street, Tel. 830/997-4379, open daily 8am to 5pm,* provides an historical overview of the man and of World War II in general. The outdoor exhibit includes armament from the World War II era, and a park is dedicated to presidents who served in the war. The museum building, called the Nimitz Hotel, was built in the mid-nineteenth century.

You enter a land of miniatures when you step into the **Bauer Toy Museum**, *233 East Main Street, open Wednesday to Monday 10am to 5pm.* The collection is really aimed more at adult collectors than children. Many of the toys are rare antiques, and the exhibits are strictly "hands-off."

NIGHTLIFE & ENTERTAINMENT

FREDERICKSBURG BREWING COMPANY, *245 East Main Street, Fredericksburg. Tel. 830/997-1646.*

The large Fredericksburg Brewing Company stays open late serving the beer which is brewed on the premises. The variety and flavor are excellent. You are likely to meet other weekend visitors among the friendly clientele, as the bar becomes lively in the evening.

SPORTS & RECREATION

The only truly good rock climbing in central Texas is at the base of **Enchanted Rock**, *Ranch Road 965, Tel. 915/247-3903*, which is a huge granite dome formation that reaches a height of 500 feet. Climbers and rappelling stay in the rocky cliffs at the base of Enchanted Rock. Walking though these trails on a Saturday afternoon is like entering a land of giant spiders — rappellers glide down from all around, and climbers scale up rock-face at each turn.

Campsites are available at Enchanted Rock; during most times of the year reservations are necessary. If you plan to visit the park, arriving in the early morning hours may save you the hassle of waiting for admission. Often the park fills to capacity, and you may find a line of cars waiting to get in. From Fredericksburg, go west on Main Street (Highway 290). Turn north onto Ranch Road 965, which intersects with Main just west of the center of town. You will see the awesome granite hill before you complete the 18 miles to the park entrance.

SHOPPING

A genuine five-and-dime in a small town is a true find. So go ahead and spend some time strolling the isles of **Dooley's** on Main Street. If none of the toys, trinkets or toiletries appeal to you, check out the post cards at the cashiers stands; they are the cheapest in town.

Varney's Chemist, *241 East Main,* offers a complete selection of the locally grown herbal products from the Fredericksburg Herb Farm.

One of the most unusual shops is the **Dulcimer Store**, *155 East Main Street.* Dulcimers are small stringed instruments that resemble mandolins. The factory has produced dulcimers and other stringed instruments for generations.

EXCURSIONS & DAY TRIPS

This is peach country and the roadside is dotted with stands selling fresh peaches and peach ice cream in the late summer. The place which has won the hearts and stomachs of many locals is **Das Peach Haus**. The fresh peach ice cream remains unsurpassed. From the center of Fredericksburg take Highway 87 south. You will also find many similar places along Highway 290.

The dry climate has proven excellent for vineyards and the production of wine. Most of the local wineries grow their own grapes. The operations are small enough to keep the fine art of wine-making to a level that produces excellent table wine. A trip to the **Becker Vineyards**, *Jenschke Lane, Stonewall, Tel. 830/644-2681, Fax 644-2773*, is well worth the stop. A visit to this idyllic rural corner of central Texas lets you imagine the area as it may have looked when it was first settled. The winery operates out of a nineteenth century home, made from the local stone. The small winery produces 5000 cases a year and is particularly known for its white varieties. You can take a tour and sample the wine on a walk-in basis. Jenschke Lane is about ten miles east of Fredericksburg; from Highway 290 travel south.

In the early spring wildflowers blanket the countryside in white, blue and yellow. The most spectacular stretch of road to see the beauty of this natural phenomenon is the **Wild Flower Loop**. The road twists and turns for about 20 miles, each section aglow with flowers. Many Sunday drivers flood the area and there is no parking anywhere on the loop, so expect a good deal of standing traffic. If you can go on a weekday you may have some tranquillity. The loop is not on a map, but you will find the marked turnoff just before Enchanted Rock.

The only esablishment on the loop is Harry's. The address is inexact, but you cannot miss it: **Harry's On the Loop**, *Willow City, Tel. 830/685-3553*, is a back-country road stop that has prospered with the influx of tourists. Harry's is really just a shack; but since it's the only shack within about twenty miles, it has a captive patronage. Harry's sells canned drinks, bags of snack chips and barbecue sandwiches. You can buy brisket by the pound ($5.95 per pound) or the plate (with sides of beans and bread for $5.95). The staff seems to be resentful of the tourists that crowd the small diner, but the clientele is usually friendly and you may strike up a few conversations.

LUCKENBACH

Over 20 years ago the song "Luckenbach, Texas" filled the nation's airwaves. Waylon Jennings made the town a country myth. You can visit the genuine article, which is just south of Fredericksburg and has a population of only 25 by the official count. **Luckenbach** consists of a handful of buildings and a parking area, except on July Fourth weekend, for that is when Willie Nelson holds his annual picnic and Luckenbach overflows with partying fans. It's worth the trip to Luckenbach just to say that you have been there.

The small back roads that lead to Luckenbach are not well marked. From Highway 290, south of Fredericksburg, take Farm Road 1376 south and continue for four miles. There is one bed and breakfast outside Luckenbach.

Where to Stay

THE LUCKENBACH INN, *County Road 13, Luchenbach. Tel. 830/ 997-2205 or 800/997-1124, Fax 830/997-1115. Rates: $95 to $125. Credit cards accepted.*

The ranch house is located in the rural outskirts of Fredericksburg. The lovely home sits high atop a hill, isolated from the nearest highway or town.

PRACTICAL INFORMATION

Tourist Information and a map of historic sites are available at the **Chamber of Commerce**, *106 North Adams Street, Fredericksburg. Tel. 830/ 997-6523. Monday to Friday 8am to 5pm, Saturday 9am to 5pm, closed Sunday.*

COMFORT

The small town resembles a frontier town out of an Old West movie, and the many antique stores in **Comfort** allow visitors to take home a bit of yesteryear. The center of town has over 100 historical buildings and a proud history. In 1854, the town was founded by German settlers who adored the picturesque scenery and fresh water offered by the Guadalupe River.

The Civil War erupted in miniature in Comfort, when a group of representatives from the town attempted to flee to Mexico in order to fight against slavery and the Confederate cause. The **"Treue der Union"** monument commemorates the site where fighting erupted between the Union sympathizers and Confederate soldiers.

ARRIVALS & DEPARTURES

You can reach Comfort from Fredericksburg to the north along Highway 87. From San Antonio, travel west on Interstate Highway 10, which crosses Comfort from southeast to northwest. Highway 27 runs west along the Guadelupe river and Ranch Road 473 continues east.

SPEND YOUR HOLIDAYS IN COMFORT

Traditional holiday celebrations in a small community make memorable times. The townspeople are welcoming to visitors who want to participate in holiday activities. Comfort sponsors Volksmarch, a 10 kilometer walk and Easter egg hunt on the Saturday before Easter. You can register the day of the walk and there is no fee for participation.

On July Fourth the Independence Day Parade down Main Street kicks off a day of celebration. Food, entertainment and country dancing last all day and into the evening in Comfort Park. Halloween is occasion for the fall Volksmarch, with costumed participants and a bike route. And the year draws to a sentimental close with a candlelight Christmas celebration on the first Saturday of December. In the afternoon tours of historic homes decorated for Christmas run until 5pm, then the streets alight with candles and merriment.

For more information about holiday celebrations, contact the Comfort Chamber of Commerce, Tel. 830/995-3131.

ORIENTATION

Unlike most towns, Comfort usually sleeps during the week and awakens on weekends. If you pass through during most weekdays, you may find the shops and streets deserted. Comfort is a half-hour drive from San Antonio.

WHERE TO STAY

COMFORT COMMON, *717 High Street, Comfort. Tel: 830/995-3030. Rates: $55 to $95. Credit cards accepted.*

Originally the Ingenhuett-Faust Hotel, the Comfort Common was constructed in 1880 and renovated recently. The old hotel remains true to its Victorian character, with antiques throughout. The entire ground floor is an antique shop. The former hotel has three rooms and two suites, all with private baths. The separate cottage has a single bedroom and a kitchen. The hotel is in the historic downtown area.

BRINKMANN BED AND BREAKFAST, *714 Main Street, Comfort. Tel: 830/ 995-3141. Rates: $85.*

The two country cottages that make up the Brinkmann Bed and Breakfast are in the center of the town. The furnishings are simple. You may not use a credit card for payment, although you must guarantee reservations with a credit card.

LOVETT'S LANDING, *P. O. Box 391, Comfort. Tel: 830/995-2836, Fax 830/995-2839. Rates: $125 Credit cards accepted.*

The small country house with a single attic window has two rooms for guests, each with a private bath and kitchen. The home has a unique barn which is converted into a guest-house that sleeps eight comfortably. The quaint surroundings and antique furnishings allow you to feel that you are far from modern cities and times. The house is on the Guadalupe River, and guests can swim, fish or go boating. This retreat is a good alternative to staying in neighboring Kerrville, which is a larger tourist destination. Guests who stay a full week (seven nights) receive one night free. From Interstate Highway 10 west of San Antonio, take exit 523 and travel south. Just past Cypress Creek Bridge, take a left on Hermann Son's Road. This will lead you to the bed and breakfast.

MEYER BED AND BREAKFAST, *845 High Street, P. O. Box 117, Comfort. Tel. 830/995-2304. Rates: $69 to $85.*

The stone buildings of this bed and breakfast were built by the Meyer family form the years 1857 to 1920. The earliest building was a stagecoach stop in the last half of the nineteenth century. Later the hotel building accommodated travelers arriving by train. The private cottage has a waterfront view of the Guadalupe River and offers perfect privacy, with its own kitchen and bath. The Meyer Bed and Breakfast is part of the historic downtown of Comfort.

WHERE TO EAT

ARLENE'S CAFE, *426 7th Street, Comfort. Tel. 830/995-3330. Thursday to Sunday 11am to 4pm.*

Arlene's serves home-cooked meals without the heaviness of most country recipes. The staples of this cafe, soup and salad, are a refreshing break from the chicken-fried-everything of most central and west Texas diners.

CAFE ON HIGH STREET, *814 High Street, Comfort. Tel. 830/995-3470. Thursday to Sunday 11am to 4pm.*

The downtown area is highlighted by the Cafe on High Street. Even if you are not hungry enough to fill up on a meal, stop in for a slice of pie. The deserts are famous.

CYPRESS CREEK CAFE, *Highway 27 at the Cypress Creek Bridge, Comfort. Tel. 830/995-3977.*

This old fashioned cafe, that has been around since the early 1950s, serves up hearty helpings of beef and pork prepared like a Texas grandma would make. The cafe is right on Cypress Creek and has been in operation for over 40 years. The food is inexpensive and only cash is accepted.

SHOPPING

The shopping in Comfort is more for entertainment value than serious antique browsing. Many of the stores are in very old buildings and have eclectic merchandise. **Turkey Ridge Trading Company,** *Highway 27, Tel 830/995-4265,* is a large store with western-style furniture, knick-knacks and memorabilia. The nearby **Hospice Thrift Store** is in a small stone house which has the distinctive cross-beam construction of traditional German villages. Across the street, the **Whistle Stop Tea Room** provides a quaint and quiet setting for an afternoon tea break.

EXCURSIONS & DAY TRIPS
SISTERDALE

A visit to the **Sister Creek Winery,** *FM 1376, Sisterdale, Tel. 830/324-6704 or 324-6682; open daily noon to 5pm,* gives you two experiences. The first is an historic journey. The winery of Sister Creek Vineyards is housed in a cotton gin dating from the 1890's. You walk in the front entrance, right into the renovated old gin.

The winery was founded in 1988 and cultivates vines which originated in France. The care of using traditional aging techniques pays off in rich, aromatic reds and smooth whites. Only a few varieties of wine are produced in very limited quantity each year. To reach Sister Creek Winery from Interstate Highway 10, turn north onto FM 1376 at Boerne. The winery is about 12 miles from the interstate, just south of Luckenbach.

PRACTICAL INFORMATION

Tourist information is available at the **Chamber of Commerce and Community Center,** *700 High Street, Comfort, Tel. 830/995-3131, Friday and Saturday 12:30pm to 4:30pm,* located at the corner of 7th and High Street. The quaint building dates from 1907.

KERRVILLE

For many, **Kerrville** defines the Hill Country. The small town is located west of San Antonio in an area known for its rough, rock hill tops and crisp, clear evenings.

Early settlers came to this region in the mid-1800s. They were attracted to the lovely country and fresh water of the Guadalupe River. Kerr County was created by an act signed in the Texas legislature in 1856. The small community had an active mill on the river

One of the most enjoyable events in Texas is the **Kerrville Folk Festival,** *Tel. 800/435-8249,* which takes place each year during the last week of May and first week of June. The outdoor festival lasts 18 days.

Many favorite local musicians as well as artists from around the world take the stage and families enjoy the hot days that mark the onset of summer. The evening shows take place under a brilliant canopy of stars and the cool night air.

Kerrville is a center of folk art and crafts. Seasonal celebrations at Easter and Christmas allow local artists to offer their wares as the community comes together. The **Easter Hill Country Bike Tour** and **Easter Festival & Chili Cook-off**, *Tel. 830/792-3535*, is a great reason to get out and enjoy spring. If the bike tour through the Hill Country does not tire you out, participate in the 5K or 10K run.

During Memorial Day weekend, Schreiner College hosts the **Texas State Arts and Crafts Fair**. The event began in 1971. Two hundred artisans from around the state are chosen to exhibit and sell their crafts. Paintings, jewelry, stained glass and sculpture are among the works on display. To reach Schreiner College Fairgrounds, take Highway 27 west from Interstate Highway 10. Signs will lead you to the Fairgrounds. Shuttles provide transportation from the parking to the fair. Admission to the fair is $6 for adults and $1 for children under 12 years old.

Aviation buffs will enjoy the **Southwest Regional EAA Fly-in**, which is held during the third weekend of October. Airplanes of all types from vintage models to experimental crafts can been seen, both on the ground and in the air. The Fly-in is held at Louis Schreiner Field, on Highway 27, six miles west of Kerrville. There is no admission charge for this event.

FESTIVALS IN KERRVILLE
Mid-January – Hill Country Junior Livestock Show
Last weekend of March – Easter Bike Tour through the Hill Country
Last week of May – Kerrville Folk Festival
Memorial Day Weekend – Texas state Arts and Crafts Fair
Labor Day Weekend – Kerrville Wine & Music Festival
Mid-October – Kerr County Fair
End of October – Southwest Regional Fly-in

ARRIVALS & DEPARTURES

Kerrville is located at the intersection of Highways 16 and 27, two miles south of Interstate Highway 10.

ORIENTATION

Kerrville is 66 miles northwest of San Antonio.

WHERE TO STAY

INN OF THE HILLS RIVER RESORT, *1001 Junction Highway, Kerrville. Tel. 210/895-5000 or 800/292-5690, Fax 210/895-1277. Rates: $58 to $135. Credit cards accepted.*

This 215 room inn is run by Best Western. The rooms vary from a basic hotel room to the more luxurious apartment-style suites. The extensive grounds include an indoor pool and out door pools, tennis courts, spa and gym. You do not have to venture off the grounds to go biking, hiking and fishing.

THE YO RANCH, *2033 Sidney Baker Street, Kerrville. Tel. 210/257-4440 or 800/292-2800, Fax 210/896-8189. Rates: $99. Credit cards accepted.*

The YO, once a private ranch resort, is now operated by Holiday Inn. This is the most famous of the resort hotels in Kerrville. The lobby resembles a ranch house trophy room, with enough game trophies to fill a zoo. The rooms are modern and have complete amenities such as television and telephones. The western-theme furnishings were specially made for the ranch. There are plenty of recreational activities on the ranch, including an outdoor pool, tennis courts and children's play area. Golf and horseback riding can be arranged at the front desk.

WHERE TO EAT

FARA'S RESTAURANT, *1201 Broadway Street, Kerrville. Tel. 830/896-6580. Credit cards accepted.*

Fara's is an intimate Italian restaurant in a cute little house. The intimate atmosphere compliments the good selection of pastas and traditional sauces.

SEEING THE SIGHTS

For a look back through history, visit the **Hill Country Museum**, *226 Earl Garrett Street, Tel. 830/896-8633.* The museum is housed in the Victorian homestead of Kerrville's most important founding fathers, Captain Charles Schreiner. The antiques period decor provide a backdrop for the genteel life enjoyed by the privileged settlers of the region. The museum is located near the City Park on the Guadalupe River. Earl Garrett Street is just off Highway 27, south of Sidney Baker Street.

One of Kerrville's unique attractions is the **Cowboy Artists of America Museum**, *1550 Bandera Highway, Tel. 830/896-2553, Tuesday to Saturday 9am to 5pm; Sunday 1pm to 5pm, admission $3 adults, $1 children.* This is one of the few museums that display only works portraying themes of the Old West. Some of the country's finest painters have had their works displayed here. The collection changes regularly. The museum has its own library dedicated to the study of the genre of Western painting.

NIGHTLIFE & ENTERTAINMENT

During the summer months, the Hill Country Arts Foundation sponsors evening outdoor theater performances at the **Pointe Theater**. The outdoor venue is right on the banks of Johnson Creek in nearby Ingram, Texas. During the winter, performances move to the indoor stage. For information about current and upcoming performances, call the **Hill Country Arts Foundation**, *Tel. 830/367-5121*.

SPORTS & RECREATION

The Colorado River is one of the best areas for **fly fishing** in the state. If you have never experienced the lure of this sport, a visit to Kerrville would be a great time to give it a try. Lessons, equipment and guides are available from **Pico Outdoor Company Kerrville**, *Tel. 830/895-4348 or 800/256-5873*.

The **H. E. Butt Municipal Tennis Center**, *Sidney Baker Drive, Tel. 830/257-4982*, has six lighted hard courts which are open to the public. Court fee is $2 per person. The tennis courts and pro shop are open from Monday to Thursday, 9am to 5pm; Friday and Saturday 9am to 5pm and Sunday 1pm to 5pm. To reserve a court or get information about tennis lessons, call the pro shop.

Kerrville has a fine municipal golf course, located near the center of the city and close to most hotels. The **Scott Schreiner Municipal Golf Course**, *Country Club Road, Tel. 830/257-4982*, features 18 holes of rolling greens. The facilities include a pro shop, putting green, showers and locker room. The course is open daily from 7am until dusk. Greens fees range from $8.50 to $11.50.

EXCURSIONS & DAY TRIPS

Although a granite market is all that is left to commemorate the site, Kerrville is the site of the only United States Military camel "cavalry." Camels were brought to **Camp Verde** as an experiment in 1856. The mission for the camel corps was to serve as transportation and to aid in moving supplies long distances over rough terrain. The camel is a slow and nearly untrainable beast, which may be why the experiment failed, even before the onset of the Civil War. The site of Camp Verde is one mile west of Texas 173, on Camp Verde Road.

BANDERA

Bandera has a long, interesting history. Two years after the town was founded by Polish immigrants in 1852, a group of Mormons established a colony. One of the oldest Catholic churches in the state, Saint Stanislaus, was built by the Polish settlers in 1876. The cattle drives of the pre-railroad Texas stopped in Bandera and ingrained ranching into the lifestyle. Now urban cowboys have taken over and Bandera dubs itself "The Cowboy Capital of the World." Most of the wrangling is done on dude ranches.

Tourists that stay in Bandera usually visit all-inclusive vacation ranches. Activities such as trail rides, sports, entertainment and meals are taken care of by the ranch.

ARRIVALS & DEPARTURES

Bandera is on Highway 16, west of San Antonio.

WHERE TO STAY & EAT

LOST VALLEY RESORT RANCH, *P. O. Box 2170, Bandera. Tel. 830/ 796-3299. Rates: $49 to $69. Credit cards accepted.*

The Lost Valley Ranch is for those who want a taste of the country, without total immersion in the western theme. The resort has a large outdoor pool and an 18 hole golf course in addition to hiking and riding trails. The 48 rooms have modern interiors and the large main house hosts special events for large groups. Continental breakfast is served each morning. The Lost Valley Resort Ranch is on Highway 16, 35 miles west of San Antonio.

RUNNING R RANCH, *Route 1 Box 590, Bandera. Tel. 830/796-3984, Fax 796-8189. Rates: $85 to $170 per night. Credit cards accepted.*

The 230 acre ranch feels even larger because it stands next to the beautiful woodlands of a state park. The cabins are finished off with a rustic interior and knotty pine furniture. Every guest at the Running R Ranch has two hours of horseback riding per day included with the room. You can brush up your western riding skills with special lessons form an experienced, trophy winning trainer.

NIGHTLIFE & ENTERTAINMENT

During the summer Bandera holds a rodeo every weekend. The grande finale of the season is the **Cowboy Capital PRcA Rodeo Week** on Memorial Day Weekend. You can attend the bull bustin' and barn dances and golf tournament held in conjunction with the rodeo. Rodeo admission is $10 for adults and $6 for children.

SPORTS & RECREATION

A piece of the hill country for everyone to enjoy is the **Hill Country State Natural Area**. Formerly a ranch, the 5000-plus acres of rough land is now a nature preserve. Thirty-six miles of trails traverse streams, rocky hills and canyons. Now they are open for primitive camping, hiking and swimming. To get to Hill Country State Natural Area from Bandera, take Farm Road 1077 west; the natural area is ten miles from Bandera.

The **Lost Maples State Natural Area**, *Ranch Road 187, Vanderpool, Tel. 389-8900*, is a 2000 acre preserve open for camping hiking and fishing. Not only are the maple trees here unique in the state, rare birds live in the park. Kingfishers and golden-cheeked warblers can be seen during certain times of the year. A visit to Lost Maples in early autumn lets you take in bright fall foliage, which is unusual in the southwest. From Bandera, take Highway 16 north to Medina, then continue west on Highway 337 to Vanderpool. Ranch Road 187 meets Highway 337 in Vanderpool.

Vanderpool sits close to the **Edward's Plateau**, and offers some of the best countryside in the area. Continue north on Highway 337 to enjoy one of the loveliest scenic drives in the Hill Country.

PRACTICAL INFORMATION

The **Bandera Convention and Visitors Bureau**, *P. O Box 171, Bandera, 78003. Tel 830/796-3045 or 800/364-3833*, can provide information and advanced tickets for the rodeo.

14. NORTH TEXAS

The Texas frontier meets the west in the **Panhandle** region. The vast plains were traversed by cattle drives that changed the face of the state.

A long canyon marks the northern region of Texas. **Palo Duro Canyon** is the second largest canyon in the United States, and it is here that the legend of cowboys lives most vividly. You can take part in a chuck wagon meal, watch a heard of buffalo graze or attend a rodeo. The most famous artery linking Route 66 dips through the Texas Panhandle.

DALLAS

When the city of **Dallas** was founded, it was little more than an insignificant trading post on the frontier. The city has grown into a most dynamic and diverse metropolis. Urban Dallas is surrounded by large suburbs, each with a distinctive personality. **Plano**, directly north of the city, is known as an affluent suburban area. **Mesquite**, to the east of the city, has a western appeal and holds a rodeo year-round.

Irving, on the west, is the home of the Las Colinas development, a planned upscale business area. And these are only a few of the over twenty "cities" that compose the Dallas area. Still, Dallas has a vibrant central area, with some of the best food, entertainment, shopping and cultural attractions in the nation.

ARRIVALS & DEPARTURES
DFW

The **Dallas-Fort Worth International Airport** (DFW), *Tel. 972/574-6000*, is located between the two cites. Each day over 2500 flights connect DFW to the rest of the world. Arrivals and baggage claim are located on the main level. Passenger drop-off is located on the upper level. Ground transportation is on the lower level. The airport has four passenger terminals (2E, 2W, 3E and 4E). As you drive up the main airport street, International Parkway, large signs post the current gate information for departing flights.

HELPFUL NUMBERS FOR DFW AIRPORT

*The **DFW Airport Visitor Information**, Tel. 972/574-3694, offers details about the airport including directions and assistance with ground transportation. You can also receive information about the Dallas-Fort Worth area including accommodations. The **DFW Airport Assistance Center**, Tel. 972/574-4420, can help passengers needing special attention. Foreign language information and assistance in arrangements for the handicapped are handled through this office.*

A number of shuttle services serve the Dallas area. Two of these are **Super Shuttle**, *729 East Dallas Road, Grapevine, Tel. 817/329-2000*, which offers door to airport service at any time; and **Classic Shuttle**, *3615 Ross Avenue, Dallas, Tel. 214/841-1900*. For limousine service contact **Advantage Limousine**, *Tel 972/618-7313* or **ExecuCar**, *Tel. 214/329-2002*.

Major national car rental agencies have desks at DFW Airport. One regional car rental agency is **Premier Rent-A-Car**, *Tel. 214/612-7070*. If you're renting a car, you should know that from the south, Highways 183 and 360 run to the airport. On the north use Highways 114 or 635.

Other Airports

The smaller **Love Field**, *8008 Cedar Springs Street, Dallas, Tel. 214/670-6080*, is only seven miles from downtown Dallas. **Southwest Airlines**, *Tel. 214/263-1717*, is based at Love Field.

Helicopter traffic is handled at the **Dallas Heliport**, *801 South Lamar Street, Dallas, Tel. 214/670-4338*. The heliport has a waiting area and parking lot.

Train & Bus Stations

The **Amtrak Station**, *400 South Houston Street, Tel. 214/653-1101 or 800/872-7245*, is located in the southern part of downtown. Amtrak operates one route that connects San Antonio to Chicago three times per week.

The **Greyhound Bus Station**, *205 South Lamar Street, Tel. 214/655-7082 or 800/231-2222*, is located downtown at the intersection of Lamar and Commerce Streets. The **Kerrville Bus Company**, *701 East Davis Street, Grand Prairie, Tel. 214/263-0294*, operates regular routes in the state and tours.

ORIENTATION

Dallas is a merging point for many major roads. The highway system in Dallas can be confusing, even to those who have lived in the area for

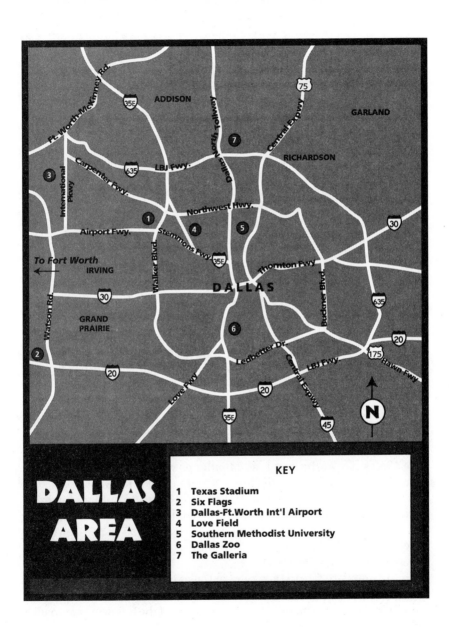

DALLAS AREA

KEY

1 Texas Stadium
2 Six Flags
3 Dallas-Ft.Worth Int'l Airport
4 Love Field
5 Southern Methodist University
6 Dallas Zoo
7 The Galleria

> ## THE COMMON NAMES OF DALLAS HIGHWAYS
> *Highway 635: LBJ or Johnson Freeway*
> *Highway 75: Central Expressway*
> *Interstate Highway 45: Schepps Freeway*
> *Interstate Highway 35: Stemmons Freeway*

awhile. Interstate Highway 35 runs through Dallas from north to south. This is the east branch of the interstate, which splits south of the city; the western branch runs through Fort Worth.

Interstate Highway 20 approaches Dallas from the east and skirts the city to the south; it continues west to Fort Worth. Interstate Highway 30 cuts east-west through central Dallas and also through Fort Worth. Highway 635 loops around the northern and eastern sections of the city. In the south, Highway 635 merges into Interstate Highway 20. Highway 75 runs north-south through the city center. Loop 12 makes a circle of the central area. The Dallas North Tollway runs from Interstate Highway 35, just west of downtown, to North Dallas.

GETTING AROUND TOWN

The **Dallas Area Rapid Transit** (**DART**), *Tel. 979-1111*, serves the Dallas area with bus service and rail service. The urban train went into operation recently. The line begins at the Dallas Convention Center and serves the Dallas Zoo and West End entertainment district. The line will expand to the north and is currently under construction. One-way adult fare for bus and rail service is $1.

The **McKinney Avenue Trolley** is a restored antique transportation that connects the Dallas Museum of Art with the restaurant area of McKinney Street. The cars date from the early 1900's and were used until the 1950's. Today the line is a reminder or yesteryear and an enjoyable way to get around the sometime congested downtown streets. The Trolleys run Sunday to Thursday, 10am to 10pm and until midnight on Friday and Saturday nights. One way adult fare is $1.50. McKinney Avenue is located just west of Interstate Highway 35 in the downtown area. You can begin your trolley trip at the Dallas Museum of Art, where there is ample parking.

The standard fare for taxi rides in Dallas is $1.50 for the first mile and $1.20 for each following mile. A charge of $1 is assessed for each additional person. You might want to call one of the following companies if you need a taxi:

• **Allied Taxi**, *Tel. 214/819-9999*
• **Checker Cab**, *Tel. 817/469-8880 or 469-1111*

• **Cowboy Cab**, *Tel. 214-428-0202*
• **West End Cab**, *Tel. 214/902-7000*
• **Yellow Cab**, *Tel. 214/426-6262 or 800/749-9422*

WHERE TO STAY

THE ADOLPHUS, *1321 Commerce Street, Dallas. Tel. 214/742-8200 or 800/221-9083, Fax 214/742-8200. Rates: $135 to $215. Credit cards accepted.*

The Adolphus is Dallas' most prestigious historic hotel. The building was built in 1912, and it retains the elegance of antiquity while benefiting from the most up-to-date renovation. Today the twenty-one story hotel is practically dwarfed by the surrounding skyscrapers. Yet its character stands firm. The standard rooms are slightly small compared to more spacious floor plans in modern buildings. But this is made up by the charm of the decor. The rooms have elegant furnishings which reflect the simplicity of the Chippendale period. The warm tones of the carpet and upholstery add to the antique feeling. The restaurant offers excellent French food. The hotel is a short walk from the downtown Neiman Marcus and the West End entertainment district.

CRESCENT COURT, *400 Crescent Court, Dallas. Tel. 214/871-3200 or 800/654-6541, Fax 214/871-3272. Rates: $195 to $280. Credit cards accepted.*

The Crescent Court is housed in one of the most unique buildings in Dallas. The Crescent Building was designed by the famous architect, Philip Johnson. Its classic French design is built on a grand scale. At all times you will find each accent in the lobby polished to perfection. The rooms reflect the emphasis on comfort and the decor exudes distinction. The 40 suites offer the plushest accommodations in Dallas. Beau Nash, the hotel's cafe, offers excellent dining in a comfortable setting. The more formal Conservatory is an elegant and intimate setting for fine dining.

Some of the finer shops in Dallas are located in the shopping center surrounding the courtyard of the hotel. The Crescent is located close to the excellent restaurants on Routh Street, and the McKinney Avenue Trolley. The hotel offers babysitting.

FAIRMONT HOTEL, *1717 N. Akard, Dallas, Tel. 214/720-5249 or 800/527-4727. Rates: $179 to $199. Credit cards accepted.*

Attention to detail has made the Fairmont among the finest hotels in the south since it opened nearly thirty years ago. The hotel is located in the heart of downtown Dallas, walking distance from many of the city's best attractions. The luxury suites in the north and south tower have fantastic views. The hotel has one of the city's best restaurants on its premises. The Pyramid is recognized as one of Dallas' best restaurants. Elegant decor combine smartly with the equally elegant menu choices. Romantic setting, courteous service and live music make this an excellent choice for honeymoon or anniversary dinners. Six-course, $36 fixed-price menu available (or $58 with wine).

THE MANSION ON TURTLE CREEK, *2821 Turtle Creek Boulevard, Dallas. Tel. 214/559-2100 or 800/442-3408 (in Texas), 527-5432 (outside Texas), Fax 214/528-4187. Rates: $280 to $320. Credit cards accepted.*

The location of the Mansion is exemplary, in the lovely park-like surroundings of Turtle Creek. The hotel, which is regarded by many distinguished guests as the *only* place to stay when in Dallas, offers 140 rooms. The hotel has a gym, outdoor pool and salon on premises. The rooms have lavish decoration, each adorned with furnishings made specifically for the hotel. The hotel's restaurant prepares some of the most exquisite food in the city.

RAMADA PLAZA, *1101 South Akard Place, Dallas. Tel. 214/421-1083 or 800/527-7606, Fax 214/428-6827. Rates: $89 to $99. Credit cards accepted.*

This hotel recently underwent a complete renovation. Many small comforts were added, such as hair dryers and coffee makers in every room. Each of the 236 spacious rooms has a balcony that overlooks Dallas. A modern gym and indoor pool is available. When you stay at the Ramada, you receive complimentary parking and shuttle service to the airport or anywhere within a five mile radius of the hotel. The Ramada is located close to the convention center and the West End entertainment district.

DALLAS' INTIMATE, HISTORIC HOTELS

THE MELROSE, 3015 Oak Lawn Street, Dallas. Tel. 214/521-5151 or 800/635-7673, Fax 521-9306. Rates:Credit cards accepted.

The historic Melrose dates from the roaring twenties. The independently run hotel is an intimate size by Dallas standards, with 142 rooms. The Library is a sophisticated bar attracting young Dallasites for early evening cocktails.

THE STONELEIGH, 2927 Maple Street, Dallas. Tel. 214/871-7111 or 800/255-9299, Fax 214/871-9397. Rates: 170 to $395. Credit cards accepted.

Nearly one-third of the 153 rooms at the Stoneleigh are suites. This exemplifies the standard of luxury that the hotel maintains. The historic building was built in 1923 and the decor lovingly recreates the 1920s. The rooms reflect the character of this time, when one settled into a place, not merely passed through. Many of the suites have parlor areas. The hotel offers an outdoor pool and two of the area's finest restaurants.

Central
   HYATT REGENCY, *300 Reunion Boulevard, Dallas. Tel. 214/651-1234 or 800/233-1234. Rates: $105 to $235.*
   The bright glass Hyatt blends into the modern skyline. The Hyatt is located near the convention center and the downtown area. The hotel is most notable for its size, thirty stories and 950 rooms. The feeling of this hotel is somewhat cool, possibly due to the modern decor or the fact that many large groups choose this location. Reunion Tower is part of the hotel complex; the tower restaurant overlooks the entire city. The hotel has extensive fitness facilities, including a large pool, track and gym.
   WYNDHAM ANATOLE HOTEL, *2201 Stemmons Freeway, Dallas. Tel. 214/748-1200, Fax 761-7520. Rates: $149 to $235. Credit cards accepted.*
   The mammoth glass and steel Anatole is an entire complex unto itself. The grandiose scale reflects the bigger-than-life character of metropolitan Dallas. Sixteen hundred rooms sprawl over 27 floors. The indoor atriums are so large and manicured that you feel like you're outdoors. The hotel has all the recreational facilities you could need — an indoor pool, tennis courts and a complete fitness center — and each is of the finest quality. The hotel's premier restaurant, Nana Grill, *Tel. 214/761-7479*, virtually created Southwestern cuisine in the Dallas area. Now this is the hip place to have an excellent meal. The food combines with the stunning skyline view for an incredible dining experience.
   CLASSIC MOTOR INN, *9229 Carpenter Freeway, Dallas. Tel. 214/631-6633 or 800/662-7437, Fax 214/631-6616. Rates: $42 to $49. Credit cards accepted.*
   This 134 room motel recently underwent a complete renovation. The simple rooms have brass beds and sparse furnishings. Continental breakfast is served every morning. The hotel has a small fitness room. Stay here if you don't want a large chain hotel.
   DAYS INN CENTRAL, *4150 Central Expressway, Dallas. Tel. 214-827-6080 or 800/325-2525, Fax 214/827-0208. Rates: $50 to $80. Credit cards accepted.*
   This location is just a few miles up Central Expressway from downtown Dallas. The hotel is convenient for those who want a location near the cultural sights and have a car to get around town. Children under the age of 12 years stay free with parents. The hotel offers an outdoor pool and free continental breakfast.

North
   WESTIN GALLERIA, *13,330 North Dallas Tollway, Dallas. Tel. 972/934-9494 or 800/228-3000 Rate; $194 to $254. Credit cards accepted.*
   The Westin is part of the large Galleria complex that includes a shopping mall and office tower. The 431 room hotel rises 21 stories above

the surrounding north Dallas neighborhoods. Recreational facilities include a heated outdoor pool and jogging track. You are located in the middle of shopper's paradise. The modern refinement of Dallas is reflected in the sleek decor and attentive staff of the Westin.

THE GRAND KEMPINSKI, *15,201 Dallas Parkway, Dallas. Tel. 972/ 386-6000 or 800/426-3135, Fax 972/404-1848. Rates: $174 to $195. Credit cards accepted.*

The elegant Grand Kempinski rivals other Dallas luxury hotels by maintaining the standard of service of their grand European hotels. The hotel has a nightclub, complete gym, indoor pool and tennis courts.

COURTYARD BY MARRIOTT, *2201 Airport Freeway, Bedford. Tel. 817/545-2202 or 800/321-2211, Fax 817/545-2302. Rates: $92 to $102. Credit cards accepted.*

The Courtyard is located close to Dallas Fort Worth International Airport. This hotel delivers the good service that Marriott is known for, while providing an upscale motel environment. The hotel has a fitness room and outdoor pool. Laundry facilities are on the premises.

Bed & Breakfast

Bed and Breakfast Texas Style, *Tel. 214/298-8586 or 800/899-4538, Fax 214/298-7118*, can help you find the right accommodations for your stay in the area. One of the very best B&B's in Dallas is:

COURTYARD ON THE TRAIL, **8045 F**orest Trail, Dallas. Tel. 214/ 553-9700 or 800/484-6260, Fax 214/553-9700. Rates: $95 to $125.

The house overlooks White Rock Lake, Dallas' only urban park setting with a lake. A stay here allows you to remove yourself from the rest of the world, especially since there are only two rooms for guests, each with luxurious baths decorated with marble. A pool in a garden setting is yours to enjoy. Both rooms have French doors that open to the courtyard. From Loop 635 north, take the Skillman Exit. Head south on Skillman to Kingsley, then turn left on to Kingsley. Follow this to White Rock Trail, turn right and proceed to Forest Trail.

WHERE TO EAT

Downtown

AMERICANA, *3005 Routh Street, Dallas. Tel. 214/871-2004. Credit cards accepted.*

If America is a melting pot, this eclectic restaurant represents the country. The upscale dining establishment serves American cuisine with unusual twists. Indian influence adds flare to the menu. Fine dining combines well with an extensive wine list. Try the regional nightly specials to sample the chef's true abilities. Americana maintains Routh Street's reputation as a place for excellent dining.

DREAM CAFE, *2800 Routh, Dallas. Tel. 214/954-0486. Credit cards accepted.*

The fanciful decoration is a prelude to the dreamy food. Expect a wait, especially for weekend brunch, as this place's reputation has grown considerably in the past months. Try the Eggs Oscar, a variation on Eggs Benedict made with crab-meat and a decadent dill-hollandaise sauce. So much of the food is downright healthy, you can enjoy eating something that is good for you. The Green Plate ($6.50), mashed potatoes, basmati rice and organic black beans with the fresh vegetable of the day . Many of the light lunch specials are full of flavor, such as the Ensenada Quesadillas ($7), marinated beef tenderloin with roasted bell peppers in whole wheat tortillas.

The bakery always has specialty bread, such as apricot walnut sourdough. Go ahead, get a whole loaf. Dream Cafe is in the Quadrangle Building. *The original location is 1133 Zang, Tel. 214/943-6448.*

DAKOTA'S *550 North Akard Place, Dallas. Tel. 214/740-4001. Credit cards accepted.*

A downtown classic offering chic nouvelle cuisine in an elegant setting. The bread that starts your meal comes warm from the oven. The unpretentious environment and straightforward good food keep patrons returning. Most of the food is grilled over a mesquite smoke, eliminating the need for fancy sauces or spices. Every evening the "twilight menu" ($15.95) offers a set three course meal. The restaurant is located below street level. (You ride an elevator from the street). Reservations required.

GREEN ROOM, *2715 Elm Street. Tel. 214/748-7666. Credit cards accepted.*

An adventure for the passive-aggressive gourmet, this restaurant offers a "Feed Me" four-course dinner ($34), in which the chef decides your meal. Most listed choices reflect the former Star Canyon chef's penchant for Asian flavorings. The mussels steamed with ginger are succulent. Nothing is out of the reach of the chef, who combines diverse tastes like Cajun and Asian. The upbeat atmosphere will get you geared up to explore the rest of Deep Ellum, Dallas' main action-packed nightlife district. This spot is small and very popular so expect a wait. Fortunately you can hang out on the roof top bar until you get a table.

SAM'S CAFE, *100 Crescent Court, Dallas. Tel. 214/855-2233. Credit cards accepted.*

The airy, comfortable atmosphere of this restaurant describes the entire dining experience. Sam's serves southwestern food that are ripe with delicate flavors. The creamy chipotle cheese that is served with fresh bread sticks is good enough for a meal in itself. But don't stop there — five types of quesidillas are stuffed with grilled vegetables and meat. The simple pasta dishes are consistently good, and vegetarians will enjoy the grilled portabello sandwich. The food is reasonably priced; meals are under $15. The restaurant is located in the Crescent Building.

SAMBUCA, *2618 Elm Street. Tel. 214/744-0820. Credit cards accepted* .

To say that jazz dominates the atmosphere at this popular Deep Ellum night spot and restaurant would be to overlook the excellent food. Inviting entrees come carefully prepared with fresh sauces. The menu features dishes with a Mediterranean influence, such as a Spicy Beef Couscous ($10.95) appetizer served with roasted garlic yogurt. Or have couscous as an entree. The Couscous Marakesh combines artichokes, sun-dried tomatoes and olives with smoked chicken ($14.95) — delicious. The pasta selection is extensive, and the Herbed Gnocchi served with forest mushrooms and romano cheese ($12.95) is a vegetarian delight. An entire menu of specialty drinks and coffee drinks is available. *Sambuca has a north Dallas location at 15,207 Addison Rd., Addison, Tel. 972/385-8455.*

SIPANGO, *4513 Travis Street, Dallas. Tel. 214/522-2411. Credit cards accepted.*

Succulent, juicy seafood pasta dishes are hard to pass up, but all choices are sure to please in this darkly lit, sparsely decorated night spot. Classic Italian dishes, such as veal Marsala with polenta and wild mushrooms, are exquisitely prepared. Try one of their fine Texas wines or beers. Romantic spot for dinner in spite of its simple setting. The sorbetto is made in-house. Entrees under $20.

STAR CANYON, *702 Ross Street, Dallas, Tel. 214/744-3287. Credit cards accepted.*

The Star Canyon prides itself as one of the latest haute Southwestern restaurants. Try the shrimp and papaya enchiladas with avocado-tomatillo salsa; very fresh. Favorite Texas meats like quail and venison are combined with unusual combinations of spices for extraordinary entrees. The Star Canyon is an expensive restaurant, with entrees averaging over $20. Do not even think about walking in, as reservations are absolutely necessary.

Greenville Avenue

CAFE IZMIR, *3711 Greenville Avenue, Dallas. Tel. 214/826-7788. Credit cards accepted.*

The true star of the Greenville scene is this unassuming Mediterranean restaurant that claims to have mom in the kitchen cooking. The best way to experience the delicious variety of food is to just sit back and enjoy the menuless experience. The fixed-price selections ($14) change daily. Plates of richly flavored Mediterranean influenced food are brought to your table, one after the other. The stuffed dolmas are pungent and very tasty. The grilled vegetables and lamb are extraordinary. Sides include couscous, tabouli and a variety of others. You cannot find better hummus in the state. The food selection can be completely or only partially vegetarian. The wine selection includes excellent European table wine. **DADDY JACK'S**, *1916 Greenville, Dallas. Tel. 214/826-4910. Credit cards accepted.* When Daddy Jack's opened it appeared to be just a "chowder house" on restaurant row. But don't be fooled by the casual atmosphere. The excellent seafood does in fact include chowder, as well as other New England-style seafood dishes. The reputation of this small place has grown exponentially and it is truly a Dallas favorite. Daily specials highlight the freshest seafood. *The second location is in downtown in Deep Ellum, 2723 Elm Street, Dallas, Tel. 214/653-3949.*

FLYING BURRO, *2831 Greenville Avenue, Dallas. Tel. 214/827-2112. Credit cards accepted.* Fun, inventive New Mexican variations on classic Tex-Mex fare. Try the killer queso to start, but don't expect what you're used to. It comes with lots of green chiles and tomatoes and a little cheese, but the chunky texture and mild flavor are a delightful change. The same holds true for the entire menu, with such offerings as pizzaritos and green chile and turkey burritos. The service is minimal, yet so are the prices.

MARIANO'S MEXICAN CUISINE, *5500 Greenville Avenue, Dallas. Tel. 214/691-3888. Credit cards accepted.* What makes this restaurant unique to Dallas it that it claims to be the original home of the frozen margarita. It shares this claim with a few other restaurants in Texas, but no other restaurant has a shrine to frozen drink machines as you enter. If you're looking for something with a little more pizzazz than cheese enchiladas, Mariano's has a lively menu of Tex-Mex variations at very reasonable prices. The poblano al carbon with chicken is tender and tasty without being overwhelmingly spicy. *(Mariano's is in the Old Town Shopping Center; there's also a downtown location, 1402 Main Street, Tel. 214/742-2521.*

Central

ANZU, *2620 McKinney Street, Dallas. Tel. 214/526-7398. Credit cards accepted.* You could characterize the food as nouvelle Japanese. The stark yet sophisticated decor allows you to concentrate solely on the great food. The food covers the entire spectrum from east to west. You can dine on lamb served with no frills or indulge in something more exotic like Mongolian beef fajitas made of lamb, with five spices served over eggplant and tomato salad. Entrees cost under $20.

CAFE BRAZIL, *6420 N. Central Expressway. Tel. 214/691-7791. Credit cards accepted.* Coffee brings people to Café Brazil. They typically offer about eight of their special house blends at a time, in large comforting mugs which you can refill as much as you want. Breakfast blend is rich and aromatic, and their flavored coffees are daring and fun. It's the food, though, that keeps people coming back. Veggie empanadas (a heavy Brazilian pastry pocket), with grilled potatoes in rosemary cream sauce and your choice of eggs will keep you satisfied all day. They also offer sumptuous build-your-own crepes and a variety of tantalizing soups and sandwiches. The Lakewood location tends to offer a bit more warmth in atmosphere and slightly better food. Cafe Brazil never closes.

CAMPISI'S EGYPTIAN RESTAURANT, *5610 E. Mockingbird Lane, Dallas. Tel. 214/827-0355. Credit cards accepted.*

Revered by Dallas as having the best pizza in town, this inexplicably named restaurant boasts a fine menu of traditional Italian food – if you're not in the mood for pizza, try the decadent lasagna. What really stands out about Campisi's though, is the atmosphere. Darkly lit, with old red booths and ancient juke boxes at each table, it's clear this place hasn't changed much in its over 50 years in Dallas. At a circular booth in the back of the restaurant you can see a large portrait of the original owners, Frank and Joe Campisi, now both deceased. Ask for a table in the back room so you can soak up the photo gallery of Frank and Joe with such brat pack-era luminaries as Frank Sinatra and Sammy Davis, Jr.

EL FENIX, *1601 McKinney Ave. Dallas. Tel. 214/747-1121. Credit cards accepted.*

A venerable Tex-Mex chain established in 1918, El Fenix has stood the test of time in the turbulent world of Dallas restaurants. The menu, which was inventive fifty years ago, offers the standard Tex-Mex fare that everyone now enjoys. Corn tortillas are the standard for enchiladas and the cheese tacos are terrific. Lunch specials are delivered to your table in five minutes or less. The downtown location is just north of the West End off Field Street. Six other locations ensure that Dallas receives its requirement of Tex-Mex food.

JAVIER'S GOURMET MEXICANO, *4912 Cole Street, Dallas. Tel. 214/521-4211. Credit cards accepted.*

Dark, heavy Caribbean decor reminiscent of Colonial Mexico matches the cuisine. Offerings range from Mexican classics to tasty seafood as well as wild game. Javier's is well known for the generous portions of excellent food. You can order truly traditional Mexican food, such as cabrito, young goat. The sauces are spicy but not overpowering. The salsa verde, made from tomatillos, is unbeatable.

KATHLEEN'S ART CAFE, *4424 Lovers Lane, Dallas. Tel. 214/691-2355. Credit cards accepted.*

Tiny bistro-style restaurant with periodically changing menus offers slightly askew fare, not dissimilar to the mismatched furniture. Somehow it works; everything including the food comes together in a pleasant, cozy environment. The pasta specialties are always very good. This is a great place to talk over the excellent wine offerings. The menu changes daily. **LOVER'S EGGROLL**, *5360 W. Lover's Lane, Dallas. Tel. 214/358-1318. Credit cards accepted.*

Somewhere between fast food and gourmet meals stands Lover's Eggroll. Tucked inside the Inwood Shopping Center, this casual Chinese restaurant is probably overlooked by most tourists, but Dallasites know it's the best and often cheapest place to get authentic Chinese food. Many just drop by for take-out, but you can eat in too. Very generous portions, so consider splitting an order with at least another person if you are a light eater.

MAI'S RESTAURANT, *4812 Bryan, Suite #11, Dallas. Tel. 214/826-9887. Credit cards accepted.*

The family that runs Mai's Restaurant serves the most delicious and authentic Vietnamese dishes you will find anywhere outside of Vietnam. The cuisine is not altered to fit trendy tastes or compromised in any way. Many dishes are versions of the cuisine of central Vietnam, the most flavorful of the country. The ingredients are fresh and tasty and the dishes come with the traditional accompaniment of a tray of bean sprouts, cilantro and peppers.

The soups are meals in themselves and for $4 per bowl, they're one of the best deals in Dallas. Mai's version of the classic Vietnamese spicy chicken soup (bun ga hue) is full of noodles and the broth has a full flavor and marvelous aroma. The house specialties are seafood dishes, such as charbroiled shrimp wrapped in sugar cane ($5.95) or sautéed catfish in clay pot ($6.95). Vegetarians have a variety of choices from soup to curry. Lunch specials ($4.50) are served from 11am to 3pm on weekdays. If you're here for dinner, the best way to begin your meal is with an appetizer of summer rolls, soft rice paper filled with salad and served with peanut sauce. And don't forget a cup of the genuine and potently sweet Vietnamese coffee after the meal is over.

Mai's restaurant is located about 1.5 miles east of Central Expressway (Highway 75). Exit Fitzhugh and travel east about 1.3 miles. Take a right on Bryan Street and you will find Mai's just south of the intersection of Fitzhugh and Bryan Streets. Open Monday to Thursday, 11am to 9:30pm; Friday to Saturday 11am to 10:30pm, closed Sunday.

THE MANSION ON TURTLE CREEK, *2821 Turtle Creek, Dallas, Tel. 214/526-2121. Credit cards accepted.*

As the finest and possibly only truly world class restaurant in Dallas, this is the place for the beautiful people who want to eat exquisite food. The Mansion became famous for daring Southwestern cuisine and awe-inspiring prices. What gives the cuisine such a sterling reputation is the amazing juxtaposing tastes and textures that create something fresh and agreeable. Duck crepes and venison fajitas are examples of the innovative extras. Game is the centerpiece of the dinner selections. The menu is continually refreshed and reinvented. A $65 four course fixed-price menu available. Sunday brunch ($29.95) served from 11am to 2:30pm.

MATTITO'S CAFE MEXICANO, *4311 Oak Lawn, Dallas. Tel. 214/ 526-8181. Credit cards accepted.*

"Little Matt's" off-shoot of the famous Matt's El Rancho in San Antonio. Offers lively Mexican specialties including fabulous chili rellenos, in a bright, playful decor. The food is fresh, and the excellent lunch specials always draw a crowd. The big margaritas are a happy-hour favorite.

SONNY BRYAN'S SMOKEHOUSE, *318 North Central Expressway, Dallas. Tel. 214/562-5484. Credit cards accepted.*

Dallas businessmen and women arrive early and sit on their cars to eat, because Sonny Bryan's has no chairs and when the food's gone the smokehouse stand closes for the day. But for those who yearn to have tangy sauce dribbling down their chin as they devour chopped beef sandwiches, there is no substitute for Sonny's magical combination of mesquite smoke and zesty marinade. The humble smokehouse stand has such an ardent following that it finally had to accept its destiny and become a proper restaurant. *Other locations: 302 N. Market St., Tel. 214/ 744-1610; 325 North St. Paul Street, Tel. 214/979-3003.*

In the South Suburbs

LA CALLE DOCE, *415 West Twelfth Street, Dallas. Tel. 214/941-4304. Credit cards accepted.*

La Calle Doce, in an unassuming blue house, is a haven for those who long for Veracruz-style seafood. Most every dish on the menu has seafood, and it is more than a house specialty; at La Calle Doce it is an art. Before you begin your Mexican coastal meal, remember the margaritas. The frozen margaritas are so smooth they are almost creamy and are served in large glasses to assure you they last the entire meal.

Seafood specials ($8.35-$10.95) come with a cup of fish soup which has delicate broth and flaky white fish. Another excellent soup is the Caldo Xochitl, which is the house version of the chicken soup made in the southern Mexican state of Oaxaca. Try the chile relleno de mariscos, a mild poblano pepper stuffed with shrimp, scallops, octopus and fish and blanketed with thick, white cheese sauce. Shrimp Veracruzana is a mixture of large shrimp, bell peppers and black olives in light tomato sauce and gentle spices, served with rice. On weekends you can indulge in paella, seafood, chicken and pork prepared in the special Spanish style with rice.

For those who do not love seafood, there is an entire section on the menu devoted to meat dishes and a few vegetarian choices. The flan, or Mexican custard, is deliciously authentic. A small breakfast menu of egg dishes is served from 11am to 2:30pm daily. No reservations are accepted. Open daily 11am to 11pm.

In the Nortth Suburbs
BARBEC'S, *8949 Garland Road, Dallas, Tel. 214/321-5597.*
In a sea of cookie-cutter look-a-like diners, Barbec's stands alone as a Dallas original. Breakfasts are traditional, quick and cheap with the best beer biscuits in the entire world. Lunch and dinner specials vary but offer a standard and consistent fare of old-fashioned Southern home cooking. If you're looking for breakfast on the weekend, expect a brief wait, but rest easy in the knowledge that you'll be offered one of their fabulous biscuits to make the time go by easier.

SEEING THE SIGHTS
Dallas leapt into the future with its downtown, choosing design over practical aspects of office construction. The tall downtown area is almost ironic in a city that places little value on distance and an emphasis on individual convenience. In such a city there is no need for a downtown at all; and in fact many who live in Dallas never venture into the downtown area. But to miss the amazing architectural marvels of the Dallas skyline would be to ignore a living museum of architecture.

Fountain Place, *1445 Ross Avenue,* is a geometrical mixture of triangles and rectangles that seems to change the shape of the building from different angles. Even more striking than the building itself is the two acre water fountain and garden at the entrance. Many think of I. M. Pei as the man who shaped the Dallas skyline. The Fountain Place and the Wortham Center are both his designs.

Probably the most distinctive building is the **Texas Commerce Tower**, *2200 Ross Avenue,* with its six story "hole" near the top of the structure. The result seems to be an optical illusion, but is really a window through the center of the 55 story building. The tallest building is the **Nations Bank Plaza**, *901 Main Street,* which has 72 stories.

Thanksgiving Square is a piece of tranquillity in the center of the city. The park is intended to give people a place for meditation and pause for giving thanks. A non-denominational chapel with a modern spiral shape stands in the park. The design is the work of Philip Johnson. The park is bordered by Pacific Avenue, Bryan Street and Ervay street.

The humble beginning of the city stands proudly in the central business district. Surrounded by skyscrapers, the **John Neely Bryan**

Cabin remains intact. Erected in 1841 by the city founder, this tiny log cabin, set incongruously in the middle of downtown, served as both Bryan's home and a trading post. Imagining the solitary wooden house standing on empty plains is nearly impossible. The cabin is in the Dallas County Historical Plaza on Commerce Street.

Located on the southern end of the downtown area is the infamous **Dealy Plaza**, where President Kennedy was shot and killed while his motorcade drove down Elm Street. The plaza was made in 1938 and is located at the intersection of Elm Street, Commerce Street and Houston Street. The John **F**. **Kennedy Memorial Plaza** is located on Commerce Street, one block north of Dealy Plaza. The stark monument is a haunting tribute designed by Philip Johnson.

The official collection that records for history the assassination of President John F. Kennedy is the **Sixth Floor Museum**, *411 Elm Street, Tel. 214/653-6666*. Naturally this museum is located on the infamous sixth floor of the **Texas School Book Depository** and is dedicated to the memory of President John F. Kennedy. It contains more than 400 photographs as well as video and other artifacts and displays. If you look up at the building from the street you will notice that a window on the sixth floor is open. This is believed to be the place from which the fatal bullets were fired.

The most unusual **Conspiracy Museum**, *110 South Market Street, Tel. 214/741-3040, Open daily 10am to 6pm, Admission $7 adults, $6 students*, stands defiantly on the same block as the official museum that commemorates the assassination of President Kennedy. The Conspiracy Museum capitalizes on Dallas' unfortunate notoriety following the assassination, and through its text-intensive exhibits attempts to link assassinations in the 20th century. You can purchase hard-to-find books about presidential assassinations and various other government cover-ups. Some of the texts were written by the curator of the museum

Dallas Museum of Art, *1717 Harwood Street, Tel. 214/922-1200*. The permanent collection includes masterworks of Western art by Matisse, Monet, and Rodin. The extensive pre-Columbian wing shows rare and amazing artifacts and art by the Native Americans of Meso and South America. Excellent traveling and exhibits routinely visit. Thursdays admission is free. The beautiful building is one of I. M. Pei's architectural designs that contribute greatly to the modern character of the city.

The **Dallas Memorial Center for the Holocaust**, *7900 North Haven Road, Tel. 214/750-4654, Open daily 10am to 4pm*, is an archive of the experiences of the survivors of the Holocaust. The museum exhibits documents, photos and artifacts from the Nazi destruction of European Jewry. The large archive includes a library of books and videos. The center is open year-round and free to the public.

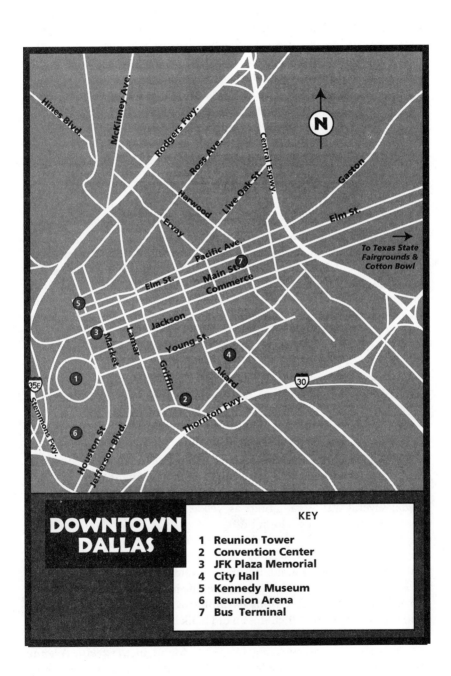

DOWNTOWN DALLAS

KEY

1 Reunion Tower
2 Convention Center
3 JFK Plaza Memorial
4 City Hall
5 Kennedy Museum
6 Reunion Arena
7 Bus Terminal

A large collection of African art is on display at the **African-American Museum**, *3536 Grand Avenue, Tel. 214/565-9026, Tuesday to Thursday and Sunday noon to 5pm, Friday noon to 9pm Saturday 10am to 5pm.* The museum is in Fair Park. The exhibits provide a fascinating perspective of the richness of African American heritage.

Some of the nation's best examples of monumental art deco architecture are found close to downtown Dallas. **Fair Park**, *3939 Grand Avenue, Tel. 214/421-4500*, was named a National Historic Landmark because of the grandiose deco buildings. But it is also known as the home of the State Fair of Texas; this complex houses museums, the Music Hall, the Cotton Bowl, an IMAX theater, even a restaurant open year-round. Fair Park also frequently hosts local cultural festivals. Take the kids to **Science Place**, an interactive museum that fosters a hands-on approach to science. Other museums on the premises include the **Age of Steam Railroad Museum** and the **Dallas Aquarium**; all are open year-round.

Crowds turn out en masse to see the "Spring Blooms" at the **Dallas Arboretum and Botanical Garden**, *8525 Garland Road, Tel. 214/670-6374*. The gardens have seasonal floral exhibits for year round enjoyment. This spot is often chosen for celebrations. You can spend hours enjoying the 66 acres of cultivation. The Arboretum frequently offers seminars in various horticulture techniques.

Kids will love the **Dallas Zoo**, *621 East Clarendon, Tel. 214/670-5656, Open daily 9am to 5pm, Admission $3 adult, $1.50 child.* The Wilds of Africa monorail exhibit includes a nature trail and a gorilla conservation center. Other more standard exhibits feature over 2,000 animals. The zoo has been undergoing extensive renovation for several years and promises more extensive and habitat-like conditions. From Dallas, take Interstate Highway south, exit Ewing Street, and follow the signs.

A wide ranging variety of mostly fighter planes expertly restored to their original condition is housed at the **Cavanaugh Flight Museum**, *4572 Claire Chennault, Addison Airport, Tel. 214/380-8800*. The collection includes several WWI- era fighters as well as some intimidatingly modern crafts. A must-see for aviation buffs.

The **Freedman Cemetery** *2470 Five Mile Parkway, Tel. 214/333-0983*, is a pre-Civil War African-American cemetery has been preserved as a state and local historical landmark. The **Old City Park Museum**, *1717 Gamo Street, Tel. 214/421-5141,* preserves life in turn-of-the-century Dallas through recreations of various examples of historical architecture relevant to Dallas culture. Includes an old bank building and an antebellum mansion.

A piece of genuine living history is found in the **Swiss Avenue Historical District**. The boulevard is lined with painstakingly restored Prairie-style late Victorian homes. Most were converted into apartments during World War II and have been returned to their original glory through the efforts of individuals reclaiming the turn-of-the-century neighborhood. To reach Swiss Avenue from Central Expressway (Highway 75), take Fitzhugh Street east.

NIGHTLIFE & ENTERTAINMENT

The **Dallas Opera**, *3102 Oak Lawn Street, Suite 450, Tel. 214/443-1000*, offers five performances in a season. The performances feature talent of international acclaim. The venue is the **Morton H. Meyerson Symphony Center**, *2301 Flora Street, Tel. 214/670-3600*, a modern masterpiece with flowing lines designed by I. M. Pei. The center is the latest gem in Dallas' cultural arts crown.

The venue for many summer concerts is the **Starplex**, *Fair Park, Tel. 214/373-8000*. It defines, for the time being at least, the easternmost border of Fair Park. Bring an umbrella if it looks like rain, because you can't go back to your car once you enter the grounds. Name acts like Fleetwood Mac appear at Starplex.

The grandeur of the 1920's is evident in the **Majestic Theater**, *1925 Elm Street, Tel. 214/880-0137*. The fabulous theater, built in the 1920's, is adorned with Art Deco murals. A painted starlit sky hangs overhead. Originally vaudeville acts played this venue. Today you can see touring performances on the restored stage.

Dallas has a number of downtown areas that are centers of nightlife. The Greenville Avenue venues have been around longest. **Lower Greenville** offers many restaurants and casual bars in a neighborhood setting. The **West End Marketplace**, *603 Munger Avenue, Tel. 214/748-4801*, is a shopping and entertainment development located in what were once deserted warehouse buildings. Many restaurants and distractions from movies to bars guarantee the family will have something fun to do at the West End. From Highway 75, exit McKinney Avenue and go east.

For decades the area was nearly abandoned. Today, **Deep Ellum** has blossomed into an entire district filled with fine local restaurants and the best live music in the city. Over sixty clubs, restaurants and interesting shops are packed into this roughly nine block area. You can easily visit a number of clubs in one night, as the streets are filled with "club hoppers." As more buildings offering loft apartments open, the traffic and congestion become worse. This is the place to be for a night on the town. The area is bordered by Elm Street on the north, Canton Street on the south, and Hall Street on the east. Deep Ellum is located just north of Interstate Highway 30 and east of Highway 75, to the east of downtown.

The **West End Taste of Dallas** is a giant outdoor culinary extravaganza held at the West End Historic District, *Tel. 214/665-9533*, in the middle of July. You can sample the many flavors of Texan cooking as well as international dishes. Admission is free.

SPORTS & RECREATION
Golf
Dallas has long been a center for golf. For over seventy years the **Cedar Crest Golf Course**, *1800 Southerland, Tel. 214/670-7615, Fax 670-7641*, has been a challenging test of skill. The rolling hills and tall trees make this a beautiful setting for the 18 hole par 71 course. You can rent clubs, take lessons and practice on the putting green here. Greens fees range from $11 to $14. Cedar Crest is located south of the city, off Interstate Highway 35.

One of the most difficult private courses in the area is open to the public. The **Sleepy Hollow Country Club**, *4747 South Loop 12, Tel. 214/371-3430, 371-5466*, has one 18 hole, par 71 course that non-members may use. The club facilities include a restaurant, locker room, driving range and putting green. Greens fees range from $20 to $30; gulf cart rental $10.

Tennis
The **Hyatt Bear Creek Golf and Racquet Club**, *West Airfield Drive, Arlington, Tel. 972-615-6882, Fax 453-6410,* is an excellent public facility. The club offers two golf courses with bent grass greens. Of the seven tennis courts, three are indoor; ten racquetball courts are available. The Hyatt Bear Creek Club is located near Dallas Fort Worth International Airport.

Biking
Bicycling, jogging and walking enthusiasts will enjoy **White Rock Lake**, off Loop 12 east, which has over 11 miles of trails and lovely scenery.

Spectator Sports
Dallas is full of sports excitement. The renowned **Dallas Cowboys** meet head-to-head with other NFL teams at **Texas Stadium**, *2401 East Airport Highway, Irving, Tel. 972/556-2500*. The football season runs from September through December.

The excitement of professional basketball is brought home by the **Dallas Mavericks** at Reunion Arena, *777 Sports Street, Tel. 214/748-1808.* You can see them play from November through April.

And the all-American sport, baseball, is played by the **Texas Rangers** at the Ballpark in Arlington, *1000 Ballpark Way, Arlington, Tel. 817/273-5100*. The Rangers play in the American League.

Dallas is proud to have the only major league professional hockey team in the state, the **Dallas Stars**, *901 Main Street, Tel. 214/GO-STARS.* Even polo is represented in Dallas. The **Dallas Dragons**, *5210 McKinney Avenue, Suite 280, Tel. 214/979-0849,* play every Sunday in the spring and summer. Occasional Saturday matches are held in the fall. The home games are held at the Polo Range in Red Oak, about 20 miles from the city. From downtown Dallas, go south on Interstate Highway 35. Take the Ovilla Exit and travel east.

There is almost always a rodeo in Dallas. The **Mesquite Rodeo**, *1818 Rodeo Drive, Mesquite, Tel. 972/285-8777 or 800/833-9339,* is held Friday and Saturday night form April through September. You can see all the real live action of bull riding, roping and barrel racing. A barbecue buffet is offered and the kids will enjoy the petting zoo. From Loop 635 East, take Exit 4 to Mesquite and follow the signs to the rodeo.

SHOPPING

The flagship store for **Neiman Marcus**, *1618 Main Street, Tel. 214/741-6911,* is located downtown. The building was constructed for the department store in 1914, and since then the elite of Dallas will not shop anywhere else.

The shopping area of the **Galleria**, *Loop 610 and Dallas North Tollway, Tel. 214/702-7100,* is but one piece of this amazing complex. A high-rise office tower and first class hotel are located here as well. You can easily spend at least an entire day shopping in this deluxe mall. The Galleria features over 200 stores, including Nordstrom and Tiffany & Co.

Northpark Mall, *Loop 12 and Central Expressway, 214/363-7441,* has 160 shops, including Lord & Taylor, Neiman Marcus and Tiffany.

EXCURSIONS & DAY TRIPS

On most days you might drive through **Canton** and barely notice the tiny town. But on the weekend preceding the first Monday of each month, the town of 3000 blossoms into a Mecca. Thousands flood the 100-acre flea market known as **Canton First Monday Trade Days**. You can find everything from antiques to livestock. And you are sure to take back vivid impressions of country life. The vendors cannot reserve spaces, so each month the entire market changes.

The first Monday tradition began in the 1870s, when stray horses were auctioned once per month. Despite the name, you will not find much of a market left on Monday; all trading is done on the weekend. Take Interstate 20 east about 63 miles; Canton is at the intersection of Interstate Highway 20 and Highway 64. Admission is free; parking $3.

Do not expect to find J. R. Ewing at the **Southfork Ranch**, *3700 Hogge Road, Parker, Tel. 214/442-7800*. The old farm house used for the television series draws many tourists; unfortunately, there is little of interest among the "Dallas memorabilia" that people pay to see. To get to the attraction, take Highway 75 north to the Parker Road exit, then continue east, following the signs.

PRACTICAL INFORMATION

The **American Automobile Association** has two offices in Dallas; the main one is *4425 North Central Expressway, Tel. 214/526-7911*; for 24-hour road service, *Tel. 214/528-7481*.

You can find out what hot in Dallas through the **Dallas Events Hotline**, *Tel. 214/746-6679*.

FORT WORTH

The name **Fort Worth** conjures up images of cattle drives and cowboys. The town actually was a fort before the cattle industry took over. Fort Worth stands in the shadow of the larger, more metropolitan Dallas. Yet its personality gives a more diverse representation of all of Texas. The western character is maintained, even in the midst of a thriving urban center. The city has a reputation for being a center of visual and performing arts as well; five institutes of higher learning are based in Fort Worth.

The Fort Worth area celebrates its artistic heritage and cultural diversity with the **Main Street Arts Festival**. For one long weekend in mid-April, Main Street is closed for this pedestrian fair. Stages come alive with dance and musical performances, many which highlight the contributions of different cultures to Fort Worth. The street is filled with booths where artisans sell their crafts. And exhibitions of fine art are featured. Special activities for children both entertain and challenge their imaginations.

ARRIVALS & DEPARTURES

The **Dallas-Fort Worth International Airport** is located between the two cities for which it is named. The clear skies over Arlington often look like a highway for air traffic, especially at night with the frequent takeoffs and landings. **Airport Van Service**, *1000 East Weatherford Street, Fort Worth, Tel. 817/334-0092*, provides transportation from the airport to Fort Worth. One-way fare to or from the downtown area is $8.

The Amtrak route that serves Fort Worth originates in San Antonio, with a stop in Austin, and continues north to Chicago. The train station is located at *1501 Jones Street, Fort Worth, Tel. 817/332-2931*.

If you're driving, Interstate Highway 30 runs from Dallas to the central part of Fort Worth. Interstate Highway 20, which enters on the south side of the city, also runs east-west. Interstate Highway 35 West bisects the city on a north-south axis. This highway splits into two branches south of the Dallas-Fort Worth area. The east branch runs to Dallas.

ORIENTATION

The arts district is located on the western side of the city center. From Interstate Highway 30, take the University Exit north. To get to the Stockyards, exit Commerce and go north on Commerce to the complex.

GETTING AROUND TOWN

The bus system in Fort Worth is called simply "**The T**," *Tel. 817/870-6200*. Special routes cover areas of interest to visitors. The 73A and 73B bus travels between the downtown area and the Stockyards. The standard adult fare is 75¢. Private tours of city attractions are offered through **Gray Line**, *Tel. 817/429-7563*.

A number of taxi companies operate in Fort Worth. **Yellow Cab**, *Tel. 817/534-5555 or 800/749-0900*, serves the entire Dallas-Fort Worth area.

WHERE TO STAY

THE WORTHINGTON, *200 Main Street, Fort Worth. Tel. 817/870-1000 or 800/433-5677, Fax 817/335-3847. Rates: $185 to $375. Credit cards accepted.*

The beautiful Worthington is the premier hotel in Fort Worth. Located in the heart of the city, right in the Sundance Square entertainment district, this modern twelve story hotel is adjacent to the city convention center. The 504 rooms are spacious and some have lovely views of the city. This is the only four star hotel in the area and strives to provide exemplary service. On the premises you will find four restaurants, a gym and outdoor pool.

STOCKYARDS HOTEL, *109 East Exchange Avenue, Fort Worth. Tel. 817/625-6427 or 800/423-8471. Rates: $135 to $165. Credit cards accepted.*

You will get a taste of the Old West at the Stockyards Hotel, which is located on historic Exchange Street. The building was built as a hotel in the early 1900's and has hosted the famous and infamous, like the real Bonnie and Clyde gangster duo. You can simply mosey down the street for daytime entertainment. The western theme decor is downright kitschy, with rooms styled like a Victorian parlor or Wild West abode. This hotel is a favorite of foreign tourists who want to get a full dose of cowboy atmosphere. There's a restaurant and bar on the premises.

MISS MOLLY'S HOTEL, *109 West Exchange Avenue, Fort Worth. Tel. 817/626-1522 or 800/996-6559, fax 817/625-2723. Rates: $95 to $170. Credit cards accepted.*

Miss Molly's is the most unusual place to stay in the city. In the good old days, this hotel was not exactly intended for overnight guests. The eight room esablishment was once a house of ill repute. The painted ladies have long since left, and today this is a cozy and unique luxury hotel. The decor is reminiscent of the past, with plenty of red fabric and Victorian style accents. Breakfast is included with your stay.

RADISSON PLAZA, *815 Main Street, Fort Worth. Tel. 817/870-2100 or 800/333-3333, Fax 817/335-3408. Rates: $120 to $158. Credit cards accepted.*

The Radisson has over 500 rooms and is located in the downtown area. The hotel first opened in 1921, as Fort Worth's finest luxury hotel and only high-rise. This hotel is famous as the last place that President Kennedy stayed before his fateful trip to Dallas. The on-site restaurant has buffet meals for breakfast, lunch and dinner. Amenities include a heated outdoor pool on the rooftop and a fitness area. The hotel is within walking distance of the convention center and restaurants and bars.

REMINGTON HOTEL, *600 Commerce Street, Fort Worth. Tel. 817/332-6900, Fax 877-5440. Rates: $49 to $120. Credit cards accepted.*

This 300 room hotel is near the center of town, and convenient for the various tourist area in the city. The modern rooms are comfortable. The hotel has a restaurant, lounge and fitness facilities on the premises.

THE PARK CENTRAL, *1010 Houston Street, Fort Worth. Tel. 817/336-2011 or 800/848-Park, Fax 817/336-0623. Rates: $50 to $85. Credit cards accepted.*

This motel has 121 rooms and is located close to the Convention Center. The hotel has an outdoor pool, but no other recreational facilities. Children may stay with parents at no additional charge.

HOTEL TEXAS, *2415 Ellis Avenue, Fort Worth. Tel. 817/624-2224 or 800/866-6660, Fax 817/624-7177. Rates: $49 to $109. Credit cards accepted.*

The Hotel Texas was built in 1921 as the luxury accommodation for the Stockyards business district. The two story building is made of yellow brick. The twenty-one rooms have the old-time western feeling but are completely modern. Children under the age of 18 stay free with parents.

Bed and Breakfast

BLOOMSBURY HOUSE, *2251 Lipscomb Street, Fort Worth. Tel. 817/921-2383 or 888/652-7378. Rates: $99 to $110. Credit cards accepted.*

The home was built at the turn-of-the-century and is complete with a carriage house in the back. The three rooms in the main house have old-fashioned furnishings and offer a tranquil hideaway close to major attractions in the city. Guests enjoy a hearty breakfast in the morning and a light dessert in the evening. You can dine in your room or on the bright patio downstairs.

AZALEA PLANTATION BED AND BREAKFAST, *1400 Robinwood Street, Fort Worth. Tel. 817/838-5882 or 800/687-3519. Rates: $89 to $110. Credit cards accepted.*

The Azalea Plantation is located north of downtown Fort Worth, still within a short drive from major attractions and entertainment. The lovely old home has four rooms for guests and two rooms which are used as a common area for visitors. The home is located on lovely property with large trees and a secluded feeling. On weekends a full breakfast is served. Children under the age of six years may stay for no charge with parents.

TEXAS WHITE HOUSE, *1417 English Avenue, Fort Worth. Tel. 817/ 923-3597 or 800/279-6491, Fax 817/923-3597. Rates: $85 to $105. Credit cards accepted.*

This charming house has three guest rooms. Recreational facilities area located nearby, including a golf course. Adults only are welcomed to stay at this house.

WHERE TO EAT

CACHAREL, *2221 East Lamar Street, Arlington. Tel. 817/640-9981. Credit cards accepted.*

This is not just another French restaurant with the standard fare. The charm of provincial French cooking is found at Cacharel, but here it is done with the influence of Texas. The inventive recipes recreate traditional French dishes with American flare. Fresh fish from the Gulf, ostrich meat and tropical fruit among other non-French ingredients are used. The intimate dining room overlooks metropolitan Fort Worth. The set course ($34.95) meals are recommended. Each night the menu changes. From Fort Worth, travel east on Highway 30; take Highway 360 south and exit Lamar Boulevard.

CATTLEMEN'S STEAK HOUSE, *2458 Main Street, Fort Worth. Tel. 817/624-3945. Credit cards accepted.*

With all the fancy grilling and smoking that has overtaken current cooking trends, it is not easy to find a charcoal broiled steak – except at Cattlemen's, where that is the norm. You can also select from a variety of seafood or juicy ribs. The logical place for a steak house is right next to the stockyards, which is where you will find Cattlemen's.

JOE T. GARCIA'S, *2201 Commerce Street, Fort Worth. Tel. 817/626-4356.*

Dining at this restaurant is a tradition for most residents of Fort Worth, and part of the ritual is a very long wait. The Tex-Mex food tastes as though you were sitting down for dinner cooked in a family's kitchen.

You could toss a coin to decide what to order — really, you have but two choices, either enchiladas or fajitas. The dishes are equally popular and delicious. The enchiladas are made in the old-fashioned way, which means heavy on the oil. The margaritas complete the experience of a meal at Joe T. Garcia's. The prices are so low, that the restaurant accepts neither credit cards nor reservations. You can go around the corner to Joe T. Garcia's bakery for dessert.

PARIS COFFEE SHOP, *700 West Magnolia Avenue, Fort Worth. Tel. 817/335-2041. Credit cards accepted.*

This place is all coffee shop, and no Paris. The food is southern cooking at its best. Nothing fancy, but the sort of plates you would get from your grandma's kitchen. Lunch is usually a meaty dish, like chicken fried steak or meatloaf. Breakfast comes in huge portions, with plenty of eggs, sausage and (of course) grits. The corn bread arrives at the table hot, and the gravy has the full flavor that means it can be only homemade.

PULIDO'S, *2900 Pulido Street, Fort Worth 817/732-7571. Credit cards accepted.*

People from all around the metroplex come to Pulido's. While the food is good, they often come for the music. On Friday nights, Pulido's features a harp player from Veracruz, Mexico. He is the foremost musician in this particular style of music, and he has played Carnegie Hall among other notable venues. As you enjoy the tropical decor of the restaurant and absorb yourself in the harp melodies, do not forget to order. Among the selections are many combination platters, such as the Caballero Platter which comes with a 10 ounce sirloin, enchilada, beans and potatoes ($9.95). The homemade tamales are exceptional (five for $6.30). And for dessert you can get fluffy sopapillas, light puff pastry served with honey.

SEEING THE SIGHTS

There is no doubt that the **Stockyards**, *140 East Exchange Avenue, Tel. 817/624-4741*, are the primary attraction in the city. The many turn-of-the century buildings were the center of life in Fort Worth at one time. Today the entire area is renovated for visitors. The area recreates the Old West, with shops, restaurants and entertainment. The **Stockyards Museum**, *131 Exchange Avenue, Tel. 817/624-4741*, shows the importance of the cattle industry during Texas in the early twentieth century. The exhibits reveal the economic and social impact of ranching.

Every Saturday evening, from April through September, a rodeo is held at the Stockyards. The cowboys are some of the finest professional around and are sure to put on a good show. The stockyards are located north of Interstate Highway 30; take the Commerce Street exit. You can take a steam train, the **Tarantula**, *Tel. 817/625-7245 or 800/952-5717,* from the Stockyards to the Arts District.

Life in the early days of Fort Worth is reconstructed at the **Log Cabin Village**, *2250 University Drive, Tel. 817/926-5881.* You can walk through the homes that are decked out as though the pioneers were still living in them. The arts district is north of this area on University Drive.

The **Kimball Art Museum**, *3333 Camp Bowie, Tel. 332-8451, Tuesday to Thursday and Saturday 10am to 5pm, Friday and Sunday noon to 5pm,* is often referred to as the finest art museum in Texas. The museum was based on a private collection and over the years has grown into one of the most comprehensive representations of art to be found anywhere. Much of the lighting is natural, allowing masterpieces to be seen in a unique manner. The permanent collection includes an exemplary collection of primitive art and work by masters such as Monet and Picasso. The museum is best known for attracting the finest touring exhibitions.

The work of current artists is displayed at the **Modern Art Museum**, *1309 Montgomery Street, Tuesday to Sunday noon to 5pm.* Exhibits change regularly. Educational programs add to the offerings of this museum.

The new **Museum of Science and History**, *1501 Montgomery Street, Tel. 817/732-1631, Monday to Friday 9am to 5pm, Saturday and Sunday 9am to 9pm, Admission adult $5, child $3,* is a welcome high-tech learning center in the city arts district. The hands-on exhibits allow children to dig like an archaeologist, experience the galaxy in the planetarium and take fun and educational workshops. The museum's **Omni Theater**, *Tel. 817/732-1631,* shows movies from 10:30am to 11:30pm; daily schedules vary.

Sid Richardson made his fortune in Texas oil, but he left his mark by the many endowments he made. The **Sid Richardson Collection of Western Art**, *309 Main Street, Tel. 817/332-6554,* is one such gift. The museum highlights masterpieces that portray life in the Old West. The collection breathes depth and passion into the lore of the cowboy.

The **Fort Worth Botanical Garden**, *3220 Botanic Drive, Tel. 817/332-2272,* has acres of outdoor gardens that replicate a variety of habitats. The conservatory offers a more formal look at fauna and presents educational programs. The Japanese Garden is a tranquil and meditative abode sculptured in the formal Japanese style.

The **Fort Worth Zoo**, *1989 Colonial Parkway, Tel. 817/871-7050, Open daily 10am to 5pm, Admission $5.50 adult, $3 child,* represents the amazing bio-diversity of the planet. As home to over 5,000 animals, the zoo provides habitats for reptiles, birds of prey, primates and a special area for Asian animals. The zoo has received kudos as one of the finest in the nation. From Interstate Highway 30, take the University Street Exit south to Colonial Street.

NIGHTLIFE & ENTERTAINMENT

The **Fort Worth Convention Center**, *1111 Houston Street, Tel. 817/ 332-9222*, is a large complex that has stages for performances by the **Fort Worth Symphony**, *Tel. 817/926-8831*, **Fort Worth Ballet**, *Tel. 817/763-0207*, and the **Fort Worth Opera**, *Tel. 817/731-0833*.

According to legend, when Butch Cassidy and the Sundance Kid were hiding from the law, they came to Fort Worth. The town had a rough area known as Hell's Half Acre, which was the setting for debauchery cowboy-style. Times have indeed changed, and the convention center stands on what was once Hell's Half Acre. But to keep the memory of bygone wild days intact, a small historic square bears the name of Cassidy's partner. **Sundance Square** covers fourteen downtown blocks and is full of casual restaurants, bars and entertainment. The area is within Second and Fifth Streets, to the north and south, and Throckmorton and Commerce on the east and west.

To the west of Fort Worth you will find **Six Flags Over Texas**, *Tel. 817/2640-8900*, which is not a history lesson, but a grand Warner Brothers amusement park. This was the first of the parks in Texas, but continual additions keep the rides as looping and frightening as technology allows. Like the twin cities of Dallas and Fort Worth, there are twin Six Flags. Hurricane Harbor is a giant water park, with the tallest water raft ride in the nation. From Fort Worth, take Highway 30 west, then Highway 360 south.

Billy Bob's Texas, *2520 Rodeo Plaza, Tel. 817/624-7117*. The definition of "honky tonk" is Billy Bob's Texas. And this dance hall seems to be about as big as Texas; the dance floor alone is over 1500 square feet. If you want to be a cowboy — even just for one night — this is the place to go. The dance floor is full of people sporting cowboy hats and boot-cut jeans. The club is an institution in Fort Worth, and certainly the most famous country-western scene in the state. Billy Bob's is open every night. Live entertainment is featured some nights; there is always a cover charge.

Caravan of Dreams, *312 Houston Street, Tel. 817/877-3000*. One of the southwest's premier venues for live jazz music. The complex has a club that attracts music enthusiasts and a theater that incorporates nature into its construction. The performing arts stage holds productions in the spring through the late summer. The Caravan of Dreams is part of the civic center and hosts excellent performances during the year.

SPORTS & RECREATION

The finest animals in the state are found at the **Fort Worth Stock Show and Rodeo**, *Tel. 817/877-2400*, which is held at the end of January. The events span three weeks and include a rodeo, parade, and of course, a livestock show. The **Will Rogers Memorial Center**, *3400 Burnett-Tandy Drive*, is the site of the celebration. The Center is west of the center of town; from Interstate Highway 30, take the Montgomery Street exit north. Admission to the show and rodeo is $16.

The **Texas Rangers** thrill fans at The Ball Park in Arlington, *Tel. 817/ 273-5100*. The season begins in April and runs through September; games are held in the evening. You can tour the stadium for a behind-the-scenes perspective of the game. Also the **Legends of the Game Baseball Museum and Learning Center**, *Tel. 817/273-5099*, is on the complex grounds. From Interstate Highway 30, exit Collins Street south. The Ballpark is close to the highway.

EXCURSIONS & DAY TRIPS

American Airlines chose the Dallas-Fort Worth area as its home base, and consequently the museum that chronicles American's history is located near Dallas Fort Worth Airport. The **American Airlines C. R. Smith Museum**, *4106 Highway 360, Tel. 817/967-1560, Wednesday to Saturday, 10am to 6pm, Sunday noon to 5pm, Admission free*, displays chronicle the history of commercial flight through American Airlines' perspective. From Highway 183, take Highway 360 south.

Nature lovers will enjoy the wildlife at **Fossil Rim Wildlife Center**, *Highway 67, Glen Rose, Tel. 817/897-2960*, a preserve for living animals. Visitors drive along nine and one-half miles of trails through the homes of giraffes, large cats, zebras and an array of other animals. Prehistory is well represented at Fossil Rim; guests can walk along nature trails and hunt for fossils. Fossil Rim is an educational facility. Part of the preservation efforts include breeding endangered species such as the white rhino. Taking a guided tour will acquaint you with the science behind managing the preserve. The cozy lodge provides a luxurious vacation in the country. The more adventurous can take an African-style tent safari. The only shots fired on the safari will be with a camera, though. From Fort Worth, take Loop 820 south, exit Highway 67 and go south to Glen Rose. Fossil Rim is three miles south of Glen Rose on Highway 67.

The **Dinosaur Valley Park**, *Farm Road 205, Glen Rose, Tel. 806/897-4588*, is named for the fossilized dinosaur footprints found there. You can view some of the tracks at the park's museum. The exhibits provide information about the geography of the area in the age of the dinosaurs. The park offers primitive campsites and those with hook-ups. Six miles of hiking trails lead through the interesting river landscape. You can swim in the Brazos River. From Fort Worth, take Highway 67 south to Glen Rose. Then head west on Farm Road 205. Dinosaur Valley is on Park Road 59, four miles from Highway 67.

PRACTICAL INFORMATION

American Automobile Association (AAA), *5431 South Hulen Street, Fort Worth. Tel. 817/370-3000.*

Fort Worth Convention and Visitors Bureau, *415 East Street, Fort Worth. Tel. 817/336-8791 or 800/433-5747.*

The **Arts Council of Fort Worth**, *Tel. 817/870-2564*, provides information about performing arts events in the city.

The **Stockyards Visitor Center**, *130 East Exchange Street, Fort Worth. Tel. 817/626-7921*

ABILENE

Abilene stands alone, between the Dallas-Fort Worth urban center and the beginnings of west Texas, at the Midland and Odessa area. Abilene is a center of higher education; Abilene Christian University, Hardin-Simmons University and McMurray University are located in the city. The wide open plains of this region made Abilene a hub of the cattle trade in the late 1800s. Although oil played a minor role in the shaping of this city, Abilene has always taken its character from the lore of the cowboys.

In September, the glory days of cattle drive come back to life in Abilene. The **Western Heritage Classic**, held at the Taylor County Expo Center, *1700 Highway 36, Abilene, Tel. 915/677-4376*, revisits the lifestyle of working the range. Of course a rodeo is held, but the event runs for ten days and is far more than just roping and riding. The vittles are served up at the Championship Chuck Wagon Cook-off. The melodious lyrics of Cowboy Poets are celebrated. And the entire event winds up with the Rhinestone Gala. Arts, crafts and food are for sale every day.

ARRIVALS & DEPARTURES

Interstate Highway 20 crosses Abilene from east to west. Highway 87 runs north to south through the city.

GETTING AROUND TOWN

Public transportation is provided by the **Abilene Transit Authority**, *Tel. 915/676-6403*, which operates the bus service.

WHERE TO STAY

BOLIN'S PRAIRIE HOUSE, *508 Mulberry Street. Abilene. Tel. 915/675-5855 or 800/673-5855. Rates: $50 to $65. Credit cards accepted.*

Bolin's bed and breakfast is located close to the center of town. Built in 1902, the quaint two story home is a pleasure to visit. The house offers four guest rooms. Two of the rooms have private baths and all guests have use of the downstairs living area. A country-style breakfast is served.

KIVA INN HOTEL, *5403 North First Street, Abilene. Tel. 915/695-2150 or 800/592-4466, Fax: 915/698-6742. Rates: $49 to $54. Credit cards accepted.*

The Kiva Inn has conference center facilities, including meting rooms. Both a lounge and full service restaurant are located on the premises. A pool enclosed in an atrium with a fitness center provides recreational opportunities. The inn has a game room with ping pong tables and other diversions. The simple rooms are adequately comfortable.

HOLIDAY INN EXPRESS, *1625 Highway 351, Abilene. Tel. 915/673-5271 or 800/465-4329, Fax 915/673-8240. Rates: 56 to $62. Credit cards accepted.*

This new hotel has an outdoor pool and is located near attractions and public transportation. Continental breakfast is included with every room. This is a convenient place to stay if you're taking a highway trip.

WHERE TO EAT

BETTY ROSE'S LITTLE BRISKET, *2402 East 7th Street. Abilene. Tel. 915/673-5809.*

Years ago, if you filled up at Betty Rose's you would have been putting gas in your car. The restaurant is a former filling station. The retro roadside attraction atmosphere adds to the experience of eating truly good barbecue. The brisket is the specialty of the house. Side dishes include macaroni and potato salad. The beans are good, but the desserts are better. They do not take credit cards, but the meals only cost about $5.

SEEING THE SIGHTS

In 1851, a fort was established to protect the town from hostile attacks. Today **Fort Phantom Hill** is a ghost fort, with an eerie, desolate character. Three buildings remain intact and many lie in ruins on the hilltop preserve. After only three years, the fort was deserted, in part due to difficult conditions in this dry area. The fort stands on private property and is open to the public. There are no facilities or museum buildings at the site. From Interstate Highway 20 in Abilene, take Farm Road 600 north and continue for 14 miles. The fort overlooks a lake which shares its name.

Abilene has a respectable arts community housed in the interesting **Grace Museum Center**, *102 Cypress Street, Tel. 915/673-4587.* Located in the historic Grace Hotel, built in 1909, the hotel was the premier accommodations in the area when it was built. A section of the hotel has been restored for viewing.

The **Abilene Fine Arts Museum**, *102 Cypress Street, Tel. 915/673-4587, Tuesday to Friday 9am to 5pm and Saturday and Sunday 1pm to 5pm, closed Monday*, displays regularly changing exhibits of work by local artists and of interest to the community. Children will get a kick from the whimsical world of discovery at the **Abilene Children's Museum**, also housed in the Grace Museum complex.

Hardin-Simmons University, which is in central Abilene, has an arts area open to the public. The **Frost Visual Arts Center**, *Hardin-Simmons University, 2200 Hickory Street, Tel. 915/677-7281*, highlights the work of students, faculty and renowned artists.

Air travel has been of primary importance since its beginnings, perhaps because Abilene is far from the nearest city, or maybe because the Texas skies are clear and bright in this region. The **Dyess Air Force Base**, *Tel. 915/696-2863*, has been in operation since just after World War II. The base has a collection of vintage and modern aircraft that can be viewed by the public through an arranged tour. The tours are free, but you must call in advance. Dyess Air Force Base is located west of the city. From the business loop of Interstate Highway 20 West, take Loop 312 south to the base entrance.

The Abilene Municipal Airport Has a collection of World War II fighter planes. The **Phantom Squadron**, *Abilene Municipal Airport, Hanger 2, open Saturday and Sunday noon to 5pm*, can be viewed on weekend afternoons only. From Interstate Highway 20, take Highway 322 south to the Abilene Municipal Airport.

NIGHTLIFE & ENTERTAINMENT

The historic **Paramount Theater**, *310 North Willis Street, Tel. 915/676-9602*, presents classic films and theatrical and musical performances. The beautiful theater has been renovated, and the building itself is a piece of art.

SPORTS & RECREATION

Attractive **Abilene State Park**, *121 Park Road 32, Tuscola, Tel. 915/572-3204*, was once inhabited by the Tonkawa Native Americans. The park has a long and complex history, as cattle land, a stop on the Western Cattle Trail, and finally as a natural preserve. Rolling hills, large pecan trees and steams characterize the landscape. Lake Abilene is only a half mile away. The park has hiking trails and wildlife observation spots, many picnic sites and a swimming pool. Camping facilities include over 90 campsites, from tent areas to full hook-up facilities. From Abilene or Interstate Highway 20, take Farm Road 89 south for sixteen miles, then look for the signs indicating the park road.

EXCURSIONS & DAY TRIPS

You can gain insight to the real Old West at **Fort Griffin State Historical Park**, *Route 1, Box 125, Albany, Tel. 915/ 762-3592, Fax 915/ 762-2492*. Some of the original frontier buildings of Fort Griffin remain standing. Reconstructed buildings and a visitors center provide a complete picture of life in this trading outpost. In some ways this was a rougher settlement than those of the western region of Texas. Gunfights were a leading cause of death here in the late nineteenth century. Twice a year Civil War battles are reenacted by members of a history club. The park arranges trail rides throughout the year. Fort Griffin is north of Abilene on Highway 283. Take highway 351 north from Abilene. At Albany go north on Highway 283 and continue for 15 miles.

A mix of authentic frontier buildings and new tourist attractions is found at **Buffalo Gap**, *Tel. 915/572-3365*. An old courthouse, jail and log cabins are among the nearly 20 old buildings. A doctor's office, a barber shop and a print shop are modern reconstructions. The plain white chapel is one of the oldest houses of worship in the region. To get to Buffalo Gap, from Abilene or Interstate Highway 20, take Farm Road 89 south. It's about 15 miles south of Abilene.

LUBBOCK

Lubbock was once a twin city. Monterey became incorporated to Lubbock in 1890. The city stands near low, rolling canyons, which mark the beginning of the Llano Estacado geological region. Recent history distinguishes Lubbock from the other cattle towns of north Texas. This is the birthplace of rock n' roll legend Buddy Holly. The city is the home of **Texas Tech University** and has an active cultural life.

ARRIVALS & DEPARTURES

Highway 87 divides Lubbock on a north-south axis. Highway 85 runs from northeast to southwest and is crossed by Highway 84, which runs northwest to southeast. The Lubbock airport is just to the east of Interstate Highway 30, north of the city.

ORIENTATION

The streets in central Lubbock make a nearly perfect gird, as do the county line surrounding the city. Loop 289 completely encircles Lubbock. Texas Tech University and the museum district are in the northwest region of the city.

GETTING AROUND TOWN

A metropolitan bus system, *Tel. 806/767-2380*, serves the city of Lubbock.

WHERE TO STAY

ASHMORE INN, *4019 Loop 289, Lubbock. Tel. 806/785-0060 or 800/785-0061, Fax 806/785-6001. Rates: $62 to $67. Credit cards accepted.*

The Ashmore Inn offers 100 rooms in an agreeable motel setting. The rooms are large, with ample sitting areas. Continental breakfast is offered each morning at no cost to guests. From Monday to Thursday, a free cocktail hour takes place in the early evening.

LA QUINTA, *4115 Brownfield Highway, Lubbock. Tel. 806/792-0065 or 800/531-5900. Rates: 63 Credit cards accepted.*

The six story hotel is in the vicinity of the Texas Tech University campus. The modern building is built around the atrium lounge. Continental breakfast is complimentary. The hotel has an outdoor pool. La Quinta is located on Highway 82, just south of Highway 62. Free shuttle service to the airport is available. La Quinta also has a location on Avenue Q, near the civic center.

SHERATON FOUR POINTS, *Avenue Q, Lubbock. Tel. 806/747-0171 or 800/925-3535, Fax 806/747-9243. Rates: $79 to $89. Credit cards accepted.*

The Sheraton Four Points is often the choice of business travelers. The hotel has computer data ports on phones and ample space for meetings in the conference rooms. The hotel is located in the city center. An indoor pool and a lounge offer leisure time activities.

WHERE TO EAT

GABRIEL'S, *8201 Quaker Avenue, Lubbock. Tel. 806/794/5444. Credit cards accepted.*

Gabriel's is usually packed in the evenings. One of the most appreciated restaurants in the city, the menu takes regular Italian dishes, such as lasagna, and brings them up-to-date. Using the best ingredients, rich cheeses, imported vinegar, and the freshest fish, the food is a joy to eat. The wine list offers a variety to suit every palate. Expect to spend at least $20 for a meal here. Reservations are highly recommended, especially on weekends.

GRAPEVINE CAFE, *2407 B 19th Street, Lubbock. Tel. 806/774-8246. Credit cards accepted.*

You could easily pass by the Grapevine and not look twice. This small, unassuming eatery is not often found by visitors. The refreshing menu offers light fare for lunch, like generous salads, fresh soup and crepes. Dinner has a more extensive selection. The pasta dishes are very satisfy-

ing, and the combinations of ingredients is the focus of the taste, not the sauce. The desserts are excellent. The cafe is open until 11pm nightly. **LALA'S**, *1110 Broadway Street, Lubbock. Tel. 806/747-2334. Credit cards accepted.*
The time to eat at Lala's is when you wake up really hungry, yearning for a filling breakfast. The eggs and omelets come with a big side of crispy potatoes. You can order breakfast well into the afternoon. Lala's is open Monday to Saturday.

SEEING THE SIGHTS

You may be surprised by how many famous entertainers hail from west Texas. The **Walk of Fame**, *8th Street and Avenue Q,* has bronze plaques to Roy Orbison, Tanya Tucker and Waylon Jennings, among many others. The centerpiece of the walk is a giant bronze statue of the most revered Lubbock native, Buddy Holly.

The park that surrounds **Lubbock Lake Landmark**, *North Loop 289, Tel. 806/741-0306,* has archaeological excavations that date to 12,000 BC. Extraordinary fossil evidence records fauna unique to the region.. The ongoing dig has yielded artifacts from a hunt that may be 10,000 years old. You can take a guided tour of the excavation site while the dig is in progress. The park's museum explains the significance of the finds and our current understanding of the prehistory of the region. The park is on the south of the city at Loop 289 and Highway 84.

Texas Tech University, *400 Indiana Avenue, Tel. 806/742-2490, Tuesday to Saturday, 10am to 4pm, admission free,* has archives that range from art history to science. The **Texas Tech Library**, *Tel. 806/472-3758,* has the nation's second largest archives of documents dealing with the Vietnam War.

NIGHTLIFE & ENTERTAINMENT

The **Depot District**, *at 19th Street and Avenue Q,* is the center of nightlife and live music in Lubbock. You can find a variety of distractions in this trendy area, from live rock music to country western dancing. Lubbock's own microbrewery, **Hub City Brewery**, is located here. This historic **warehouse area** is popular with the Texas Tech crowd.

EXCURSIONS & DAY TRIPS

The buffalo roam at **Caprock Canyon State Park**, *Ranch Road 1065, P. O. Box 204, Quitaque, Tel. 806/455-1492 or 800/792-1112.* The park hosts occasional safari-style tours to view buffalo herds and other wildlife. Visitors can marvel at the excavation of a 10,000 year old Native American buffalo kill. Another unusual site is an abandoned railroad tunnel, one of the few in the nation. The park also has herds of Proghorn Antelope and many other types of wildlife. Over 13,000 acres and 24 miles of hiking trails and paths for mountain bikes await the adventurous at Caprock Canyon. The land rises high above the riverbeds and is the backdrop for beautiful sunsets. At **Big C's Trading Post**, you can rent canoes and paddle-boats to use on small **Lake Theo**. Facilities include camp sites, both primitive and with hook-ups, and a small lodge. From Lubbock, take Interstate Highway 27 north to Tulia, then Highway 86 east past Silverton to the park.

In the winter, migratory cranes flock to the **Muleshoe National Wildlife Refuge**, *Highway 214, Muleshoe, Tel. 806/946-3341*. As many as 100,000 cranes nest in the tall grasses along the lake. You can follow motor routes or hiking trails through the refuge. Regardless of when you visit, you should catch a glimpse of birds. Over 280 species inhabit the area during the year. From Lubbock, take Highway 84 north. At Muleshoe, go south on Highway 214. When you reach the park entrance, you will have to drive about two miles on a rugged road to reach the refuge headquarters.

One of the largest and most acclaimed wineries in the state is the **Llano Estacado Winery**, *Highway 84, Lubbock, Tel. 806/745/2258, Fax 806/748-1674, open daily noon to 4:30pm*. Llano wine includes 12 varieties, and 75,000 cases are produced annually. Wine tasting is conducted at the modern visitors building.

PRACTICAL INFORMATION

The **Lubbock Chamber of Commerce**, *1400 Avenue K, Lubbock, Tel. 806/747-5232 or 800/692-4035, has information about attrac*tions in the area.

AMARILLO

You can get your kicks just outside of **Amarillo** on the old Route 66! From the Cadillac Ranch to the local art museum, Amarillo is a good stop wherever you're going.

ARRIVALS & DEPARTURES

Amarillo is in the center of the Texas panhandle, at the crossroads of Interstate Highway 40, which runs east to west, and Highway 87, which runs north to south.

The **Amarillo International Airport**, *10,801 Airport Boulevard, Amarillo*, is in the west part of the city. American, Delta and Southwest have service to and from Amarillo. From Interstate Highway 40, exit Airport Boulevard. Taxi service is available from the airport.

GETTING AROUND TOWN

The **Amarillo Transit Authority**, *Tel. 806/378-3094*, provides public bus service for the city.

Taxi companies in Amarillo include:
- **Bob's Taxi Service**, Tel. *806/373-1171*
- **Royal Cab**, *Tel. 806/376-4276*
- **Yellow Cab**, *Tel. 806/374-5242*

WHERE TO STAY

PARKVIEW HOUSE, *1311 South Jefferson Street. Amarillo. Tel. 806/ 373-9494, Fax 373-3166. Rates: $65 to $105. Credit cards accepted.*

This Victorian home is located near central Amarillo, and is the home of the former Mayor. The home later became a hotel, then a boarding house. Renovated to reflect the charm of the early 1900's, Parkview House has special touches, such as local antiques and stained glass windows. The English Room is a small suite with a private bath. The Victorian Rose Room offers the most romantic decor and has an antique tub in the bath. A private cottage is available for rental. From Interstate Highway 40, exit Jefferson Street and proceed north to 14th Street.

WHERE TO EAT

BIG TEXAN STEAK RANCH, *7701 Interstate Highway 40 East. Tel. 806/3726000. Credit cards accepted.*

Come here for a good, old fashioned meat-and-potatoes meal. The steaks here are big enough to suit the biggest Texan you could imagine. Seventy-two ounces of beefy delight is the house specialty, and the steak that put this restaurant on the map for every beef lover. The restaurant occasionally features entertainment. A full meal is well under $20.

OHMS, *619 Tyler street, Amarillo. Tel. 806/373-7476. Credit cards accepted.*

This art gallery and restaurant combination has the best of both. The atmosphere is upbeat and trendy. The recipes take chances, bringing together Asian influences, like pungent ginger, and Tex-Mex selections. The menu covers all the bases including Italian, Cajun and a bit of standard Texas fare. The very casual restaurant does not have a wait staff, but instead you serve yourself from the cafeteria-like line. OHMS is a good place to enjoy a cup of coffee and take in the surroundings.

SEEING THE SIGHTS

One of the oddest works of monumental art is the **Cadillac Ranch**, a row of ten vintage Cadillacs standing in the ground headlong. The Cadillac Ranch is west of Amarillo on Interstate Highway 40.

More mainstream art can be found in the city. The **Amarillo Art Musuem**, *Amarillo College, 2200 Van Buren Street, Tel. 806/371-5050, Tuesday to Friday 10am to 5pm, Saturday and Sunday 1pm to 5pm*, features art by the students and faculty of Amarillo College, and also offers exhibits of interest by national artists.

The **American Quarter Horse Heritage Center and Museum**, *Quarter Horse Drive at Interstate Highway 40, Tel. 806/376-5181*. The history of breeding is shown through standard museum exhibits. The facility includes a research library and rotating exhibits.

The **Amarillo Zoo**, *Thompson Park, Highway 287, Tel. 806/381-7911*. The zoo is a natural preserve for animals that are native to the state, and in need of protection. You can watch a herd of buffalo graze. The petting area is the main attraction at the zoo.

NIGHTLIFE & ENTERTAINMENT

The **Amarillo Symphony**, *1000 Polk Street, Tel. 806/376-8782*. The Amarillo Symphony began filling the city with classical music in 1927. The symphony performs in the **Civic Center**, *Tel. 806/359-5941*, located at 3rd Street and Buchanen. Guest musicians and touring concerts are also hosted in this venue.

For a fun bar, try:

THE BREWPUB, *3705 Oleson, Tel. 806/353-2622*.

This unpretentious bar with a strong showing of regulars serves its own brew on tap. Special beers are regularly featured and pub food is served. The lively atmosphere is often the place to be on weekend nights. Credit cards accepted.

EXCURSIONS & DAY TRIPS

Native Americans used the distinctively colored flint from this region for thousands of years. The **Alibates Flint Quarries National Monument**, *Highway 136, Fritch, Tel. 806/857-3151*. Guided tours during the summer at 10 am and 2pm. During other months, tours can be made by reservation. The quarry mounds are located at the end of a one-mile trail that includes a number of stone steps. It takes about two hours to complete the tour. The park is about 40 miles north of Amarillo. Take the Lake Meredith Recreational Area exit then follow the signs to the ranger station. From Amarillo, take Highway 136 north; signs clearly mark the monument.

The national park at **Lake Meredith**, *Highway 136, Fritch, Tel 806/857-3151*, is a popular area for boating enthusiasts. Primitive campsites are free of charge. From Amarillo, take Highway 136 north; the lake is 30 miles north of Amarillo.

A worthwhile stop in the small town of Canyon is the **Panhandle-Plains Historical Museum**, *West Texas State University, Canyon, open Monday to Friday 9am to 5pm, Sunday noon to 6pm*. As you walk in, note the decoration of cattle brands. The museum pays tribute to the cultures of north Texas. Displays show the archaeological findings from Native American sites. A recreation of a chuck wagon gives insight to how cowboys actually lived. And the petroleum wing shows the beginnings of the technology of the oil industry. The museum building is an unusual mix of art deco design and native limestone. The structure dates from 1933. Mural-sized paintings depict the history of the Amarillo area. Canyon is 15 miles south of Amarillo on Interstate Highway 27.

Route 66 has been overshadowed by Interstate Highway 40. Still the old route, in parts a ghost highway, covers nearly 180 miles, running straight across the panhandle from east to west. Most diners and businesses long ago moved to more traveled territory. Still, a trip along **Route 66** appeals to the truly nostalgic. The one stronghold for travelers is the **Old Route 66 Musuem**, *Old Route 66, Kingsley, Tel. 806/779-2225*, that features barbed wire as the mainstay of the collection. The museum has on display over 450 types of barbed wire and the machines that made the fencing. Artifacts and memorabilia from the glory days of Texas Route 66 are also shown throughout the museum. There is no admission charge.

HOW BARBED WIRE CHANGED THE WEST

Barbed wire changed the face of Texas, especially in the panhandle. Before its invention in 1874, the vast expanse of land allowed cattle and cowboys to roam free. Soon ranchers ended this by stringing up cheap and effective barbed wire. Millions of acres of land became impenetrable, thanks to the fencing which was invented in Illinois, not Texas. With their land and cattle secure, the ranchers soon provided fodder for the railroad industry, which soon connected Texas to the larger markets in the east.

PRACTICAL INFORMATION

American Automobile Association (AAA), *2607 North Wolfin Village, Amarillo, Tel. 806/354-8288.*

The **Amarillo Visitor Center**, *7703 East Interstate Highway 35, Tel. 800/894-9103*, offers information about the panhandle region.

15. EAST TEXAS

HOUSTON

Houston, the fourth largest city in the United States with a population of 1.7 million, traces its beginnings to the vision of two brothers. The city of Houston was founded in 1836 by the Allen brothers, who changed a small settlement into a metropolis. When the Allens arrived, the village of Frottstown had been in existence for 14 years. They had visions of transforming the tiny frontier community into a grand commercial center.

Even in infancy, Houston relied on waterway access for trade and growth. The brothers laid out the city blocks in orderly fashion, and these same streets remain the center of Houston's business district today. The city became the capital of the fledgling nation of The Republic of Texas in 1837.

Market Square was the meeting place of merchants and the site of local government buildings throughout the nineteenth century. This area fell into economic depression, then was used as a parking lot. Market Square once again is a center of commerce. The Market Square Park, which offers a striking view of the downtown skyscrapers, is surrounded by restaurants.

During the nineteenth century, the city was a rugged place, and women were not permitted downtown. So when the wealthy merchants built their homes, they went to what was then the outskirts of town. East Texas cotton farmers soon made Houston their center of commerce. The **Houston Cotton Exchange** on Travis Street, built in 1884, shows that cotton was indeed king to the Houston economy.

Houston remained in the shadow of neighboring Galveston, which had a larger port and thriving economy at the turn-of-the century. Galveston rivaled New Orleans in importance as a shipping center until the hurricane of 1900 devastated the coast. That fierce storm washed the city away, and permanently devastated its commercial port. Trade quickly shifted to Houston.

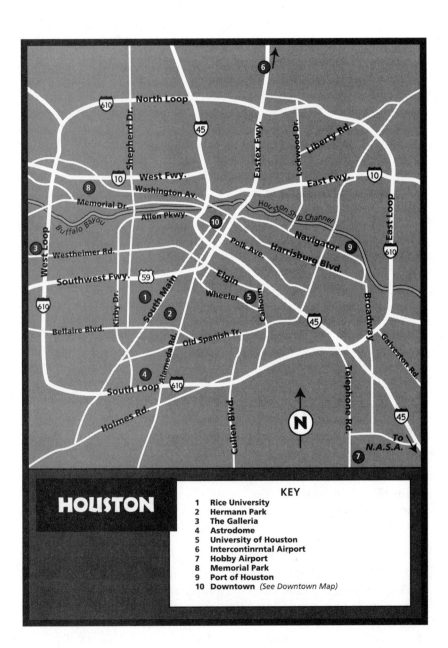

KEY

1	Rice University
2	Hermann Park
3	The Galleria
4	Astrodome
5	University of Houston
6	Intercontinrntal Airport
7	Hobby Airport
8	Memorial Park
9	Port of Houston
10	Downtown *(See Downtown Map)*

HOUSTON

SAM HOUSTON

The city's namesake, **Sam Houston**, *arrived in what is downtown Houston in 1836. Although the city was named for him, Houston lived here only while serving as president of the Republic of Texas. The small wooden buildings which served and the seat of the government have long since disappeared.*

After Texas joined the United States, Sam Houston went on to become a United States senator, then governor of the state of Texas. Opposed to Texas joining the Confederacy, Houston lost that battle and resigned the governorship in 1861. He moved to Huntsville, north of Houston, where he lived his remaining years with his wife and family.

Houston's big boom came with the oil industry. The large **Port of Houston** sits amid many smaller port cities, making the area an artery for the oil trade. Much of the city took shape in the 1970s and early 1980s; the style gives the high-dollar gloss to Houston's facade. The image of the urban cowboy remains strong in the hearts and minds of Houstonians.

You can step into the boots of an urban cowboy at the largest rodeo in the world — which is, of course, held in Houston. The annual winter event has grown in size every year since its founding in 1932. The **Houston Rodeo** starts in mid-February and lasts two weeks. The weeks before the rodeo include festivities like the annual Trail Ride and Rodeo Parade. For more information on the rodeo, see *Sports & Recreation* below.

ARRIVALS & DEPARTURES

By Plane

Houston has two major airports. **George Bush Intercontinental Airport** (airline code IAH), recently renamed in honor of the president who calls Houston home, is one of the 15 largest airports in the world. Bush Intercontinental has four terminals with a total of 89 gates. An underground train connects terminals A, B, C, the Mickey Leland International Terminal and the Marriott Hotel, which is on the airport grounds.

Many area hotels and motels run courtesy vans to the airport for their guests. Public METRO buses serve each terminal, as well as a passenger pick-up area for taxi cabs. Fares to Houston range from $29 to the north of the city to $64 to the Clear Lake area.

Inexpensive shuttle service to the airport and central Houston is provided by **Airport Express**, *2222 Cleburne Avenue, Houston, Tel. 713/ 523-8888.* The buses serve downtown, the Medical Center, the Astrodome, the Galleria, Greenway Plaza and the west side of town. Special shuttles connect Bush Intercontinental to Hobby Airport. Fares range from $16 to $21 one way. Children under 12 years old are charged $5.

Galveston and the Bay Area are served by **Galveston Limousine Service**, *Tel. 800/640-4826.* Fares range from $18 to $26 for a one-way ride to League City, Texas City and Galveston. Children under 12 years old are charged half-fare.

William P. Hobby Airport, named for a former state governor, handles domestic flights to over 60 cities and is used by Conquest Airlines, Southwest Airlines, Northwest Airlines, American Airlines, Delta Airlines and TWA. Many hotels have courtesy vans for guests arriving and departing from Hobby Airport. To get to Hobby Airport, take Gulf Freeway (Interstate Highway 45) south from Loop 610.

Airport Express, *Tel. 713/523-8888,* charges between $11 and $21 for shuttle service to Houston. Taxicabs have a passenger pick-up station just out the doors by the first floor baggage claim. Taxi rates to different areas in Houston range from $17 (downtown) to $52 (north Houston). The rates are fixed and a schedule is available from drivers. The city METRO bus service has a bus stop in the same area.

Both airports have car rental desks and all major national car rental agencies serve Houston.

By Bus & Train

The **Greyhound Bus Terminal** *2121 Main Street, Tel. 800/231-2222 or 713/759-6565* is near the business district.

The **Amtrak Station**, *902 Washington Avenue, Tel. 800/USA-RAIL (872-7245),* is located downtown. From Interstate Highway 10, exit Smith Street, take Franklin Street to Bagby and continue to Washington.

Houston is on the Amtrak Sunset Limited route which travels between Los Angeles and Miami. The eastbound train arrives on Tuesday, Thursday and Sunday at 8:30am and departs at 8:45am. The westbound train arrives Wednesday, Friday and Sunday at 11:48pm and departs at 11:59pm. From Houston the Sunset Limited goes to San Antonio, Del Rio, Sanderson, Alpine and El Paso. Passengers going to Dallas transfer to the Amtrak Throughway Bus.

From Houston to Central America

Houston is a port for **Norwegian Cruise Lines**, which sails to Cozumel, Mexico and Roatan, Honduras. The cruises currently offered are seven day western Caribbean itineraries.

ORIENTATION

Loop 610 encircles the central part of Houston. Unlike Dallas, which is a conglomeration of small cities, Houston is one large urban area. All highways lead to city center, which has two main commercial areas.

Interstate Highway 10 cuts through the city's northern half from east to west. The western part of Interstate Highway is called Katy Freeway, and the eastern section is East Freeway. Interstate Highway 45 connects Dallas to the north and Galveston to the south. The southern part of Interstate Highway 45, which leads to the Gulf of Mexico, is known as Gulf Freeway.

The business center of Houston is bordered by the historic district to the north and the theater district to the east. The University Area, just south of downtown near Rice University, is home to the major art museums, many cafes, and lovely tree-lined residential areas. Montrose Street and Westheimer Road are popular areas for shopping and nightlife.

HOUSTON HIGHWAYS & THEIR CHANGING NAMES

When you get directions for highway driving in Houston, the name of the highway may not match the name on the map. Each highway in Houston has a given name which lets you know more specifically which part you will travel on.

- *Katy Freeway, the western section of Interstate Highway 10*
- *East Freeway, the eastern section of Interstate Highway 10*
- *Gulf Freeway, the southern section of Interstate Highway 45*
- *Southwest Freeway, Highway 59*
- *North (South, East, West) Loop, Loop 610*
- *Tollway 8, Sam Houston Tollway*

GETTING AROUND TOWN

Taxi cabs charge $1.50 per mile and 30¢ for standing time; a $1 late night surcharge is added to all rides from 8pm to 6am. The rates are not high, but fares can add up for the long distances in Houston driving. No additional charge is levied for up to four passengers.

- **American Liberty Cab**, *Tel. 713/999-1096*
- **Fiesta Cab**, *Tel. 713/236-9400*
- **United Cab**, *Tel. 713/699-8040*
- **Yellow Cab**, *Tel. 713/224-4445*

Major national car rental agencies have offices in Houston; most have more than one. A few local companies rent automobiles and trucks:

- **Bay Area Auto & Truck Rental**, *2800 Gulf Freeway, Houston. Tel. 281/337-1529*
- **Hillcroft Ford**, *6445 Southwest Freeway, Houston. 281/588-5000*
- **PV Car & Truck Rental**, *1201 Crawford Street, Houston. Tel. 800/ASK-PVPV*

Private limousines are plentiful and can be arranged through a hotel or travel agent. **Miles of Success Limousine Service**, *13,150 Northwest Freeway Suite 665, Houston, Tel. 713/896-6999*, offers cars for rent by the hour or day. Sedans and full-size limousines, both with a professional driver, are available. Another area company is **Corporate Limousines of Houston**, *3006 Sawdust Road, Suite 206, The Woodlands, Tel. 281/298-5466 or 888/298-LIMO*.

Houston has an extensive public bus system, the **METRO**, *Tel. 713/635-4000*, that reaches all parts of the metropolitan area. High Occupancy Vehicle (HOV) lanes on the highways allow the buses to stay on schedule. During weekdays buses run on 20 minute intervals, and during rush hour this increases to every 10 minutes. In the evenings service cuts back to 20 minute intervals. On Saturdays the buses come every 20 minutes all day; on Sunday every 30 minutes. Fare is $1 for adults and 25¢ for children. A **Convention Pass** allows unlimited rides for seven days and costs $5. The route that serves most areas that visitors will want to go is the 15 Hiram Clarke. This route runs from the downtown business district through the Medical Center to the Astrodome. One transfer will take you to the Galleria area. Twenty-two hotels are on this route.

Tours

You can take a variety of tours of Houston and the surrounding area. Those who love to walk can check out the underground tunnel system, historic district or restaurants with **Discover Houston Tours**, *P. O. Box 22072, Houston, Tel. 713/840-WALK*. Walking tours are scheduled daily and can be customized for groups with special interests.

Tours with a personal touch are offered by **Annette's Tours**, *Tel./Fax 281/492-1042*. A three hour tour featuring all major sights in central Houston costs $28 per person. A rural tour of the countryside west of Houston lasts seven hours and costs $65 per person.

Grey Line Tours, *Tel. 713/223-3451*, offers a city tour by bus for $3 per person. These tours depart from the Hyatt Regency and the Westin Galleria four times daily.

Excursion tours designed to fit the interests of a small or large group can be arranged through **Star Shuttle & Charter**, *Tel. 713/540-6700 or 800/341-6000*. The multilingual guides speak Spanish, French, German or Japanese and offer different modes of transportation from motor-coach to limousine.

WHERE TO STAY

Downtown

DOUBLETREE HOTEL, *400 Dallas Street, Houston. Tel. 713/759-0202 or 800/222-TREE, Fax 713/752-2734. Rates: $135. Credit cards accepted.*

The golden glass Doubletree is located in the heart of downtown, near the Convention Center. You can walk to the historic section of downtown and the theater district. All 341 rooms are geared to business travelers with computer hook-ups and desks. Dover's Restaurant specializes in fresh seafood dishes prepared with garden-fresh ingredients. Guests can enjoy a complimentary happy hour in the lobby lounge. The hotel shuttle serves the downtown area. The hotel is in the Allen Center at the intersection of Dallas and Bagby Streets, just off Interstate Highway 10. Doubletree has two other hotels in Houston, one on Westheimer Road and the other on Post Oak Boulevard in the Galleria area.

THE LANCASTER, *701 Texas Avenue, Houston. Tel. 713/228-9500 or 800/231-0336, Fax 713/223-4528. Rates: $200 to $350. Credit cards accepted.*

The Lancaster, between the business and theater districts, manages to present a cozy and friendly atmosphere in grand style. The homey interior is a relief from Houston's fast-paced urban style. The hotel's decor is elegant 1920's style, the period when it was built. Many of the antiques pre-date the building itself. Fresh flowers accent the romantic rooms, which have modern amenities of compact disc players and speaker phones. Theater-goers enjoy after-performance cocktails at the Bistro Lancaster. The food at the Bistro mixes the spiciest flavors of the American south and the Mexican Yucatan to make an unusual and delicious cuisine. Breakfast, lunch and dinner is served.

FOUR SEASONS HOTEL, *1300 Lamar Street, Houston. Tel. 713/650-1300 or 800/332-3442, Fax 713/650-8169. Rates: $185 to $295. Credit cards accepted.*

The lovely Four Seasons Hotel is adjacent to the George R. Brown Convention Center. Each of the 399 rooms offers modern comfort and luxury. After a workout in the fitness center, guests can indulge in European spa treatments. The imposing Houston skyline is visible from the rooftop pool. The twentieth-floor takes elegance to a grandiose level with VIP suites offering security and stunning views.

HYATT REGENCY, *1200 Louisiana Street, Houston. Tel. 713/654-1234, Fax 713/951-0934. Rates: $179 to $215. Credit cards accepted.*

This 963 room hotel feels even larger because of the generous open spaces in the lobby and large rooms. The atrium reaches 33 stories high.

The Hyatt makes getting around Houston easy; the hotel is on the downtown tunnel network and has shuttle service to the airports and Galleria. The Spindletop Restaurant revolves, offering a complete view of the city skyline. When embarking on a Norwegian Star Cruise from the Port of Houston, package rates including room, breakfast and transfers. There's another location near Bush Intercontinental Airport.

Central

HOUSTON PLAZA HILTON, *6633 Travis Street, Houston. Tel. 713/ 313-4000 or 800/445-8667, Fax 713/313-4660. Rates: $99 to $178. Credit cards accepted.*

Located four miles south of downtown and one mile from the museum district in the fashionable West University neighborhood near Rice University., this 15 floor hotel is well equipped for business travelers, with computer connections and voice mail in each room. The hotel stands on manicured grounds that have an outdoor pool and jogging track for guests. Courtesy transportation is provided to major attractions within three miles of the hotel. Other Hilton locations include the University of Houston, Hobby Airport and West Houston. Complimentary hors d'ouevres served in the lounge during early evening.

LA COLOMBE D'OR, *3410 Montrose Boulevard, Houston. Tel. 713/ 524-7999, Fax 713/524-8923. Rates: $195 to $275. Credit cards accepted.*

Possibly the most sought-after vacation address in Houston, La Colombe d'Or has only six guest rooms. Each room is exquisitely decorated in a different style, and named after a painter. The overwhelming theme is European elegance and you can be assured the staff will attend to your every need. The French restaurant in the hotel has an impeccable reputation. The entire interior was an antique ballroom which was transported in entirety to Houston.

RENAISSANCE HOTEL, *6 Greenway Plaza East, Houston. Tel 713/ 629-1200 or 800/HOTELS-1, Fax 713/ 629-4702. Rates: $119 to $169. Credit cards accepted.*

The high-rise Renaissance Hotel has 389 rooms, many with excellent views of the city. One restaurant and two bars offer a full range of meal selections, and room service is available. The outdoor heated pool and fitness room are available to guests. The hotel shuttle offers complimentary rides to the Galleria. The Renaissance Hotel is across from the Summit Arena close to Highway 59.

WYNDHAM WARWICK, *5701 Main Street, Houston. Tel. 713/526-1991 or 800/996-3426, Fax 713/639-4545. Rates: $150 to $195. Credit cards accepted.*

The Warwick is one of the city's grand old hotels. The 12-story hotel was built in 1922 and underwent a complete renovation in 1995. The hotel has an ideal location in the museum district near Rice University and Hermann Park. Men's and women's saunas and outdoor pool compliment the fitness room. The Hunt Room is the hotel's restaurant and specializes in steak. The less formal cafe serves Italian food. Wyndham has another location in the Greenspoint area.

MARRIOTT FAIRFIELD INN, *3131 West Loop South, Houston. Tel. 713/961-1690 or 800/228-1690, Fax 713/627-8434. Rates: $62 to $67. Credit cards accepted.*

The motel-style inn has an outdoor pool and no charge for breakfast or local calls. The Summit Arena is only two miles away; the hotel is six miles from downtown. The Bristol Bar & Grill has steakhouse selections such as New York strip. On weekdays, the Bristol has happy hour specials. The Fairfield Inn is located between Westheimer Road and Richmond Street on the east side of West Loop (610) near the Galleria.

LA QUINTA INN, *8017 Katy Freeway, Houston. Tel. 713/668-8941 or 800/531-5900. Rates: $65 to $73. Credit cards accepted.*

La Quinta offers a no-frills approach to accommodations. Children under the age of 18 stay with adults without charge. A light breakfast is included with your stay. Houston has 17 La Quinta Inns spread throughout the urban area. To find the Inn closest to the attractions you want to be near, call the toll free number.

Galleria Area

HOLIDAY INN CROWNE PLAZA, *2222 West Loop South, Houston. Tel. 713/ 961-7272 or 800/327-6213, Fax 713/961-3327. Rates: $$139 to $159. Credit cards accepted.*

This high-rise is conveniently located on Loop 610, near the Galleria area. The 23 story building has rooms with excellent views of Houston. Fitness facilities include an indoor pool and spa. The Crown Plaza has two good restaurants. The Signet Restaurant is more formal and offers an excellent selection of wine to accompany your meal. The Cafe Royale has breakfast and lunch buffets with a good selection of delicious food. On Sunday the lobby bar serves a champagne brunch which is frequented by visitors and locals alike.

THE HOUSTONIAN, *111 North Post Oak Lane, Houston. Tel. 713/ 680-2626 or 800/231-2759, Fax 713/680-2992. Rates: $180 to $359. Credit cards accepted.*

George Bush slept here; in fact, he called the elegant resort his Texas "home." The Houstonian is an elegant combination of country tranquillity and superior accommodations. The no-frills names of the dining facilities do not do justice to the posh atmosphere and impeccable service. The Cafe, which overlooks the hotel's eighteen fabulous manicured acres, could be a secluded lodge. The light food is perfect for lunch or a mid-day

RESORTS IN THE HOUSTON AREA

THE WOODLANDS RESORT, 2301 Millbend Drive, The Woodlands. Tel. 713/367-1100 or 800/533-3052 (in Texas) or 800/433-2624 (outside Texas), Fax 713/364-6338. Rates begin at $125. Credit cards accepted.

The tall pines of The Woodlands provide a beautiful backdrop for The Woodlands Resort. The Woodlands is a planned city just north of Houston. The attraction is privacy, recreational facilities and access to nature. The golf courses include 36 holes on three courses and host the Houston Open. Nature trails stretch throughout the area and are open to joggers and bicycles. The area has its own shopping mall. To get to The Woodlands, take Highway 59 north. The Woodlands exits are clearly marked.

DEL LAGO RESORT, 600 Del Lago Boulevard, Montgomery. Tel. 713/350-5023 or 800/833-3078. Rates: $115 to $145. Credit cards accepted.

The manicured grounds of the Del Lago Resort let you enjoy the more refined aspects of a vacation, such as golf, boating, tennis or relaxing in a private villa. The resort is self-contained and has a restaurant, lounge, business center and children's center. The main building is a high-rise hotel. For those who desire more privacy, cottages on the golf course and villas on the waterfront are available. Lake Conroe is a freshwater lake perfect for water skiing and fishing. The resort is 65 miles north of central Houston. Take interstate Highway 45 north to Highway 105. Travel east on Highway 105 to Walden Road. Turn onto Walden Road; this will lead you to the resort.

SOUTH SHORE HARBOUR RESORT, 2500 South Shore Boulevard, League City. Tel. 713/334-1000 or 800/442-5005, Fax 713/334-1157. Rates: $119 to $165. Credit cards accepted.

League City is about half-way between central Houston and Galveston Island, on Clear Lake. The South Shore Harbour Resort has large rooms with ultra-modern decoration. The more traditional style of the Paradise Reef and Harbour Club provide a nice atmosphere for intimate dinners and romantic evenings. Many rooms have lake views.

snack. The Manor House serves health-conscious American food and is exclusively for guests of The Houstonian. The most exclusive suite is $1,150 per night.

LUXURY COLLECTION HOTEL, *1919 Briar Oaks Lane, Houston. Tel. 713/840-7600, Fax 713/840-0616. Rates: $ 125 to $225. Credit cards accepted.*

The Luxury Hotel Collection is the former Ritz-Carlton. Even though the high-rise, 232 room hotel is in the heart of the Galleria district, it manages to feel like a small, intimate establishment. Polished marble and elegant accents exude a feeling of refinement. Although the atmosphere conveys the finest in accommodations, the service can be less than "Texas friendly." The hotel offers a small fitness center and an outdoor pool. Valet parking is mandatory for guests with cars.

North
RAMADA LIMITED, *15,350 J. F. K. Boulevard, Houston. Tel. 713/442-1830 or 800/2-RAMADA, Fax 713/987-8023. Rates: $60 to $68. Credit cards accepted.*
The 126 room inn is located close to the Bush Intercontinental Airport. Facilities include an exercise room and outdoor pool. All rooms use electric key locks for added safety. Guests can take the Ramada shuttle service to the airport or nearby Greenspoint Mall. J. F. K. Boulevard runs from the airport to Beltway 8 (Sam Houston Parkway). The Ramada is to the east of this intersection. Ramada has five locations, including hotels near the Galleria and the Astrodome.
LEXINGTON HOTEL SUITES, *16,410 Interstate Highway 45 North, Houston. Tel. 713/821-1000 or 800/53-SUITES. Rates: $79 to $99. Credit cards accepted.*
Lexington Suites provides the amenities of a hotel, such as dry cleaning service and on-site complimentary breakfast. Business rooms and services cater to corporate travelers. The comfort of one or two bedroom suites include kitchen and living areas. Special rates for long-term stays are offered. The hotel is only three miles from Spring, a fun shopping area. To reach Lexington Suites travel 11 miles north from Bush Intercontinental Airport on Interstate Highway 45.

West
ADAM'S MARK, *2900 Briar Park, Houston. Tel. 713/978-7400 or 800/444-ADAM, Fax 713/735-2726. Rates: $160 to $179. Credit cards accepted.*
The glitz that makes Houston famous is the hallmark of Adam's Mark. The interior style is neo-art deco on a grand scale. In the atrium lobby, glass elevators soar above tall stained glass lights that dominate the lobby bar. Fitness facilities include a pool and sauna. The hotel is a 35 minute drive from both Intercontinental and Hobby airports. From the Sam Houston Tollway, exit Westheimer Road.
MARRIOTT WESTSIDE, *13,210 Interstate Highway 10, Houston. Tel. 713/558-8338 or 800/228-9290, Fax 713/558-4028. Rates: $124. Credit cards accepted.*
This 400 room sprawling glass and steel hotel is west of downtown. The grounds resemble a first-class office building; a manicured lawn and

water fountains complement the indoor gardens. The lobby garden has plenty of fresh air, with full-size trees and a large water pool. The hotel has 26 meeting rooms that can handle anywhere from 15 to 1500 people. A large outdoor pool and lighted tennis courts let guests unwind outside. The hotel restaurant features Sunday brunch with live Dixieland music. Marriott has hotel s at the Medical Center, Bush Intercontinental Airport, Greenpoint (north) and the Galleria.

Bed & Breakfast in The Heights

The Heights, Houston's oldest and most historic neighborhood, has beautiful historic homes and tree lined streets. Although the area is close to downtown, the elegant atmosphere of Houston's first subdivision provides an escape from the concrete-and-steel city lifestyle. The Heights is just west of Interstate Highway 45, between Loop 610 and Katy Freeway (Interstate Highway 10).

SARA'S BED & BREAKFAST INN, *941 Heights Boulevard, Houston. Tel. 713/868-1130 or 800/593-1130, Fax 713/868-1160. Rates: $55 to $150. Credit cards accepted.*

The fourteen room inn has a private garden which provides the setting for continental breakfast. The largest suite can accommodate four and has adjoining bedrooms, each with its own bath, plus living and dining areas.

WEBBER HOUSE, *1101 Heights Boulevard, Houston. Tel/Fax 713/864-9472. Rates: $75 to $110. Credit cards accepted.*

Each of the four rooms is furnished in a different theme that compliments the Victorian home. The Attic Hideaway is a private, romantic guest suite with an antique footed tub.

The Bay Area

The cities that surround the bay east of Houston are known as the Bay Area. Many who are just passing through Houston proper choose to stay in the Bay Area to avoid the urban congestion of the city.

HOLIDAY INN, *300 South Highway 146, Baytown. Tel 713/427-7481. Rates: $45 to $70. Credit cards accepted.*

This hotel was recently renovated and offers comfortable rooms with standard amenities such as cable television and room service. The location is good for those who want easy access to attractions in the south of Houston, while avoiding staying in the center of the metropolitan area. When traveling from Houston, take Interstate Highway 10 to Baytown, exit Highway 146 (Alexander Drive) and travel south about 10 miles; the Holiday Inn is on the west side of the highway. Baytown is located east of Houston on Interstate Highway 10.

MARRIOTT RESIDENCE INN, *525 Bay Area Boulevard, Houston. Tel. 713/486-2424 or 800/331-3131. Rates: $89 to $125. Credit cards accepted.*

This hotel has the feel of an apartment community. Rate incentives are offered for long-term stays. Some rooms have fireplaces, kitchenettes and ceiling fans. Larger suites include two bedrooms and living areas.

TEXAS CITY FAIRFIELD INN, *10,700 East Lowry, Texas City. Tel. 409/986-3866 or 800/228-2800. Rates: $68 to $75. Credit cards accepted.*

A stay at the Fairfield inn includes continental breakfast. The hotel has an indoor pool. From Interstate Highway 45, exit Lowry Expressway. The hotel is at this intersection. Suites are available for a nominal extra charge.

Camping

SOUTH MAIN RV PARK, *10,100 South Main, Houston. Tel. 713/667-0120 or 800/626-Park, Fax 713/668-7343. Daily $16.65; weekly $94.50.*

This large recreational vehicle park has 72 spaces with electricity and full hook-ups, including telephone. This is more of a residential community than a vacation spot, but the location on South Main allows easy access to the downtown business area and museum district. Special monthly rates are available and change by season.

WHERE TO EAT

Central

BIBA'S GREEK RESTAURANT, *607 Gray Street, Houston. Tel. 713/523-0425. Credit cards accepted.*

No matter what hour you crave a gyro or Greek salad, Biba's on Gray Street will fill your stomach. The location on West Gray is open around the clock. The blue awnings tell you that the Mediterranean influence remains strong. The stuffed dolmas are not to be missed. Weekday happy hour includes a buffet of Greek food.

BRENNAN'S, *3300 Smith Street. Houston. Tel. 713/522-9711. Credit cards accepted.*

The flavors of New Orleans are brought to Houston at Brennan's. The French decor and beautiful indoor and outdoor dining is actually a spot of tranquillity amid the hustle of Houston. Who would think that turtle soup could be so delicious? The bread pudding is so good, it is famous. Entrees are in the $20 range.

BUFFALO GRILLE, *3116 Bissonnet, Houston. Tel. 713/661-3663. Credit cards accepted.*

Known for the huge breakfasts, Buffalo Grille is a great casual meal at any time of the day. The pancakes are exceptional. The menu offers a

variety of light fare. Meals cost under $10. Open Monday to Friday 7am to 2pm; Saturday and Sunday 8am to 2pm.
FRESH MARKET CAFE, *6560 Fannin Suite 120, Houston. Tel. 713/ 799-9211. Credit cards accepted.*
The Fresh Market has a bounty of healthy food in a deli-style restaurant. All the menu items down to the sauces are prepared from scratch and made with healthy eating in mind. The fixings — cheese, sprouts — come separate from the sandwich, so each person can suit their own taste. The Healthy Hero is an all-time favorite, with marinated vegetables and mozzarella cheese. Stop in for a guiltless snack. The Chocolate Fix is non-fat chocolate frozen yogurt topped with chocolate sauce and bits of brownie.
GOODE CO., *5109 Kirby Drive, Houston. Tel. 713/522-2530. Credit cards accepted.*
Goode calls its food "Texas barbecue," and no words could better describe the selection, which ranges from duck to Czech sausage. In addition to exemplary beef brisket, you will find turkey breast or jalapeno sausage, which are unusual items for many barbecue houses. The choice can be difficult, so the combo dinners (two meat selections, $7.95) is a sure winner. The Jambalya Texana is the best, spiciest side dish. Vegetarians need not feel left out; loaded baked potatoes ($2.75), baked beans, and coleslaw are filling in themselves. The restaurant is located two blocks south of Highway 59.
KIM SON, *7531 Westheimer Road, Houston. Tel 713/783-0054 . Credit cards accepted.*
Kim Son is probably the most successful Vietnamese restaurant in the state. The restaurant takes traditional Vietnamese food and transforms it into modern cuisine. The hot pot dishes are made with the succulent mix of spices that cannot be duplicated by any other type of cooking. Brave new combinations, such as Vietnamese Fajitas, actually come together in a delicious way. *Other locations include 2001 Jefferson, Tel. 222-2461, and 8200 Wilcrest, Tel. 498-7841.*
MAXIM'S, *3755 Richmond Avenue, Houston. Tel. 713/877-8899. Credit cards accepted.*
This intimate French restaurant glows with the warmth of Europe elegance. Seafood, steak and pasta are specialties. In the evening the piano bar adds to the lavish surroundings. The wine cellar holds vintages that were bottled before the opening of Maxim's in 1950. Maxim's is located near the Summit arena.
MIYAKO JAPANESE RESTAURANT & SUSHI BAR, *6345 Kirby Drive, Houston. Tel. 713/520-9797. Credit cards accepted.*
The freshest, most expertly prepared sushi and sashimi around. Every weekday the sushi happy hour offers discounts on the tasty sushi

morsels. Tempura specialties and beef are also made. Lunch specials are featured on weekdays. All locations feature a brunch buffet every Sunday from noon to 3pm. *Other restaurants at 6345 Westheimer Road, Tel. 781-6300 and 910 Travis Street (in the bank One Building), Tel. 752-2888.*

PATRENELLA, *813 Jackson Hill Street, Houston. Tel. 713/863-8233. Credit cards accepted.*

This cozy Italian restaurant is one of the best kept secrets in Houston. It is located in an off-beat neighborhood. The place is so popular that the waiting crowd spills out onto the patio. Once you are seated, take your time to enjoy the splendid food. Each night a variety of specials are featured, but for me the standard red sauce is unbeatable. The pasta is prepared in the kitchen; the gnocchi is exceptional. Wine by the bottle is very affordable. Entrees are around $10.

THAI PEPPER, *2049 West Alabama, Houston. Tel. 713/520-8225. Credit cards accepted.*

Inside Thai Pepper, the elegant, modern atmosphere sets the stage for the great food. The extensive menu offers a wide variety of authentic Thai dishes, both heavy on spice and sweet sauces that distinguish the cuisine. The Clay Pot chicken comes over crystal rice noodles, with rich aromatic undertones. The Pad Thai is made with red sauce, and is a dark, sweet version of the traditional dish. Seafood is the specialty of the house. The Royal seafood is a succulent mixture of shrimp, scallops, and crawfish with light garlic sauce ($14.95). If you are lucky, the Cashew Crab – Alaskan King crab with cashew nuts and straw mushrooms – will be in season. The food is prepared according to your preference of spiciness; MSG is never used.

Galleria Area

HARRY'S AMERICAN BAR & RESTAURANT, *1717 Post Oak Boulevard, Houston. Tel. 713-622-0022. Credit cards accepted.*

Hemingway could have dined here — the dark wood decor and elements of by-gone eras transport you to another time. The food is far from standard; Welsh rarebit and lamb chops are two wonderful dishes. Italian fare is well represented with pasta dishes. Enjoy the rich flavors of European inspired cuisine while piano music fill the air during weekend evenings. Open Monday to Friday 11am to 11pm; Friday and Saturday 11am to midnight.

HUNAN, *1800 Post Oak Boulevard, Houston. Tel. 713/965-0808. Credit cards accepted.*

The exotic cuisine of Hunan China is prepared to perfection at Hunan. The classic dishes that you already know are prepared with the zest and flare of fine dining. Elegantly understated atmosphere is the hallmark of this restaurant, which has been open since 1976 and remains one of the best in Houston. Hunan is located in the Pavilion shopping center in the Galleria area.

JIMMY G'S, *3009 Post Oak Boulevard, Houston 713/629-5380. Credit cards accepted.*

Its hard to find a good Houston restaurant that can limit itself to only two locations. Jimmy G's is just that; despite its success, it has managed to limit itself to a size that permits the quality of the seafood to remain constant. This is a necessary stop for seafood lovers who want a real taste of the Gulf of Mexico. The food and spices of the coasts of Louisiana and Texas combine for spicy Cajun creations. The stuffed red snapper is excellent. Start the meal with a crawfish sauté or a creamy crabmeat au gratin. *Jimmy G's has another location at 307 Sam Houston Parkway, Tel. 713/931-7654, located near the Transco Tower.*

RIVER OAKS GRILL, *2630 Westheimer, Houston. Tel. 713/520-1738. Credit cards accepted.*

This restaurant has an upbeat and airy atmosphere where you will hear the clamor of the crowd. The extraordinary food features steak. Filet mignon ($22.50), Veal Parlante, veal on wilted spinach with white wine sauce, and grilled quail ($19.95) are good selections. The focus is also on lobster, a refreshing choice in an area where it is difficult to find. The lobster bisque ($6.50) is a perfectly smooth soup. The Lobster Capellini ($6.95) made with brandy cream sauce, is sinfully delicious. For a particularly good side, try the baby artichokes, prepared with red pepper and basil. You can choose from a very good selection of wine.

ROTISSERIE FOR BEEF AND BIRD, *2200 Wilcrest, Houston. 713/977-9524. Credit cards accepted.*

The Rotisserie specializes in serving feasts of wild game. You step inside to the warmth of an American colonial home. For special occasions guest can dine in the wine cellar, surrounded by vintage reserves. Seafood and Maine lobster highlight the non-meat menu choices. Meals average over $30 per person. During the week the restaurant is open for lunch from 11:30am to 2:30pm and dinner 6pm to 10:30pm; only dinner is served on Saturday; closed Sunday.

THE STABLES, *3734 Westheimer Road, Houston. Tel. 713/621-0833. Credit cards accepted.*

Although the name of this restaurant does not conjure up the most inviting images for dining, The Stables is a lovely restaurant. At times the ambiance goes overboard and the atmosphere can be described as snooty. *The second location 7325 South Main, Houston. Tel. 713/795-5900.*

Outside the Loop

59 DINER, *3801 Farnham, Houston. Tel. 713/523-2333. Credit cards accepted.*

A genuine diner, complete with daily Blue Plate Specials. The down-home comfort food includes chicken pot pie, homemade meatloaf and liver & onions. The menu also includes burgers ($4.59), sandwiches and deluxe plates, like chicken fried chicken ($7.25). The side dishes feature daily vegetables, and standards like cornbread dressing and baked sweet potatoes.

BRENNER'S, *10,911 Katy Freeway, Houston. Tel. 713/465-2901. Credit cards accepted.*

It's like being out on a ranch at this cozy restaurant. Brenner's has been a favorite of Houstonians since it opened in 1936. The Texas meat and potatoes fare fills the menu. All the sauces are family recipes.

CIMARRON, *3000 North Loop, Houston. Tel. 713/688-0100. Credit cards accepted.*

The menu borrows heavily from the tastes of the southwest and is decorated with west Texas images. The food is of an exceptional standard, with specialties such as fresh Gulf shrimp over filet mignon or pasta primavera. Cimarron is in the Houston Medallion Shopping Center, at the intersection of Loop 610 and Highway 290.

GUADALAJARA MEXICAN GRILLE & BAR, *Towne & Country Village, Katy Freeway, Houston. Tel. 713/461-5300. Credit cards accepted.*

Texas-style Mexican food is prepared a step above the usual standards at the Guadalajara Bar & Grille. The standards, like beef fajitas, chicken enchiladas and carne asada are made with the freshest vegetables and authentic Mexican spices. Quail grilled over mesquite chips is a house specialty. Happy hour specials are featured from 3pm to 7pm on weekdays.

KELLY'S DEL FRISCO STEAKHOUSE, *14,641 Gladebrook Drive, Houston. 713/893-3339. Credit cards accepted.*

Many find this to be one of the best steakhouses anywhere. Steak and lobster highlight the traditional selections on the menu. After your meal, relax in Resa's Piano Bar. From Interstate Highway 45 North, exit Farm Road 1960 and travel west. Gladebrook intersects with Farm Road 1960.

OLD HEIDELBERG INN, *1810 Fountainview, Houston. Tel. 713/781-3581, Fax 713/781-3350. Credit cards accepted.*

For more than 20 years, the Old Heidelberg Inn has served traditional German food in a European atmosphere. Good selections include fried camembert, vichyssoise, and the veal schnitzel "Heidelberg style." The goulash soup tastes like it was made in Budapest. There is little for the vegetarian here. Open Monday to Saturday 11:30am to 2am.

TASTE OF TEXAS, *10,505 Katy Freeway, Houston. Tel. 713/932-6901. Credit cards accepted.*
This is what you might imagine a Texas steakhouse a la theme park might look like. The restaurant is large and filled with Texas-style decor. You can hand-pick the steak you want to have prepared for your dinner. The menu itself is reminiscent of a tourist attraction, and is available in 12 languages. Nonetheless, the steaks are good and the food is guaranteed to fill you up.

SEEING THE SIGHTS

You can walk through Texas history by visiting Houston's historic downtown parks. Modern Houston's history began at **Allen's Landing Park**, *1001 Commerce Street*, where the Allen brothers first set foot on Texas soil. The city hall once stood on Market Square. The square, which was once the heart of the commercial district, became a parking lot. In 1976 a revitalization began, and today the area is a renovated historic district.

The center of historic Houston is **Sam Houston Park**, *1000 Bagby, Tel. 713/655-1912, Monday to Saturday 10am to 4pm; Sunday 1pm to 5pm*. Plan to spend a few hours to really take in all the history that is documented on the 19-acre museum complex and park in the city center. The indoor and outdoor exhibits recreate over 150 years in Houston through seven restored residences of prominent residents and a museum. The earliest example of life in Houston is the Old Place, a rendering of the first colonial houses constructed in 1826, while Texas was part of Mexico. Tours of the homes are conducted until 3pm each day. The **Museum of Texas History** has temporary and permanent exhibits from the time of the sixteenth century Spanish colonial explorers to the present. Finish your trek through time at the museum's tea room, a cafe located in a reconstructed nineteenth century store.

Houston is a modern marvel as well as an historic one. The famous Houston skyline is a virtual museum of monumental architecture. The downtown business district has the greatest concentration of skyscrapers. Among the most notable is **Pennzoil Place**, *700 Milam*, a large, split building with a glass pyramid entrance. Pennzoil Place and neighboring postmodern **Nation's Bank** (formerly Republic Bank) *700 Louisiana Street*, which has large-scale elements of traditional European design and soars to 56 stories, were both designed by the famous architect Philip Johnson.

TRANSCO TOWER

The skyscraper most deserving a visit in Houston is not found downtown. The **Transco Tower**, *2800 Post Oak Boulevard, is the world's largest building in a suburban area. Of course a Houstonian will tell you that the Transco Tower is not in a suburb at all, but in Houston's "second downtown," the Galleria area. Transco is located at Post Oak Road and West Alabama Street, near Loop 610 West.*

The design of the building is as ominously futuristic as its name; this is another masterpiece by Philip Johnson. The tall, shiny, dark tower reaches straight into the sky to over 50 stories. The Wall of Water is a large semicircular water fountain standing on the Transco grounds. You can walk through the neo-Romanesque facade into a thundering waterfall.

A network of **pedestrian tunnels** connects Houston's skyscrapers, historic district and theater district. The tunnels were designed primarily for business people who need to comfortably and safely walk through the business district. During the sweltering summer months, walking underground is preferable to baking in the daytime sun, which seems to be magnified by the glass and steel buildings. The main network of tunnels runs roughly north to south, and much of it resembles a shopping mall. Numerous small shops and eateries line the central junctions. Some segments of the tunnels connect small groups of buildings that are not part of the main tunnel system.

The **Houston Chronicle Building**, *801 Texas Avenue*, is the only entrance in the historic district which connects to the main tunnel system. The **Alley Theater**, *615 Texas Avenue*, and its parking garage are a good starting point to enter the tunnels from the theater district. The large Allen Center Garage, *3 Allen Center, Polk Street*, has a tunnel entrance.

The Four Season's Hotel and the Hyatt Regency Hotel have entrances to the tunnel system. The Doubletree Hotel and the Lancaster Hotel are both across the street from entrances to the tunnel system.

Houston is known to offer some the finest medical care in the world. The sprawling complex of **The Texas Medical Center**, *1155 Holcombe, Tel. 713/790-1136*, is sometimes called "Houston's Third Downtown." And the buildings do make their own mark on the Houston skyline. Research, treatment and education are conducted in the 100 buildings of the Medical Center. Many patients seeking specialized care for cancer and heart disease make Houston their first choice. You can arrange a tour of the facilities by contacting the medical center; people with all interests are welcome.

The Museum District

The Museum District is just south of downtown Houston, where Montrose Boulevard and Main Street intersect at the Mecom Fountain. Hermann Park is located on Hermann Drive, which also intersects with the Mecom Fountain traffic circle.

The **Museum of Fine Arts**, *1101 Bissonnet, Tel. 713/639-7300, closed Monday, Tuesday to Saturday 10am to 5pm; Sunday 12:15pm to 6pm, admission $3 adults, $1.50 children, students and seniors*, is the centerpiece of the arts district. Major exhibits from around the world are shown in the large gallery space. The permanent collection features paintings and sculpture from Europe, Africa and Oceania. Touring exhibits of international fame regularly grace the halls of the main gallery. Cafe Express, the museum's in-house cafe, offers light lunches and snacks. This is the most convenient place in the area to get food while touring the exhibits.

The museum hosts a lunchtime series called "Drop-in Tours," held Tuesday to Friday at noon. Every Thursday admission to the permanent collection is free, and the museum stays open until 9pm. Admission for traveling expositions varies; on Thursday, a discounted rate is offered. The museum is located on the corner of Bissonnet and Main Street. Parking in the lot across the street from the main entrance is free.

The museum's art school, the **Glassell School of Art**, *5101 Montrose Boulevard, Tel. 713/639-7500*, has temporary exhibitions and educational programs. Frequent lectures for adults and workshops for children are conducted throughout the year. Most are free or have a nominal admission. The museum sponsors on-going art films, *Tel. 713/639-7515*, which are shown on Friday evenings and weekends.

The freshly renovated **Contemporary Arts Museum**, *5216 Montrose Boulevard, Tel. 713/526-6749, Fax 713/526-6749, Tuesday to Saturday 10am to 5pm, free admission,* hosts unusual and thought-provoking modern art exhibitions that change frequently. Just down the street from the art museums is the **Lillie Hugh and Roy Cullen Sculpture Garden**, *Bissonnet at Montrose, 9am to 5pm*. This is a refreshing place to appreciate fine art outdoors.

Houston has its own museum dedicated to kids, and creative learning is the element that puts fun into the **Children's Museum**, *1500 Binz Street, Tel. 713/522-1138, Tuesday to Saturday 9am to 5pm, Sunday noon to 5pm, closed Monday, admission $5 adults and children*. A variety of topics from science and technology to health are covered with inventive exhibits that allow hands-on activity. Children from the ages of 6 to 12 years will find the material to their liking. The museum is six blocks southwest of the Museum of Fine Arts.

A trip to the **Museum of Health and Medical Science**, *1515 Hermann Drive, Tel 713/521-1515, Tuesday to Saturday 9am to 5pm; Sunday noon to*

> ## THE JUNG CENTER IN HOUSTON
>
> *During his lifetime, Carl Jung made some of the most important contributions to the field of analytical psychology. In 1954 two students of Jung opened the **C. G. Jung Educational Center**, 5200 Montrose Boulevard, Tel. 713/524-8253. The center primarily serves the community as an educational facility. During the year numerous short courses are offered, and frequent lectures are held. Dance, art and writing are taught on an ongoing basis. Some of the programs are offered free to the public. The bookstore offers an array of hard-to-find books that deal with spirituality and psychology, among other topics.*
>
> *For thirty years the center's annual conference has drawn academics, professionals and students from around the globe. The three-day conference is held in July and features lectures and workshops.*

5pm, is good for your body and mind. Interactive exhibits teach you about the way a body works and is put together. The museum is full of health and nutrition information. Even the snack bar and the gift shop sell treats that are good for you. Children's programs sponsored by the museum include films and artistic programs.

The chilling photographs of the Holocaust are perhaps the most vivid memories to take away from **The Holocaust Museum**, *5401 Caroline Street, Tel. 713/942-8000, Fax 713/942-7953*, but the entire experience leaves an emotional impression. Although the subject matter may be difficult to confront, the power of remembering tribulation is an important tool for learning from the past. The exhibits strive to reach into the hearts and minds of visitors, providing not only the historical account but also the human side of the Holocaust. The Memorial Room allows you to rest and consider the powerful information that the museum delivers. Movies, research facilities and teaching programs are part of the museum's outreach efforts.

Hermann Park

The most popular attraction in Hermann Park is the zoo, more formally known as the **Houston Zoological Gardens**, *1513 North MacGregor Street, Tel. 713/525-3300, open daily 10am to 6pm, admission $2.50 adults, $2 seniors, 50¢ children*. The zoo takes up 55 acres of Hermann Park. The large grounds provide a variety of habitats for the more than 3500 animals at the zoo.

Natural history from the age of the dinosaurs down through space exploration is chronicled in the **Museum of Natural History**, *One Hermann Circle Drive, Tel. 713/639-4629, admission $3.50 adult, $2 children*. Three stories of live butterflies are a larger-than-life exhibit. The planetarium and IMAX theater have daily shows that bring the vastness of the universe within reach.

Outside the Museum District

The private collection of John and Dominique Menil is one of the most extraordinary assemblages of art you will see in Texas. **The Menil Collection**, *1515 Sul Ross Street, Tel 713/525-9400, Wednesday to Sunday 11am to 7pm, closed Monday and Tuesday.* The extensive assortment of art spans the breadth of time from the era of Byzantium to modern times. Works by modern masters grace the walls. Art and artifacts from all over the world are on display; of particular interest is the collection of African art. The Menil Collection is behind the University of St. Thomas. From Interstate Highway 59, exit Montrose and go north to Sul Ross Street.

Next door to the Menil Collection stands the **Rothko Chapel**, *3000 Yupon Street, Tel. 713/524-9839, open daily 10am to 6pm*, a non-denominational religious sanctuary designed by abstract expressionist painter Mark Rothko. The simplicity and unity of his painting is reflected in the architectural design, which unifies spiritual experience by allowing visitors to meditate in a temple devoid of religious imagery.

The decor is sparse, but the furnishings are undeniably Gothic in the **American Funeral Service Museum**, *415 Barren Springs Drive, Tel. 713/876-3063, Monday to Saturday 10am to 4pm; Sunday noon to 4pm, admission $5 adults, $3 children.* This is one of the more unusual collections you will find anywhere. Among the exhibits is a collection of caskets from the time of the Civil War, a group of hearse sleighs and a replica of Abraham Lincoln's coffin. The museum is north of downtown. From Interstate Highway 45, take the Airtex Exit and travel west. Turn north onto Ella Boulevard; Barren Springs is the first intersection.

In a city as hot as Houston, it seems appropriate that there would be a fire museum. **The Houston Fire Museum**, *2403 Milam, Tel. 713/524-2526, Tuesday to Saturday 10am to 4pm*, features displays on Houston firefighting. The first firefighters were the volunteer residents who were organized by city founder Augustus Allen. They are remembered as the Bucket Brigade because buckets were their tools of fire fighting. Exhibits include the city's oldest fire fighting wagons, and trace the history of firemen up to today.

Part of the Museum of Fine Arts is the former residence of prominent Texan Ima Hogg. She was the daughter of the state's first governor to be born in Texas. For her entire life she collected American antiques, and that collection remains in her home at **Bayou Bend Collection and Gardens**, *1 Westcott Street, Tel. 713/639-7750, closed Monday, open Tuesday to Saturday 10am to 2:45pm, Saturday 10am to 5pm, Sunday 1pm to 5pm,* *admission $10 adults, $5 children.* The gardens are open Tuesday to Saturday 10am to 5pm, Sunday 1pm to 5pm. Bayou Bend is one of the most extensive collections of its type open to the public. You will gain a rare glimpse into the life one of the most powerful families in Texas at the turn-of-the-century. The grandeur of the home is matched by the elegantly manicured gardens. The collection is free to families with small children on the third Sunday of each month.

The **Port of Houston**, *7300 Clinton Drive, Gate 8, Wharf 7, Tel. 713/ 670-2614*, is one of the largest ports in the world. You can view the ships from the observation deck or take a free sightseeing cruise. The ninety minute trip is sponsored by the port authority and you must make reservations at least two months in advance to get a seat. The Port of Houston is accessible from Loop 610 east.

Clear Lake Area

Clear Lake is the closest body of water to central Houston, and therefore popular for boating, wind-surfing and sunbathing. The area is the home of NASA, which has been an important part of the Houston area for several decades. **The Space Center Houston**, *1601 NASA Road 1, Tel. 713/244-2100 or 800/972-0369. Monday to Friday, 10am to 5pm, Saturday and Sunday 7pm*, brings to earth the marvels of man's encounters with outer space. A visit to the Space Center takes at least four hours to see the many films and exhibits. The Space Center has an extensive collection of space suits, the Apollo 17 module, and the Saturn V rocket, among others. But there is far more than museum-style exhibits.

The interactive displays let you experience the feeling of repairing a satellite in space and landing a space shuttle. Movies explore the far reaches of space and the question of man's destiny in space. The Space Center is an amazing trek to where we have been and will go in our universe. From Memorial Day to Labor Day the Space Center has extended hours, daily 9am to 7pm. To get to NASA from Houston, take Interstate Highway 45 (Gulf Freeway) south to the Space Center/NASA Exit. The clearly marked signs lead you to the center.

You can visit the **Budweiser Brewery**, *755 Gellhorn, Tel. 713/670-1695*. The brewery is open year-round and there is no admission charge. A tour will take you through the entire process of brewing beer. From central Houston, take Interstate Highway 10 east to Gellhorn.

NIGHTLIFE & ENTERTAINMENT

Astroworld, *Loop 610 South, Tel. 713/799-8404*, is one of the Six Flags amusement parks featuring Warner Brothers characters Bugs Bunny and Batman. This is the largest theme park in Texas and its newest ride, the

Dungeon Drop, plummets 237 feet. Of the 34 rides, nearly one-third are twisting, spiraling roller coasters that can keep you occupied all day. Or you can take a water break at **Waterworld** next door. In the summertime Waterworld features stunt shows and even more rides. The parks are open almost every weekend through the year and during the weekdays in summer.

The immense **Astrodome** is not just a venue for major sports and concert events, it is a tourist sight in itself. Reaching a height of 18 stories, the Astrodome is a feat of modern engineering and design. Tours are held each day at 11am, 1pm and 3pm. To reach the Astrodome, take Loop 610 south to Kirby Drive; you can't miss the arena.

Houston has a vibrant and active arts scene. Both the **Houston Grande Opera** and **Houston Ballet** perform regular seasons in the **Wortham Center**, *510 Preston Boulevard, Tel. 713/237-1439*. This modern theater complex is part of the Houston Civic Center. You can purchase tickets at the Ticket Center, *550 Prairie Street*. The world-class performances of the **Houston Symphony** are held at the **Jesse H. Jones Hall**, *615 Louisiana Street, Tel. 713/222-3415*.

You can enjoy the arts and culture of Houston in the heart of Hermann Park. The **Miller Outdoor Theater**, *Hermann Park, Concert Drive, Tel. 713/520-3290*, hosts evening performances and daytime festivals. The symphony, ballet and theater companies perform here throughout the year. General admission is free; you may purchase tickets for reserved seating. Children's shows are held on many weekend mornings from March to October. Some of the recent performances include Ambassadors International Ballet Forlklorico, the Houston Grand Opera and the Houston Youth Symphony.

For nearly two decades the annual festivals at the Miller Outdoor Theater has drawn huge crowds and the best talent in the country. In March, the Sounds and Dance of Puerto Rico brings the color and festivity of the island to Houston. The Pan African Cultural Festival, a celebration of African-American heritage, is held for three days at the end of May and includes one evening performance. A Freedom Festival and Blues Festival celebrates Juneteenth, on June 19, the day slavery ended in Texas. In mid-October, Asian food, music and dance, and martial arts exhibition performances fill the day for the Asian-American Festival.

Houston's first professional dramatic company, the **Alley Theater**, *615 Texas Avenue, Tel. 713/228-8421*, holds performances during the week. The **Ensemble Theater**, *3535 Main Street, Tel. 713/520-0055*, is Houston's African-American professional theater. For 20 years this company has produced the highest quality plays. In addition to the regular season, youth programs and community outreach projects are held during the year.

Bars & Clubs

THE FABULOUS SATELLITE LOUNGE, *3616 Washington Avenue, Tel. 713/869-2665.*

Fabulous live music. Jazz and swing tunes set the stage for the martini-and-cigar crowd. The bands that play here often are not well known, but they are usually very good. Occasionally the dance floor is hopping.

THE HOUSTON BREWERY, *6224 Richmond Avenue, Tel. 713/953-0101. Credit cards accepted.*

This is Houston's largest brew pub. The large dining room serves food during the day and in the evening. The bar area has a somewhat more cozy feeling. The best way to enjoy the pub is to bring your own crowd of beer lovers. Each day a different stout, bitter or ale is featured in the special. The beer is exceptional.

LA CARAFE, *813 Congress Avenue. Tel. 713/229-9399.*

The downtown area, long deserted in the evening, is once again becoming the place for going out. La Carafe is unquestionably the bar with the most personality in Houston – possibly in the entire state. The dark, cozy bar remains untouched by time, and takes you back to the days of the Old West. The bar overlooks Market Square. From the tall bar windows you can see the skyscrapers of downtown. La Carafe serves beer on tap and wine by the bottle.

SOLERO, *910 Prairie Street, Tel. 713/227-2265. Credit cards accepted.*

Solero stands in a fabulous antique building amid the skyscrapers of downtown Houston. This bar serves tapas all day, and many come here for dinner. It is easy to spend hours over the delicious small servings of marinated mushrooms, Spanish tortilla and Manchego cheese with apples. You can also try not-so-Spanish selections such as Tempura vegetable medley and grilled chorizo with potatoes. The tapas can be ordered in small or large servings ($3.95 to $6.95). The crowd, mostly young and beautiful, throw back martinis and wine by the bottle late into the evening.

For a night on the town, you can join trendy Houstonites at the **Richmond Avenue District**. This area, which runs from the 5600 to the 6500 block of Richmond Avenue, has many bars, restaurants and night clubs. Pedestrians crowd the sidewalks and establishments.

THE HOUSTON INTERNATIONAL FESTIVAL

The Houston International Festival celebrates world cultures during the last half of April. The main events focus on music and art and are held on the last two weekends of April. During the week, free outdoor concerts are held downtown during the lunch hour. On the weekends twenty blocks of downtown are taken over by the festival. Food, dance, music and art from just about every culture you can imagine are here. For more information, contact the offices of the Houston International Festival, 1221 Lamar Suite 715, Houston, Tel. 713-654-8808, Fax 654-1719.

SPORTS & RECREATION

The Rodeo

The **Houston Rodeo**, *Astrodome, Tel. 713/791-9000*, takes place in mid-February and is open daily from 9am to 8pm. A pass for admission to all events costs $20. One admission to watch rodeo events and the music performance is $10; admission to the Livestock Show is $5. The Trail Ride and Rodeo Parade are the big events.

The **Trail Ride** is a unique event that takes days to complete. Over 6,000 riders, some from nearly 400 miles away, reenact an old west trail ride. Some of the riders are organized in clubs, others are individuals. The western-clad riders convene in Memorial Park, with their horses, covered wagons and gear to participate in the **Rodeo Parade**. The parade greets the arriving Trail Ride, and the riders and parade come together for a rodeo kick-off celebration. After the Rodeo Parade, the World Champion Barbecue Cook-Off gets underway in the Astrodome. The event draws over 150,000 hungry rodeo fans.

During the two weeks that the rodeo runs, events take place every night. The prizes amount to $700,000 and 500 participants, both men and women, compete. Events include bull riding, steer wrestling, barrel racing and chuckwagon races. Country music performances and fireworks wind down every night's events. The **Livestock Show** accompanies the rodeo, and gives ranchers a chance to exhibit their best stock and compete for $500,000 in prizes.

Enjoying Nature

The natural surroundings of Houston provide an abundance of natural beauty. A variety of plants from tropical palm trees to evergreen pines thrive in Houston's hot, humid climate. You can enjoy the flora almost all-year round at any of the area's nature preserves and gardens. **The Houston Arboretum and Nature Center**, *4501 Woodway, Tel. 713/*

681-8433, open daily 8:30am to 6pm, has five miles of trails for easy hikes and self-guided tours. The **Discovery Room**, *open daily 10am to 4pm*, in the Nature Center is an educational facility that provides resources for children's groups to have a hands-on learning experience in nature. Classes about the native flora and fauna take place throughout the year.

For a more formal approach to the outdoors, visit the **Houston Garden Center**, *1500 Hermann Drive, Tel. 713/529-3960*. The garden areas include flower beds, rose gardens, a sculpture garden and a Chinese-style pavilion. **Hermann Park**, *6001 Fanin Street, Tel. 713/522-8490*, is the home of the **Japanese Garden**, *Tel 713/520-3283, open daily 10am to 6pm, admission $1.50 adults, $1 seniors, 25¢ children*, which is a tranquil place for a casual stroll and some tranquillity. The garden was designed by one of the most famous landscape architects, Ken Nakajima.

Kids have a place of their own at Hermann Park. The **Playground For All Children** is a large recreational area with challenging and enjoyable outdoor activities.

Biking enthusiasts will enjoy the **Alek Velodrome** *in Cullen Park, 19,008 Saums Drive, Tel. 281/578-0858*. This is a full Olympic-size arena and is open to the public for training. Hours of the velodrome vary by season: from March to October, Tuesday to Thursday 5pm to 9pm, Saturday to Sunday 4pm to 8pm; from November to February, Monday, Wednesday and Friday 5pm to 9pm, Saturday and Sunday 2pm to 6pm.

The Houston Parks Department operates the **Memorial Fitness Center**, *6402 Arnot, Tel. 713/802-1662*, which has aerobic classes, weight training facilities and a swimming pool that are open to the public.

Tennis

Houston has a number of public tennis courts:
- **Homer L. Ford Center**, *5225 Calhoun, Tel. 713/747-5466*
- **Memorial Tennis Center**, *6000 Memorial Loop Drive, Tel. 713/861-3765*
- **Le Clear Tennis Center**, *9506 Gessner, Tel. 713/772-0296*

Golf

Golf is a very popular recreational activity in Houston, in part because of the excellent weather year-round. Municipal golf courses offer easy access to the game for a nominal greens fee. Public courses have seasonal hours: summer, daily 6am to 6pm; winter, daily 7am to 8:30pm. Some good courses include:
- **Hermann Golf Course**, *6201 Golf Drive, Tel. 713/526-0077*
- **Melrose Golf Course**, *401 East Canino Road, Tel 281/847-1214*
- **Memorial Golf Course**, *6001 Memorial Loop Drive, Tel. 713/862-4033*
- **Wortham Golf Course**, *7000 Capital, Tel. 713/921-3227*

Spectator Sports

The **Houston Aeros** are the city's professional hockey team that plays in the International Hockey League (IHL). They are one of ten teams in the western conference and play national teams from San Antonio, Chicago, Las Vegas and Manitoba. Games are held at the Summit, which seats over 15,000 spectators. The season runs from October through March

Horse races are held in the spring and summer at the **Sam Houston Race Track**, *Sam Houston Tollway, Tel. 281/807-7223*. Class 1 thoroughbreds races are run in the late summer from July to September.

SHOPPING

The **Galleria**, *5075 Westheimer Road, Tel. 713/621-1907*, is Houston's premier shopping mall, with Marshall Field's, Lord & Taylor and Neiman Marcus as the major stores. The Galleria has three sections and some 300 merchants: the Galleria I, on the east and home to the Westin Oaks Hotel; Galleria II, the central area which has a high-rise office building; and Galleria III, on the west side. The Galleria also has an ice skating rink. An express parking entrance is located at Post Oak boulevard and Westheimer Road, or valet park at Neiman Marcus or one of the Westin hotels.

The entire area along Post Oak Boulevard just south of Loop 610, known as the Galleria area, has upscale shops and fine restaurants.

The Heights

The charming old streets of The Heights are lined with Victorian homes that now hold antique shops, gift stores and cafes. You can spend at least an afternoon here browsing through the art and artifacts. One of the largest stores is **Antiques on Nineteenth**, *345 West 19th Street, Tel. 713/ 869-5030*, which has over 5000 square feet of furniture and memorabilia. The **Heights Station**, *121 Heights Boulevard, Tel. 713/868-3175*, is a conglomeration of 15 small stores which sell small antiques, glassware and collectibles. Those with high-end collections may find something at **Chippendale**, **Eastlake**, **Louis & Phyfe**, *250 West 19th Street, Tel. 713/862-3035*. The art stores in the area have off-beat collections that are unusual even for the southwest. **Yubo's Ethnic & Folkart Gallery**, *1012 Yale, Tel. 713/862-3239*, has handmade crafts from the far reaches of Mexico and South America.

The Heights is located just north of downtown, in the nine blocks west of Interstate Highway 45, between Loop 610 to the north and Katy Freeway to the south.

Spring

If you desire the surrounding of a small town, venture to **Old Town Spring**, just north of Houston on Interstate Highway 45. The renovated shopping district has 150 small shops in antique homes. Many of the arts and crafts are hand-made by the shop owners themselves. Spring was once a small town isolated from Houston. Now it has become a suburb and a fashionable area for young professionals to call home. To get to Spring, take Interstate Highway 45 North to the Spring Cypress exit (70-A). Go east one mile.

Naturally a city the size of Houston has bargain hunters, and they shop at the **Lone Star State Factory Stores**, *Interstate Highway 45, LaMarque, Tel. 409/938-3333*. This outlet center advertises that its prices are from 30 to 70 percent below retail. The stores include national clothing, kitchenware, china and shoe stores. From Houston, take Interstate Highway 45 south to exit 13. The outlet center is open seven days-a-week.

EXCURSIONS & DAY TRIPS

The final battle in the Texas war for independence was fought at San Jacinto. The battleground at San Jacinto is both a State and National Monument. The **San Jacinto Monument**, *3523 Highway 134, La Porte, Tel. 713/479-2431 or 479-2411, open daily 10am to 5:30pm*, stands 489 feet tall and marks the final military victory of Sam Houston's Texas forces over the Mexican Army of General Santa Anna. The bottom floor houses a visitor's center and provides elevator access to the observation deck on the top. A thirty-five minute film describes the military victory and its implications to the history of Texas, Mexico and the United States.

The San Jacinto State Historical Park, *3523 Highway 134, La Porte, Tel. 713/479-2431 or 479-2411*, covers 1000 acres of coastal plains. The park offers areas for fishing and bird watching. Picnic facilities have shelters. The battlefield has a trail of markers that describe the event. You can also visit an important part of twentieth century history at the park. The World War I **Battleship Texas**, *Wednesday to Sunday 10am to 5pm*, is open to the public. The ship served in both world wars.

To reach the park, take Loop 610 east to Highway 225. Travel east on 225, then exit Highway 134 and travel north.

LIBERTY

Liberty is one of the few towns in Texas that was once a Spanish settlement that was not a mission. In the eighteenth century a small Spanish military post stood here. After the decline of the steamboat industry, Liberty ceased to maintain its economic importance. Today the town is remembered as the one-time home of Sam Houston, who practiced law here.

Liberty is about 50 miles east of Houston on US Highway 90. Beaumont lies about 60 miles east of Liberty on the same highway. Many notable historic monuments are north of the town. The Liberty Chamber of Commerce, 1915 *Trinity Street, Liberty, Tel. 409/336-5736*, offers tourist information.

The **Geraldine D. Humphreys Cultural Center**, *1710 Sam Houston Street, Tel. 409/336-8901, open Monday to Thursday 9am to 6pm, Friday 1pm to 5pm, Saturday 10am to 4pm*, located in the historic downtown, sponsors plays and houses a small museum.

LIBERTY'S BELL

When the founding families of Texas planted their roots, they aspired to reproduce the idealism and independence of the American Colonies. Town names such as Liberty, Lexington and William Penn are hardly coincidental. In Liberty, the town took their homage to the American colonists one step further – they commissioned their own Liberty Bell. The bell was made by the same British foundry which produced the Liberty Bell in Philadelphia, Pennsylvania. The bell stands next to the Humphreys Cultural Center, in the center of town. The Texas version is in working order, and on special occasions you can hear freedom ring in Liberty, Texas.

Texas history buffs will love the **Sam Houston Regional Library and Research Center**, *Texas Highway 146, Liberty, Tel. 409/336-8821*, which is part of the Texas State Library system. Part of the research collection is on display in the museum. The early development of Texas is shown through original documents, such as written accounts of the first Anglo settlers in the region. Sam Houston, his life and achievements is the focus of a section of displays. Two historic nineteenth century homes stand on the library grounds and are open to the public. From Houston, take Highway 90 east to Liberty. Turn north on Highway 146 and travel two miles. Signs clearly indicate the entrance.

PRACTICAL INFORMATION

The **American Automobile Association** (AAA), *3000 Southwest Freeway, Tel 713/524-1851; for 24 hour road service, Tel. 713/521-0211,* provides information and assistance for AAA members.

American Express has six travel service locations in Houston, three of which have mail service for card holders. The most centrally located office is American Express Travel Services, *5015 Westheimer Road, Houston, Tel. 713/626-5740,* which can assist with travel arrangements.

A number of international air carriers have offices in Houston:

• **Air France**, *500 Dallas Street, Suite 2850, Houston, Tel. 713/654-3600*
• **Aeromexico**, *4900 Woodway, Suite 750, Houston, Tel. 713/939-0077*
• **American Airlines**, *5858 Westheimer Road, Suite 207, Houston, Tel. 281/878-0005*
• **Aviateca Guatemalan Airways**, *5821 Southwest Freeway, Suite 100, Houston, Tel. 713/665-3090*
• **British Airways**, *10,700 North Freeway, Suite 900, Houston, Tel. 281/878-2700*
• **Continental Airlines**, *George Bush Intercontinental Airport, P. O. Box 4607, Houston, Tel. 800/525-0280*
• **Delta Airlines**, *340 North Sam Houston Tollway, Suite 216, Houston, Tel. 800/221-1212*
• **KLM Royal Dutch Airlines**, *One Allen Center, Suite 2810, Houston, 713/658-9741*
• **Lufthansa German Airlines**, *1221 Lamar Street, Suite 1313, Houston, Tel. 800/ 645-3880*
• **TACA Costa Rican Airlines**, *5821 Southwest, Suite 100, Houston, Tel. 713/665-3090*
• **United Airlines**, *George Bush Intercontinental Airport, P. O. Box 60909, Houston, Tel. 281/230-8100*

You can find out anything you may need to know about all aspects of visiting or living in Houston from the **Greater Houston Convention and Visitors Bureau**, *801 Congress, Houston, Tel. 713/227-3100 or 800/4-HOUSTON, Monday to Friday 8:30am to 5pm.* The bureau sells T-shirts, coffee mugs and other gifts emblazoned with "Houston proud" phrases. And you are only a phone call away from what is happening in Houston, thanks to the **Downtown Events Hotline**, *Tel. 713/654-8900.*

GALVESTON

In its infancy, east Texas was dominated by river trade. River boats and stage coaches brought the traffic that shaped the land into a spill-over of the deep south. The rich soil in the area grows cotton among other crops. The combination of riverboat trade and cotton farming created an area ripe for southerners to move into and establish new homes and farms. Galveston grew up at the hub of this trade.

In 1900, an extremely powerful hurricane pounded the coast, with high winds and tidal surges. Perhaps as many as 10,000 people died. The city took many years to recover from the devastation. Today, Galveston still remembers its days of grandeur as the greatest port city on the Gulf of Mexico. Those who built the landmark structures attempted to temper the rough reputation Galveston earned as a haven for pirates and sailors. The decoration and theme of the town reflects the elegance of Victorian times, with such decorative touches as art nouveau filigree ornamentation, stained glass and extravagant use of crystal chandeliers.

Today, on the first weekend of December, the wheels of time turn back to Victorian days for **Dickens on the Strand**. Merchants, with shops decked out for an old time Christmas, extend seasonal warmth. Many people don Victorian outfits for the occasion.

Mardi Gras has always been celebrated in a big way in Galveston. The entire city turns out for the parade that marks Fat Tuesday. Beads and token coins fill the air as the Strand celebrates and rejoices.

ARRIVALS & DEPARTURES

Galveston is located on Interstate Highway 45, about 50 miles south of Houston. Galveston lies on the northern portion of the Padre Island chain.

ORIENTATION

Past the bridges that connect the barrier island to the mainland, the highway turns into Broadway, the main thoroughfare that bisects Galveston. Broadway dead-ends into Seawall Boulevard, which runs along the waterfront. Seawall Boulevard becomes Farm Road 3005 outside the city.

GETTING AROUND TOWN

The **Galveston Island Trolley**, *Tel. 409/763-4311*, is a system of real antique trolleys that run from Seawall Boulevard to the Strand and to major hotels. The main station is located at 21st Street and Seawall Boulevard.

You can take a tour by trolley on the **All About Town Yellow Trolley**, *Tel. 409/744-6371*. The entire program lasts one hour; a narrator tells the stories behind the historic sites in the city.

A large paddle wheel boat takes tours of Galveston Bay. **The Colonel**, *22nd and Wharf Streets, Tel. 409/763-4666 or 713/280-3980*, runs both day and night. The evening cruises include dinner and music.

WHERE TO STAY

HOTEL GALVEZ, *2024 Seawall Boulevard, Galveston. Tel. 409/765-7721 or 800/392-4285. Rates: $104 to $145. Credit cards accepted.*

The majestic hotel of the Gulf Coast offers the best accommodations in the area. Built in 1911, the 228 rooms have the beauty of the town's majestic Vicorian era. The completely modern and luxurious renovation makes every room comfortable. The hotel is across from the beach, so you can hear the pounding of the surf from sea view windows. The expansive outdoor pool has crystal blue water.

THE TREMONT HOUSE, *2300 Ship Mechanics Row, Galveston. Tel. 409/763-0300 or 800/874-2300, Fax 409/763-1539. Rates: $89 to $175. Credit cards accepted.*

The 117 rooms of the Tremont House offer the most luxurious accommodations. The hotel is in the center of the historic downtown area. So you are only a short walk away from shopping, entertainment and dining. Each room has period-style modern rooms with hardwood floors. The furnishings reflect the past, with elegant decor throughout. You feel as though you are visiting a piece of living history. The service at the Tremont is exemplary.

HARBOR HOUSE, *28 Pier Twenty-one, Galveston. Tel. 409/763-3321 or 800/874-3721. Rates: $132 to $219. Credit cards accepted.*

This is a unique hotel; the building was a warehouse that has been renovated into a hotel. The result is a building with the trendy, modern flair of urban living. The inn has 42 crisp, comfortable rooms that overlook the historic pier. The furnishings are modern and stylish. You can sail right up to the boat slips. The hotel is the anchor of a large retail project and has a restaurant on the wharf.

THE VICTORIAN CONDO HOTEL, *6300 Seawall Boulevard, Galveston. Tel. 409/740-3555 or 800/231-6363, Fax 409/744-3801. Rates: $49 to $199. Credit cards accepted.*

This large condominium-style hotel allows you to practically set up a temporary residence while visiting Galveston. The suites have small kitchens and living areas with modern, simple furnishings. Recreational facilities include tennis courts, children's play area and an outdoor pool. Many rooms have balconies overlooking the beach.

WHERE TO EAT

CHRISTIE MITCHELL'S BEACHCOMBER, *401 Broadway, Galveston. Tel. 409/762-8648. Open daily 11am to 9pm.*

At this casual eatery on Stewart Beach you can get some of the freshest seafood on the gulf coast. The location makes this a favorite of Galveston residents. The restaurant is right on the beach, and the sound of the surf sets the atmosphere for every meal. During lunch on weekdays, a buffet is offered.

THE STRAND BREWERY, *23 Street, Galveston. Tel. 409/763-4500. Credit cards accepted,*

This microbrewery prepares four specialty beers made in the German style. The brewery is in middle of the lively Strand area. From the roof-top deck you can look over the city or harbor. The delicious food includes selections like hamburgers, individual pizzas and pasta. The artichoke ravioli served in cream sauce is recommended. Open Sunday to Thursday 11am to 10pm. On weekends, the Strand Brewery has live music and stays open until 2am.

SEEING THE SIGHTS

The dramatic filigree **Old Red**, *310 University Boulevard, Tel. 409/772-2618*, exemplifies neo-Renaissance design in Victorian architecture in Texas. This is the main building of the University of Texas Medical Branch in Galveston. Tours of the entire campus are conducted weekdays from 9am to 4pm and begin at Old Red.

The classic tall ship, the *Elissa*, is docked permanently at the **Texas Seaport Museum**, *2100 Seawall Boulevard, Tel. 409/763-1877*. You can walk aboard the magnificent vessel, a product of the age when wind-power still ruled the seas. The museum has a multi-media presentation on the history of clipper ships.

The sprawling botanical learning center, **Moody Gardens**, *1 Hope Boulevard, Tel. 800/582-4673, open daily 10am to 9pm*, is an interesting and enjoyable trip through the climates of the world. A large glass pyramid provides a tropical environment for fauna from Asia and South America. Birds fly freely and fish are bred in naturalistic ponds; you can visit a bat cave room to get a rare look at the creatures up close. The large complex includes an IMAX theater. When you've finished with the gardens, you can dine at the restaurant on the premises.

NIGHTLIFE & ENTERTAINMENT

Modern musical performances are held amidst the opulent setting of the **Grand 1894 Opera House**, *2020 Postoffice Street, Tel. 409/765-1894 or 713/480-1894*.

SPORTS & RECREATION

Wide open beaches perfect for fishing, surfing, and swimming beckon visitors to **Galveston Island State Park**, *14901 Farm Road 3005, Tel. 409/737-1112*. Flounder, redfish and drum are some of the fish native to these waters. There are covered picnic tables with grills, 150 campsites with complete hook-ups and four miles of easy hiking trails. The park is six miles south of Galveston on Seawall Boulevard (Farm Road 3005).

SHOPPING

The center of Historic Galveston is the street known as the **Strand**. Both Strand and Mechanic Streets are designated National Historic

Landmarks. Many restaurants, art galleries, and shops line the Strand, which has been restored to its Victorian grandeur.

EXCURSIONS & DAY TRIPS

Angleton, south of Galveston on Highway 35, is a small town with history and wildlife. The **Brazoria National Wildlife Refuge**, *1212 North Velasco Street, Angleton, Tel. 409/849-6062*, has one of the nation's largest populations of snow geese during winter migration. A six-mile hiking trail offers a self-guided tour of the refuge and a chance to see some of the over 200 types of birds that inhabit it.

Brazoria County Museum, *100 East Cedar Street, Angleton, Tel. 409/849-5711 extension 1208, Tuesday to Friday, 9am to 5pm, Saturday 9am to 3pm, Sunday 1pm to 4pm* is housed in the historic county courthouse built in 1897. The centerpiece of the museum is an exhibit about Stephen F. Austin's colony, which was one of the original settlements in Texas. Native American history of the region is the focus of other exhibits.

The protected land of the **Big Thicket**, *Farm Road 420, Kountz, Tel. 409/246-2337*, is a short drive from Beaumont. Much of east Texas was covered in swampy woodlands so dense that even the Native Americans of the region left places unexplored. Development has cleared much of these lands; what remains is 96,000 acres that spreads into 12 counties.

Village Creek State Park, *Lumberton, Tel. 409/755-7322*, has camping, hiking and birdwatching areas. This small but lush park offers easy access to the Big Thicket. The Village Creek is a quiet waterway, perfect for an easy-going canoe ride. Canoes are available for rental on the creek.

To get to Big Thicket and Village Creek from Galveston, take Interstate Highway 45 north. Continue on Highway 146 north to Interstate Highway 10; travel east. From Beaumont, take Highway 96 north. For Big Thicket, from Highway 96 north continue on Highway 287 north. Farm Road 420 is about 20 miles from the turn-off.

PRACTICAL INFORMATION

You can obtain maps, information about the historic homes and recreational activities at the **Strand Visitors Center**, *2016 Strand, Tel. 409/765-7834, open daily 9:30am to 5pm*.

COLUMBUS

Columbus claims the distinction of being the oldest continually occupied town in Texas. From before the time of Spanish exploration, the area of Columbus was occupied by a settlement of Native Americans.

Columbus is part of the heartland of the Republic of Texas. Pick up the local paper and you will see it was established in 1857. Cattle barons ruled the city at the turn of the century. Their grand homes and the buildings they sponsored are now historic buildings open to the public.

Town square surrounds the courthouse, and is a trip into the past. The old fashioned barber shop with its peppermint-candy striped pole stands next to the meat market on Milan Street. Antique stores and a small cafe are nearby.

Columbus celebrates Columbus Day in a non-traditional way — with a German festival. The **Fall Festival** has contests for the best strudel, sauerkraut and sausage. Of course you can partake of the cuisine while listening to "oom-pa" music. The festival is held on Milam Street in the center of town and lasts through the day into the evening.

ARRIVALS & DEPARTURES

Columbus is located on the business loop of Interstate Highway 10, about 78 miles east of Houston.

WHERE TO STAY

RAUMONDA, *1100 Bowie Street, Columbus. Tel. 409/732-2190 or 732-5135. $60 to $100. Credit cards accepted.*

Guests step into the past when they enter the Raumonda. This gorgeous mansion was built by German settlers and retains the old world character in the details of its decoration. Guests can relax among the antiques which adorn the home. The Gant House is a German-style cottage behind the main house. The walls have the original stenciled decoration.

COLUMBUS INN, *2208 Highway 71, Columbus. Tel. 409/732-5723, Fax 409/732-6084. $35 to $50. Credit cards accepted.*

This no-frills, 72 room inn has clean rooms and plenty of parking. All rooms come with morning coffee and a newspaper. Two-room suites are spacious. The outdoor pool has a hot tub attached. From Interstate Highway 10, exit 696.

WHERE TO EAT

BOOTHILL BAR AND GRILL, *512 Spring Street, Columbus. Tel. 409/732-3245*

This honkey-tonk style food joint serves hamburgers and sandwiches. In the evening, it's basically a bar.

SEEING THE SIGHTS

The **Magnolia Homes Tour Office**, *Tel. 409/732-5135*, offers guided tours of the city's historic sites and homesteads. The Magnolia office is located next to the Opera House, just behind the courthouse.

The first judicial court of the Republic of Texas was held under a tree on what is now the grounds of the **Colorado County Court House**, *Courthouse Square, Walnut Street,* in 1837. The courthouse was not built until 1890, long after Texas was a state. Note the Masonic symbol engraved in the granite cornerstone. Visitors can step inside the District Court Room for a look at the green stained glass ceiling.

Outside the court house, a tall castle-style tower stands on the southwest corner of the square. This was the watershed for the city from 1883 to 1926. It took 400,000 hand-made bricks to build the tower's 32 inch-thick walls.

SPORTS & RECREATION

The Columbus Lions Club sponsors the **Rolling Hills Challenge**, a 100 mile bicycle ride through east Texas. The bike ride is held on the second weekend in May.

PRACTICAL INFORMATION

The **Columbus Convention and Visitors Bureau**, *Tel. 409/732-8383, Fax 732-5881,* has information about the productions at the Stafford House, maps of downtown and wildflower trails and information.

LA GRANGE

La Grange has the dubious distinction of being famous for its once illicit reputation. The Chicken Ranch, the institution upon which the play and movie *The Best Little Whorehouse in Texas* is based, was in La Grange. The Chicken Ranch burned down years ago.

Since the beginning of known history, La Grange has been the center of a crossroads. La Grange stands near the site of **La Bahia Trail**, a throughway for Native Americans, and the Colorado River. Later, early settlers of Texas passed through La Grange. The town was settled in 1837.

ORIENTATION

La Grange is 128 miles west of Houston, at the intersection of Highways 77 and 71.

WHERE TO STAY

MEERSCHEIDT HAUS, *458 North Monroe Street, La Grange. Tel 409/ 968-9569. Rates: $69.*

This offbeat place is for those who like to visit the unusual places in a community. The Meerscheidt Haus is part emporium, part bed and breakfast. The four guest rooms are upstairs in the Victorian home. The downstairs is a showroom for the antique furnishings, which are for sale.

WHERE TO EAT

BON TON RESTAURANT, *Highway 71 West, La Grange. Tel. 409/ 968-5863.*

You will get a full dose of small town Texas hospitality at the Bon Ton. This old-fashioned diner has been feeding La Grange since 1929. The menu includes steak, sandwiches and Tex-Mex dishes like enchiladas. The prices are low and the atmosphere is unbeatable. There is always a buffet and salad bar. The Bon Ton serves breakfast, lunch and dinner.

SEEING THE SIGHTS

La Grange shows the French influence in east Texas; the name of the county is LaFayette. The first settlers in the area were French and the Marquis de LaFayette settled the area. Some of the most significant buildings were built in Victorian times. The **County Courthouse**, *Business Highway 71 between Main and Washington Streets,* built in 1891, is in imposing neo-Romanesque style. The **Saint James Episcopal Church**, *156 Monroe Street*, was built in 1885.

Those who trace their family history back to the La Grange area will be interested in the **Fayette Heritage Museum and Archives**, *855 South Jefferson Street, Tuesday to Friday 10am to 5pm; Saturday 10am to 1pm, Sunday 1pm to 5pm*, which has information about the founding families of the area. Displays also feature local artwork.

When German immigrants came to La Grange, they molded the Texas resources into the traditions of their homeland. The **Kreische Brewery State Historic Site**, *Spur 92, Tel. 409/968-5658*, offers a fine example of this. The three-story commercial brewery and family were built entirely of the stone and resources of the land. This was of one of the first breweries to produce on a large scale in Texas. The water system relied on the flow of natural springs. Now the brewery is in ruins and can be visited as part of a state park. Tours along outdoor trails explain the brewing process and Kreische Family history.

Monument Hill and visitors center is part of this state park, and has a lovely view of the beautiful countryside. The monument honors the Texas soldiers who died in the Mier Expedition in the Texas War for Independence. Guided tours are offered every Saturday and Sunday at 2pm and 3:30pm; tours of the house are held on Sunday at 1:30 and 3:30pm. Take Highway 77 south of La Grange for one mile. Turn onto Spur 92 and go west. Signs lead to the park.

EXCURSIONS AND DAY TRIPS

Among the many groups of European immigrants to arrive in Texas were the **Wends**, Slavic people who lived in eastern Germany. Wends began arriving in 1849 and settled in east Texas. They brought the culture and traditions of Lusatia to the town which later became Serbin, Texas.

The Wendish culture is celebrated at the **Texas Wendish Heritage Museum**, *Farm Road 2239, Serbin, Tel. 409/366-2441, Sunday to Friday 1pm to 5pm, admission $1 adults, free to children under 14 years old.* From Highway 71, exit Farm Road 2104, which is between Bastrop and La Grange. Travel north on farm Road 2104 to Farm Road 2239. Head east to Serbin.

PRACTICAL INFORMATION

Tourist information is available at the **La Grange Area Chamber of Commerce**, *129 North Main Street, La Grange, Tel 409/968-5756*, located on the old town square.

BRENHAM

The rolling hills and picturesque ranch land of **Brenham** were part of the first land grants given to the founders of Texas by the Mexican government. The personality of the area was carved by the German and European settlers who cleared the land for cattle. The green hills, manicured ranches and white fences seem far removed from the cowboy image of Texas.

Most visitors to Brenham stop in as a retreat from the city life of Houston or Dallas. The old downtown is undergoing a revitalization, including the opening of a number of antique and gift shops and a mural project depicting the city's life and history.

ARRIVALS & DEPARTURES

Brenham is located between Houston (to the east) and Austin (to the west) on US Highway 290.

WHERE TO STAY

Brenham operates a **Bed and Breakfast Registry**, *Tel. 409/836-3695*, which can make reservations at the local establishments for you.

ANT STREET INN, *107 West Commerce Street, Brenham. Tel. 409/836-7393 or 800/481-1951. Rates: $85 to $160. Credit cards accepted.*

This may be the only inn in Texas that has an antique elevator as the centerpiece of one of its guest rooms. You will not be able to go anywhere in the elevator — it's merely a conversation piece in the already interesting Ant Street Inn. The inn, built in 1900, stands in the heart of restored downtown Brenham. The 14 rooms have decorations reminiscent of the year of its construction and private baths. The bar offers occasional nightlife in sleepy Brenham. A luscious, fresh breakfast is included for each guest.

THE BRENHAM HOUSE, *705 Clinton, Brenham. Tel. 409/ 830-0477.
Rates: $70 to $75. Credit cards accepted.*
The Brenham House gives visitors the flavor of old Brenham. It is in the center of the historic town, so you can take an evening stroll through the city or walk to the museums. The four rooms are loving furnished with antiques and homey accents. As you relax in one of the libraries or the sun porch, you can make friends with one of the cats.

HEARTLAND COUNTRY INN, *Route 2 Box 146, Brenham. Tel. 409/ 836-1864.*
This large home dates from the early 1900's and has 14 guest rooms. One pastime that guests enjoy are picnic lunches on the 158 acres of beautiful land that surrounds the farmhouse. To reach the Heartland Country Inn, take County Road 68 north/south from Brenham for 10 miles.

NUECES CANYON BED AND BREAKFAST, *9501 U. S. Highway 290 West, Brenham. Rates: $75. Tel. 409/289-5600 or 800/925-5058.*
Nueces Canyon has 11 guest rooms on a working ranch that sits on 80 acres of land. Every day begins with a hearty country breakfast. There is plenty to do right on the ranch — horseback riding and hiking trails and fishing can fill your days. Special events include hay rides and western-style cookouts. The inn is ideal for group events and special arrangements can be made for activities and group rates.

THE SCHUERENBERG HOUSE, *503 West Alamo Brenham. Tel. 409/ 830-7054 or 800/321-6234. Rates: $85 to $120. Credit cards accepted.*
This beautiful home was held in the family of the original land owners for four generations. The home has been renovated into a modern guest house, but the grandness of the Victorian era remains intact. Throughout the house, Schuerenberg family furnishings add authentic accents that make a stay in this historic landmark much like a night in a museum.

SECRETS BED & BREAKFAST, *405 Pecan Street, Brenham. Tel. 409/ 836-4117. Rates: $65 to $85.*
The Victorian theme of Secrets is carried through the decor and antique shop. There are only three bedrooms, each with special touches such as hand-made quilts. Breakfast is included. The house is six blocks from downtown Brenham.

PREFERENCE INN, *201 Loop 290 East, Brenham. Tel. 409/830-1110, Fax 409/830-0826. Rates: $42 to $46. Credit cards accepted.*
This older 99 room motel on Highway 290 has an outdoor pool and small restaurant. The simple rooms have standard amenities such as television and telephone.

RAMADA LIMITED, *2217 South Market Street, Brenham. Tel. 409/836-1300 or 800/272-6232. Rates: $49 to $59. Credit cards accepted.*
The newer Ramada has large rooms with comfortable modern decor.

The motel facilities include an outdoor pool, gym and safety deposit boxes at the front desk.

WHERE TO EAT

FLUFF TOP ROLL RESTAURANT, *210 East Alamo, Brenham. Tel. 409/836-9411.*

The restaurant is named for their trademark light and fluffy Lucas rolls. The rolls have made Fluff Top locally famous, but out-of-towners enjoy stopping in for a full serving of the small town atmosphere, as well as the home-style cooking. The rolls come out of the oven all day and accompany lunch. The restaurant is open daily until 2pm.

MUST BE HEAVEN, *107 West Alamo, Brenham. Tel. 409/830-8536. Credit cards accepted.*

This recreation of an old-time soda shop will be heaven for anyone with a sweet tooth. It's hard to not start lunch with the dessert selection of homemade pies, hand-dipped Blue Bell ice cream and freshly baked cookies and cakes. The restaurant has two rooms. You enter through the ice cream parlor. The larger dining room has a cafeteria-style sandwich shop that offers selections like grilled chicken breast sandwiches ($4.75) to peanut butter and jelly ($3) served on homemade bread. Diferent kinds of quiche is made daily. Must Be Heaven is open Monday to Saturday from 8am to 5pm.

SEEING THE SIGHTS

The most famous thing about Brenham is not its history, but the **Blue Bell Creamery**, *Farm Road 577, Tel. 409/830-2197 or 800/327-8135.* The Blue Bell company bills itself as a local creamery which captures the flavor of simple country goodness in its product. Indeed, many Texans will confirm that Blue Bell is the best ice cream around. The operation is large-scale and modern, although the scenery is quaint and rural. The creamery conducts 45 minute tours during the week (Monday to Friday at 10am, 11am, 1pm, 1:30pm, 2pm, and 2:30); reservations are required for groups of 15 or more; during March and April reservations are necessary for all tours. The admission fee is $2 for adults and $1.50 for children over 6 years old. After the tour, participants receive a complimentary sample of ice cream.

The **Blue Bell Creamery Country Store** is open from 9am to 3pm on Saturday, although the creamery is closed for tours on Saturday. The creamery is located on FM 577. From Highway 290, take 577 north. The creamery is on the east side of the road; look for the signs.

The history of Brenham is preserved in the **Brenham Heritage Museum**, *105 South Market Street, Tel. 409/830-8445, Wednesday 1pm to 4pm, Thursday to Saturday 10am to 4pm, closed Sunday and Monday,* which houses exhibits showing life in the heart of Texas farming country. The museum's centerpiece is an early steam-powered fire engine, restored to mint condition. The museum building was constructed as a post office in 1915, and since that time has remained in constant use. Donations are accepted as admission charge.

For an even keener insight to life in this historic part of Texas, contact the **Heritage Society of Washington County**, *Box 1123, Tel. 409/836-1690*, to arrange a tour of the historic homes which are not open to the general public.

SHOPPING

The **Antique Rose Emporium**, *9300 Lueckemeyer Road, Tel. 409/836-5548, Fax 409/836-7236, Monday to Saturday 9am to 6pm; Sunday 11am to 5:30pm*, is a unique shop that specializes in wild rose bushes. This particular type of rose was commonly used in elegant gardens of the late nineteenth century. Today the flowers are somewhat a rarity. The shop is in a beautiful Victorian house in the farming area north of Brenham. From Highway 290 in Brenham, travel east on Highway 105, then go north on Highway 50 for about nine miles.

EXCURSIONS & DAY TRIPS

Set in the rural hills near Brenham, you can visit the **Pleasant Hill Winery**, *Farm Road 345 and Salem Road, Brenham, Tel. 713/350-3685 or 409/830-VINE*. Only 650 cases of wine are produced each year. The close attention given to the wine-making process is evident, because the vintages are excellent. The public is invited to take free tours of the wine cellar and estate grounds and to enjoy a wine tasting.

Visitors to Brenham can take the short, scenic trip to see the seat of the independence movement of the Texas pioneers at **Washington-on-the-Brazos State Park**, *Farm Road 1155, Box 305, Washington, Tel. 409/878-2214*. The park has an excellent museum and a scenic drive. The 154-acre park has reconstructed homes of the pioneers of the state of Texas. A small wood cabin, Independence Hall, was the place where the Texas Declaration of Independence from Mexico was signed. The **Star of the Republic Museum** in the park provides a thorough overview of the road to independence and later statehood for Texas. This excellent collection has reproductions of photographs, portraits and artifacts from the period of the Republic of Texas. Many of the famous men for whom Texas counties are named are profiled here, as are the leaders of the Republic of Texas. On the drive to the park you can see some of the estate homes of the first settlers of Texas, which are private residences to this day.

Most visitors who come to the **Monastery of Saint Clare**, *Highway 105, Brenham, Tel. 409/836-9652*, do not make the pilgrimage for religious reasons but to see the farm of miniature horses. The Franciscan nuns raise miniature horses that stand only 15" tall. The horses and arts and crafts produced by the sisters are for sale to the public. You can take a self-guided tour of the horse farm; from April through June you may arrange a guided tour. The horse farm is open daily from 2pm to 4pm. From US Highway 290 near Brenham, take Highway 105 north for ten miles. There is no admission charge, but the sisters greatly appreciate donations to the monastery.

PRACTICAL INFORMATION

For tourist information and local events information, contact the **Washington County Convention and Visitors Bureau**, *314 South Austin Street, Brenham, Tel. 409/836-3695.*

BURTON

If you have never had the opportunity to see a genuine tractor pull, don't miss the **Burton Cotton Gin Festival**. The country festivities commence on a Friday in mid-April and include goat milking, goose plucking, and a pie eating contest. Indoor activities are held in one of the few remaining working cotton gins in the nation. The three day celebration features plenty of regional music and dance, such as zydeco, polka and country. For more information, contact the festival directly, *Tel. 409/289-FEST.*

ARRIVALS & DEPARTURES

To reach Burton, exit US Highway 290 12 miles west of Brenham. Signs will indicate the route to Burton.

WHERE TO STAY & EAT

THE KNITTEL HOMESTEAD, *520 Main Street, Burton. Tel. 409/289-5102, Fax 836-1056. Rates: $75 to $85.*

The Victorian home is located in the center of Burton, at the corner of Main and Washington Streets. A full breakfast is included with your stay, and arrangements can be made for dinner or special meals. The common area, the home's sitting room, has a television and VCR. The owner serves an adult-only clientele and does not accept credit cards.

THE LONG POINT INN, *Route 1 Box 86-A, Burton. Tel. 409/289-317. Rates: $65 to $125. Credit cards accepted.*

The Long Point Inn is a modern building on a working cattle ranch. The pastoral setting offers opportunity for relaxation. Only two guest rooms, each with private bath, are equipped with furnishings for small children. The inn is a lovely retreat, and is especially recommended to travelers who enjoy indulging in culinary delights. Lunch and dinner, prepared with produce from the ranch's own organic garden, can be arranged in advance. The 175 acres of land exemplify the natural beauty of the area.

INDEPENDENCE

This is one of the oldest towns in the state, founded in 1823 as Coles Settlement. Thirteen years later, when Texans declared their independence from Mexico, they met in log cabins in the piney woods along the Brazos River. Thus the town of **Independence** earned its name.

Sam Houston chose this as the site of his homestead when he settled the area as a land grant from Mexico. The 300 families who colonized this land were led by Texas founding fathers, including William B. Travis and Stephen F. Austin. Many of the individuals who were drawn to Texas came from the southern United States. The few homes from the early period of statehood exhibit the charm and stateliness of the American south.

Today, the town is a tiny community of less than 150 people.

ARRIVALS & DEPARTURES

From Houston, take Highway 290 west. At Brenham, take Highway 105 north and travel five miles. Turn north onto Ranch Road 50 and continue nine miles. Independence is at the intersection of Ranch Roads 50 and 390.

WHERE TO STAY

CAPTAIN TACITUS T. CLAY'S HOUSE, *Route 5, Box 149, Independence, Tel. 409/836-1916. Rates:*

The farmhouse was built in 1852 and remains true to that period. The gracious home sits on rolling acreage and miniature horses romp in the back pasture. Wine and cheese in the afternoon and home cooked breakfast the following morning are included. From Brenham, take Highway 50 north, travel 12 miles to Farm Road 390.

SEEING THE SIGHTS

Independence also was important in the founding of the Baptist church in Texas. The **Independence Baptist Church** is the oldest Baptist congregation in the state, active since 1839. The historical center next to the church holds artifacts of Texas Baptist history.

This town is the site of the founding of Baylor University, originally Baylor College, which moved to Waco in 1887. Only a few pieces of the walls and parts of the foundation of Baylor College buildings remain in **Old Baylor Park**, *Farm Road 390, one-half mile west of town.* The park has serene rolling hills and picnic tables. The historic home which is the birth place of the founder of Baylor University, John Coles, stands in the park and may be visited by making an appointment with the **Washington County Convention and Visitors Bureau**, *314 South Austin Street, Brenham, Tel. 409/836-3695.*

Although the rustic log houses of the first settlers no longer remain, reproductions stand at **Washington-on-the Brazos State Park**. On this quiet bend of the Brazos River, the Declaration of Independence of the Republic of Texas was signed. The men who would guide Texas into statehood, and some who would die for her freedom, met here. The new **Star of the Republic** museum and visitors complex at Washington-on-the-Brazos State Park promises to draw increasing numbers of visitors to the region. This museum offers the best introduction to Texas history that can be found. Full of pictures, memorabilia and maps, the museum brings the founding fathers of the state to life.

CHAPPELL HILL

The first stagecoach line that blazed its way through Texas stopped in the small town of **Chappell Hill**.

ARRIVALS & DEPARTURES

Chappell Hill is on Highway 290, 75 miles west of Houston. From Highway 290, take the Ranch Road 1155 exit; this scenic road continues north through Chappell Hill to Washington-on-the-Brazos State Park.

SEEING THE SIGHTS

Museum of Chappell Hill, *Church Street, Wednesday to Saturday 10am to 4pm; Sunday 1pm to 4pm*, traces the state's early history and shows the contributions Polish immigrants made to the state. The museum building was one of the first women's colleges in Texas; unfortunately, the school is no longer in operation.

WHERE TO STAY

THE BROWNING PLANTATION, *Route 1 Box 8, Chappel Hill. Tel. 409/836-6144 or 713/661-6761. Rates: $85.*

The elegant Browning Plantation is a mansion built in the Greek Revival style. You will feel as though you have entered a movie set in the old South. The genteel atmosphere is somewhat unique in the state. Guests can relax under the shade trees or in the pool. Breakfast is served in the formal dining room.

THE STAGECOACH INN, *Main and Chestnut Streets, Chappel Hill. Tel. 409/836-9515. Rates: $90.*

The stately elegance of the Stagecoach Inn offers a trip through time, to the mid-eighteenth century. The architecture is accented with Greek Revival touches, and the furnishings are of museum quality collection. This is unusual for Texas, which has few landmarks from pre-Victorian times. The inn includes a separate guest house and sits on five acres of manicured grounds. The significance of the Stagecoach Inn is noted by its inclusion in the National Register of Historic Places.

BRYAN/COLLEGE STATION

Bryan and neighboring **College Station** are the cities which grew up around **Texas A&M University**. The two cities merged around the university and are indistinguishable from each other. The university began as an agricultural institute and the home of the Corps of Cadets.

The weekend following Thanksgiving marks the most important football game of the season, when the Texas Aggies face their arch-rival the University of Texas Longhorns. To prepare for the game, a large bonfire is held at the university. Thousands of students prepare for and watch the fire. The **Aggie Bonfire** is a major event for the Aggies and marks one of their most cherished rituals.

ARRIVALS & DEPARTURES

Bryan/College Station is located on Highways 6 and 21. From Austin, take Highway 290 east, then Highway 21 north. From Houston, take Highway 290 west and Highway 6 north.

WHERE TO STAY

LA QUINTA INN, *607 Texas Avenue, College Station. Tel. 409/696-5900 or 800/531-5900, Fax 409/696-0531. Rates: $59 to $69. Credit cards accepted.*

The La Quinta is a comfortable hotel located near the main entrance of the university. You get a complimentary breakfast of pastries, fruit and juice. The hotel has an outdoor pool and offers shuttle service to guests. Children under the age of 18 stay free with parents.

VINEYARD COURT HOTEL, *216 Dominik, College Station. Tel. 409/693-1220, Fax 764-1250. Rates: $59. Credit cards accepted.*

This establishment offers apartment-style accommodation near the university. Many families and faculty use this as temporary housing while relocating in the area, so there is a professional atmosphere. Each suite of rooms has a full kitchen. Business services such as fax and copy machines are available for guest use. The hotel is located near a university shuttle bus stop, so you can easily visit the university area. Recreational areas include an outdoor pool and yard.

Bed and Breakfast
MESSINA HOF WINE CELLARS, *4545 Old Reliance Road, Bryan. Tel. 409/778-9463, Fax 409/778-1729. Rates: $79.95. Credit cards accepted.*
One of the more unusual and private places to stay is the Vintor's Loft at Messina Hof Wineries. The modern single room is located over the visitor's center, and has a television but no telephone. A night here is for the true wine lover; breakfast features wine jelly and port wine chocolates. Only one room is available, so reservations are essential.

WHERE TO EAT
CAFE ECCELL, *101 Church Avenue, College Station. Tel. 409/846-7908. Credit cards accepted.*
The casual atmosphere at Cafe Eccell reflects the easy going nature of this university town. The restaurant is located in the building which used to be the city hall. The interior is now refreshingly modern. The menu includes individual pizzas, grilled meat and fish. The pizza is cooked in a wood burning oven until the crust is crisp yet tender. The grilled selections have the full flavor of mesquite smoke. The prices are reasonable; meals average around $15. On weekends, from 8am to 2pm Cafe Eccell features a brunch menu.

SEEING THE SIGHTS
Texas A&M University, *Rudder Hall Visitor's Center, College Station, Tel. 409/845-5851*, has been in operation since 1876. It is famous for the elite Corps of Cadets, which now constitutes a small portion of the student body. The university's enrollment tops 42,000. The excellent teaching facilities are highlighted by several museums on campus. During the academic year you can watch excellent collegiate sports.
When you arrive at the university, enter through the main entrance on Texas Avenue. Take the road that veers left, Lubbock Street. This will take you to the Rudder Complex and a public parking garage on Houston Street.
A taste of old world charm is found near Aggieland. The family who founded the **Messina Hof Wine Cellars**, *4545 Old Reliance Road, Bryan, Tel. 409/778-9463, Fax 409/778-1729*, traces its roots back through six generations of wine-makers from Italy. Messina Hof began producing wine 15 years ago and has an annual bottling of 100,000 gallons. The 45 acres of grounds is the tranquil setting for festivities that celebrate wine, including grape stomping competitions. The winery offers tours Monday

to Friday at 1pm; Saturday 11am, 12:30pm, 2:30pm and 4pm; and Sunday 12:30 and 2:30pm. There is no charge for the tour, but reservations are necessary.

NIGHTLIFE AND ENTERTAINMENT

The Dixie Chicken, *307 University Drive, College Station, Tel. 409/846-2322.* For years, the casual western atmosphere and pitchers of beer has made the Dixie Chicken the place for some collegiate country-style fun. The place is usually packed with university students. The dance floor is full of country buffs, from novice to expert. So don't be shy; get up and dance.

EXCURSIONS & DAY TRIPS

The town of **Anderson** stands on land that was once on a Native American trail. The Spanish also journeyed through the area, and part of El Camino Real, the old Spanish Royal Way, went through Anderson.

One of the first postmasters in Texas, Henry Fanthrop, built his home here in 1834. The house soon became an important stop on the road for travelers traversing the state and is known as the **Fanthrop Inn**, *Main Street, Anderson, Tel. 409/873-2633.* Today the inn is a state park, and visitors can tour the rooms where Sam Houston and Stonewall Jackson are said to have stayed. You can relive the past on the second Saturday of each month with a ride in a stagecoach. The stagecoach rides are from 1pm to 4pm in the afternoon. Anderson is located on Highway 90.

CALDWELL

The old buildings that line Main Street downtown are reminiscent of the idealistic simplicity of small town life in the first half of this century. Unfortunately, many of the businesses are now closed. **Caldwell** pays homage to the Czech settlers who founded the area, many of whose families still call Caldwell home, through its September **Kolache Festival**.

Caldwell proudly calls itself the Kolache Capital of Texas. Kolaches are sweet pastries, and the variety baked in Texas is actually better than the authentic Czech version. The town is a quiet repose for those who enjoy getting out of the big cities and getting to know the locals.

For the Kolache Festival, the baker who produces the most delicious kolache takes home the $100 state championship award. The best part is that everyone can sample the entries. The festival offers more than just food. Polka, folk and country bands provide entertainment all day. Classes teach traditional Czech arts and crafts as well as kolache baking. Antiques and art from the region are on display and on sale.

ARRIVALS & DEPARTURES

Caldwell is on Highway 21 at the intersection of Highway 36, about 25 miles south of Bryan.

WHERE TO STAY

CALDWELL MOTEL, *1819 Highway 21, Caldwell. Tel. 409/567-4000 or 567-9293. Rates: $29 to $31. Credit cards accepted.*

The 48 room motel offers rooms with kitchenettes and extra-large beds. All rooms have standard amenities such as telephone and cable television. The restaurant is open all day. Discounted rates for long stays.

SURREY INN, *403 Highway 21, Caldwell. Tel. 409-567-3221. Rates: $34, to $36. Credit cards accepted.*

The surrey inn is a comfortable road-side stop when traveling through east Texas. The inn has a homey feeling and rooms are neat and comfortable. You can enjoy the outdoor pool or the fishing pond, which is on the grounds. The Surrey Inn is at the intersection of Highways 36 and 21. The Surrey Inn restaurant serves home cooked meals, a salad bar and offers daily lunch specials.

WHERE TO EAT

CRAZY HORSE BBQ & STEAKHOUSE, *Highway 36, Caldwell. Tel. 409/567-7722.*

All the meat is prepared fresh, from the cutting to the smoking. Even the sausage is made fresh. If you prefer your meat cooked quickly, try the steaks which are grilled as you order. Home-made side dishes include potato salad and cole slaw. Daily specials are featured at lunch and dinner. Monday to Thursday 10am to 8pm, Friday and Saturday 10am to 9pm.

KOLACHE CAPITAL BAKE SHOP, *Highway 21, Caldwell. Tel. 409/567-3474.*

This bakery claims the grand prize as having the best professionally baked kolaches in the state, as decided by the Kolache Festival judges. The sandwiches are served on fresh bread and stacked tall. Baked potatoes and soup round out the lunch menu.

SEEING THE SIGHTS

The **Burleson County Czech Heritage Museum**, *212-A West Buck Street, Tel. 409/567-3218, Fax 409/567-0818*, exhibits everyday items of Czech settlers in Texas. Much of the tiny museum educates people about the Czech culture. A display of woodcarving and musical instruments from Moravia provides an interesting glance at a part of the world that at first seems far removed from Texas. The museum is upstairs in the Chamber of Commerce building.

The small Victorian home of Thomas Kraitchar, Jr., is open to the public by appointment. The area historical society restored **Kraitchar House**, *corner of Buck and Porter Streets*, to represent the Victorian era in Texas. To schedule a tour of the Kraitchar House, call the Caldwell Chamber of Commerce, *Tel. 409/567-3218*.

A unique opportunity awaits those with an interest in small-scale self-sufficient farming. The **Purple Gate Farm**, *Ranch Road 5, Box 88E, Tel. 409/567-9824*, relies on wild vegetation, solar power and water conservation to provide a sustainable environment for the family farm. Native plants are used for decoration and as a learning tool about the uses of wild fauna. Private tours of the farm may be arranged by appointment.

PRACTICAL INFORMATION

Tourist information is provided by the **Caldwell Chamber of Commerce**, *212-A West Buck Street, Caldwell, Tel. 409/567-3218, Fax 409/567-0818*.

PALESTINE

In **Palestine**, the annual **Dogwood Trails Heritage Festival** starts the spring with a celebration of the dogwood season. Downtown Palestine is the site of a carnival and theater productions. Square dances and a bicycle tour throughout he countryside get the community and visitors active. The festival takes place on the last two weekends of March and the first weekend of April.

ARRIVALS & DEPARTURES

Palestine is on Highway 287, which can be reached by Interstate Highway 45 from Dallas in the north or from Houston in the south.

WHERE TO STAY

SPIRIT INN, *921 North Sycamore Drive*, and **SPIRIT HOUSE**, *109 East Pine, Palestine, Texas 75801. Tel. 903/723-9565 or 800/224-0999. Rates: singles $45 to $65; doubles $65 to $85.*

The Spirit Inn and Spirit House are two historic homes about one block from each other which offer comfortable accommodations in the heart of one of Palestine's most historic neighborhoods. The Spirit Inn has four rooms, all with cable television; the Spirit House has three rooms and an outdoor courtyard with a hot tub. Both houses were built in the first part of the century and retain their historic charm. Children are welcome and a bassinet can be rented for infants. Weekend stays include a delicious country breakfast, usually served outdoors. From Highway 79, turn north onto Sycamore Street.

ASH-BOWERS MANSION, *310 Magnolia Street, Palestine. Tel. 903/ 729-1935.*

The beautiful home was built in 1878 in simple Italian architectural design. Years later the Victorian trim was added to the facade. The home is completely restored and offers four guest rooms.

COUNTRY CHRISTMAS TREE FARM, *514 North Sycamore, Palestine. Tel. 903/729-4836 or 729-2671, Fax: 729-0322. Rates: $60 to $85. Credit cards accepted.*

Located in the historical district, the inn has several rooms with different names. The Sunday House is a two-bedroom country-theme residence with kitchen and dining room. The Carriage House is a studio residence located above the garage. You can also make arrangements to stay at the rural tree farm. The modern house has four guest rooms, the bunkhouse has two rooms, and two private cottages. They also have a small, modern guest cottage on their tree farm in rural east Texas. Arrangements can be made to stay at the farm; call for details.

DAYS INN, *1100 East Palestine Avenue, Palestine. Tel. 903/729-3151 or 800/DAYS INN. Rates: $35 to $79.*

This 65 room hotel is a standard hotel with a fitness room, outdoor pool, tennis courts and ample parking areas. The Gazebo Restaurant serves food all day. Palestine Avenue is Highway 79.

Camping

RED ROCK RANCH, *Route 8 Box 121, Palestine. Tel. 903/723-1836. Camp sites $12 to $27.*

Round Rock Ranch is a small private park and campground located just a few miles from Palestine. Facilities include a picnic area, bathrooms and showers. Entrance to the park is $3 per car. Rustic campsites are available, and priced according to the number of people camping. Call ahead to reserve a space and get directions to the campground.

WHERE TO EAT

EILENBERGERS BAKERY, *512 North John Street, Palestine. Tel. 903/ 729-2253. Credit cards accepted.*

The bakery is an institution in Palestine. Eilenbergers once supplied east Texas with baked bread. Today the bakery specializes in fruitcake and pastry. The tea room is a cozy spot for a light snack and coffee. Here you will taste the flavor of baked goodies that make an east Texan feel at home.

RANCH HOUSE, *301 East Crawford, Palestine. Tel. 903/723-8778. Credit cards accepted.*

The Ranch House is the family dining spot of choice for locals. The generous steaks, hearty side dishes and children's plates please everyone. The restaurant is known for their fresh salads.

OLD BOSTON SANDWICH SHOP, *119 West Main Street, Palestine. Tel. 903/ 729-4099.*

This small shop makes fresh deli sandwiches and soup of the day. Stop in for ice cream and a soda when visiting the historic section of downtown.

SEEING THE SIGHTS

In the center of the city you will find the landmark buildings of Palestine's past. The **Anderson County Courthouse**, *Courthouse Square, Lacy Street,* was built in the neo-Classical style in 1914. The courthouse is located between Fanin and Dechard Streets. The beautiful **Carnegie Library**, *502 North Queen,* is now used as the Palestine Chamber of Commerce.

In 1851, Colonel Howard built his home in Palestine. **Howard House Museum**, *1011 North Perry Street, Tel. 903/584-3225*, has a collection of antiques from the mid-nineteenth century reflecting the lifestyle of the merchant class of east Texas. Visitors must schedule an appointment to visit the museum.

Local history is preserved in an exemplary fashion at the **Museum for East Texas Culture**, *400 Michaux Street, Tel. 903/723-1914*. The building was once the only high school in Palestine, then later served as the junior high school. The park surrounding the museum has picnic tables and tennis courts that are open to the public.

SHOPPING

If you appreciate the work of artisans, then take the time to find an out-of-the-way shop, **Old Farmhouse Pottery**, *Country Road 1805, Maydelle, Tel. 903/795-3779*. True to its name, the shop is indeed in a farm house dating from the 1930's. The resident artist, David Henly, is a master of hand-made pottery who makes functional stoneware and gallery-quality art. You can visit the studio from Thursday to Monday 1pm to 5pm or by appointment.

To get here, travel east from Palestine on US Highway 84. Turn north onto County Road 1804, which turns into County Road 1805 after a half mile. The shop is on the east side of the road, about three-quarters of a mile from the highway.

EXCURSIONS & DAY TRIPS

The **National Scientific Balloon Facility**, *Tel. 903/729-0271,* is open to the public. Tours of the facility are free, but you must call in advance to make arrangements. To reach the facility, take Highway 287 west for five miles.

Every September the tomato harvest is celebrated at the **Jacksonville Tomatofest**. The festivities include the Miss Tomato Pageant, barbecue cooking and hot sauce making contests and lots of games for kids. Jacksonville is at the intersection of US Highways 69, 79 and 175, about 25 miles northeast of Palestine.

TEXAS' ONLY NATIVE AMERICAN EARTH MOUNDS

*The only Native American structures in the state are earthen mounds at the **Caddoan Mounds State Park**, Highway 21, Route 2 Box 85C, Alto, Tel. 409/858-3218, open daily 10am to 6pm. The mounds were constructed just after the turn of the first millennium, and they have been studied by American archaeologists since 1919. A reconstructed Caddoan home and a museum are open to the public. Visitors can take a self-guided tour on a 3/4 mile trail. From Rusk, take Highway 21 south approximately ten miles.*

Steam Trains

The years when the steam engines tamed the American frontier were the glory days of east Texas. The Palestine-Rusk Railroad was a working industrial line from 1896 to 1921. **The Texas State Railroad Historical Park** captures the bygone railroad days with working tourist trains.

Today the Texas State Railroad operates locomotives which run from Palestine to Rusk from March through November. Eight antique locomotives make the 25 mile trip. The one-way journey takes one-and-one-half hours and passengers must return the same day. Trains leave both Rusk and Palestine at 11am and return to the city of origin at 1:30pm. Each station is reconstructed in the turn-of-the-century style and has a visitor's center, gift shop and restaurant. Round trip fare is $15 per adult and $9 per child. Evening trains run once in the spring and once in the summer. To make reservations, call the **Texas State Railroad**, *P. O. Box 39, Rusk, Tel. 800/ 442-8951 (in Texas), 903/683-2561 (outside Texas).*

Both train depots are surrounded by state parks offering picnic areas and playgrounds. The Rusk park has camping sites and tennis courts. To reach the Palestine Station and State Park, from Loop 256 take Highway 84 and travel east two miles. The Rusk Station and State Park is on Highway 84, three miles west of downtown.

To venture even farther back in history, visit a bit of the Spanish legacy in east Texas. The first Spanish mission built in Texas was not an adobe compound in west Texas, but a small log cabin in the east Texas woods built in 1690. Mission San Francisco de los Tejas no longer is standing, but a replica of what the building may have resembled commemorates the site at the **Mission Tejas State Historical Park**, *Route 2 Box 108, Grapeland, Tel. 409/687-2394*. The park has over three miles of hiking trails, picnic areas, a playground, campsites with full hookups and a fishing pond. From Crockett, travel north on Highway 21 for 22 miles.

PRACTICAL INFORMATION

The visit to the **Palestine Chamber of Commerce**, *502 North Queen Street, Palestine*, is worth the trip to see the Carnegie Library Building alone. The information and maps are an added perk.

RUSK

The small town of **Rusk** is responsible for several "firsts" in Texas. The town is named for Thomas Jefferson Rusk, one of the human cornerstones of the state and a leader of independent Texas. He signed the Texas Declaration of Independence and served as the Republic's Secretary of War. After Texas joined the United States, Rusk became one of the first United States Senators to represent Texas. Among the famous who claim Rusk as their home was Texas Governor Jim Hogg, the first native Texan to become governor. (He may be even better known as the man who named his daughter Ima Hogg). Jim Hogg State Park has a replica of the Hogg family home.

Most visitors to Rusk spend only a few hours in the city as a stop on the Texas State Railroad historic steam engine. For more information about the city, contact the **Rusk Chamber of Commerce**, *P. O. Box 67, Rusk, Texas 75785, Tel. 903/683-4242 or 800/933-2381*.

ARRIVALS & DEPARTURES

Rusk is on Highway 84, just east of Palestine.

WHERE TO STAY

Rusk has a number of booking services for its numerous bed and breakfasts. **AAA Reservations**, *Tel. 800/299-1593*, and **Classic B&B Inns**, *Tel. 800/468-2627*, provide information and reservations.

THOMAS J. RUSK HOTEL, *105 East Sixth Street, Rusk. Tel. 214/683-2556 or 800/634-6513. Rates: $70 to $115. Credit cards accepted.*

This historic hotel sits on the town square. Built in the 1920's, the 36-room hotel is full of history. The spacious suites are well worth the extra cost. Breakfast is not included with rooms, but a lunch buffet is served on weekends.

ATHENS

This unassuming town created America's staple food, the hamburger. Every September the city commemorates the inventor, Fletcher Davis, with a **Hamburger Cook-off and Trade Fair**.

ARRIVALS & DEPARTURES

From Interstate Highway 45, take Highway 31 east. Highway 31 meets Interstate Highway 45 at Corsicana, about 55 miles south of Dallas. continue on Highway 31 for 37 miles. Athens is at the intersection of Highways 175, 31 and 19.

WHERE TO STAY

CARRIAGE HOUSE, *Hickory Hill Farm, Route 2, Box 2153, Athens. Tel. 903/677-3939 or 800/808-BEDS. Rates: $90 to $120. Credit cards accepted.*

Hickory Hill Farm is only three miles from Athens, but it is very much in the country. Rolling hills and a rustic setting provide a perfect getaway. The carriage house of the old farm has been remade into three guest rooms, each furnished with antiques and a private bath. The upstairs is actually a private suite. All rooms include breakfast and a snack in the afternoon. From downtown Athens, take Highway 19 south for three miles. Turn west on Farm-to-Market Road 753. Travel about two and one-half miles; the farm is on the north side of the road.

SEEING THE SIGHTS

The **Texas Freshwater Fisheries Center**, *5550 Flat Creek Road, Tel. 903/676-BASS, Fax 903/676-FISH, open daily 10am to 5pm, admission $4 adults; $3 seniors; $2 children*, lets you into the world of game fish. The Texas Parks and Wildlife Department runs the complex that includes the Edwin L. Cox visitors center, pond and reservoir, and casting pond. The wetlands and alligator pond show the fearsome American alligator, an east Texas native.

During the dive show, the theater turns into a 26,000 gallon dive tank, and the diver answers audience questions. If learning about the fish makes you want to eat one, you can get casting lessons and catch fish in the casting pond. Scientific research is conducted at the fish hatchery, which is open for tours.

TYLER

Tyler is the "Rose Capital of the US" due to the prominence of the rose growing industry. The centerpiece of the city is the nation's largest public rose garden. Tyler is best know for its annual **Rose Festival**, which has been held for more than 64 years. This old-fashioned remnant of southern society is part floral celebration and part pageantry. Tyler became a city in 1848, and grew when the railroad became the main artery of transportation through the area. Today Tyler is a small town with a big tradition of rose growing.

The **Annual Texas Rose Festival** is held in mid-October. The highlight of the five day event is the Rose Festival Parade, which takes place near downtown. Stadium seats require a ticket ($5 admission), and spectators can stand along the closed parade route ($3 admission). Numerous other events, such as square dance, a car show and informative lectures about roses are open to the general public. The coronation of the Rose Queen is the main event for Tyler locals. An entire year of preparation culminates in the fanciful Coronation performance (tickets $20 or $25), where you can see area debutantes dressed in giant hoop-skirted ball gowns.

For more information or an order form for tickets, contact the **Texas Rose Festival Association**, *P. O. Box 8224, Tyler, Texas 75711, Tel. 903/579-3130*. Tours of the **Tyler Nursery** are by reservation only (no admission charge). To arrange a tour, contact the Convention and Visitors Bureau, *Tel. 903/592-1661, extension 229*.

ARRIVALS & DEPARTURES

Air traffic in Tyler uses **Ponds Field Airport**, which is about seven miles west of the city on Highway 64.

If you're driving, Tyler is south of Interstate Highway 20. Take Highway 69 south from Interstate Highway 20 to reach Tyler.

ORIENTATION

Highway 69 bisects the city from north to south; Loop 323 circles the city. Highway 110, which is in the southeast corner of Tyler, is also called Troupe Highway.

WHERE TO STAY

ROSEVINE INN BED AND BREAKFAST, *415 South Vine Street, Tyler. Tel. 903/592-2221, Fax 593-9500. Rates: $85 to $150. Credit cards accepted.*

The Rosevine Inn is a two story brick home located a few blocks from downtown. The neighborhood is a good area for long, quiet strolls. Although the house itself is not very old, the antique furnishings provide a quaint atmosphere. The rooms are large with warm decor. You can enjoy the perks of staying in a modern home, such as the hot tub and sauna and private baths for each room. Guests receive complimentary refreshments and a full breakfast.

WOLDERT-SPENCE MANOR, *611 West Woldert Street, Tyler. Tel. 800/965-3378 or 903/533-9057, Fax 903/531-0293. Rates: $65 to $95. Credit cards accepted.*

The family that built the house was a prominent landholder in Texas when it was an independent republic. The home was built in 1859 and no doubt was a landmark in its time. The single-story home close to downtown has beautiful antiques throughout and stained-glass windows in many of its rooms. Large shade trees adorn the property. Guests can relax in the large yard or outdoor hot tub.

BED OF ROSES COUNTY INN, *Highway 69 north, Tyler. Tel. 800/265-7673, Fax 903/882-3597. Rates: $55 to $65. Credit cards accepted.*

This home, built in 1953, has three guest rooms with a shared bathroom and quaint furnishings. Each room has a telephone.

HAMPTON INN, *3130 Troupe Highway, Tyler. Tel. 903/596-7752, Fax 903/596-7765. Rates: $63 to $89.*

Rooms have amenities such as microwave ovens, small refrigerators and hair dryers. Some rooms have spa bathtubs. From Interstate Highway 20, exit Highway 69, go south to Loop 323. Take 323 south to Troup (Highway 110) exit. Take Troupe Highway north for about five miles.

LA QUINTA INN, *1601 West Southwest Loop 323, Tyler. Tel. 903/561-2223, Fax 903/581-5708. Rates: $59 to $66. Credit cards accepted.*

This comfortable motel offers free continental breakfast to its guests. Children under the age of 18 stay free with their parents. The La Quinta is located on the southwest part of Loop 323. From Interstate Highway 20, take Highway 69 south to Loop 323. Travel south on 323, exit Old Jacksonville Road.

RESIDENCE INN, *3303 Troup Highway, Tyler. Tel. 903/595-5188 or 800/331-3131, Fax 903/595-5719. Rates: $69 to $89. Credit cards accepted.*

Studio-style rooms have kitchen and living areas. The Residence Inn has fitness facilities that include a heated pool and spa. Pets may stay in rooms for an extra charge. Complimentary breakfast is provided, as is free shuttle service to the airport. From Interstate Highway 20, exit Highway 69. Travel south to Loop 323, then go east to Highway 110. The motel is 17 miles form the airport and four miles from the city center.

WHERE TO EAT

BERNARD CASE'S, *7701 South Broadway, Tel. 903/581-0744. Credit cards accepted.*

This restaurant is a few miles from the center of the city, but you will feel as though you are eating in Louisiana. A combination of delicate French sauces and the zeal of Cajun cooking make the meals exceptional. Seafood is the house specialty, and steak and chicken are also on the menu.

SEEING THE SIGHTS

The hallmark of Tyler, roses, are grown to abundance in the **Tyler Municipal Rose Garden**, *1900 West Front Street, Tel. 903/531-1370, open daily 8am to 5pm*. The garden covers 22 acres and has the latest variations and some of the most unusual rose bushes in the 500 varieties grown here. A museum dedicated to the Annual Rose Festival is on the garden grounds.

The former Carnegie Library is now the **Carnegie History Center**, *125 College Street, open Tuesday to Sunday 1pm to 5pm*, has a good collection of pieces of daily life from the time of the Republic of Texas. Exhibits focus on life in Texas during the Civil War. The museum is free.

An interesting glimpse into the past is revealed at the **Goodman Museum**, *624 North Broadway, Wednesday to Sunday 1pm to 5pm*. The musuem is in a Greek Revival home built in 1859. The stately manor holds an extensive collection of furniture and medical instruments from the years before the Civil War.

SPORTS & RECREATION

The **Tyler State Park**, *789 Park Road 16, Tel. 903/597-5338*, allows guest to enjoy the beautiful nature of the Piney Woods area. Wooded hiking trails and an 8.5 mile mountain bike trail take visitors into the serene wilderness. Swimming and fishing are permitted in the park's small lake. Campsites with full hook-ups and picnic areas are available. From Tyler, travel north on Farm Road 14. The park is two miles north of Interstate Highway 20.

PRACTICAL INFORMATION

You can learn more about Tyler by contacting the **Convention and Visitor's Bureau**, *P. O. Box 390, Tyler, Texas 75710, Tel. 903/592-1661 or 800/235-5712*.

SAN AUGUSTINE

This city shares the name of a larger city in Florida for good reason. The first road to cross Texas was mapped out by the Spanish in the seventeenth century. The Royal Way ran from Mexico City to San Augustine, Florida. Part of Highway 21 covers the same ground as the old Spanish Imperial route.

The small town stands in the heart of the Texas piney forest region. The landscape is characterized by rolling hills and tall evergreen trees. The winters are cold and crisp, with frequent morning frost. The summers are very hot and humid.

ARRIVALS & DEPARTURES

San Augustine is located on Highway 96 near the Louisiana border. Highway 21 takes you directly into town.

WHERE TO STAY

CAPTAIN E. E. DOWNS HOUSE, *301 East Main Street, San Augustine. Tel. 409/275-2289, Fax 409/275-3444. Rates: $45 to $75. Credit cards accepted.*

The twentieth century Victorian home is in the center of town, just off the town square. Its five rooms are furnished with antiques which bring the historic character of the home to life. The lovely neighborhood provides ample opportunity for a stroll. The largest room, the master suite, is spacious and accommodating. A light breakfast is served in the morning.

THE WADE HOUSE, *128 East Columbia Street, San Augustine. Tel. 409/275-5489. Rates: $40 to $80. Credit cards accepted*

The historic highlight of this relatively modern home is a large collection of hats. This home does not reflect the long history of the area. But the friendly atmosphere is inviting, and you will leave with a sense of really getting to know the small town. Three of the five guest rooms have private baths.

SEEING THE SIGHTS

In the early 1700's, the Spanish established a mission in San Augustine. The **Mission Senora de los Dolores de los Ais**, or Dolores Mission, was the site of conflict between the French and Spanish, and was deserted by the late 1700's. Nothing remains of the Spanish settlement, although the site of the Dolores Mission is commemorated with an historical marker. To find the Mission grounds, walk four blocks south from the courthouse.

The most important historic home in town is the **Home of Ezekiel W. Cullen**, *at the corner of Congress and Market Streets, open Thursday to Sunday 1pm to 5pm; closed Monday to Wednesday*, which was built in 1839. Cullen was a judge, and the house is evidence of his wealth and political power. The Greek Revival structure has a full-sized ball room which takes up the entire top story.

The main attraction in the area is the beautiful national forest preserves. Eleven miles north of San Augustine on Texas Highway 147, you will find the **Angelia National Forest**. The large **Sabine National Forest** is only five miles west of San Augustine on Farm-to-Market Road 353.

CHRISTMAS CELEBRATIONS IN EAST TEXAS & LOUISIANA

Texans are not known as sentimental folk, but venture to east Texas during the Christmas season and you'll find old-time country celebrations. Marshall, famous for its Christmas light decorations that include an illuminated courthouse with five million lights, is only part of the month-long seasonal celebration. Jefferson offers a more traditional candlelight trail of the city's historic homes. Jacksonville has an old-fashioned Christmas parade, sing-a-long and boat parade on Lake Jacksonville during the second week of December.

Cross the border to Shreveport, Louisiana for Lights On Line, a five-mile light show on Line Avenue. The American Rose Center in Shreveport has a show of light sculptures. Bossier, Louisiana strings lights along the Barksdale Air Force Base water tower and hosts an annual Christmas parade. On the first Saturday in December, Natchitoches, Louisiana holds its Christmas Festival, which includes a parade, fireworks and lights.

Marshall is on Interstate Highway 20. Jefferson is just north of Marshall, on US Highway 59. Shreveport and Bossier City, Louisiana, are east of Marshall on Interstate Highway 20. Natchitoches is south on Interstate Highway 49, which crosses Interstate Highway 20.

PRACTICAL INFORMATION

The **San Augustine Chamber of Commerce**, *West Columbia Street, San Augustine, open Monday to Friday 9am to 4pm*, provides area information.

JEFFERSON

In the late 1800's, when **Jefferson** refused a railroad in order to concentrate on the established steamboat business, the town could not have realized that it was freezing its growth potential. Today the town is a time capsule of prosperous Victorian Texas. Jefferson grew quickly from a frontier village of log cabins to a city of elegant homes of wealthy merchant families.

The city is full of historic homes, many of which are bed and breakfast establishments. You can take city-sponsored tours of historic homes or you can take a self-guided tour. Most homes charge admission fees.

ARRIVALS & DEPARTURES

Jefferson is located at the crossroads of Highway 59, which runs north-south, and Highway 49.

GETTING AROUND TOWN

To catch a glimpse of the history of Jefferson the easy way, jump aboard one of the trolley-style buses that offer tours. The tours include all major places of interest and fill tourists in on the regional folklore. Tours leave at 11am, 1pm and 3pm daily form the **Historic Jefferson Tours Headquarters**, *222 East Austin Street, Tel. 903/665-1665.*

For a different take on the tour route, the **wagon tours** depart across the street from the Jefferson Historical Society Museum. The small wagons are pulled by mules, so the pace is leisurely.

WHERE TO STAY & EAT

You can easily find a bed and breakfast by using the **Book-A-Bed-Ahead Reservation Service**, *P. O. Box 723, Jefferson, Texas 75657, Tel. 903/665-3956 or 800/486-2627, Fax 903/665-8551*, which offers accommodation at 15 historic inns of Jefferson. There is no charge for the service and rates range from $60 to $145 per night.

THE CAPTAIN'S CASTLE AND CARRIAGE HOUSE INN, *403 East Walker Street, Jefferson. Tel. 903/665-2330. Rates: $75 to $115.*

The main house is built in the style of the grand homes of Tennessee. Tall trees and manicured gardens highlight the beauty of the simple, southern architecture. The main house has three rooms, each furnished with period antiques. Adjacent to the house is the smaller carriage house, which has three guest rooms, each with a private bath. The private cottage has a fireplace and romantic sitting room. Guests awaken to fresh coffee and muffins in the morning. A full breakfast is served in the dining rooms.

HOTEL JEFFERSON, *124 West Austin, Street, Jefferson. Tel. 903/665-2631. Rates: $ 64 to $100. Credit cards accepted.*

When this hotel first opened for business its guests were cotton — the building was a warehouse until 1900. When the railroad finally squelched the steamboat as a practical mode of shipping, the need for cotton warehouses consequently dried up. Tourism still played a role in Jefferson, so the Hotel Jefferson opened its doors. The modern, renovated Hotel Jefferson has a variety of room sizes, from those with a standard full bed to the luxurious master suite.

McKAY HOUSE BED & BREAKFAST, *306 East Delta Street, Jefferson. Tel. 903/665-7322 or 800/468-2627, Fax 903/665-8551. Rates: $95 to $125. Credit cards accepted.*

The McKay House has a sturdy front porch and a white picket fence, the perfect home away from home. Each of the four rooms and one suite in the main house has a private bath. The Sunday House, the cottage, has two suites each with its own bath and living areas. The home is decorated with furnishings from the late 1800's. But the genteel charm goes beyond the material surroundings. Southern hospitality fills the inn, making each visit an extraordinary trip through history. A generous breakfast is served in the conservatory. Reservations are recommended.

SEEING THE SIGHTS

The **Twin Oaks Plantation**, *Farm Road 134, Tel. 903/665-3535, Wednesday to Saturday 4 and 5pm, is worth a* visit simply because it is an uncommon type of house in Texas. The mansion represents more closely the life of Louisiana and the deep south. Working plantations were not common in Texas, although there were slave-holding families. The Twin Oaks Plantation was a working farm. The home has original decor, with a notable collection of European art which was fashionable in the south at the time. The Twin Oaks Plantation is open for tours only which are given at 4pm and 5pm. Special arrangements can be made for group tours.

The **Carnegie Library**, *301 Lafayette Street, Tuesday to Friday noon to 5pm, closed Monday, Saturday and Sunday, has serve*d the community since it was built in 1907. Displays about the history of the area are free to the public. The building itself is a living museum of the life, history and community of the area.

The best way to see big **Cypress Bayou** is by boat. Small tourist boats make 45 minute tours daily. The boat dock is located under Polk Street Bridge on US Highway 59, *Tel. 903/665-2222.* The tranquillity of the Cypress Bayou envelops visitors. You can see some of the last remaining untouched bayou areas in Texas. Thick trees and calm, glassy water are the backdrop for the 45 minute boat ride. Fare is $5.50 per person (either adult or child); group rates are available.

16. SOUTH TEXAS

Beautiful **south Texas** comprises a dramatic patchwork of cultures. The stark coastal plains are the birthplace of the American cowboy, and the place where Longhorn cattle were first raised in the state. Windswept beaches spotted with palm trees oleander blossoms make up the tropical part of the state. The rich Latino culture contributes the bright, cultural flare that characterizes the area.

SAN ANTONIO

San Antonio stands on the border of central and south Texas. The city offers the benefits of both regions, beautiful central Texas hill country and the rich traditions of the Texas-Mexico border. San Antonio is a beautiful blend of American and Mexican traditions. San Antonio has historically been situated at the crossroads of many cultures. The city was once part of Mexico, a center of German immigrant settlement and a major trade center for North America. The varied history lives on in the quaint residential communities, picturesque downtown and thriving arts scene.

The San Antonio area was one of the first areas to be settled during the Spanish colonization of North America. Catholic missionaries braved the rugged terrain and long dry summers to establish religious centers. The city absorbed many armed conflicts during the birth of the state of Texas. The famous **Alamo** still stands at the center of the city. The Mexican Army marched on San Antonio twice in 1842, with one significant battle resulting, the Battle of Salado Creek.

Although San Antonio played an important role as a point on the trade route that connected Mexico and North America, for decades it remained little more than a frontier town with mud streets. Downtown Houston Street was part of the Old San Antonio Highway and was the route for traffic traveling to Mexico City. In the late 1800's, mule-drawn trolleys provided public transportation downtown.

Today, San Antonio has a population of over 950,000. The metropolitan area sustains slow, consistent growth, allowing the city to maintain its turn-of-the-century demeanor. The center of tourism lies downtown along the famous **River Walk**. The factories and rail-yards which once sustained the city are now incorporated into its metropolitan character. San Antonio is home to five military bases and is a major Air Force and medical center.

San Antonio hosts conventions throughout the year, with the spring (from February to April) being high season. On certain weekends, such as Valentine's Day or Easter, you may find all the hotels downtown booked full. San Antonio celebrates the many aspects of its rich history with festivals throughout the year. The **San Antonio Rodeo** is held at the beginning of the year, and is the major rodeo in south Texas.

Fiesta, a week-long celebration of Hispanic heritage, lights up the city in April. Concerts, parades, outdoor activities and festivals fill the days. La Villita is the site of "A Night in Old San Antonio," a celebration of the city's history and culture and a number of formal dances and balls are held. Some events are free to the public, and admission prices vary for others. For a complete schedule of events, contact the **Fiesta San Antonio Commission**, *122 Heiman Street, San Antonio, Texas 78205*.

Every August, the **Institute of Texas Cultures**, *801 South Bowie Street, Tel. 210/558-2300*, holds the **Texas Folklife Festival** to bring together the traditions of the many peoples of San Antonio. Over 80,000 people turn out to share food, music, dance and costumes from all over the world.

A number of festivities celebrate Christmas. In early December, the Christmas season is welcomed with the **Las Posadas**, a candle-lit parade that lines the River Walk. The San Antonio Museum of Art sponsors a Saturday Market called **Bazaar Sabado**, with crafts and art from Mexico. And Sea World displays a driving tour of lights.

ARRIVALS & DEPARTURES

San Antonio International Airport is conveniently located only 13 miles from downtown and is seldom crowded. For airport information, *Tel. 210/821-3411 or 800/428-4322*. For parking information, *Tel. 210/821-3465*. The airport is located at the intersection of Highways 281 and 410, in the north of the city.

The **Star Shuttle Service**, *Tel. 210/341-6000*, runs mini-vans between the airport and the San Antonio area. The fare from the airport to central San Antonio averages $6, about half the cost of a ride by taxi. Taxi pick-up is just outside the main doors of the airport.

The **Amtrak Station**, *1174 East Commerce Street, Tel. 210/223-3226 or 800/872-7245*, is located downtown. Trains run to Dallas/Fort Worth, Houston, El Paso and connect to out-of-state routes.

To get to the **Greyhound Bus Station**, *500 N Saint Mary Street, Tel. 800/231-2222*, from Interstate Highway 35, take the Lexington Street Exit, turn left and cross under the highway. Continue on Lexington Street for five blocks, then turn right onto St. Mary's Street; the station is three blocks down. **Kerrville Bus Company**, *Tel. 210/227-5669 or 800/335-3722*, serves south Texas with regular routes, charters and tours.

ORIENTATION

In Texas, it seems that all roads lead to San Antonio. Both Interstate Highway 35, which bisects the state from north to south, and Interstate Highway 10, which cuts across from east to west, run through central San Antonio. Interstate Highway 35 branches off into Interstate Highway 37, which connects the Texas Gulf Coast.

Loop 410 circles the city and provides access to many major attractions that lie outside the center. Highway 281 is a picturesque freeway connecting downtown to the airport and the parks in the northwest areas.

The San Antonio River runs through the center of the city. The downtown area has the famous **River Walk**, a serene stretch of hotels, restaurants and bars located near the Alamo. Large trees provide shade along the twenty block pedestrian zone that sits below the street level of downtown. This is the city's center of tourism, entertainment and recreation. In the evening, music enlivens the atmosphere, as bars and nightclubs come alive.

Just south of downtown, off St. Mary's Street, you'll find the historic neighborhood of the **King William District**. First settled by German merchants when the territory was still part of Mexico, the 25-block area has marvelous restored Victorian homes, some of which are open to the public. The King William Conservation Society sponsors walking tours of the area. The **Mission Trail** is found just south of the King William District.

GETTING AROUND TOWN

If you plan to stay only a few days in San Antonio, a car is not necessary. Most points of interest are within walking distance of the River Walk and public transportation provides excellent routes for tourist attractions.

Local car rental agencies include:
• **A&P Recreational Vehicle Rental**, *Tel. 210/667-1838*
• **Capps Van and Car Rental**, *Tel. 210/822-8655*
• **Chuck's Rent-a-Clunker**, *Tel. 210/922-9464*
• **Rent-a-Van**, *Tel. 210/340-8267*

Taxis in San Antonio charge $2.80 for the first mile and $1.10 for each mile following. Two companies that serve the San Antonio area are **Checker Cab**, *Tel. 210/222-2151,* and **Yellow Cab**, *Tel. 210/226-4242.*

San Antonio has an excellent, modern bus system, **VIA Metropolitan Transport**, which has nearly 100 routes across the city and trolley-style buses that serve the central tourist district. Route 7 serves the Alamo, McNay Art Museum, Witte Museum, Zoo and Botanical Gardens. Route 40 runs from the Alamo to the historic San Antonio Missions in the southern suburbs. Special express buses run to Sea World and Six Flags Amusement Park. The VIA Metropolitan Transport Information Office is located close to the River Walk, *112 Soledad, Monday to Friday 7am to 5pm and Saturday 8am to 5pm, Tel. 210/227-2020.*

Generally people do not take a horse-drawn carriage to actually get anywhere, but just to enjoy a fun ride for a bit. In San Antonio, the carriages are most easily found in the park in front of the Alamo. They generally follow a route along the older streets of downtown. Two services which can be hired for special events are **Lone Star Carriage**, *Tel. 210/656-7527,* and **Yellow Rose Carriage**, *Tel. 210/225-6490.*

The popular deck-boat river cruises are a pleasant way to see the buildings along the River Walk. The drivers give a tour during the 40 minute cruise. Unfortunately you may have to stand in line longer than 40 minutes to get on a boat. Standard fare is $4 for adults and $1 for children under the age of 5 years. For more information or to charter your own boat for a special event, call **Yanaguana River Cruise**, *Tel. 210/244-5700 or 800/417-4139.* You can arrange a dinner river cruise for a group through **Zuni Restaurant**, *Tel. 210/227-0864.*

Bus tours of San Antonio and specific tours of the Mission Trail are offered by **Gray Line Tours**. Gray Line also ventures to Laredo, Texas and Nuevo Laredo, Mexico for shopping trips and conducts tours of the Texas Hill Country. The Grey Line information office, *Tel 210/226-1706 or 800/472-9546,* is located across the street from the Alamo.

WHERE TO STAY
Downtown
ADAM'S MARK HOTEL, *452 Soledad, San Antonio. Tel. 210/354-2800 or 800/444-ADAM, Fax. 210/354-2700. Rates: $140 to $200. Credit cards accepted.*

This brand new 400 room hotel stands at the heart of the River Walk, close to the convention center. The recreational facilities on the premises include a full health club with an indoor spa and outdoor pool. The hotel restaurant features southwestern cuisine; two bars provide entertainment into the night. The Adam's Mark offers both a parking lot and valet service.

THE CAMBERLY GUENTER, *205 East Houston Street, San Antonio. Tel. 210/227-3241 or 800/555-8000, Fax 210/227-3299. Rates: $ 149 to $169. Credit cards accepted.*

The Camberly Guenter has a rich history that reflects the character of San Antonio. When the hotel opened in 1909, not only was it the mainstay of the San Antonio skyline but was hailed as the most modern hotel between the east and west coast. The Guenter cost $1 million to build, and the price tag itself made news. The spot where the hotel stands has a long history. It was the site of San Antonio's first inn in 1837, first military barracks in 1851, and two subsequent hotels. The Mahncke Hotel was famous as the home of newly arrived German immigrants. The center of the social scene quickly found itself in the Guenter. Famous guests include President Harry Truman, John Wayne and Mae West.

The elegant Guenter is a pleasure to visit. The hotel is located across from the Majestic Theater, in the center of San Antonio. From the moment you enter the lobby, you know you're in a landmark. The 312 rooms and 10 suites are furnished in historic grand style. During the afternoon you can enjoy high tea; in the evening Muldoon's Bar serves cocktails.

CROCKETT HOTEL, *320 Bonham, San Antonio. Tel 210/225-6500 or 800/292-1050. Rates: $85 to $150. Credit cards accepted.*

The Crockett is a downtown landmark, most distinguished by the large neon sign that spelled out its name. The property was built in 1907 by a fraternal organization known as the International Order of Odd Fellows. A second wing was added in 1927. The Crockett was painstakingly restored in the 1980's to replicate the grandeur of the days when it was built. This hotel overlooks the Alamo and offers very comfortable accommodations at good rates. Holiday Inn operates six other hotels in San Antonio, including one near Sea World.

THE FAIRMONT, *401 South Alamo Street, San Antonio. Tel. 210/224-8800 or 800/642-3363. Rates: $165 to $225; suites: $195 to $550. Credit cards accepted.*

This charming hotel was moved from its former site to preserve the building. Much of the hotel is the original building from 1906. The lobby and the restaurant are accented with authentic lamps and crystal chandeliers. With only 37 rooms, 17 of which are suites, the Fairmont provides a luxurious and secluded setting in the heart of the city. The location on the River Walk is one of the most serene and picturesque. Each room of the Fairmont is furnished in turn-of-the-century style. The master suite is an extravagant apartment, with a spa bath, hard wood floors and two bathrooms.

HYATT REGENCY RIVER WALK, *123 Losoya Street, San Antonio. Tel. 210/222-1234 or 800/233-1234. Rates: $195 to $ $220. Credit cards accepted.*

The Hyatt is one of the most convenient places to stay on the River Walk because the lower floors of the hotel have a lovely miniature mall with fountains, food, and the area's foremost club, Jim Cullum's Landing. The hotel was a landmark when it was built because it incorporated the River Walk into a modern high-rise. A series of fountains runs though the hotel, bringing the feeling of the river through the building.

HILTON PALACIO DEL RIO, *200 South Alamo Street, San Antonio. Tel. 210/222-1400 or 800/445-8667. Rates: $150 to $253. Credit cards accepted.*

The tall Hilton stands on the River Walk; many of its rooms have balconies that overlook the river and downtown. This was one of the first high-rise hotels on the San Antonio River, and the entire building was recently renovated. The hotel is convenient to the convention center and Alamodome.

LA MANSION DEL RIO, *112 College Street, San Antonio. Tel. 210/225-2581 or 800/292-7300, Fax 210/226-0389. Rates: $165 to $290. Credit cards accepted.*

This beautiful hotel offers guests the warmth of traditional Mexican style. From the tiled floors to the white-washed walls, you step into the atmosphere of a refined hacienda. The Mexican decor carries into the spacious and comfortable rooms. Las Canarias, the hotel's main restaurant, serves authentic Mexican food. La Mansion offers the most beautiful views of San Antonio's River Walk from the outdoor seating at the restaurant. Even if you don't stay here, stop in for coffee and dessert.

THE MENGER, *204 Alamo Plaza, San Antonio. Tel 210/223-4361; Fax 228-0022. Rates: $112 to $162. Credit cards accepted.*

When the Menger was built in 1859, it had fifty rooms and two stories. Eight subsequent additions expanded the hotel. The 1909 renovation added much of the decoration that makes the Menger famous today, including marble, columns and ornamentation. The halls leading to the reception area are lined with photos showing the rich history of the hotel. And the baby grand player piano in the lobby hauntingly fills the air with music in the evenings. The hotel itself is a rambling conglomeration of additions. Requesting the oldest section will give you the best location and most pleasing decor. The hotel is built around two large gardens and has lots of windows. Just across the street you will find the Alamo and the River Walk.

EMILY MORGAN RAMADA, *705 East Houston Street, San Antonio. Tel 210/225-8486 or 800/824-6674; Fax 210/225-7227. Rates: $129 to $179. Credit cards accepted.*

The historic building, which dates from the mid-1920s, was built as the city's first medical center. In 1985 it was renovated into a modern hotel. The Emily Morgan offers an excellent location near the Alamo and some of the most reasonable rates downtown. Most of the 177 rooms have a spa bathtub and all have hair dryers and irons. You can wake up to complimentary coffee and newspapers in the lobby each morning. The Yellow Rose dining room serves buffets at breakfast and lunch. Room service is also offered. The hotel has a full health club and sauna rooms.

PLAZA SAN ANTONIO MARRIOTT, *555 South Alamo, San Antonio. Tel. 210/229-1000 or 800/421-1172; Fax 210/229-1418. Rates: Credit cards accepted.*

This Marriott blends the Mexican and American aspects of San Antonio. Sitting on six acres of manicured grounds, the Plaza offers the feeling of a resort in the center of town. The beautiful health club has an indoor gym and outdoor tennis courts, croquet area and jogging routes. The rooms are thoroughly modern with a western style that emphases comfort. This hotel places a premium on service, with two standard room cleanings per day and an evening turn-down service to prepare your bed. All rooms receive morning coffee and a daily newspaper.

MARRIOTT RIVER CENTER, *101 Bowie Street, San Antonio. Tel. 210/224-4555 or 800/228-9290. Rates: $179 to $235. Credit cards accepted.*

The Marriott River Center can be seen when approaching the city; the 1000 rooms are a major part of the River Center Mall. A variety of activities go on each night in the mall; just a few steps away is the River Walk. This hotel is very popular with large tour groups and conventions.

MARRIOTT RIVER WALK, *711 East River Walk. Tel. 210/224-4555 or 800/228-9290. Rates: $179 to $235. Credit cards accepted.*

The older of the two neighboring Marriotts, this one is half the size of the newer hotel. The hotel is rather non-descript in its decor, but remains an adequate travel center. The indoor pool is under a glass atrium and many of the rooms have a pool view.

BED AND BREAKFAST ON THE RIVER, *129 Woodward Place, San Antonio, Tel. 210/225-6333 or 800/730-0019. Rates: $99 to $150. Credit cards accepted.*

The stately old home stands just over the San Antonio River, offering the only bed and breakfast rooms in the center of town. Inside you enter a comfortable Victorian setting with antique accents. The charming rooms have private baths, some have spa baths and balconies. The large penthouse room on the top floor has a large spa bath and French doors that open to a private balcony.

North

DOUBLETREE CLUB HOTEL, *1111 North East Loop 410, San Antonio. Tel. 210/828-9031 or 888/444-CLUB, Fax 210/828-3066. Rates: $59 to $124. Credit cards accepted.*

This newly renovated 227 room hotel is close to the San Antonio International Airport. A fitness room and outdoor pool provide recreation. Business facilities include a lounge with data port computer hookups at each table. Informal dining is available throughout the day. The rooms are large and have areas for working. There is plenty of free parking available.

QUALITY INN AND CONFERENCE CENTER, *10811 Interstate Highway 35, San Antonio. Tel 210/590-4646 or 800/797-1234; Fax 210/967-6717.*

Conveniently located on the major north/south thoroughfare, this is not your typical economy lodging. The grounds are lovely, including a large outdoor pool and a chapel for wedding ceremonies. The motel has only 128 rooms, many are suites and all are spacious. Business travelers will find everything they need for life on the road, including in-room hair dryers, coffee makers, microwaves, alarm clocks and irons. Breakfast is included with all rooms; airport shuttle service is available.

HYATT REGENCY HILL COUNTRY RESORT, *9800 Resort Drive, San Antonio. Tel. 210/647 1234, Fax 210/681-9681. Rates: $190 to $425; Suites $485 to $1700. Credit cards accepted.*

Each morning you greet the day with a splendid breakfast and set off to enjoy all the recreational pleasures of the hill country. The Hyatt resort stands on 200 acres in the west of San Antonio. Designed in the style of a stately ranch house, the resort gives a majestic elegance to the serene hill country setting. The splendid pools have a natural area with a beach and a river for floating. The 18-hole golf course has spectacular views

For those who want true rest, the day spa offers facials, massage and salon services such as manicures and hair cuts. The resort is an ideal retreat for families; special children's activities are held each day. And guests under the age of 18 years can stay free with their parents. Package prices are offered throughout the year.

King William District

A YELLOW ROSE, *229 Madison Street, San Antonio. Tel. 210/229-9903 or 800/ 950-9903. Rates: $95 to $145. Credit cards accepted.*

When the Mueller House was built in 1878, it was a grand residence. Today you can relive a bygone era when you stay at A Yellow Rose. The five rooms each are finished with antique furnishings and have private baths. The largest, the Magnolia Room, can accommodate four adults. Breakfast is served at 9am and prepared with the inn's own recipes.

BECKMANN INN AND CARRIAGE HOUSE, *222 East Guenther, San Antonio. Tel. 210/229-1449 or 800/945-1449. Rates: $90t o $130. Credit cards accepted.*

This historic inn, built in 1886, has five guest rooms, three in the main house and two in the separate carriage house. This elegant home was the residence of one of San Antonio's most prominent families and is on the National Register of Historic Places. You can enjoy the beautifully landscaped yard from the front porch, which wraps around the house. The carriage house rooms each have a sitting area. All rooms have queen size beds, private baths and refrigerators. The gourmet breakfast is served in the main dining room. A two-night minimum stay is required on weekends.

VICTORIAN LADY, *421 Howard Street, San Antonio. Tel. 210/224-2524 or 800/879-7116, Fax 210/224-2524. Rates: $70. Credit cards accepted.*

The stately Victorian home has seven guest rooms, each furnished in the period style. The home was built in 1898, at the height of the fancy architecture for which the Victorian period is famous. Children under the age of nine years may not stay at the house.

WHERE TO EAT
River Walk

ACAPULCO SAM'S BURGER JOINT, *212 College Street, San Antonio, Tel. 210/212-SAMS. Credit cards accepted.*

Thick, juicy burgers are featured here. A variety of appetizers such as nachos go with seven fruity types of frozen margaritas. The huge warehouse style restaurant attracts many who want the festive atmosphere of a nightclub. This is a good place to come for an informal meal and a few hours of noisy fun.

THE BAYOUS RIVERSIDE, *517 North Prensa, San Antonio. Tel. 210/223-6403. Credit cards accepted.*

A mild touch of Louisiana flavors mixes with the unusual combination of Creole and southwestern spices. The seafood of The Bayous Riverside is fresh and specialties include fresh fish from the Gulf of Mexico. The riverside patio seating is an excellent place to enjoy a long Sunday brunch, served every Sunday from 11:30am to 3pm. Monday to Thursday and Sunday 11:30am to 11pm; Friday and Saturday 11:30 to midnight.

BOUDRO'S, *421 East Commerce Street, San Antonio. Tel. 210/224-8484. Credit cards accepted.*

The aroma of steaks hot off the grill whets the taste buds upon entering this restaurant. The repertoire featured on the menu is not that of an ordinary steak house. The Creole roots of the cooking is accented by southwestern spices. The cactus margarita is the current specialty drink of choice. Monday to Thursday and Sunday, 11am to 11pm; Friday and Saturday 11am to midnight.

CASA RIO, *430 East Commerce, San Antonio. Tel. 210/225-6718. Credit cards accepted.*

You are sure to eat genuine Tex-Mex food here – Casa Rio practically invented it. The restaurant first opened in 1946 and is one of the first establishments on the River Walk. The recipes reputedly have been passed down in the family. Open daily 11am to 11pm.

DICK'S LAST RESORT, *406 Navarro Street, San Antonio. Tel. 210/ 224-0026. Credit cards accepted.*

Be certain to bring your sense of humor to Dick's, where both beer and ribs are served by the bucketful. The informal atmosphere, rows of picnic tables, and offbeat wait staff make for a fun, informal meal. You can chow down on just about any fried treat imaginable, such as "Fried Shrimpies" ($6.95) and onion rings ($1.95). The sandwiches are the best on part of the menu, the Marinated Chicken Breast is best with the bacon and cheese option. The burgers are under $4 and downright juicy. The rowdiest establishment on the River Walk. Open daily, 11am to 2am.

THE FIG TREE, *733 River Walk, San Antonio, Tel. 210/224-1976. Credit cards accepted.*

The Fig Tree is part of the restored La Villita Shopping Center. The charming restaurant serves the finest traditional dishes, like lobster and beef Wellington. The pricey menu and elegant decor are sure to impress diners. Taking the time to savor the food and the atmosphere is worth it, since the dining here should be a total experience in indulgence. Open daily 6pm until late.

IBIZA PATIO BAR & RESTAURANT, *715 River Walk, San Antonio. Tel. 210/270-0773. Credit cards accepted.*

This is one of the few Spanish restaurants in San Antonio. The menu offers dishes with a Mediterranean flair. Tapas are the specialty, and there is no better place to enjoy tapas and cocktails than this brightly colored restaurant. The full menu includes breakfast, lunch and dinner. Bands perform on weekends. Round off your meal with the excellent cappuccino and luscious deserts. Monday to Thursday and Sunday 6:30am to midnight; Friday and Saturday 6:30am to 2am.

PAESANO'S, *111 East Commerce, San Antonio. Tel. 210/22-PASTA.*

The first Paesano's opened its doors in 1969 and quickly became the standard of Italian food in south Texas. The best dishes on the menu are still the traditional Italian specialties, such as Veal Marsala ($15.95) and Osso Buco Milanese ($15.95). Fish, pizza and a long list of pasta give all tastes a good deal of choice. The wine selection includes Italian reds that perfectly accompany the food.

PRESIDIO, *245 East Commerce Street #101, San Antonio Tel. 210/472-2265. Credit cards accepted.*

Italian cooking highlighted with Mediterranean influences comprise the menu. Non-traditional use of spices and sauces bring together European and Mexican cooking for such creations as Grilled Game Hen Mole ($12.95). The distinct tastes come together for bold and pleasing creations. The Snapper Ancho ($15.95) has a spicy sauce of ancho chiles and pesto, with artichoke hearts and shitake mushrooms on top. Presidio offers an extensive selection of wine and cigars. Sunday to Wednesday 11am to 11pm; Thursday to Saturday 11am to midnight.

ZUNI GRILL, *223 Losoya, San Antonio. Tel 210/227-0864. Credit cards accepted.*

Zuni Grill joins the flavors of Mexico and New Mexico. The menu is an eclectic collection of nuevo Tex-Mex cuisine. The mesquite smoke flavored salsa exemplifies how Zuni takes a standard (like red salsa) and puts a Texan twist to it (adding smoked flavor). You will find surprises on the menu, like the appetizer of Applewood Smoked Salmon ($7.95) served with bagels. The food is lighter and probably far healthier than traditional Tex-Mex cooking. The Blue Corn Enchiladas ($10.95) are a sure bet, with smoked chicken and spicy green sauce. Vegetarians will find the Grilled Vegetable Fajitas ($11.95) flavorful and more than filling.

Central San Antonio

EARL ABEL'S, *4200 Broadway, San Antonio. Tel. 210/822-3358. Credit cards accepted.*

Since 1933, Earl Abel's has been serving the flavor of home-cooked meals in a neighborhood setting. The decoration dates from the same era, as do the bee-hive hairdos that some of the waitresses sport. The best meal of the day here is breakfast. Long-time customers know the staff on a personal basis, and they come in for leisurely conversations with their meals. Oatmeal, pancakes and eggs highlight the breakfast selections. Heartier appetites will enjoy the hot roast beef sandwich ($5.50) or the Hand Breaded Beef Cutlet ($6); both come with fluffy mashed potatoes. But the real centerpiece of the menu is the list of desserts. The lemon chess pie and the chocolate ice box pie are legendary. All the desserts are made at Earl Abel's. Open daily, 6:30am to 1am. Take Broadway north from downtown to get to Earl Abel's.

CARRANZA'S, *701 Austin Street, San Antonio. Tel. 210/223-0903. Credit cards accepted.*

Carrranza's stands alone, both in the dining experience and location. The restaurant is in the family store, a building that dates from 1920 and is located in an area which was once an industrial and railroad center. The unusual location is enhanced by the unique interior, walls made of rough limestone and tall old west-style windows that overlook the neighboring train tracks. The menu offers fish, mesquite smoked barbecue and Tex-Mex and Italian dishes. The variety does not lower the quality. The fish is accented with your choice of six delicate sauces. The scallops ($11.95) are best with Venustiano sauce, a lemon butter sauce. Try the Vera Cruz, a spicy tomato sauce, with the Red snapper ($16.50). The Italian cuisine is bursting with flavor. During lunch you can order brisket ($6.95), pork ribs ($7.95) or combination plates. The downstairs deli serves food-to-go. Carranza's is just southeast of the intersection of Interstate Highway 35 and Highway 281. Open Monday to Saturday, lunch 11am to 2pm (weekdays only), dinner 5pm to 11pm.

LA MARGARITA, *120 Produce Row, San Antonio. Tel. 210/227-7140. Credit cards accepted.*

La Margarita is known for serving large plates of fajitas, giant margaritas and blazingly spicy salsa. The tables outdoors give diners a festive atmosphere right on Market Square. The food is moderately priced and tame enough for the most sensitive palates.

MI TIERRA, *218 Produce Row, San Antonio. Tel. 210/225-1262. Open daily, 24 hours. Credit cards accepted.*

You can satisfy your Tex-Mex craving anytime at Mi Tierra, since the restaurant is open round the clock. This family-owned establishment has been serving food since 1941. Mariachis stroll through the restaurant offering serenades during dinner. Mi Tierra is a tradition for natives and tourists alike. The food is known as good, standard Tex-Mex; the chicken mole enchiladas are the most exotic dish on the menu.

PECAN STREET MARKET DELI, *152 East Pecan Street, San Antonio, Tel. 210/227-3226.*

Hams and sausage hang in the window, giving away the fact that this is an authentic old-fashioned deli. In the heart of San Antonio's business district, Pecan Street Deli caters to the hurried business crowd. This does not mean they serve fast food. The mufallettas are overstuffed, and the vegetarian pita will not disappoint. Mediterranean specialties such as hummus, couscous and Greek salads round out the menu. Monday to Friday 7:30am to 5pm; Saturday 10am to 6pm.

SCHILLO'S, *424 East Commerce Street, San Antonio. Tel. 210/223-6692.*

At Schillo's you can get a taste of San Antonio's German Heritage. Schillo's serves weinerschnitzel, bratwurst and their very own root beer. This is a San Antonio tradition you should not miss. Monday to Saturday 7am to 8:30pm.

SEA ISLAND, *322 West Rector, San Antonio. Tel. 210/342-7771.*

This informal seafood house is no secret to locals, who crowd in for lunch and dinner. The secret recipes for the breading, the highest quality seafood and large charcoal grills come together for seafood that surpasses most formal restaurants. The Coho Salmon ($7.75) is a large fillet with lemon and butter, and Lemon Pepper Fish ($7.95) almost melt right into your tastebuds. The Charcoal Broiled Shrimp Platter ($8.50) is three kabob skewers full of shrimp grilled to perfection. The platter is almost more food than you can eat, with french fries, cole slaw and hush puppies. You can always substitute a baked potato or corn on the cob.

The excellent lunch specials ($4.25 to $5.95) draw a crowd large enough to cause a 30 minute wait even on weekdays. Sea Island is located next to North Star Mall.

SEEING THE SIGHTS
The Alamo
For many, the **Alamo** symbolizes the Texas. *Located at 300 Alamo Plaza, in the center of downtown near the River Walk. Tel 210/225-1391, open Monday to Saturday 9am to 5:30pm; in the summer hours are extended until 6:30pm; admission free; donations accepted.* The siege of the Alamo is remembered as the single battle that represents the sacrifice that led to the making of Texas. On March 6, 1836, the Alamo fell after a 13 day siege.

The defenders of the Alamo knew that they would face certain death against the 4000 soliders under the command of one of Mexico's strongest leaders, General Santa Anna. Many of the founding fathers of Texas died in the siege, including Colonel James Bowie and Colonel William Barret Travis. Many of the 189 defenders of the Alamo were not Texans, including Davy Crockett and his Tennessee Boys. A number of women and one child survived the attack. Over 600 Mexican soldiers were killed.

The Alamo is actually the **Mission San Antonio do Valero**, and was the first colonial structure built in the area. The name "Alamo" comes from the commander of Mexican forces who used the Alamo as a military camp at the turn of the nineteenth century. A museum presents a multimedia account of the siege of the Alamo. Part of the grounds are reconstructed to show the daily life of the clergy and Native Americans who inhabited the mission. The Alamo Library is open to the public for research and photocopy services.

When you visit the Alamo, you see the famous inner building that has been portrayed in movies and novels. This small stone structure actually stood in the center of the Alamo grounds, surrounded by the outer walls. In the park in front of the Alamo stands a modern monument to the defenders. The names of the 189 men who died defending the Alamo are engraved on the monument.

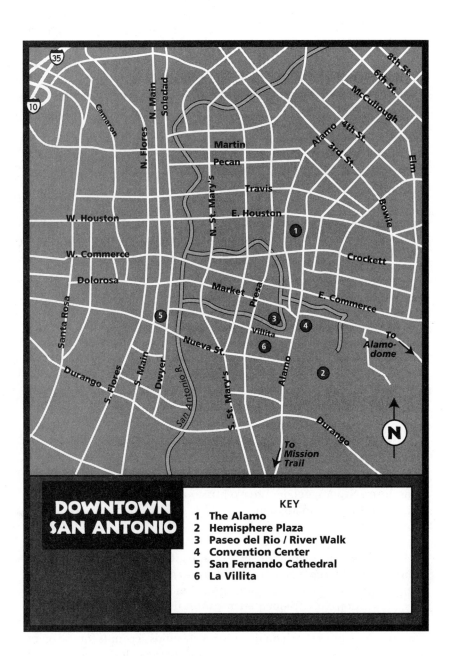

**DOWNTOWN
SAN ANTONIO**

KEY

1 The Alamo
2 Hemisphere Plaza
3 Paseo del Rio / River Walk
4 Convention Center
5 San Fernando Cathedral
6 La Villita

The River Walk

The main entrance of the **River Walk**, *315 East Commerce Street,* is located across the street from the Alamo. The pedestrian thoroughfare follows the San Antonio River through the downtown area. Tour deck-boats scoot along the river all day and into the night. Restaurants, shops and bars line the way. The **Rivercenter Mall**, *100 Alamo Plaza*, has a multitude of department and specialty stores, restaurants and entertainment. The **IMAX theater**, *River Center Mall, Tel. 210/225-4629*, shows special IMAX films and occasionally runs new releases.

For the flavor of the past and the shopping and dining experiences of today, visit **La Villita**, *418 Villita, Tel. 210/ 207-8610, daily 10am to 6pm* – the Little Village. It is a group of twenty adobe and wood homes that date from the period of Mexican rule. The buildings have been restored; some are shops and there is an historical exhibit. Large shade trees make this a comfortable retreat from the afternoon sun. Along the River Walk you will see the tiered park which serves as outdoor seating for **Arneson Open Air Theater**. The stage is across the river in the rock wall. During the summer frequent musical performances grace the stage. La Villita is located across the street from the convention center. You can reach La Villita by the River Walk or downtown between South Alamo and Nueva Streets.

The Missions Of San Antonio

Just south of downtown you can visit the sites of some of the first colonizations in Texas. The Spanish missions are the legacy of Franciscan Friars. The Alamo was part of this trail of missions, but is now regarded as more of a war memorial than a religious settlement. To reach the **Mission Trail**, from highway 281 south, take highway 90 west. Exit Mission Street and follow the Mission Trail Signs.

From north to south you will find:
• Nuestra Senora de la Purisima Conception Mission
• San Jose y San Miguel de Aguayo Mission
• San Juan Capistrano Mission
• San Francisco do la Espada Mission
Each is described below:

The **Nuestra Senora de la Purisima Conception Mission**, *807 Mission Street, open daily 9am to 6pm; admission free,* is partially restored and there are no tours of the grounds or services held in the church. Due to this, the mission is less frequented by visitors than the others, but this adds to its charm. The mission was settled in 1731, but took 20 years to build. The massive stone church on the mission grounds accounts for the many years that went into construction. This is one of the oldest stone churches in North America. Anyone interested in not only seeing but feeling the history of the mission settlements will enjoy a peaceful stop at Conception Mission.

San Jose y San Miguel de Aguayo Mission, *6539 San Jose Street, Tel. 210/932-1001, open daily 8am to 5pm; admission free*, is the largest of the missions and the first to be established. In the year 1720 ground broke on the famous mission, but the main building phase did not conclude until more than 60 years later, when the church was completed in 1782. This was a working mission, with granary facilities, a flour mill and various workshops on the grounds. Tours of the grounds, which include quarters for Native Americans, offer a glimpse of a bygone era.

Mass is held daily at 8am. On Sunday the service is in Spanish at 7:45am and in English at 9am and 10:30am. At noon Mariachi Mass is held featuring traditional Mariachi music.

The beautiful grounds of **San Juan Capistrano Mission**, *9101 Graf Street, open daily 9am to 6pm; admission free*, are an idyllic setting for an afternoon picnic. There are no tours of the mission, but the buildings are lovely. Mass in English is held Monday to Wednesday, 6:30pm; Saturday, 5pm. Spanish Mass is held Friday 6:30pm; and Sunday 10:30am.

The smallest of the missions, **San Francisco do la Espada Mission**, *Espada Road, open daily, 9am to 5pm; admission free*, is not completely reconstructed. The mission was built in 1731. The grounds overlooking a creek are probably the loveliest of all the missions. You can walk among the ruins of the original walls and housing quarters. The church is restored but public services are not held. Tours are available. To reach the mission, take Espada Road to the very end; it leads directly to the mission.

King William District

The **San Antonio Conservation Society**, *107 King William Street, Tel 210/224-6163*, provides brochures which detail a walking tour of the King William District and describe the history of the area. After working hours you may pick up a brochure from the box on the front gate of the Conservation Society office.

San Antonio is home to one of the nation's largest flour mills, Pioneer Flour. The **Guenther House**, *205 East Guenther, Tel. 210/227-1061, open Monday to Saturday 9am to 5pm; Sunday 8am to 2pm; admission free*, holds a collection of historic items that trace the history of the mill. This house is one of the historic German mansions of the King William Historic District, and viewing the Guenther House alone is well worth the trip. The museum restaurant is open during regular museum hours. This is a pleasant setting for a light lunch or afternoon coffee.

The **Steves Homestead Museum**, *509 King William Street, Tel. 210/ 225-5924, open daily 10am to 4:15pm*, provides a glimpse into the daily life of the prestigious German merchant community of the nineteenth century. This Victorian house has been restored to its original splendor. The furnishings represent the period and the grounds are maintained according to the original style.

Museums

The **San Antonio Museum of Art**, *200 West Jones Avenue, Tel 210/978-8100, Monday to Saturday 10am to 5pm; Tuesday 10am to 9pm; Sunday noon to 5pm; admission varies, free on Tuesday from 3pm to 9pm*, boasts an exceptional representation of art from around the world as well as excellent traveling exhibitions. The permanent collection includes Latin American and European masterpieces in oil and some sculpture. The museum is housed in the former Lone Star Brewery. The renovation is a beautiful mix of rough, old texture and modern improvements.

The small but impressive collection of the **McNay Art Museum**, *6000 North New Braunfels Road, Tel. 210/824-5368, closed Monday; Tuesday to Saturday 10am to 5pm; Sunday noon to 5pm; admission fee*, includes work from the masters Picasso, Van Gogh and Monet, among others. The beautiful museum was once a private home. The grounds are a relaxing park-like setting with flowers and fountains. Touring exhibits of painting, photography and are featured throughout the year. The McNay Museum is located at the intersection of US Highway 81 and New Braunfels Road.

San Antonio Children's Museum, *305 East Houston Street, Tel. 210/ 21-CHILD, closed Monday; Tuesday to Saturday 9am to 6pm; Sunday noon to 5pm; admission fee*, features exhibits that encourage children to participate and learn. Children from as young as two years old to the age of ten will find something of interest at this museum. The goal is to encourage children to participate in learning about the cultures of San Antonio.

What could be more fun than climbing a giant tree-house? This is just one of the interesting exhibits at the **Witte Museum**, *3801 Broadway, Tel. 210/357-1900, Monday to Saturday 9am to 6pm*. This science museum has a number of permanent displays that deal with the history and wildlife of Texas. The ancient rock paintings of the Pecos Valley are featured. You can tour the three restored historic homes on the museum grounds.

The Texas Rangers are a legendary part of Texas history. Their story is displayed at the **Pioneer, Trail Drivers and Texas Rangers Memorial Museum**, *3805 Broadway Street, Tel. 210/822-9011, open daily 11am to 4pm; admission fee but children under five years of age get in free*. The cattle drives that shaped the lore of Texas are documented in this museum housed in the historic Memorial Building dating from 1936. The ruggedness of the frontier is portrayed with displays featuring guns and weapons, accounts of the Texas Rangers stories and a memorial to Rangers who died in the line of duty. The museum is located in Brackenridge Park, next to the Witte Museum.

One of the only museums dedicated to the lonely life of the frontier, **The Cowboy Museum**, *209 Alamo Plaza, Tel. 210/229-1257, open daily 10am to 7pm; admission fee,* is a private collection of memorabilia. The museum contains a replica of a frontier town.

In the heart of downtown San Antonio, you will find the **Hertzberg Circus Museum**, *210 Market Street, Tel. 210/207-7810 or 207-7819, Monday to Saturday 10am to 5pm; from June to August open Sunday 1pm to 5pm; closed Sunday during other months.* The museum is an entertaining tribute to the history of the traveling circus of yesteryear. The museum has unique pieces from turn-of-the-century circus shows. On weekends the Hertzberg Museum sponsors films and entertainment, such as shows of juggling and magic. The Hertzberg Museum is on the corner of South Prensa and West Market Streets.

The various cultures that make up Texas are represented at the **Institute of Texas Cultures**, *801 South Bowie Street, Tel. 210/558-2300, closed Monday; Tuesday to Sunday 9am to 5pm; $5 admission includes 2 hours parking.* The Institute is far more than a museum portraying the life of the Texas frontier. This is a learning experience, worthwhile for anyone who wants to gain a greater understanding of the foundations of modern Texan culture. You will see replicas of frontier families and the homes in which they lived. The Native American cultures of the Texas territory are well represented. The Institute is part of the University of Texas at San Antonio and publishes excellent books about the peoples of Texas. The Dome Show, a multimedia show, gives insight to the diversity of the people of Texas. The Institute of Texan Culture is located at the HemisFair Park, at the corner of Bowie and Durango Streets.

The **Lone Star Brewery**, *600 Lone Star Boulevard, Tel. 210/270-9467, open daily 9:30am to 5pm; admission fee,* has two museums on its grounds. You can tour the brewery and enjoy a drink afterward, and then visit the museums. The **Buckhorn Hall of Horns**, **Fins and Feathers** has on display 3,500 stuffed animals that have been hunted throughout the world. The Hall of Feathers features game birds, and likewise, the Hall of Fins exhibits fish. The **Texas History Wax Museum** and the San Antonio home of William Sidney Porter, **O. Henry House**, are also on the brewery grounds.

One of San Antonio's more unusual collections is housed in the **Texas Transportation Museum**, *11731 Wetmore Road, Tel. 210/490-3554, Thursday to Sunday 9am to 4pm, donations accepted.* Horse-drawn carriages and trains show the development of transportation, which was crucial in the taming of the Texas frontier. The museum is located in McAllister Park.

Military Museums of San Antonio

San Antonio has a long history as a military stronghold. The military bases in the area specialize in aviation and medical training. Military buffs will find hours of fascinating displays at the museums housed at San Antonio's bases.

The **Fort Sam Houston Museum**, *Harry Wurzbach Road, Building 123, Fort Sam Houston, Tel. 210/221-1886, Wednesday to Sunday 10am to 4pm,* traces the history of the United States military in the San Antonio area. Fort Sam Houston is a piece of history as well. The base first began operations in the mid-1800s as a cavalry headquarters. The officers quarters are grand old homes from the first half of this century. The museum is located on the corner of Harry Wurzbach Road and Stanley Road.

Across the street you will find the **US Army Medical Department Museum**, *Harry Wurzbach and Stanley Roads, Fort Sam Houston, Tel. 210/221-6358, closed Monday, Tuesday to Sunday 10am to 4pm; admission free,* which shows how medical care was administered during wartime. Displays feature medical equipment from foreign countries including Russia, Germany and China.

The displays inside the **Lackland Aviation Museum**, *Lackland Air Force Base, Tel. 210/671-3055, Tuesday to Saturday, 8am to 4:45pm, closed Sunday and Monday; admission free,* show the inner workings of airplanes and the history of early military aviation. While outside you will find the planes themselves, a collection of 43 historic planes on display throughout Lackland Air Force Base. You can walk through military aviation history at the park-like display of planes. Among the older planes are the C-119 Flying Boxcar and P-38 World War II fighters. This is one of the few places you can see an SR-71 Blackbird, the fastest plane ever developed, which was used for high-level aerial reconnaissance during the Cold War. To reach the base from Interstate Highway 10 west, take Highway 90 west, exit Military Drive and follow the signs to Lackland Air Force Base. The military police officer at the gate will ask you to present photo identification and will provide directions.

The **Edward H. White Memorial Museum**, *Brooks Air Force Base, Tel. 210/536-2203 or 531-9767, Monday to Friday, 8am to 4pm; closed weekends; admission free,* also known as **Hangar 9**, traces the history of modern military medicine and aviation. Of particular interest is the section which deals with the development of aerospace medicine. Attached to the museum is the Flight Nursing Annex, which shows the history of flight nurses. The hangar itself is a museum piece, built entirely of wood and dating from the World War I period. The museum is named for Edward White, the first astronaut to walk in space.

Parks

The largest park in San Antonio, **Brackenridge Park** is the home of the **San Antonio Zoo**, *3900 Saint Mary's Street, open daily 9:30am to 5pm; admission $6 adults, $4 children.* The zoo has the third largest animal population of all the zoos in the United States. The wildlife of each continent is represented. You can ride atop a camel during the summer. The zoo has an aquarium section that takes you under the sea.

Various climates of Texas are represented on the city's 33 acre **Botanical Gardens**, *555 Funston Street, Tuesday to Sunday 9am to 6pm.* Wildflowers, a fragrance garden and a biblical garden are featured. The gardens have a 90,000 square foot conservatory which replicates desert and tropical environments. The tea room is a quiet place to relax and enjoy greenery.

A lovely, tranquil place for a stroll is the **Japanese Tea Garden**, *3800 North Saint Mary's Street, Tel. 210/821-3120, daily 8am until nightfall, admission free.* The native Texas plants arranged in a Japanese-style setting are offset by paths and water.

NIGHTLIFE & ENTERTAINMENT
Nightlife

CHAMPION'S SPORTS BAR, *Rivercenter Mall, San Antonio. Tel. 210/226-7171.*

Champion's is the armchair quarterbacks' retreat. The walls are full of antique sports memorabilia, and the modern sports scene is represented with 16 television sets which bring the latest events via satellite. Should you not want to sit inside and watch sports, the bar has outdoor tables along the River Walk. On weekends a DJ plays loud dance tunes. Open daily from 11am to 2am.

JIM CULLUM'S LANDING, *123 Losoya Street, San Antonio. Tel. 210/223-7266.*

The Landing brings sophistication to the River Walk. This small jazz club is brimming with talent. Inside every night except Sundays you can hear the modern jazz great Jim Cullum and his band. Standard bar drinks and light fare is served. The small outdoor patio has its own band. Monday to Friday 4pm to 1am; Saturday and Sunday noon to 1am.

HARD ROCK CAFE, *111 Crockett Street, San Antonio, Tel. 210/224-ROCK. Credit cards accepted.*

The gingham tablecloths in the Hard Rock Cafe give this chain restaurant an more-than-casual feeling. The food is standard, and service not always on par. Naturally most of the clientele are tourists. The entrance is near the River Walk. Open daily 11am to 2am.

MAD DOG'S BRITISH PUB, *123 Losoya Street, San Antonio. Tel. 210/ 222-0220.*

A pub in San Antonio stands out as different from the usual bar. Just the place to sip on a single malt scotch or a pint of British brew. British-style pub food is served until midnight. Open daily 10am to 2am

THE LABORATORY BREWING COMPANY, *7310 Jones Maltsberger, San Antonio. Tel. 210/824-1997.*

The Laboratory is located in an historical building which was formerly the Alamo Cement Company. The brew pub always offers six varieties on tap. The signature brews such as Alamo Amber Ale are made by one of the best brew-masters in the region. On Wednesdays and weekends you can enjoy live music.

Entertainment

MAJESTIC THEATER, *212 East Houston Street, San Antonio. Tel. 210/ 226-3333.*

The Majestic is an historic theater, home of the San Antonio Symphony. The theater is on Houston Street, which was a major street in the early part of the century. The beautiful old buildings show off the glamour of yesteryear.

SIX FLAGS FIESTA TEXAS, *17,000 West Interstate Highway 10, San Antonio. Tel. 210/697-5050. Tel 210/697-5050. Admission adults $31; children $21.*

This theme park has thrilling rides and a water park, but the center of the entertainment is the shows. The cartoon character theme shows are performed on five stages. The latest addition to the park is the Joker's Revenge Roller-Coaster. Or you can choose a less exciting zip through cartoon land on the Roadrunner Express ride. Special celebrations are held for Cinco de Mayo, the Fourth of July and Labor Day. Take Interstate Highway west from San Antonio to Loop 1604. The park is at Exit 555.

SEA WORLD, *10,500 Sea World Drive, San Antonio. Tel. 210/523-3611. Admission Adults $29.95, children $19.95.*

This is the only Sea World theme park in Texas. The huge complex is part zoo, part amusement park. Free shuttles, *Tel. 210/228-9776*, are available from downtown San Antonio.

RIPLEY'S BELIEVE IT OR NOT THEATER OF WAX, *301 Alamo Plaza, San Antonio. Tel. 210/224-9299.*

There's more good clean fun to be had at Ripley's Believe It or Not Theater of Wax. Over 200 wax figures of the famous and infamous. The museum contains a collection of cartoon-related memorabilia from Ripley's own collection. Sunday to Thursday 9am to 7pm; Friday and Saturday 9am to 10pm.

SPORTS & RECREATION

Spectator Sports

The **Alamodome**, *100 Montana Street, Tel. 210/207-3663*, is the largest arena in south Texas. The enormous stadium seats 65,000 hosts events and concerts. Sports events, including football games, are held here. This is the home turf of San Antonio's professional basketball team, the Spurs. You can reach the Alamodome from Interstate Highway 37 at the Market Street exit.

Just north of San Antonio, **La Retama Race Track**, *One Retama Parkway, Selma, Tel. 210/651-7000*, has horse racing from June through November. Admission ranges from $2.50 to $20. Races are run throughout the day and races from other tracks around the nation are shown in the building. The complex has restaurants, private rooms and club seating. Take exit 174-A from Interstate Highway 35.

The **San Antonio Dragons**, the city's International Hockey League (IHL) team, set the ice ablaze from October to March. They play against the 10 teams of the western conference, which includes the Houston Aeros. Tickets cost from $8 to $12 and can be purchased from the Dragon's box office, *Tel. 210/229-1524*, on the day of the game until 3pm. The **Dragon's Souvenir Shop**, *600 East Market Street*, also sells tickets.

SHOPPING

Near the Alamo you will find a store which sells Texas memorabilia. The **History Shop**, *713 East Houston Street, Tel 210/229-9855*, has interesting items and historical reproductions, which are not your average souvenirs.

The **Rivercenter Mall**, *849 East Commerce Street, Tel. 210/225-0000*, stands proudly in the center of the city. The mall is an entertainment center on the River Walk, with many restaurants including **Morton's of Chicago**, an IMAX Theater and an outdoor stage. Over 1300 stores and shops provide plenty of shopping for everyone.

The most exclusive shopping center in San Antonio is **North Star Mall**, *Loop 410 at McCullogh, Tel. 210/340-6627*. Over 200 stores and shops include some of the country's best department stores, Neiman Marcus, Saks Fifth Avenue and Marshall Field's. The mall is open Monday to Saturday 10am to 9pm and Sunday noon to 6pm.

La Villita, The "Little Village," was a group of twenty modest homes dating from the nineteenth century. Today La Villita has kept its traditional look and is now a shopping area featuring art galleries and restaurants.

EXCURSIONS & DAY TRIPS

For a trip to the wilds of Africa without leaving the comfort of Texas, visit the **Foothills Safari Camp**, *Fossil Rim Wildlife Center, Glen Rose, Tel. 800/245-0771*. This 3000 acre wildlife reserve has close to 1000 species of exotic animals, many of which are endangered. The only shots fired on these safari trips will be the shutters of cameras, though. The safari trips are similar to those of Africa; however at the Foothills Camp you are able to return to a comfortable lodge setting. For those who enjoy the thrill of the great outdoors, extended trips with overnight stays in luxury tents are available.

A piece of central Texas for everyone to enjoy is the **Hill Country State Natural Area** in Bandera. Once the more than 5000 acres of streams, rocky hills and canyons belonged to a rancher. Today the state operates the nature preserve and it is a hiker's dream, with 36 miles of trails of varying difficulty. The park is located 45 miles northwest of San Antonio.

Fishermen should not miss **Choke Canyon Reservoir**, *Callihan, Tel. 512/786-3868*. The early spring is best for catching largemouth bass, and white crappie is abundant in the late spring. This is one of the few places that has water clear enough for nighttime bow-fishing. Camping facilities from primitive sites to camper hookups are available. Play areas for children, swimming areas and nature trails offer pastimes other than fishing. From San Antonio, take Highway 281 west, exit Highway 72 and travel west for 11 miles. Take Park Road 8 to the entrance of the park.

PRACTICAL INFORMATION

American Automobile Association (AAA), *13,431 San Pedro Avenue. Tel. 210/736-4691*

Time and Temperature, *Tel. 210/226-3232*

Travel Advisories and road conditions, *Tel. 210/533-9171*

Main Post Office, *10,410 Perrin Beitel Street, San Antonio. Tel. 210/ 657-8300.*

The **Visitors Bureau**, *121 North Alamo Street, San Antonio, Tel. 800/ 447-3372*, can provide specific information about almost any attraction or event in the area.

San Antonio operates an information and reservation service for hotel and motel rooms. Contact the **Lodging Line**, *Tel. 800/858-4303*, for assistance in booking a room.

CASTROVILLE

The small town of **Castroville** is only 15 miles west of San Antonio, one of the oldest settlements of European immigrants in Texas. Henri

Castro, a Jewish Frenchman of Portuguese descent, received a land grant and founded the town in 1842. The first settlers in the town hailed from the Alsace region shared by France and Germany and came to Texas in 1844. They brought the architecture and food of their homeland, and these traditions have stood the test of time. The local Alsatian Club keeps the language a living part of the community.

Nearly 100 historic buildings fill the center of town. Many are the original handiwork of the settlers who carved a life out of the rugged riverfront territory. The quaint shops are a blend of European and Mexican frontier styles.

ARRIVALS & DEPARTURES

Little Castroville does have its own **Municipal Airport**, which is really a landing strip in the middle of farm land. The airport is used for private air traffic. The airport is located on Farm Road 471, just south of Highway 90 East.

Castroville is served by the **Kerrville Bus Company**, *Tel. 800/256-4723*, and **Greyhound/Trailways Bus Company**, *Tel. 800/231-2222*.

The **Castro Garden Club**, *Tel. 830/ 931-2298*, hosts walking tours of selected historic homes. These tours can be arranged for large or small groups by appointment.

WHERE TO STAY

LANDMARK INN, *420 East Florence Street, Castroville. Tel. 830/931-2133, Fax 538-3858. Rate: $75 to $100. Credit cards accepted.*

This was once a stagecoach stop for adventurers on El Camino Real, the King's Highway. The Inn is part of a state park which has hiking trails, fishing and canoeing on the Medina River. The inn offers eight comfortable rooms; the decor represents the 1940's, when the inn was refurbished. The 1981 renovation brought the rooms to date. Not every room is fully modern, though. Some do not have air conditioning, which could be uncomfortable in the summer. All rooms include breakfast. The Landmark Inn is not always open for visitors. Make a reservation well in advance of your expected stay. The State Park has camping facilities as well. You may camp at a primitive site or choose a cabin with electricity and water. Cabin rates range from $35 to $79 per night.

THE ALSATIAN INN, *1651 Highway 90 West, Castroville. Tel. 830/ 538-2262 or 800/446-8528. Rates: $59 to $74. Credit cards accepted.*

The Alsatian Inn is a Best Western Hotel, so you have the comfort of a modern room and facilities for your stay. The decor is true to the Alsatian theme, with French doors in each room, and historic photos of the region decorating the walls. The inn has an outdoor pool and can arrange transportation to the city golf course. Britschs' is the restaurant at the inn. The good American food is accented by a casual dining room. Entrees range from $6 to $10. The restaurant is open form 7am to 9pm each day.

WHERE TO EAT

THE ALSATIAN, *402 Angelo Street, Castroville. Tel. 830/931-3260, Fax 931-3259. Credit cards accepted.*

The Alsatian is a step back in time. Located in an historical home, the restaurant serves delicious European cuisine. The sauces, which enhance the seafood and steak, are made from Alsatian recipes. The wine selection offers a good variety of vintages, and the imported beer accompanies the heartier menu selections well. This is the most intimate spot for a meal in Castroville. Open daily for lunch 11am to 2pm; dinner Thursday to Sunday 5pm to 9pm.

LA NORMANDIE, *1302 Fiorella, Castroville. Tel. 830/538-3070. Credit cards accepted.*

La Normandie is true to its name. Traditional French food constitutes the main part of the menu. German dishes provide the right blend to make this a representation of Alsace. The romantic interior compliments the historic dwelling that houses the restaurant. Wednesday to Friday 5pm to 9pm, Saturday, 11am to 2pm and 5pm to 9pm, Sunday 11:30am to 8pm. Entrees range from $10 to $17. La Normandie is at the corner of Fiorella and Paris Streets.

HABY'S BAKERY, *207 Highway 290 East, Castroville. Credit cards accepted.*

This small bakery warms the stomach and soul with Alsatian delicacies such as cookies and pastries. The fresh bread is delicious and would be a welcome addition to a picnic. If you are passing through town, this is a good place for a coffee stop. Monday to Saturday 5:30am to 7pm; closed Sunday.

DAN'S MEAT MARKET, *Paris Street, Castroville. Tel. 830/931-2049.*

You can escape from Texas barbecue with a visit to Dan's Meat Market. The front of the store has a deli with a full selection of European-style meat and cheese. The back of the market has an old world beer hall where you can cool off with your favorite brew. Monday to Friday 8am to 6pm, Saturday 8am to 5pm.

SEEING THE SIGHTS

Religion has been at the center of life in Castroville since the first European settlers arrived. The oldest churches in the area are still used for services. There are nearly 100 structures which are recognized as historic landmarks, and many historic markers around town. The ten blocks which have the greatest concentration of historic places are in the heart of the town. From Highway 90, take either Angelo Street or Fiorella Street; these are respectively the western and eastern boundaries of the town center. Madrid Street in the north and Florence Street in the south enclose this imaginary rectangle.

The center of Alsatian heritage is Houston Square, at the corner of Angelo and Madrid Streets. From March to September, on the second Saturday of each month **Market Trail Days**, a large crafts market, is held.

The **Saint Louis Catholic Church**, which stands across from Houston Square, is one of the most predominant landmarks in Castroville. The tall sturdy steeple stands accents the somber Gothic lines of this simple church. Much of its obvious character comes from the local limestone which gives the church a style which reflects roughness of the land. You can see the layers of change in the cuts of limestone cubes over the two years of construction. The church was completed in 1870 and the pews and altars from that time remain in use. Services are held on Sunday at 8am and 10:30am. The church is open to visitors daily form 8am to 4pm.

ST. LOUIS DAY CELEBRATION

Every year the town of Castroville remembers its founding and shares its traditions with the St. Louis Day Celebration, held on the third Sunday of August. Alsatian food and drink, which most closely resembles German, is plentiful and made in the old-fashioned manner. Traditional costumes and music enliven the dances and festivities.

The older and far more humble **First Saint Louis Church**, on Moye Square, was built in 1844. The single room rectangle was used as a church by the founders of Castroville, then became a school. The rock and wood on the church are all original.

You would never guess that the adorable white home at the corner of Florence and Angelo Streets was ordered from a catalog. The Sears and Roebuck house stands as proud as it did when it was built from a mail order kit in 1911. The house is two streets south of Highway 90 on Angel Street.

NIGHTLIFE & ENTERTAINMENT

Country Gold is a Texas dance hall located on the highway just outside Castroville. Live music twangs through the air and the dance floor is often full on Saturday nights. This is an informal sort of place, so bring your own bottle and kick up your heels. Country Gold is open from 9pm to 2am and usually charges a $5 cover.

PRACTICAL INFORMATION

The **Castroville Chamber of Commerce**, *802 London Street, Castroville, Tel. 830/538-3142*, publishes a comprehensive Visitor's Guide which lists current events and is free to the public.

You can book a room through **Castroville's First Bed & Breakfast Registry**, *Tel. 830/538-9622*, which has an extensive list of the area's accommodations.

SEGUIN

Rich in history and beauty, **Seguin** is a popular retreat for weekend travelers. The town is on the border region where the hills of central Texas blend toward the coastal plains. A sense of small town pride is the hallmark of Seguin, which is named after a leader of the Texas Revolution.

Texas Lutheran University is located in Seguin, and offers cultural performances throughout the year.

ARRIVALS & DEPARTURES

Seguin is 34 miles east of San Antonio between Highway 46 and Highway 123. When traveling on Interstate Highway 10, take either of these highway exits to Seguin.

ORIENTATION

The center of town is the courthouse square, which is on Court Street. Historic buildings line the streets around the courthouse.

WHERE TO STAY

COTTONTAIL CREEK BED AND BREAKFAST, *3767 South Highway 46, Seguin. Tel. 210/379-1693. Rates: $75.*

The Cottontail Creek Ranch is five miles from Seguin. With only two guest rooms and a resident donkey on the land, the ranch is a true escape. The friendly hosts will make you feel as though you are visiting your Texas family. The Louisiana Room has a quaint dormer window and decorations from New Orleans. The Texas Room is packed with memorabilia from the Lone Star State. Your day starts with a simple yet delicious breakfast. Arrangements can be made for lunch or dinner meals. From Seguin take either Highway 46 or Highway 123 south to their intersection at Austin Street. Cash or checks are accepted.

WEINERT HOUSE, *1207 North Austin Street, Seguin. Tel. 210/372-0422, fax 303-0912. Rates: $70 to $110. Credit cards accepted.*

The breathtaking Weinert home was a landmark when it was built in 1890, and is even more so today. Each of the four rooms has a private bath and is furnished in quaint antique style. The Weinert house is centrally located, within walking distance of the historic town center and close to golf and shopping. Children under the age of nine years are not accepted as guests.

BEST WESTERN, *1603 Interstate Highway 10, Seguin. Tel. 210/379-9631. Rates: $50 to $75. Credit cards accepted.*

This 84 room motel is located at the intersection of Interstate Highway 10 and Highway 46. Fitness facilities include an outdoor pool. And the hotel restaurant is open around the clock.

WHERE TO EAT

EL RANCHITO, *983 North Highway 123, Seguin. Tel. 210/303-7802.*

For over two generations, El Ranchito has been serving the best Tex-Mex food in the area. The casual restaurant prepares large plates of enchiladas, fajitas and other regional favorites. The large, fresh margaritas are a good way to start your meal. Or visit Ciro's, the restaurant's bar, for a nightcap.

SEEING THE SIGHTS

Los Nogales Museum, *415 South River Street.* The tiny building that holds the collection is more interesting than the artifacts on display inside. In 1849 it was constructed from hand-made bricks and used as a house. The building is registered as a state and national historic landmark.

One of the earliest hotels you will find in Texas is the **Magnolia Hotel**, located on Crocket Street between Donegan and Nolte Streets, built in 1842. Stagecoaches traveling the route between Austin and Houston used the hotel.

The **Guadelupe County Courthouse**, *Court Street,* built in 1935, is a boxy limestone building reflecting the modern design movement of the time. In front of the courthouse is a large carving of a pecan, which claims that Seguin is "Home of the World's Largest Pecan."

If you would rather learn about the unknown, you can pay a visit to the **International Headquarters of the Mutual UFO Network**, *628 North 123, Tel 830/379-9216.* The center provides informative exhibits about local and international sightings of Unidentified Flying Objects. You must make an appointment for a visit and tour of the International Headquarters.

NIGHTLIFE & ENTERTAINMENT

Local and touring performances are held at **The Wupperman Little Theater**, *Texas Lutheran University, 1000 West Court Street, Tel. 210/372-8180*. The regional theater company, **One Seguin Art Center**, produces musicals on a regular basis.

The **Teatro de Artes de Juan Seguin**, *901 West New Braunfels Street, Tel. 210/401-0232*, sponsors performances of Latino folk singing and dancing. The Noche de Gala, an annual competition of ballet folklorico and mariachi music, is held in the beginning of the year.

EXCURSIONS & DAY TRIPS

The town of **Panna Maria** is the oldest Polish settlement in the United States. The name is Polish for "Virgin Mary." The town reflects the character of the European Silesian heritage of the original 100 families who settled Panna Maria in 1850. The church is still the focal point of the community.

The most significant building in the old town is the **Church of Saint Mary**, which was built in 1877 after the first church burned down. The interior of the church has much of the original woodwork and some interesting treasures. Poland gave President Johnson a mosaic, which he donated to the church, and Pope John Paul II gave the town a golden chalice.

You may attend mass, held every Sunday at 10am. The annual church fund-raiser, held on the second Sunday of October, is a festive cultural feast. The town prepares a real dinner for over 2500 people, and everyone is invited.

To visit the church and museum, simply ask in the **Visitor's Center**, *Ranch Road 81, Panna Maria, Tel. 830/780-4471, Wednesday to Saturday, 10am to 4pm, Sunday 1pm to 5pm*. The building which houses the center is the Pilcaczyk Store; the structure dates from 1875.

The city of **Goliad** was a major settlement during the days of Spanish colonization. The Mission was built in 1749. The large sturdy building remains much as it may have looked when it was used by missionaries. The mission has a museum that documents the Spanish period of Texas. From Seguin, take Interstate Highway 10 east to Highway 183. Go south to Goliad.

East of Goliad, in the town of **Shiner**, you can visit one of the oldest breweries in the state. The **Spoetzl Brewery**, *603 East Brewery Street, Shiner, Tel. 512/594-3383*, is the second oldest in the state and began operating in 1909. Spoetzl Brewery produces Shiner, an excellent beer named for the town.

South of Goliad, on Highway 183, is another town of great importance to the Spanish and to Texans, **Gonzales**. The battle for independence is said to have begun in Gonzales. It was here that the army of General Santa Anna demanded the residents return a canon that was given to them by the Mexican government. When the request was refused, shots were fired.

PRACTICAL INFORMATION

A unique way to see the area is the **"True Women" Tour** of the region. The tour is based on the novel of the same name. For more information about the tour or general travel activities, contact the **Seguin Area Convention & Visitors Bureau**, *Tel. 800/580-7322*.

CORPUS CHRISTI

The Texas coast has awe-inspiring natural beauty. The exotic mix of the cultures of Mexico and Texas draw tourists to **Corpus Christi** all year. You can pack a variety of vacations in one trip. Downtown meets the Corpus Christi Bay at the marina, which is filled with sailboats and shrimp boats. One of the best wind-surfing launches in the area is just down Ocean Drive at Oleander Point, overlooking Coal Park. The gorgeous natural beaches of **Padre Island** are only a few miles from Corpus Christi's upscale restaurants and museums.

The city-wide celebration, **Buccaneer Days**, is part carnival, part debutante ball. The parade features the season's debutantes in sparkling gowns. The summer closes with **Bayfest**, a weekend celebration held along the bay-front at the end of September. A regatta and street festival are the highlights.

ARRIVALS & DEPARTURES

The **Corpus Christi International Airport** is located in the northwest part of the city. Take Interstate Highway 37 north and look for the airport exit.

ORIENTATION

Interstate Highway 37 from San Antonio is the main route to Corpus Christi. The highway ends at Shoreline Boulevard, which turns into Ocean Drive and runs along the Corpus Christi Bay. The Harbor Bridge connects downtown to Corpus Christi Beach, where you will find a number of tourist attractions.

GETTING AROUND TOWN

The "B," *Tel. 512/883-2287*, as the city buses in Corpus Christi call themselves, serve all areas of the city.

You can shuttle under the Harbor Bridge on the Water Taxi, which connects the Convention Center and nearby museums with the State Aquarium on Corpus Christi Beach. The Corpus Christi Shuttle connects the attractions on the land. You may ride the shuttle free when you purchase a trip on the Water Taxi. These services operate during the summer only, from Memorial Day until Labor Day. Round trip fare is $2.

Taxi companies in Corpus Christi include:

• **City Cab**, *Tel. 512/881-TAXI*
• **Liberty Taxi**, *Tel. 512/882-7654 or 749-5589 (in Port Aransas)*
• **Yellow Checker Cab**, *Tel. 512/884-3211 or 800/944-4983*

WHERE TO STAY

OMNI BAYFRONT HOTEL, *900 North Shoreline Boulevard, Corpus Christi. Tel. 512/887-1600 or 800/874-4585, Fax 512/883-8084. Rates: $135. Credit cards accepted.*

This 474 room high rise overlooks the marina on the Corpus Christi Bay. The hotel offers the premier accommodations in the area. The heated rooftop pool has a striking view of the marina. You can walk to downtown restaurants and bars in the evening. During the day you can stroll to the marina to rent a boat or go deep-sea fishing. Recreational facilities include a gym, outdoor pool and racquet ball courts.

OMNI MARINA HOTEL, *707 North Shoreline Boulevard, Corpus Christi. Tel. 512/882-1700 or 800/288-4768, Fax 512/882-3113. Rates: $115. Credit cards accepted.*

This Omni is an older and slightly smaller building than its sister hotel, the Omni Bayfront. The difference in rates is minimal considering that facilities at the Omni Marina are less than adequate for a hotel in this price range. The luster has worn off this hotel, so spend the extra few dollars and treat yourself to the Omni Bayfront next door.

HOLIDAY INN EMERALD BEACH, *1102 South Shoreline Boulevard, Corpus Christi. Tel. 512/883-5731, Fax 883-9079. Rates: $115 to $169. Credit cards accepted.*

This is the only downtown hotel actually on the waterfront. The value is purely aesthetic, because the bay is used primarily for sailing. The long low rise hotel has an indoor pool and gym. The adjoining lounge tries to shed the hotel cocktail bar image. The Holiday Inn offers a convenient location for visitors who plan to drive to their recreational destinations.

RAMADA INN BAYFRONT, *601 North Water Street, Corpus Christi. Tel. 512/882-8100 or 800/688-0334, Fax 512/888-6540. Rates: $65 to 89. Credit cards accepted.*

The Ramada Inn is not on the water and can offer no views of the marina, but considering that the price is significantly lower than other downtown hotels, the view is a small sacrifice. The rooms are roomy and comfortable; downtown restaurants and the marina are just a short walk from the hotel. The Ramada is an excellent choice for families, because children under the age of 17 years stay at no charge with parents. Corpus Christi has a second Ramada Inn located near the airport.

BEST WESTERN SANDY SHORES, *3200 Surfside Boulevard, Corpus Christi. Tel. 512/883-7456 or 800/528-1234, Fax 512/883-1437. Rates: $59 to $149. Credit cards accepted.*

You can have a lovely view of downtown without staying in the center of the city if you choose Corpus Christi Beach. The coarse sand and bay water is not inviting to swimmers, so most do not come to this area for the beach. Just across the Harbor Bridge from downtown, the Sandy Shores is within walking distance from the Lexington Battleship and the Texas State Aquarium

BEST WESTERN CORPUS CHRISTI INN, *2838 South Padre Island Drive, Corpus Christi. Tel 512/854-0005 or 800/445-9463, Fax 512/854-2642. Rates: $45 to $71. Credit cards accepted.*

This hotel stands on the highway leading to Padre Island. The location is convenient for travelers who want to be near shopping centers and restaurants. The hotel has an outdoor pool and can make arrangements for golfing.

BAY BREEZE BED & BREAKFAST, *Louisiana Parkway, Corpus Christi. Tel 512/882-4123. Rates: $65 to $85.*

The Bay Breeze is located in one of the well established residential areas in the city. Only a few blocks from the bay and two miles from downtown, the location is excellent if you would like to feel as though you actually reside in the city. The Tree House, the largest of the four rooms, has a view of the bay and a patio. Each room has a private bath.

Padre Island
The island is about 15 miles from downtown Corpus Christi. The evenings on the island are quiet, with the sound of surf the only distraction. Nothing can top a moonlight stroll on the beach. But if you desire an active nightlife, staying in the city center may be a better option than on the island.

SURFSIDE CONDOMINIUMS, *15,005 Windward Drive. Corpus Christi. Tel. 512/949-8128 or 800/548-4585. Rates: $110. Credit cards accepted.*

Just 100 yards from the ocean, the Surfside Condominiums have kitchens and the conveniences of home such as televisions, stereo systems. If you use only one of the two bedrooms, lower rates apply. The facilities include an outdoor pool and laundry room. Children under the age of six years stay for free.

PORT ROYAL OCEAN RESORT, *6317 State Highway 361, Port Aransas. Tel. 512/749-5011 or 800/242-1034, Fax 512/749-6399. Rates: $ $150 to $225. Credit cards accepted.*

Port Royal is a favorite vacation spot of tourists and natives alike. The condominium resort sits quite a distance from the crowds and traffic congestion of the public beaches near Corpus Christi. And it is also a drive from the town of Port Aransas; you really can get away from it all at Port Royal. Each condo offers the comforts of home. The building is built courtyard-style around an outdoor pool and has tennis courts on the side yard. The pool is a short walk from the surf, so you can enjoy the best of fresh and salt water. One and two bedroom units are available. Rates change by season.

Campgrounds

Corpus Christi and Padre Island are popular destinations for campers. There are many private campgrounds in the area; most are located in Flour Bluff, between the mainland and Padre Island. The camping facilities at Mustang Island are excellent and allow campers to stay right on the beach. Some campers choose to set up camp for overnight stays right on the beach, usually near the sand dunes. This can be difficult. however, due to lack of facilities and high winds that can knock over a tent or disrupt a campsite.

COLONIA DEL REY RV PARK, *1717 Waldron Road, Corpus Christi. Tel. 512/937-2435 or 800/580-2435. Credit cards accepted.*

The campground, which is a Good Sam Park, sits on 12 acres and has large shade trees to offer a break from the summer heat. Camper hookups have electricity and propane can be delivered. Amenities such as a swimming pool, air conditioned laundry room and shower facilities will make traveling easier. Classes and special events are held in the recreation hall during the winter months. To reach Colonia Del Rey, when entering Corpus Christi on Interstate Highway 37, exit Highway 358. Continue on 358 for about nine miles, then exit Waldron Road and take a right. You will find the park on the left about one-half mile from the highway.

WHERE TO EAT

WATER STREET OYSTER BAR, *309 North Water Street, Corpus Christi. Tel 512/882-2211. Credit cards accepted.*

If you have only one meal in Corpus Christi, take it at Water Street Oyster Bar. The Cajun-influenced seafood specialties are the finest in town. The large airy dining room is a feast for the eyes, with a kitschy two story take-off of Botticelli's *Venus* painting and an open kitchen. Every day the fresh fish specials are listed on the blackboard. You can order your fish grilled over Mesquite smoke, sautéed or — for those with a taste for the robust — blackened. The wait-staff can offer suggestions on the best preparation to bring out the flavor of each fish. The gumbo is thick, full of seafood and probably the best in Texas. The Caldo Xochitl, a soup with aromatic chicken stock, captures the true subtlety of the Mexican version. Chicken Rockefeller ($11.99) and beef tenderloin ($12.99) are alternatives to seafood. A good selection of wine and a full bar are available.

OLD MEXICO, *3329 Leopard Street, Corpus Christi. Tel. 512/883-6461. Credit cards accepted.*

This is what a real Tex-Mex restaurant should be, unpretentious and straight-forward food. You will have no problem with the amount of spice; since the plain rice-and-beans cooking relies on you adding the salsa yourself. Corn tortillas are the basis of the food here, but you can order the more trendy flour variety. And the food stands the test of time. The traditional south Texas style has remained consistent over the decades and has won a strong local following. An average meal costs under $10.

JOE COTTEN'S BARBECUE, *Highway 77 South, Robstown. Tel. 512/767-9973.*

It's a twenty mile drive from Corpus Christi to Joe Cotten's in Robstown. But a barbecue lover would be willing to walk — the food is that good. The atmosphere may surpass the cuisine, though. You sit at a wooden table in the restaurant that resembles a Texas dance hall. A waiter takes your order and puts down a strip of butcher paper. Once your food arrives there is no limit to the number of "seconds" you can have, but most fill up after first. The cost of a meal is $8. This restaurant has served the best barbecue in south Texas for over fifty years, and included the Bush family among its distinguished clientele. Only cash is accepted.

SEEING THE SIGHTS

Corpus Christi's museums stand in Bayfront Arts and Science Park, next to the city convention center, just under the Harbor Bridge. You can spend a few hours in this area taking in the history, culture and nature of the coastal bend. Nearby Heritage Park, which is adjacent to the Bayfront Arts and Science Park, has restored historic homes which are open to the public.

Corpus Christi Museum of Science & History, *1900 Chaparral, Tel. 512/883-2862, Monday to Saturday 10am to 5pm Sunday noon to 5pm, admission $8 adult, $4 children under the age of 12*, traces the natural history of the area from prehistoric times to the present. Special exhibits geared especially for younger children include the touch tables and wharf play area. Part of the museum features an exhibit discussing the significance of the 1492 voyage of Christopher Columbus. Outside you can visit replicas of the Columbus ships, the Nina, Pinta and Santa Maria. The boats found a permanent home in the Corpus Christi Harbor soon after they visited during the 500th anniversary of his first voyage to North America. You can come aboard the **Columbus Ships**, which are surprisingly small, and see how the crew lived. Admission to the ships is included with museum entrance.

The **Art Museum of South Texas**, *1902 North Shoreline Boulevard, Tel. 512/884-3844, Tuesday to Saturday 10am to 5pm, Sunday 1pm to 5pm, closed Monday, admission $3 adult, $1 children*, overlooks the bay. The building, designed by Philip Johnson, is a work of art in itself. Exhibits change regularly and focus on art of national interest. Kids who want to get their hands active with art can visit the **Art Center**, *100 Shoreline Boulevard, Tel. 512/884-6404, admission free*. This innovative approach to children and the arts lets kids create their way to artistic expression.

Across the Harbor Bridge, **The Texas State Aquarium**, *Corpus Christi Beach, Tel. 512/881-1200, Monday to Saturday 9am to 5pm, Sunday 10am to 5pm, admission $8 adults, $5.75 children*, places the depths of the Gulf of Mexico before your eyes. The most dramatic exhibit shows the marine life that inhabits an oil rig. You can walk right up to the walls of aquariums, as though you were swimming through the legs of the rig.

The **USS Lexington**, an aircraft carrier that served in World War II, stands on Corpus Christi Beach and is open to tourists, *Tel. 800/LADY-LEX, admission $8 adults, $4 children*. You can see the engineering room, living quarters and walk on the deck. Since there is neither heat nor air conditioning, you can get an idea of some of the adverse conditions faced by the sailors aboard the Lady Lex.

NIGHTLIFE & ENTERTAINMENT

BUCKETS, *227 North Water Street, Tel. 512/883-7776.*

Sports bar, pool hall, live music venue — all these describe Buckets — under one large roof. The younger crowd of the coastal bend fills this casual downtown hang-out, downing table top mini-kegs of beer and socializing. If your tan is not up to par, you may be spotted as a tourist.

YUCATAN, *208 North Water Street, Tel 512/888-6800.*

This large party place features live music on weekend nights. The casual beach bum atmosphere was an instant hit in the city, and Yucatan's is the right mix of club and bar to keep the crowds coming back.

EXECUTIVE SURF CLUB, *309 North Water Street, Tel. 512/884-7873.*

Surfboards are tables, and the atmosphere is definitely island inspired. This small bar in the Water Street Shopping Center serves beer and fried food. Live music is featured on the weekends.

SPORTS & RECREATION

Birdwatching is a popular pastime for many residents of the Coastal Bend. The **Padre Island National Seashore**, with its miles of undisturbed beach, is a haven for water birds, notably whooping cranes and kingfishers. Guided birdwatching tours are available from **Bird Song Natural History Adventures**, *3525 Bluebonnet, Tel. 512/882-7232*. Tours range from half-day to extended trips for groups or individuals.

There are enough dive areas around Corpus Christi to keep the avid diver underwater for years. **Copeland's**, *4041 South Padre Island Drive, Tel. 512/854-1135*, offers day dives from $45 or overnight trips from $99. Another reputable dive shop, **See Sea Divers**, *4012 Weber Road, Tel. 512/853-DIVE*, offers a full range of services including equipment rental, dive trips and deep sea fishing charters.

Boating in the Corpus Christi Bay is an excellent way to enjoy the beauty of the coastline and refreshing water. You can rent sailboats by the day or week at the **Corpus Christi International School of Sailing**, *Cooper's Alley L-Head, Tel. 512/881-8503, Fax 512/881-8504*. Prices range as follows: $210 to $230 per day or $1000 to $1300 per week. The fleet of six boats includes a 38-foot sloop and are available for rental throughout the year. You can also charter a boat for a four hour cruise around Corpus Christi Bay.

The **Captain Clark**, *People's Street T-head, Tel. 512/884-4369*, docked at the city marina, offers three bay fishing trips per day during the summer. The 65-foot double-deck tourist boat has a lounge and snack bar; equipment rental is available. The Captain Clark is docked at the city marina, across from downtown.

From Port Aransas, you can embark on the area's best deep sea fishing expeditions. **Deep Sea Headquarters**, *Ferry Landing, Port Aransas, Tel. 512/749-5597*, has three boats that can hold up to 100 people for half- or full-day expeditions.

The Greyhound Race Track, *5302 Leopard Street, Tel. 512/289-9333 or 800/580-RACE*, has a club house (admission $2) and a grandstand (admission $1). If the live dogs are not enough, you can bet on six other racetracks shown on monitors. From Interstate Highway 37, take the Navigation Boulevard exit.

Golf

The city's main municipal course, **Gabe Lozano Sr. Golf Course**, *4401 Old Brownsville Road, Tel. 512/883-3696, open daily*, offers excellent no-frill facilities for golf. Two standard courses, an 18 hole and a nine hole course, are featured at this municipal park. Fees for the 9 hole course range from $4.75 to $7.25; fees for the 18 hole course range from $6.50

SOUTH TEXAS GOLF

Golf is one of the most popular sports in south Texas. Many of the winter Texans take advantage of the mild climate to play golf in every season. Many of the private clubs have reasonable greens fees, and some offer temporary memberships. The following clubs are located in small towns on the coastal bend:

Alice Country Club, Country Club Road, Alice. Tel. 512/664-3723. Open Tuesday to Sunday. Fees are $10 for weekday play; $15 for weekend play. Temporary memberships are available and include use of all club facilities. The club is located near Highway 44.

North Shore Country Club, 801 East Broadway, Portland. Tel. 512/643-1546 or 643-2798. Open Tuesday to Sunday; closed Monday. Greens fees $45 to $55 per person, including cart.

Rockport Country Club, 101 Champions Drive, Rockport. Tel. 512/729-4182 Open Tuesday to Sunday. Greens fees $40 to $50 per person, including golf cart.

to $11, depending on the day of play. The grounds have a pro-shop and snack bar. Golf carts are available for rental ($14.75 for the 18 hole course). If you don't like the sun, try the lighted driving range for evening practice.

The **Pharaoh Country Club**, *7111 Pharaoh Drive, Tel. 512/991-1490,* opens its golf facilities to the public for a fee of $25 per person on weekdays and $35 per person on weekends and holidays. Golf cart rental is included in the greens fee. The course is located in the Pharaoh Valley neighborhood close to Oso Bay. You may arrange monthly membership to the course, which ranges in price from $150 to $300 per person. To reach the Pharaoh Country Club, take Ocean Drive east (away from downtown) to Ennis Joslin Street. Turn onto Ennis Joslin Street, which begins at Ocean Drive, and go about 1.5 miles to Pharaoh Drive. Take Pharaoh Drive to the club entrance.

The **Oso Beach Golf Course**, *5601 South Alameda, Tel (512) 991-5351, open daily,* is close to Oso Bay in a pleasant residential area. The facilities include a pro-shop and a restaurant. The 18-hole regulation course is spotted with palm trees and traps of fine white sand. Fees range from $9 to $11, depending on the day of play. Special rates available for junior and senior players. Golf cart rental runs from $10.13 to $14.79, including tax.

You can play a full 18 holes on the Island at the **Padre Island Country Club**, *14,353 Commodore Drive, Tel. 512/949-8006, open Tuesday to Sunday, closed Monday, except during February and March.* The only country club on

Padre Island offers a pro-shop and club facilities. The club is not near the Gulf of Mexico, but sits amid a cozy neighborhood of beach-houses and canals for small boats. Greens fees range from $36 to $46.

EXCURSIONS & DAY TRIPS

The beautiful and in some places wild **Padre Island National Seashore** is part of a chain of barrier islands along the Texas Gulf Coast. Covering over 130,000 acres, the island offers visitors nature trails, camp sites and a variety of educational programs.

Padre Island is just east of Corpus Christi. Take South Padre Island Drive through Flour Bluff. After you cross the Intracoastal Waterway you will see the Padre Island National Seashore Offices, which can provide information about access roads to the beach.

The south end of the island has the most pristine beaches. The National Park at **Malaquite Beach** offers 47 campsites and swimming areas. To reach Malaquite beach, take Highway 22 south along the island. The road ends at the Visitor Center, which has picnic areas and showers. The national seashore extends sixty miles south of this beach, but is accessible only by four wheel drive vehicle. The drive along the water takes at least a few hours. Primitive campsites are located at Yarborough Pass, 15 miles south of Malaquite Beach.

Mustang Island State Park has camping facilities with full hook-ups. The beach has its own access road and public showers are for the use of park guests. A section of the beach reserved for swimming has a bath and dining facility. To get to Mustang Island State Park, take a left at the first stoplight, heading north on Highway 361 (Park Road 53). This highway continues to Port Aransas about 26 miles north. At **Port Aransas** you can take the free ferry boat crossing to **Aransas Pass**. Get out of your car to enjoy the sea breezes and to spot porpoises. Highway 361 continues west to Highway 181; take Highway 181 south to get back to Corpus Christi.

PRACTICAL INFORMATION

The **Corpus Christi Tourist Information Center**, *1201 North Shoreline Boulevard*, is located in the center of town.

The **Padre Island National Seashore Offices**, *9405 South Padre Island Drive, Tel. 512/949-8713, Fax 512/949-9951*, can provide information about events and nature classes.

You can book a stay at a bed and breakfast, hotel or motel through **Sand Dollar Hospitality**, *Tel. 512/853-1222 or 800/528-7782*.

KINGSVILLE

Probably more people have heard of the **King Ranch** than of **Kingsville**. With good reason — it;s larger than the state of Rhode Island and one of the most important working ranches in the world. In the mid-nineteenth century a sea captain named Richard King came to the area. He pioneered ranching in Texas and built a legacy which has endured over 130 years. Visitors come to see the King Ranch and enjoy **Baffin Bay**, a large inlet of the Gulf of Mexico.

The Christmas season is celebrated with **La Posada de Kingsville**, a traditional candlelight procession through town. The events begin during the last weekend of November and start with a parade, followed by a five kilometer run/walk through downtown and two days of festivities in the park. featuring arts events, markets and caroling. The procession itself takes place on the weekend before Christmas. For the complete schedule contact La Posada de Kingsville, *Tel. 512/592-8516 or 800/333-5032* .

ARRIVALS & DEPARTURES

The main route to Kingsville is Highway 77 which runs through Corpus Christi from the north.

WHERE TO STAY

B-BAR-B RANCH INN, *Route 1 Box 457, Kingsville. Tel 512/296-3331, Fax 296-3337. Rates: $75 to $100. Credit cards accepted.*

The adult-only guest ranch has eight rooms, each outfitted in western style. The ranch offers activities such as hay rides, hunting, fishing and cookouts. You can observe life on a real working ranch or simply lounge at the outdoor pool. A full country breakfast is prepared every day. Call for special activities or group arrangements.

BEST WESTERN KINGSVILLE INN, *2402 East King Avenue, Kingsville. Tel. 512/595-5656 or 800/528-1234, Fax 512/595-5000. Rates: $45 to $51. Credit cards accepted.*

The Best Western is located on the highway. There's an outdoor pool and spa. There is no charge for children under the age of six years. Laundry facilities are on the premises.

WHERE TO EAT

THE KING'S INN, *Farm Road 628 at Loyola Beach, Kingsville. Tel. 512/297-5265.*

At first glance you may not believe the sign on the small wooden building that proclaims "World Famous King's Inn." But don't pass it by. The thick guestbook attests with rave reviews from around the world that the King's Inn has luscious seafood. The restaurant opened in the 1940's and still serves basically the same seafood specialties. The meal comes family-style, so all you have to do is sit down and look hungry. Fresh crab and shrimp are featured daily, with chicken or steak. Choose your main dish, and the sides are brought to your table in large servings. You can eat like a king for less than $10 per person.

From Kingsville, take Highway 77 south. Turn east on Farm Road 628 and travel eight miles to Loyola Beach.

SEEING THE SIGHTS

At the **King Ranch**, you can visit the site where the first cowboys set up camp on what would become the 825,000 acre ranch. The ranch is so large parts of it are in four counties. Tours of the grounds are conducted daily. Start your visit at **The King Ranch Visitor Center**, *Highway 141, Tel. 512/592-8055, Monday to Saturday 10am to 3pm, Sunday 1pm to 4pm*, where you can watch an orientation movie and begin a guided tour.

The **King Ranch Museum**, *405 North Sixth Street, Tel. 512/595-1881, Monday to Saturday 10am to 2pm, Sunday 1pm to 5pm*, is not on the ranch but in downtown Kingsville. The museum displays antiques from the ranch and feature photographs depicting ranch life in the 1940s.

The natural history of the area is preserved at the **Conner Museum**, *Texas A&M University campus, Tel. 512/595-2819, Monday to Saturday 9am to 5pm, admission free*. The main halls are dedicated to the ecology of south Texas. Temporary exhibits about science change about 10 times a year. The trophy room displays enough hunting trophies to fill a wildlife refuge.

IT'S NEVER TOO LATE TO LEARN SOMETHING!
*Learning never stops with the **Texas A&M Kingsville Elderhostel Program**, Tel. 512/595-2111. During the winter short courses are offered in subjects ranging from birdwatching to a variety of more traditional classroom subjects. The courses usually run for one week.*

SPORTS & RECREATION

Nearby **Baffin Bay** gives you the opportunity to enjoy the coast on the calm waters of a large bay. The area is famous as a sportsman's paradise. Migratory birds flock to Baffin Bay throughout the year. Excellent salt water fishing, either from one of the many piers in the area or by boat, is readily available. However, if activity is not your desire, simply relax and enjoy the tranquil waters.

Golf

The main golf course in Kingsville is **L.E. Ramey Municipal Golf Course**, *Highway 77 South, Tel 512/592-1101 or 800/879-7263, open daily.* During the winter months, the course holds weekly tournaments for senior citizens. Tournament play begins Wednesday mornings at 9am. The facilities include an 18 hole course and driving range, as well as a pro-shop and snack bar. Greens fee range from $6.75 to $8.25; golf cart rental from $10 to $15. Memberships are available by the month, and allow unlimited play. Individual monthly membership dues are $50, and only $80 for an entire family.

During the fall football season you can watch the top-notch **Texas A&M Javalenas** play home games at Texas A&M Kingsville, *Tel. 512/595-2111.*

SHOPPING

There is no finer place to buy western riding accessories than the **King Ranch Saddle Shop**, *201 East Kleberg Street, Tel. 512/595-5761 or 800/282-KING.* You will find many local crafts for sale along with the famous King Ranch purses and backpacks.

PRACTICAL INFORMATION

The **Kingsville Visitor Center**, *101 North 3rd Street, Box 1562, Tel. 800/333-5032*, has information about the King Ranch and the city.

BROWNSVILLE

The city of **Brownsville**, resting at the southern tip of Texas, has a long and vibrant history. The area may have been one of the first parts of Texas explored by Cabaza de Vaca, who traveled up the Rio Grande in the sixteenth century.

The town was established during the mid-nineteenth century, when the United States placed a military base at the site and thereby secured the region as part of Texas. Today many of the residents of Brownsville live here for the proximity to the recreational areas of south Texas. Tourists flock into the area to visit Matamoros, Mexico and South Padre Island. The towns are so close that most people choose to stay in one and visit the others on the same trip.

ARRIVALS & DEPARTURES

Brownsville is located at the southern end of Highway 77. Highway 83 joins Highway 77 from the west and leads into Brownsville. Highway 281 runs along the Rio Grande to the west until Pharr; this highway connects to San Antonio in the north.

The **Brownsville International Airport**, *Highway 4, Tel. 956/542-4373*, is west of the city. Grey Line Tours operates shuttle service from the airport to Brownsville and South Padre Island.

ORIENTATION

The combined Highways 77 and 83 are the major north-south thoroughfare through Brownsville. The hghways end at International Boulevard, which leads to the border with Mexico. Highway 4, also called Boca Chica Boulevard, cuts east-west across the city and ends at Boca Chica Beach on the west.

GETTING AROUND TOWN

The easiest way to get around town and see the sights is with the **Historic Brownsville Trolley Tours**, *650 Farm Road 802, Tel. 956/546-3721 or 800/626-2639*. The Brownsville Convention & Visitors Bureau operate the trolleys; routes include the "Port of Brownsville" and "Historic Sites in Brownsville" tours. Adult fare is $6, and children's fare $3. Reservations should be made at least one day in advance.

To obtain information about city bus routes, contact the **Brownsville Urban System**, *700 South Iowa Street, Tel. 956/541-4881*.

WHERE TO STAY

SHERATON FOUR POINTS HOTEL, *3777 Highway 77 North Brownsville. Tel. 956/350-9191 or 800/325-7385, Fax 956/350-4153. Rates: $75 TO $85. Credit cards accepted.*

This new hotel is located north of the city. The rooms are comfortable and spacious. Workout facilities include a gym and outdoor pool. The hotel has a bar and restaurant on the premises. Special package rates for weekend travel are available. This is a good area to base yourself if you plan to drive around the lower Rio Grande Valley. Children under the age of 17 stay free with their parents.

RAMADA LIMITED FORT BROWN, *1900 East Elizabeth Street, Brownsville. Tel 956/541-2921, Fax 956/541-2695. Rates: $45 to $125.*

The 104 room Ramada Limited is located in the center of Brownsville, a short walk to the International Bridge. The hotel stands on over 10 acres of landscaped grounds and is both convenient and inexpensive. The University of Texas at Brownsville campus is nearby. Rooms include continental breakfast and the hotel has tennis courts and a pool.

WHERE TO EAT

GIO, *2325 Central Boulevard, Brownsville. Tel. 956/542-9057. Credit cards accepted.*

There is something about the sauce at Gio's that makes the meal. The only truly good Italian food south of San Antonio is right here. Excellent tomato sauce and a variety of pasta dishes and Italian specialties have made Gio a favorite of residents.

SEEING THE SIGHTS

The first true settlement in the area, **Fort Brown**, *600 International Boulevard*, is now the University of Texas at Brownsville campus. The main building dates from 1846. The Fort Brown Civic Center is the university's auditorium.

In 1928, the Southern Pacific Depot was built for first rail line through Brownsville. The design reflects the Spanish and Mexican heritage of the region. Today this historic building houses the **Brownsville Museum**, *641 East Madison Street, Tel. 956/548-1313*, which traces the history of the border, and Brownsville in particular, through photos, documents and historic objects. This museum offers a concise yet complete picture of south Texas.

The **Immaculate Conception Church**, *1218 East Jefferson Street,* is a dramatic contrast to most of the buildings in the area which have rounded mission-style facades with ornate Spanish designs. This church was built by French missionaries in 1859 and has dramatic neo-Gothic lines. You can walk through the church, which is open during the day.

Another landmark from the mid-nineteenth century is the **Stillman House**, *1305 East Washington Street, Tel. 956/542-3929*. This southern home, dating from 1850, was built by the man credited with founding Brownsville, Charles Stillman. The exhibit inside shows how the families of his era lived.

The **Gladys Porter Zoo**, *500 Ringgold Street, Tel. 956/546-2177 or 546-7187, open daily 9am to 5pm*, has one of the finest collections of animals in the southwest. The grounds spread over 30 acres and the plants are as diverse and interesting as the animals. You can scoot around the zoo in style on the Zoofari Express train. The aviary is a tropical oasis and bursts with the sounds of singing birds. A special area for children lets them explore and learn interactively. From Highway 77, exit 6th Street.

At the time of the Spanish colonization, far more of the lands of the Rio Grande Valley may have resembled the **Sabal Palm Grove Sanctuary**, *Farm Road 1419, Tel. 956/541-8034*. The preserve is an amazing natural area which contains a rare palm forest. The Audobon Society operates and conducts research in the Sanctuary. From Brownsville, take International Boulevard to Farm Road 1419. Signs will lead you to the entrance.

NIGHTLIFE & ENTERTAINMENT

The **University of Texas at Brownsville**, *80 Fort Brown, Tel. 956/544-8247*, sponsors a fine arts program which bring touring musicians to the area. Pianists, vocalists and other classical musicians of international quality grace the stage. The season runs from late September through May. Regular admission to the concerts is $7 adult and $4 children. Free concerts are offered during the season.

SPORTS & RECREATION

You know that you are playing golf near the coast since the majority of holes have water traps. The **Brownsville Golf and Recreation Center**, *Farm Road 802, Tel. 956/541-2582*, has an 18 hole par 70 course. To reach the course, take Highway 77 north and go east on Farm Road 802.

EXCURSIONS & DAY TRIPS

The Audobon Society has a 45,000 acre tropical sanctuary, the **Laguna Atacosta National Wildlife Refuge**, *Farm Road 1847, Rio Hondo, Tel. 956/748-3608, open October to April, daily 10am to 4pm*. The visitor center will provide a map of two road tours though the refuge. Hiking trails through the park remain open until sunset. From Brownsville, take Highway 77 north. At Harlingen, turn east onto Farm Road 106. Continue past Rio Hondo for 18 miles, then turn north onto the Refuge. The Visitor Center is three miles from the highway.

MATAMOROS, MEXICO

Most tourists who cross the border to **Matamoros, Mexico** go for a short day trip. The city offers bargain shopping and colorful history. Public parking is available in downtown Brownsville. When approaching the **International Bridge**, take the last turn west. The lot is only one block from the pedestrian walkway. Simply walk across the International Bridge and you are in the heart of the tourist center.

If you walk down the main street you will find yourself at the markets. Walking through the colorful old and new marketplaces can be fun, but you will find the best shopping at the city's most famous store, **Garcia's**, *Calle Alvaro Obregon, Matamoros*. Prices at Garcia's may be somewhat higher than in the market, but you will find better selection and quality. At the restaurant upstairs, Garcia's serves lunch and dinner with nightly specials. Steak costs less than $10, and of course, the margaritas are good.

To indulge in a bit of Mexico's culture, visit **Casa Mata Fort and City Museum**, *Guatemala y Santos Degollado Streets, Tuesday to Sunday 10am to 5pm*. The fort was built in 1845 as a reaction to the founding of a military base in Brownsville and was used during the Mexican-American War. Take a taxi to the museum, which is about one mile from the bridge.

PORT ISABEL

Port Isabel offers extraordinary fishing. The small surf-side city is on the mainland just across the water from the resorts of South Padre Island. The city sits on a peninsula in the calm Laguna Madre Bay. Many vacationers choose Port Isabel to escape the higher prices and crowds of tourist on South Padre Island.

If you just pass through on your way to South Padre Island, stop at the **Port Isabel Lighthouse**, *Highway 100, Port Isabel, Tel. 512/943-1172, open daily 10am to noon and 1pm to 5pm, admission $1*, and climb to the top for a spectacular view. The lighthouse stands 82 feet high and was built in 1852; it guided ships until 1902. This is one of the few lighthouses on the Texas coast.

PRACTICAL INFORMATION

You can arrange accommodations or receive more information from the **Port Isabel Chamber of Commerce**, *213 Yturia Street, Tel. 512/943-2262 or 800/527-6102*. From Brownsville, take Highway 48 east to Port Isabel.

SOUTH PADRE ISLAND

The gorgeous beaches of **South Padre Island** are unmatched in Texas. Miles of dunes and surf are reserved as park areas. Public beaches prohibit driving on the sand, leaving the waterfront unsullied by auto pollution.

The wildlife of South Padre Island is as extraordinary as the beaches. Dolphins and sea turtles swim along the coast; migrating birds nest in the wetlands. Scuba enthusiasts can take dive trips into shark territory or float alongside manta rays. A number of Spanish shipwrecks off the coast provide an historical backdrop for dives, or you can venture through a modern undersea community of sea-life on the oil rigs in the Gulf.

If you do choose to venture to the state's most radiant beaches, beware the spring break crowds. During the month of March, the Island becomes inundated with college revelry. They come from all over the nation and cause traffic and beach congestion. Hotels charge bolstered rates and add-on room charges. At motels you may find your rooms without towels and the front desk without service. The best months to visit the beach are May and September, when the summer weather is in full swing and crowds are minimal.

Be certain to book reservations well in advance; weekends and holidays often sell out months ahead.

ARRIVALS & DEPARTURES

From Highway 77, take Highway 100 west; this leads straight to Port Isabel and the Queen Isabella Bridge.

Grey Line Tours, *Tel. 956/761-4343,* operates shuttle service from the **Brownsville Airport** to South Padre Island. The tour company also has buses that run to the border ($10) or gives tours of Matamoros, Mexico ($15).

ORIENTATION

South Padre Island is at the southern end of the long, thin barrier island chain which runs along the Texas Gulf Coast. The Queen Isabella Causeway connects the Island to Port Isabel on the mainland. The concentration of hotels and restaurants covers about five miles on the island's southern tip. Padre Boulevard runs through the center of the island; Gulf Boulevard is the major north-south street connecting the beach-front condominiums on the Gulf side, and runs parallel to Padre Boulevard.

GETTING AROUND TOWN

Shuttles run along Padre and Gulf Boulevards, stopping at the major hotels and restaurants.

WHERE TO STAY

Daily, weekly and monthly rental of beach houses cam be arranged through **South Padre Beach Houses, Inc.**, *5009 Padre Boulevard, South Padre Island, Tel. 956/76-6554 or 800/377-3262.* Weekly rates range from $450 to $1375. This is an ideal way to stay if you plan an extended visit or will be traveling with a few people.

SHERATON FIESTA, *310 South Padre Island Boulevard, South Padre Island. Tel. 956/761-6551, 800/325-3535, Fax. 791-6570. Rates: $109 to $290. Credit cards accepted.*

The twelve-story Sheraton is the premier resort hotel on the Island. Tile floors and a pool-side cabana let you indulge in the south-of-the-border atmosphere. The excellent food ensures that you never have to leave the hotel. But if you do choose to venture out, recreational activities from parasailing to fishing can be arranged at the front desk. The gym overlooks the Gulf Of Mexico and the pool offers an expanse of crystal blue water.

RADISSON RESORT, *500 Padre Boulevard, South Padre Island. Tel. 956/761-6511 or 800/333-3333. Rates: $95 to $350. Credit cards accepted.*

The recreational facilities include sand volleyball courts, sea-side tennis courts, two lovely pools and outdoor shuffleboard. The 182 rooms are furnished in crisp, tropical colors and have excellent views of the Gulf of Mexico. Two restaurants on the beach and the bar at the pool provide food and entertainment. Special weekly rates are offered during certain times of the year. The hotel has two bedroom condominiums, which comfortably sleep four adults.

HOLIDAY INN SUNSPREE RESORT, *100 South Padre Boulevard, South Padre Island. Tel. 956/761-5401 or 800/531-7405, Fax 956/761-1560. Rates: $ 69 to $160.*

The Holiday Inn, designed as a fun-filled resort, is right on the beach. The hotel has complete recreational facilities including a gym, outdoor pool and planned activities. Children stay free with their parents, so this is a good choice for family travel.

RAMADA LIMITED, *4109 Padre Boulevard, South Padre Island. Tel. 956/761-4097 or 800/2-RAMADA. Rates: $65 to $180. Credit cards accepted.*

This budget-conscious accommodation is in the center of the island, but far from the beach. If you want only a room with no frills, the Ramada delivers. The hotel is new and the large rooms each have a small refrigerator and hair dryer.

WHERE TO EAT

BLACKBEARD'S, *103 East Saturn Street, Port Isabel. Tel. 956/761-2962. Credit cards accepted.*

You will have to venture back across the Queen Isabella Bridge to eat at one of the most frequented seafood restaurants on the coast. Blackbeard's serves most of its dishes — shrimp, crab, fish — batter-dipped and fried. The food is refreshingly without frills; no spicy sauces, no unusual combinations. All the food is catch-of-the day fresh, and a full meal is less than $15.

SCAMPI'S, *206 West Aries, Port Isabel. Tel. 956/761-1755. Credit cards accepted.*

When it's time to indulge in upscale seafood, south Texans come to Scampi's. Naturally the shrimp dishes are all specialties of the house. Fresh fish fillets and sauces with both European and Mexican influence highlight the daily selections. Meals are less than $20 per person.

AMBERJACK'S, *209 West Amberjack Street, South Padre Island. Tel. 956/761-6500. Credit cards accepted.*

The restaurant is located on the calm bay waters near the Queen Isabella Bridge. For a casual seafood made in a gourmet fashion, this restaurant remains unsurpassed. The layered Crab and Shrimp Enchiladas in tomatillo sauce is an exquisite mix of flavors. The sautéed Amberjack, the signature dish, is served with fresh mango creme sauce ($13.95). This restaurant sets the standard for excellent seafood on the

Island. Plan to come back a few times to explore why. Steak, chicken and sandwiches also served.

PADRE ISLAND BREWING COMPANY, *3400 Padre Boulevard, South Padre Island. Tel. 956/761-9585. Credit cards accepted.*

The only brew pub on the Island serves excellent food to accompany the fresh beer. The restaurant offers six hamburgers, all priced under $6. A pizza can be traditional or racy with toppings that include grilled quail, gorgonzola cheese or shrimp. Dinner, served from 5pm to 10pm, features eclectic entrees. The Crab Stuffed Chilies Rellenos ($12.95) are served in tomato sauce made with amber ale. The Grilled Swordfish ($14.95) has a deliciously tangy marinade of ginger and cilantro. The Beer Batter Shrimp is a sure winner for less exotic palates.

SEEING THE SIGHTS

The beach is the reason to visit Padre Island, and you will be surrounded by it. From the Isabella Bridge, turn north onto Padre Boulevard and continue past the hotels. The next ten miles are beaches with access roads.

There is a great deal to learn from the natural wonderland of the coastal bend. The **South Padre Island Aquarium**, *2305 Laguna Boulevard, Tel. 956/761-7067, open daily 10am to 10pm,* lets you enter the underwater world without getting wet. A more personal look is offered by **Sea Turtle Inc.**, *5805 Gulf Boulevard, Tel. 956/761-2544,* which is run by a lady who has devoted her life to saving the sea turtle. Periodic lectures and presentations about the sea turtle are given, call for the current schedule.

NIGHTLIFE & ENTERTAINMENT

PADRE ISLAND BREWING COMPANY, *3400 Padre Boulevard, South Padre Island. Tel. 956/761-9585. Credit cards accepted.*

The beer selection will not disappoint even the true brew connoisseur. From the refreshing Padre Island Pale Ale to the Longboard Lager, the tastes and subtleties of the beer are excellent. You will enjoy spending some time at the long bar that overlooks the dining room, where you are sure to meet locals and vacationers alike.

BLUE RAY'S, *100 Padre Boulevard, South Padre Island. Tel. 956/761-7297.*

This unique clothing Harley Davidson Motorcycle shop has a restaurant that serves light gourmet meals. Lunch specials such as blackened red snapper sandwich ($7.95) or white cheese steak sandwich with mushrooms ($6.95) will enliven your tastebuds. The pride of the kitchen is the pizza, which is made with split flatbread instead of traditional crust. During the evening entertainment is featured.

SPORTS & RECREATION

The water off South Padre Island is rich in red snapper, kingfish, wahoo and marlin. **Jim's Pier**, *209 West Whiting, Tel. 956/761-2865, Fax 761-4911*, has cruises to suit most every taste in fishing. Deep sea fishing trips take you 50 miles into the Gulf and last all day. Less intense half-day bay fishing trips start at only $15 per person. Private charters can be arranged.

Scuba divers should not pass up the opportunity to jump into the warm, inviting waters off South Padre Island. Just a boat ride away, you can dive along the warm coast or venture to an oil rig, which offers vertical ocean communities. **American Diving**, *1807 Padre Boulevard, Tel. 956/761-2030, Fax 956/761-6039*, conducts specialized dives, teaches certification courses and has dolphin watch cruises.

The **Island Equestrian Center**, *Tel. 956/761-4677 or 800/761-4677*, provides horses for riding on the beach by the hour and can arrange hay rides or cookouts.

For a bird's-eye view of the Island, jump out of a plane with **SPI Divers**, *Tel. 956/761-6026 or 233-9430*. Novice skydivers are welcome; SPI Divers specializes in tandem jumps. Each jump requires special arrangements, so call for more information.

EXCURSIONS & DAY TRIPS

Matamoros, the Mexican border city across the Rio Grande from Brownsville, is a short drive from South Padre Island. See the excursions section under Brownsville above.

PRACTICAL INFORMATION

The **South Padre Island Convention and Tourist Bureau**, *600 Padre Boulevard, South Padre Island, Tel. 800/SOPADRE*, offers information about the area.

McALLEN

The town of **McAllen**, with a population of 100,000, is one of the most popular destinations for winter tourists. For this reason, the city has good deal of large shopping centers and chain restaurants. **Reynosa, Mexico** is a charming town about 8 miles from McAllen.

Even more interesting than McAllen itself, are the many small towns surrounding the city. The personality of the Rio Grade Valley comes into focus with a visit to the nearby towns of **Mission** or **Alamo** (not to be confused with The Alamo in San Antonio).

ARRIVALS & DEPARTURES

McAllen is at the intersection of Highway 281, which runs north to San Antonio, and Highway 83, which runs east-west along the Rio Grande. The **McAllen Miller International Airport**, *Tel. 956/682-9101,* is located just south of the city.

ORIENTATION

Most of what you will need to find in McAllen is along Highway 83, which crosses through the center of town. Highway 336, which runs to Hidalgo and the Mexican border, is also called 10th Street.

WHERE TO STAY

DOUBLETREE CLUB HOTEL, *101 North Main Street, McAllen. Tel. 956/631-1101, 800/222-8733. Rates: $49 to $99.*

This historic building underwent a complete renovation in 1989. The three story, 158 room hotel offers the excellent service and comfort of a Doubletree, with the historic charm of McAllen. Each room has a coffee maker and hair-dryer; some have views of the outdoor pool. The hotel has a restaurant and a lounge. Complimentary shuttle service takes guests to the nearby golf course and airport.

McALLEN AIRPORT HILTON, *2721 South 10th Street, McAllen. Tel. 956/687-1161 or 800/346-2878, Fax 956-687-8651. Rates: $64 to $74. Credit cards accepted.*

The 149 room hotel is located in close proximity to the airport. The fitness facilities include a tennis court and an outdoor pool. The hotel can arrange access to a nearby golf course. The shine has somewhat faded from this Hilton, although it remains the business traveler's choice for service and convenience.

COURTYARD BY MARRIOTT, *2131 South 10th Street, McAllen. Tel. 956/668-7800 or 800/321-2211, Fax 956/668-7801. Rates: $75.*

This hotel is at the corner of 10th Street and Wichita Street. The Courtyard offers a gym and outdoor pool. Children under the age of 17 stay free of charge with parents.

WHERE TO EAT

COUNTRY OMELETTE, *2025 North 10th Street, McAllen. Tel. 956/687-6461. Credit cards accepted.*

When you sit down for a meal at the Country Omelette, you get a slice of local life. The waitresses know almost everyone in the restaurant by name. So, you can catch up on the local gossip while you await a No Imagination Omelet (one ingredient, $4.05) or Super Omelet (five ingredients, $5.25). The menu includes lunch and dinner. Beef fajitas

($6.35) and Chicken Fried Steak are reputed to be the local favorites. The daily "happy hour" lets you fill up on all the ice tea or coffee you can drink for 65¢. The lottery tickets sold here are a major pastime and point of conversation.

1318 CAFE & PATIO, *1318 North 10th Street, McAllen. Tel. 956/687-2520. Credit cards accepted.*

The 1318 serves lunch only, and does an exemplary job of it. A number of classic sandwiches are offered such as Ham and Cheese, but the menu beckons you to try something wild. Unusual combinations come together for Tony's Sandwich, hard boiled eggs and avocado with cucumber yogurt sauce ($5.95), and the Po Boy, which is made with chicken breast and spicy chile orange mayonnaise ($5.75). The soup is made from scratch each day.

LA GUACAMAYA GRILL, *400 Nolana Street, McAllen. Tel. 956/668-7230. Credit cards accepted.*

For a real adventure in dining, try La Guacamaya Grill. You may begin your meal at the salad bar, which is always fresh. The seafood entrees are not shy in flavor. Bold flavors borrowed from Mexican cooking, such as strong garlic and spicy peppers, accent the entrees, which are under $15.

SEEING THE SIGHTS

The **McAllen International Museum**, *1900 Nolana, Tel. 956/682-1564, Tuesday to Saturday 9am to 5pm, Sunday 1pm to 5pm, admission adult $2, students $1*, has interesting collections focusing on the arts and crafts that have developed in northern Mexico and the Rio Grande Valley. The permanent collection includes pieces from Europe and Latin America. The emphasis of the exhibits and learning programs is to nurture the artistic expression of the area's youth.

For a look at the indigenous flora, walk along one of the trails at the **McAllen Nature Center**, *4101 West Business 83, Tel. 956/682-1517, open daily 8am to dark*. The center is the home of some of the beautiful coastal birds who inhabit the Valley.

EXCURSIONS & DAY TRIPS
REYNOSA, MEXICO

Reynosa is about eight miles south of McAllen. Take Highway 336 (10th Street) south to Hidalgo. There is a shopping center and parking lots just to the west of the International Bridge.

Once you cross over the bridge you will be in the shopping area. Continue down the main street and you will reach the town square. If you cut across the square to the left a large pedestrian street leads you along the city marketplace for residents. Here you can buy music, food and various sundries. As you move away from the square the merchandise becomes more utilitarian and the crowd thickens. Should you want to stay the night in Reynosa, the hotels in the town square are clean and reasonably safe.

HOTEL SAN CARLOS, *970 Plaza Hidalgo, Reynosa. Tel. 89/22-12-80 or 22-40-00. Credit cards accepted. Rates: $28 to $35.*

This five story hotel over looks the main plaza. The rooms are clean and comfortable, and the friendly staff speaks some English. The hotel restaurant serves good, inexpensive food. And you are just two blocks away from the cafes on Zaragoza Street.

HOTEL MIRABEL, *830 Plutarco Elias Calles, Reynosa. Tel. 89/22-25-90 or 89/22-26-30. Rates: $30. Credit cards accepted.*

This 53 room hotel is just around the block from the main street that leads to the border crossing. The neighborhood setting is quiet and just a four block walk to Plaza Hidalgo, the main square.

CAFE SANCHEZ *Calle Zaragoza, Reynosa. Open daily 8am to 7pm.*

This small diner is packed with locals grabbing a quick meal. The food is good and the atmosphere authentic. The best part of the place is that there probably will not be other tourists. Do not expect anything exceptional, and you will be very satisfied.

CAFE PARIS, *Calle Zaragoza, Reynosa. Open daily 7am to 7pm.*

This upscale cafe serves excellent breakfast for about US$1.50. You can buy fresh pastry, muffins and sweetbread to take away or eat there with coffee. For lunch and dinner, each day a different set menu special features soup, a meat dish (like chicken and peppers) with rice and beans for about US$2.

TREVINO'S, *30 Virreges, Reynosa. Tel. 89/22-14-44.*

This is the best known bar, and the one most frequented by tourists. It is stumbling distance from the border, and it earned its reputation by making excellent margaritas. On weekend nights Trevino's still gets festive, although it can be empty on weeknights.

WEST OF McALLEN

A few miles south of Mission, **La Lomita Chapel**, *Farm Road 1016, Mission*, is a worthwhile side trip. The small, white chapel with a shingle roof was a rest stop for travelers along the Rio Grande. Built in 1865, the chapel is not only standing but occasionally used for religious services. In 1899 the building was moved to its present location. From McAllen, take Highway 83 west; go south on Farm Road 1016.

In January, Mission is the site of the **Texas Citrus Festival**. This celebration of fruit culminates in a parade which features entire floats made from citrus — peel, leaves and seeds.

The small town of **Los Ebanos** has a bit of living history connecting the United States and Mexico. This is the site of a hand-drawn ferry. You may cross the Rio Grande with your car or on foot. The small boat holds two average-sized vehicles. The ferry conductor stands at the front and pulls the ferry across, hand over hand. There is nothing of interest on the Mexican side of the border, just a dirt road that leads to a village. From McAllen, take Highway 83 west 14 miles past Mission to Farm Road 886. Turn south and this road leads to the ferry.

EAST OF McALLEN

The town **Alamo** has nothing to do with the famous mission in San Antonio; it was named for a local agricultural company. Lovers of uncultivated nature will want to visit the **Santa Ana National Wildlife Refuge**, *Farm Road 907, Alamo, Tel. 956/787-3079*. Thousands of acres of sub-tropical forest are home to many animals more commonly seen in Mexico. Nature trails run through the preserve and a tram takes visitors on tours (fare adult $3 children $1) with a skilled guide. From McAllen, travel west on Highway 83 to Alamo. Take Farm Road 907 south to Highway 281, then head west.

Harlingen, founded in 1905, is a hub for area citrus farmers. The **Rio Grand Valley Museum**, *Harlingen Industrial Park, Harlingen, Tel. 956/430-8500, Wednesday to Saturday 10am to 4pm, Sunday 1pm to 4pm, closed Monday*, gives an interpretive look at life in south Texas. History is traced through art, recreations of businesses and photos of documents. The museum helps visitors understand history through the perspective of the residents of the Rio Grande Valley. The enthusiastic guides relate stories and folklore. From McAllen, take Highway 83 east to Loop 499 in Harlingen. The museum is across from Texas State Technical College. Harlingen has its own Chamber of Commerce, *Tel. 800/531-7346*.

Rio Grande City has one of the more unusual landmarks in south Texas, a replica of the Lourdes Grotto, *305 North Britton Street, Rio Grande City*. The grotto was built by Father Gustave from 1927 to 1928. Tranquil recorded music gives a haunting quality to the 90-foot tall stone grotto. From the highway, turn toward the courthouse.

La Borde House, *601 East Main Street, Rio Grande City*, was the house of a French businessman, and today is a lovely inn. The establishment may not be open, but this curiosity is worth a stop, simply to appreciate the historic French architecture which is so unusual in the area. La Borde House has the charm of French style and the beauty of a preserved landmark. The rooms are richly furnished in antiques, and the restaurant downstairs has a patio for drinks and dining.

PRACTICAL INFORMATION

The **McAllen Convention & Visitors Bureau**, *Tel. 800/250-2591*, can answer questions about city's attractions.

LAREDO

Laredo stands on the Texas-Mexico border. Interstate Highway 35 passes through Laredo and continues south as the major Mexican highway to Mexico City. As the gateway to the United States, Laredo is a busy center of trade and commerce. In the last few years truck and car traffic across the border has increased dramatically.

Both Laredo and **Nuevo Laredo, Mexico** used to be one city. They split after the United States-Mexico War. Laredo was founded early in the Spanish attempt to colonize their northern territory. In 1755 the San Augustin Plaza, or town square, was the core of the community. Later the business district took over as a downtown area. Today the older parts of the city are in decline, while the suburban malls and shopping centers blossom.

Every year Laredo throws a big celebration for the birthday of George Washington. The tradition stems from the celebration of the end of Spanish and European rule on the continent. For nearly 100 years parades, celebrations and a lot of home cooking pay homage to Washington and freedom.

ARRIVALS & DEPARTURES

The **Laredo Airport** is on the north of the city. Take Loop 20 from Interstate Highway 35. American, Continental, Conquest and the Mexican carrier TAESA serve Laredo.

ORIENTATION

The main access to Laredo is via Interstate Highway 35, which runs south from San Antonio. Highway 59 connects Laredo to Houston from the northeast.

GETTING AROUND TOWN

Ole Tours, *Tel. 956/726-4290*, takes groups on sightseeing and shopping tours of Laredo and Nuevo Laredo. The four and one-half hour tour includes hotel pick-up and costs $15 per person. They also have daily tours to Monterey, Mexico.

The **Laredo Municipal Transit System**, *401 Scott Street, Laredo, Tel. 956/722-0951*, operates the city bus service.

WHERE TO STAY

LA POSADA, *1000 Zaragoza Street, Laredo. Tel. 956/722-1701, Fax 956/722-4758. Rates $79 to $300. Credit cards accepted.*

The premier hotel in Laredo stands on the historic San Augustine Plaza. Beautiful Mexican decoration fills this hotel, which offers the charm of an historical setting and the luxury of first-class accommodations. Each of the 204 rooms and suites is comfortably furnished, and you can expect the highest standard of service. Many of the rooms overlook the pool and tropical courtyard. The Tack Room, the hotel restaurant, is popular with local diners; El Cafe serves less formal Mexican meals. La Posada provides free airport shuttle service to all guests.

CONEXION BED AND BREAKFAST, *907 Zaragoza Street, Laredo. Tel. 956/725-7563. Rates: $75.*

The Conexion stands just off Laredo's historic old square. The location is ideal for tourists who want to walk to Nuevo Laredo; the International Bridge is only a few blocks away. The comfortable rooms are on the second floor of an old home. The shared baths and large kitchen will make you feel right at home. The rooms have tall ceilings, hardwood floors and plenty of windows. A long balcony overlooks the Rio Grande.

HOLIDAY INN CIVIC CENTER, *800 Garden Street, Laredo. Tel. 956/727-5800 or 800/HOLIDAY, Fax 956/727-0278. Rates: $59 to $85. Credit cards accepted.*

The Holiday Inn is a short drive from the border, and offers the comfort and convenience of nearby retail shopping centers. Two restaurants, one which remains open around the clock, a small gym and indoor parking are on premises. Children under the age of 12 stay free with parents, and during certain seasons they eat free at the hotel restaurant. The hotel is located just across from the Laredo Civic Center close to Interstate Highway 35.

BEST WESTERN FIESTA INN, *5240 San Bernardo Street, Laredo. Tel. 956/723-3603 or 800/460-1176, Fax 956/724-7697. Rates: $55.*

The Fiesta Inn offers the best service-oriented budget accommodations in the area. Located near Interstate Highway 35, about four miles form the border, this is a good choice for travelers passing through. Each room includes continental breakfast. The large pool in the center of the courtyard-style hotel is a great way to cool off after along day of sightseeing. Free shuttles to the border and airport are provided.

WHERE TO EAT

CHEZ MAURICETTE, *500 Flores Avenue, Laredo. Credit cards accepted.*

This French restaurant offers a break from the Mexican influenced food of south Texas. The servings are large and the food more hearty than typical French fare. The highlight of your meal are the eight superb soups from which to choose. The aromatic garlic soup perfectly accompanies ribeye steak in wine sauce. Monday to Friday 11:30am to 5:30pm and Thursday to Saturday 7pm to 11pm.

ROSITA'S, *1402 San Bernadino, Laredo. Tel. 956/722-4599. Monday to Saturday 10am to 9pm.*

This simple cafe serves home-made Tex-Mex food. Here you can taste the flavors that south Texans grow up with, like the rich chicken-broth of the caldo, or soup, and the heavy enchiladas. Prices are reasonable.

SEEING THE SIGHTS

San Augustine Plaza has been the center of town since the days of Spanish rule. When approaching from Interstate Highway 35, Zaragoza Street veers west just before International Bridge 1; San Augustine Plaza is only two blocks from the highway.

The **San Augustine Roman Catholic Church** is on the San Augustine Plaza, the city's historic district. The white walls of the church are an element of understatement in the simple Gothic-style design. Inside beautiful wooden carvings and vivid stained glass windows provide aesthetic tranquillity.

In the midst of turmoil on the frontier, a group of ranchers, lawyers and businessmen decided to take politics into their own hands. They declared the region an independent state, free from the governments of Mexico and Texas, and Laredo was the capital. The **Capitol of the Republic of the Rio Grande Museum**, *1009 Zaragoza Street, Tel. 956/727-3480, Tuesday to Saturday 9am to 4pm, Sunday 1pm to 4pm,* is the only institution that pays tribute to these brave individuals. Three rooms document the battles, and are furnished with pieces from the nineteenth century. The small republic attempted to operate as an independent state from 1839 to 1841. The declaration of independence was signed at a constitutional convention on a ranch near Zapata, Texas. The "revolution" received far less attention than that of the larger Republic of Texas, which was at war with Mexico at the time. The museum holds free Historic Walking Tours of Laredo every Friday and Saturday at 10:30am and 1:30pm.

NIGHTLIFE & ENTERTAINMENT

Most head to the bars of Nuevo Laredo across the border for entertainment and nightlife.

SPORTS & RECREATION

Laredo has a modest horse racing track at the **Laredo International Fair and Exposition Grounds**, *Highway 59, Tel. 956/722-5662.*

EXCURSIONS & DAY TRIPS
NUEVO LAREDO, MEXICO

International Bridge 1 is the main pedestrian and passenger car route into Laredo. Just after you cross the bridge, continue straight on Avenida Gurrero. This is the center of shops for tourists, and the streets with recommended restaurants cross this road.

I recommend the following restaurants in town:

VICTORIA, *Calle Victoria No. 3020, Nuevo Laredo. Tel. 871/2-69-00 or 3-30-20.*

The colorful decoration of Victoria puts you in the mood for some festive, truly Mexican food. This restaurant serves the type of cuisine you would expect in an international city, and the menu comes in English. The sauces are flavorful and not shy with spices, and the appetizers are not to be missed. The bean soup is creamy and delicious; queso flameado, white cheese with peppers and mushrooms eaten in tortillas, is excellent. The main dishes will not disappoint. The selection includes steak, chicken and shrimp specialties made with the rich sauces and styles of southern Mexico. For dessert, round your meal off with flan, custard in caramel sauce and a cup of cafe Mexicana, dark coffee with cinnamon and spice. An entire meal including drinks costs under $20. The restaurant is located to the west of the main street that connects to the border.

EL DORADO, *Avenida Ocampo and Calle Belden, Nuevo Laredo.*

To Texans, this is still the Cadillac Bar, the famous restaurant that concocted the Ramos Gin Fizz. Many long nights have begun in this unassuming restaurant-bar. The food is good, an authentic version of what Tex-Mex should be. And the atmosphere is always festive, since the clientele are tourists. The hunting trophies on the walls betray the foundations of this bar, as one of the favorite of Texas hunters and ranchers since 1926.

SENOR FROG'S, *351 Avienida Ocampo, Nuevo Laredo. Tel. 87/13-30-31 or 13-30-11.*

Nuevo Laredo's link in the infamous Carlos n' Charlies' restaurant chain is just across the street from the time-honored El Dorado. Senor Frogs serves good food, and better drinks with the brightly colored "in-your-face" style of fun for which they are famous.

For shopping in Nuevo Laredo:

Practically the entire town of Nuevo Laredo is an open shop, with small alleyways lined with shops, merchants calling you in, markets old and new. The finest of all shops on the border is **Marti's**, *2923 Calle Victoria, Nuevo Laredo, Tel. 87/12-3337 or 12-21-83*. Three floors are packed with the finest crafts from all over Mexico. The top floor holds lovely, rustic hacienda-style furnishings, sculpture and decorations. The second floor has an array of ceramics and glass. The first floor has cases of gold and silver jewelry, clothes and accessories. You can rest assured that the items are the finest quality, and credit cards are accepted.

For a more adventurous approach to shopping, visit the **El Cid Glass Factory**, *3861 Avenida Reforma, Nuevo Laredo*, where you can watch the pieces being hand-blown. The shop, which is open daily, is located about two miles from the border.

SAN YGNACIO

A short drive south from Laredo on Highway 83 is **San Ygnacio, Texas**, a border hamlet founded in the eighteenth century. The town was little more than a large ranch and reflects the architecture of northern Mexico of the time. Small stucco buildings accented with Spanish-style decoration dating from the nineteenth century compose an historic district. To reach the historic district from Highway 83, exit to Mina Street.

Every September the town throws the **San Ygnacio Anniversary Celebration**, a small yet jubilant festival providing a glimpse into the current life and history along the Rio Grande. The town grew up around and received protection from the Jesus Trevino Fort, 1830-1871. The main threats to frontier life were hostile bandits that roamed the desolate borderlands. Armed rebellion has also been a common occurrence on the Texas frontier. The Our Lady of Refuge Church dates from 1875. The preservation in the town is remarkable, considering that the historic sites are not open for tourists.

The Falcon Reservoir is surrounded by **Falcon State Park**, which offers fishing, swimming, boating and camping. Known primarily as a location for bass fishing, Falcon Reservoir is also a birdwatcher's paradise. Highway 83 runs along the eastern coast of the reservoir.

PRACTICAL INFORMATION

American Automobile Association (AAA), *7100 San Bernando Avenue, Laredo, Tel. 956/727-3527.*

The **Laredo-Webb County Chamber of Commerce**, *2310 San Bernardo Avenue, Laredo, Tel. 956/722-9895 or 800/292-2122*, provides tourist and historical information.

A **Texas Department of Highways Travel Information Center** is located on Interstate Highway 35, six miles north of Laredo. Blue signs indicate the exit.

17. WEST TEXAS

Open desert, dramatic canyons and succulent plants characterize west Texas. The dry climate and lack of city lights make the **Davis Mountains** an ideal location for stargazing. The University of Texas operates **McDonald Observatory**, which is open to the public for daytime and nighttime stargzing.

The **Rio Grande** marks the southern border between Texas and Mexico. The snaking waterway cuts through the mountains of Big Bend. Driving distances through west Texas are long. While Interstate Highway 10 is seldom empty, smaller roads may often be deserted.

SAN ANGELO

The name **San Angelo** conjures up images of dusty cattle drives and burnt orange sunsets. As the cattle industry settled into ranching, San Angelo became a hub of the wool trade. **San Angelo State University** is a major contributor to the cultural life of the city.

The wild west lives on in San Angelo. You can visit a preserved house of ill repute over a saloon, then venture to the frontier stronghold of **Fort Concho**, which provides a lasting reminder of how the west, and San Angelo, was conquered.

If you want to be a cowboy — and who doesn't — join in the festivities at the annual **Cowboy Gathering** on the last weekend of August at San Angelo State Park, *Farm Road 2288, Tel. 915/949-4757*. Genuine barbecue and other cowboy culinary delights are on the menu. There are songs, rope tricks and other sorts of family fun to be had.

ARRIVALS & DEPARTURES

San Angelo is at the crossroads of Highways 67, 87 and 277, which meet in the center of town. To the south stands Twin Buttes Reservoir; the North Concho River flows into OC Fisher reservoir on the northwest.

ORIENTATION

Old Ballinger Highway is the business branch of Highway 67 which cuts through town from the northeast to the southwest. Highway 87, which passes over OC Fisher Lake in the north, makes a diagonal cross with Highway 67. Highway 87 and Bryant Street are the same road.

GETTING AROUND TOWN

San Angelo Public Transportation, *Tel. 915/655-9952*, operates bus service in the city.

WHERE TO STAY

HINKLE HOUSE, *19 South Park Street, San Angelo. Tel. 915/653-1931. Rates: $60 to $65. Credit cards accepted.*

The Hinkle House was built in 1921 and retains the charm of the architecture of the roaring twenties. Hardwood floors run throughout the house and porches let you enjoy the outdoors. There are only two guest rooms in Hinkle House, so you pretty much have the entire house to yourselves. Breakfast is prepared each morning, and guests may choose from menu selections. The Garden Room is decorated with a floral motif. French doors lead to the private patio. The Concho Room is full of antiques. The home is located west of downtown, off Beauregread Street.

INN OF THE CONCHOS, *2021 North Bryant Street, San Angelo. Tel. 915/658-2811 or 800/621-6041, Fax 915/653-7560. Rates: $41 to 46. Credit cards accepted.*

This is an old fashioned motel. And although the shine may have worn off the fixtures, you will have a clean and comfortable room for a very reasonable rate. The inn has a certain charm to it simply because it is not affiliated with a large chain.

HOLIDAY INN CONVENTION CENTER, *441 Rio Concho Drive, San Angelo. Tel. 915/658-2828 or 800/465-4329. Rates: $79 to $87. Credit cards accepted.*

The Holiday Inn is the largest motel in the city and offers the nicest facilities. The fitness center includes an indoor pool, spa and gym. The hotel is located in the heart of the city and is within walking distance of city sights.

BEST WESTERN INN OF THE WEST, *415 West Beauregard Street, San Angelo. Tel. 915/653-2995 or 800/582-9668. Rates: $43 to $50. Credit cards accepted.*

This Best Western is a good, standard motel close to the city center. The fitness facilities include a gym and indoor pool. There's a restaurant and lounge on the premises.

WHERE TO EAT

OLD TIME PIT BAR-B-QUE, *1805 South Bryant Street, San Angelo. Tel. 915/655-2771. Credit cards accepted.*

This simple, no-nonsense barbecue house serves the best brisket any cowboy could expect to sink his teeth into. Simply load up your plate at the counter and sit down at one of the picnic tables to enjoy your meal. The potato salad is creamy and slightly sweet. A meal costs about $6.

SEEING THE SIGHTS

The town of San Angelo grew up around a military base in the late nineteenth century. To understand the hardships and lifestyle of the Texas frontier, visit **Fort Concho**, *213 Avenue D, Tel. 915/657-4441, Tuesday to Saturday 10am to 5pm, Sunday 1pm to 5pm, closed Monday; admission, adult $1.50, student $1.* This is one of the most interesting and extensively preserved sites remaining from the old west. Besides preserved buildings, the fort has two museums. The **Danner Museum of Telephony** has early telephones tracing the development of communication on display. The **Robert Wood Johnson Museum of Frontier Medicine** shows the cutting edge of frontier medical care. Admission to both museums is included in park admission.

After discovering the hardships faced by the soldiers of Fort Concho, you can see the illicit pleasures they had at their disposal. The saloon and ladies quarters of the ladies of the evening is now **Miss Hattie's Museum**, *18 East Concho, Tel. 915/655-1166, Tuesday to Saturday 9:30am to 4pm, closed Sunday and Monday; admission.* Miss Hattie's operated for nearly a century. The rooms remain with original decoration.

The 7000 acre **San Angelo State Park**, *Farm Road 2288, Tel. 915/949-4757*, stands on the shore of the **OC Fisher Reservoir**. The ancient remains of dinosaurs were found here, and this is one of the few areas where you can see Native American petroglyphs. You can reach the park by taking Farm Road 2288 from either Highway 67 or 87; follow the signs to the state park.

EXCURSIONS & DAY TRIPS

Fort McKavett, *FM 854, Menard, Tel. 915/396-2358, Wednesday to Sunday 8am to 5pm*, was built on the San Saba River in 1852 as a post against Native Americans who were hostile to settlers. The fort was under construction for four years, then abandoned only three years later when troops moved north. In 1869 the fort reopened, and the 24th Infantry of Buffalo Soldiers were stationed there.

Today you can visit the reconstruction of the fort. Replicas of frontier buildings, including military barracks, a post office and school are open to the public. From San Angelo, take Highway 87 east (about 45 miles) to Highway 83. Head south on 83 to Menard. From the town of Menard, take U.S Highway 190 south to Farm-to-Market Road 854. Signs will show the entrance to Fort McKavett.

PRACTICAL INFORMATION

The **San Angelo Convention & Visitors Bureau**, *500 Concho Drive, San Angelo, 915/653-1206 or 800/375-1206*, can provide information about events and destinations in the region.

JUNCTION

The city of **Junction** thrives from the local hunters who pour into town in the spring and fall. Turkey is probably the most popular game in the area; deer, javelina and exotic game fill the local ranches.

Junction's only unusual monument is a tall Christmas Tree-shaped sculpture made of deer antlers called the **Deer Korn Tree**, standing in a tiny park in front of Kimbell Processing Company on Main Street. The Women's Professional Business Club donated the Deer Korn Tree to the city.

Barbecue lovers head to Junction on July 4th for the annual **Brisket Cook-off**, *2341 North Main, Tel. 800/397-3916*. The three-day event includes live music and picnic games on ten acres of beautiful Hill Country. The best brisket brings home a $1500 purse. The best part is that everyone can sample the cooking. The cook-off takes place near the intersection of North Main and Interstate Highway 10.

ARRIVALS & DEPARTURES

To reach Junction, take Exit 456 or Exit 457 from Interstate Highway 10.

WHERE TO STAY

DAYS INN, *111 Martinez Street, Junction. Tel 915/446-3730 or 800/ 329-7466, Fax 915/446-3730. Rates: $49 to $64. Credit cards accepted.*

The 50 room motel stands on a bluff overlooking the countryside, offering rooms with spectacular vistas. The hotel has an outdoor pool and areas for walking your pet. The building is rather new, so the rooms still have a crisp feel. Continental breakfast included with each room. Recreational facilities include an outdoor pool. This is probably the most comfortable hotel in the city. The Days Inn is located just off Interstate Highway 10; take Exit 457.

LA VISTA MOTEL, *2040 Main Street, Junction. Tel 915/446-2191. Rates: $42.94 Credit cards accepted.*

Reasonably comfortable older motel which is popular with the hunting crowd. The small older hotel is quaint, but musty. Those with an appreciation for neon signs and 1950's roadside architecture may enjoy the La Vista.

SLUMBER INN, *2343 North Main Street, Junction. Tel. 915/446-4588. Rates: $43. Credit cards accepted.*

This is the newest of the hotels in Junction. The rooms are large and immaculate with modern furnishings. The Slumber Inn offers by far the best deal in the area. The hotel is located close to Interstate Highway 10, behind the Dairy Queen on Main Street, and it is difficult to see the inn when approaching from either road.

SUN VALLEY MOTEL, *1161 Main Street, Junction. Tel. 915/446-2505. Rates $40.68. Credit cards accepted.*

The large neon sign marks the center of Main Street. This hotel has a swimming pool and the rooms are decent, but the weekly and monthly rates attract clientele who are not the standard campers or travelers.

Camping

KOA, *2145 North Main Street, Junction. Tel. 915/446-3138.*

The KOA campground is located on the banks of the Guadalupe River, less than one-half mile from Interstate Highway 10. You can fish and swim in the river. The campground has electrical hook-ups at each site. If you left your RV at home, the campground has three small but cozy cabins.

WHERE TO EAT

ISAAC'S, *1606 Main Street, Junction. Tel. 915/446-4202. Credit cards accepted.*

The neon sign outside of Isaac's let's you know that this is an old-fashioned establishment. Isaac's is a down-home diner overflowing with friendly atmosphere and good food. The onion rings, with their flaky, almost sweet batter, could pass for gourmet food. Sirloin steaks are carefully prepared ($8.95); the chicken fried steak ($6.95) is more than a meal. Dinners come with salad and French fries or a baked potato. The menu includes sandwiches, a small salad bar and delicious home-made pie. Open daily 6 am to 10pm.

COME 'N' GIT IT, *2341 Main Street, Junction. Tel. 915/446-4357, Fax 915/446-4476. Credit cards accepted.*

The breakfast at Come 'n' Git It will definitely fill you up. The Sombreros are giant breakfast tacos that require a knife and fork. The largest overflows with five items (try eggs, sausage, cheese, hash-browns and bell peppers as stuffing) and is only $2.35. The grits and biscuits are good, but my favorite is the Apple Jacks, flapjacks topped with fried apples. The lunch and dinner selections are no less satisfying. The salad bar is fresh and well stocked. With a twist on the traditional southern, the menu includes an array of fried food such as spicy chicken wings ($4.25), batter-fried whole onion ($4.50) and chicken fried chicken breast ($6.25). Open daily 6 am to 11pm.

SPORTS & RECREATION

Hunting leases are available for all types of land and accommodations throughout the area. Some have cabins on the property, others are only rough land. The **Kimball County Chamber of Commerce**, *402 Main Street, Junction, Tel. 915/446-3190*, publishes a list of hunting leases and also posts it outside the office.

EXCURSIONS & DAY TRIPS
ROCKSPRINGS

The seat of Edward's County is **Rocksprings**, a sleepy town settled in 1889. The area served as rest stop for weary travelers in the last century. A rock spring provided a flow of fresh water, which is the town's namesake.

The entire town is little more than the courthouse and surrounding town square. The courthouse is a late Victorian building. The town square is lined with simple white stucco establishments, at least half of which are now closed. The **Mohair Weekly Bookstore**, *Monday to Friday 8:30am to noon; 1pm to 5pm*, in the Mohair Weekly Building sells field guides and books about local history and lore. **Mary's Cafe & Bar**, *Monday to Saturday 10am to 1am*, serves inexpensive diner food.

Organized hunting trips are offered by **Helwig Hunting Services**, *P. O. Box 483, Rocksprings, 78880, Tel. 830/683-5104*. Package hunting trips cost $350 per person for two days. Hunting expeditions for exotic animals are a specialty of this service agency.

If you'd like to stay overnight, try:

MESA MOTEL, *PO Box 1043, Rocksprings. 830/683-3241. Rates: $31.70 to $39.70.*

This small stone motel has 12 older but reasonably clean rooms. As the only place in town to bunk for the night, the rates seem reasonable. The hotel is family-run. The motel is two blocks from the town square on Highway 377.

Going west on Interstate Highway 10 will bring you to the town of **Sonora**, a former trading post which is now in ranch country. The **Caverns of Sonora**, *Ranch Road 1989, Sonora, Tel 915/387-3105 or 387-*

6507, Fax 387-6508, open daily 9am to 5pm, offer breathtaking crystal formations. You can walk through one and one-half miles of gorgeous natural artwork. The caves are always a comfortable 70 degrees, and tours leave throughout the day. Camping facilities are available on the park grounds. During the summer, the **Covered Wagon Dinner Theater** provides nightly entertainment.

DEL RIO

On Saint Philips Day in 1635, a group of Spanish missionaries arrived on the banks of the Rio Grande and founded a settlement known as San Felipe del Rio. Over the next two centuries the name shortened to **Del Rio**. The charming town and quaint neighboring Acuna, Mexico are full of history. They remain free of the hearts of tourists that frequent the towns of the Lower Rio Grande Valley and make excellent destinations for leisurely trips.

The natural beauty of the area is a striking blend of the rough Hill Country and the stark desert land of west Texas. The Rio Grande has carved amazing landscapes in the canyons just north of Del Rio. **Lake Amistad** is one of the largest lakes in the state and is a favorite spot for boating, camping and diving. **Seminole Canyon** has breathtaking walking and hiking trails and at least 300 groups of ancient cave paintings.

Although he never lived in Del Rio, Judge Roy Bean, the "Law West of the Pecos," is associated with Del Rio. The judge's reputation is somewhat glorified compared to historical accounts of his life. Although Judge Bean never lived here, his grave was moved to Del Rio in 1964.

Del Rio is the home of **Laughlin Air Force Base**, which is located six miles east of town on Highway 90. Since World War I, military flights have come through the area. The base officially began operations in 1942 as a training base. The flat landscape and clear skies make the area perfect for pilot training. When driving east, you may see some planes racing across the sky.

During the first weekend in May, **Acuna, Mexico** is the site of an unusual festival called **Calcutta**. The point of this tradition is to bet on riders for the Del Rio Rodeo. Since gambling was illegal in Texas for many years, the bets were taken in the sister city of Acuna. The fun and frolicking that goes along with the Rodeo still goes on when people go to Calcutta in the evening.

ARRIVALS & DEPARTURES

Del Rio is located on Highway 90 west of San Antonio. Highway 90 approaches from the east, then shoots northwesterly. Lake Amistad is about 10 miles northwest of Del Rio.

ORIENTATION

Near the center of town, Main Street crosses Highway 90, which becomes Avenue F within the city. The old downtown area stands on Main Street. The historic neighborhood streets of Del Rio run parallel to and are on the west of Main Street. Take Main Street south from Highway 90 to Highway 277. Heading west on Highway 277 will take you to the US-Mexico border.

GETTING AROUND TOWN

You can take a **City Taxi**, *Tel. 830/775-6344*, around town or across the border. The **Del Rio Taxi Service**, *Tel. 830/775-4448*, also serves the area.

The **Lake Amistad Guide Service**, *Tel. 830/774-3484*, offers guides to show you the natural highlights and sportsman's opportunities on the lake. **Forever Resorts**, *Highway 90 West HCR-3, Del Rio, Tel. 830/774-4157 or 800/255-5561*, offers houseboat and deck cruiser rentals on Lake Amistad.

Del Rio Public Transportation, *Tel. 830/774-8670*, has information about city bus routes that serve Del Rio and the surrounding area.

WHERE TO STAY

LA MAISON DEL RIO BED AND BREAKFAST, *123 Hudson Drive, Del Rio, Tel. 830/768-1100. Singles/doubles $85 to $125. Credit cards accepted.*

Nestled in the city's oldest and most stately neighborhood, La Mansion Del Rio epitomizes the Mexican and European roots of the area's settlers. The house is built in the Mexican style with porches lining the exterior, stucco walls. The bright tile floors were shipped from Italy, and the wide beamed ceiling is Mediterranean cypress wood. Large magnolia and pecan trees shade the two acre yard. The interior is a beautiful blend of original antiques and modern renovation. A series of small murals line the main rooms; these were painted by the previous owner, Mrs. Foster.

The rooms are large and artfully decorated. The largest suite, the Judge's French Door Suite, has a large private bath and sun porch. The three upstairs rooms have queen size-beds. The Peacock Room has a private balcony and separate sun porch and private bathroom. Allow ample time in your day to relax and savor the atmosphere of this historic house, which was built in 1887. Afternoon tea and breakfast features homemade bread and fresh juice.

THE 1890 HOUSE, *609 Griner Street, Del Rio. Tel. 830/775-8061 or 800/282-1306, Fax 830/775-4667. Rates: $75 to $105. Credit cards accepted.*

The lovely 1890 House has southern comfort and tropical charm. The superbly landscaped grounds have old shade trees and graceful palm trees. Each room is furnished with Victorian decor and modern beds and baths. The in-room spa bathtubs are a particularly pleasurable amenity. The four guest rooms on the second floor of the home, are fresh and homey. The largest, the Victorian suite, has a luxurious bed and spacious modern bath. Breakfast is served in the downstairs dining room. In the evenings, guests gather in the living room to enjoy drinks and listen to piano music.

RAMADA INN, *2101 Avenue F (Highway 90), Del Rio. Tel. 830/775-1511 or 800/272-6232. Rates: $64 to $72. Credit cards accepted.*

The Ramada has a gym, heated pool and jogging track on the premises. All rooms have amenities such as hair dryers and coffee makers. The motel is located close to the center of town and a short drive from the International Bridge.

DAYS INN, *3808 Avenue F (Highway 90) West, Del Rio. Tel. 830/775-0585 or 800/DAYS-INN, Fax 830/775-1981. Rates: $36 to $58. Credit cards accepted.*

The Days Inn offers good budget accommodations just outside the center of the city. The hotel offers two bedroom suites with kitchenettes or standard rooms. A picnic area with grills is located on the hotel grounds. Continental breakfast is included with each room.

WHERE TO EAT

TEXAS ROSE RESTAURANT, *Highway 90 at Laughlin Air Force Base, Del Rio. Tel. 830/298-2286. Credit cards accepted.*

The Texas Rose is a favorite among the military families of the area. Although the building looks like a roadhouse saloon, inside it's a family restaurant. The casual atmosphere and variety of the menu is a crowd pleaser. The house specialty is barbecue, and a plate of brisket comes with beans, potato salad, onion rings and toast ($7.95). Or choose from the pasta fetuccini alfredo ($7.45) or salmon fillet ($9.95). The food here is simple and good, a home run for the unadventurous palate. To reach Texas Rose, take Highway 90 east from town toward Laughlin Air Force Base. The restaurant is on the highway, just before the turn-off to Laughlin. Open Monday to Saturday 11am to 9pm; closed Sunday.

JITRA THAI CUISINE, *800 East Gibbs Street, Del Rio. Tel. 830/775-7553. Credit cards accepted.*

The restaurant advertises that Thai-Chinese-Japanese food is served. The Thai part of the deal is authentic, and by far the best choice. Pad Thai, or rice noodles with shrimp and chicken, is light and aromatic ($6.95) and the Pad See-eew, wide noodles with meat and vegetables, is excellent. Traditional Thai salads such as Yum Nuea, beef salad ($6.95), and Yum Woon Sen, glass-noodle salad ($6.95), can be prepared as spicy as you dare to try. A variety of vegetarian dishes are available. Lunch specials run daily and include salad and soup ($3.95 to $5.95); the special dinner menu is smaller and entrees includes the same sides ($7.95). Sunday to Thursday 11 am to 9pm; Friday and Saturday 11am to 10pm; closed Tuesday.

BETTY'S RANCH HOUSE CAFE, *1312 Avenue F, del Rio .Tel. 830/775-5457. Credit cards accepted.*

This is a gem of a diner. The walls are adorned with little vases and bottles, so you feel as if you are eating in Betty's own house. Betty has run the place for years, and often is around to tell stories of the history of the building and the town. Breakfast includes real southern grits and firm biscuits. You can order breakfast throughout the day or choose from standard south Texas fare, like enchiladas. The pies are homemade and a different type is featured each day. If you are lucky enough to be there on a pecan pie day, don't pass it up — it surpasses even grandma's.

MEMO'S, *804 Losoya, Del Rio. Tel. 830/775-8104. Credit cards accepted.*

Memos' is virtually a landmark in Del Rio. The owner, a musician and local celebrity, brings in bands and plays for patrons on Tuesday nights. The food is reputed to be the best in the city. The Tex-Mex recipes at Memo's have been passed down in the family. The casual and thoroughly authentic atmosphere at Memo's brings visitors in touch with the people who have lived in Del Rio for generations.

SEEING THE SIGHTS

The oldest winery in the state, and the only one to operate legally during Prohibition, is the **Val Verde Winery**, *100 Qualia Drive, Tel. 830/775-9714, Monday to Saturday 9am to 5pm.* One of the secrets of the rich port wine produced here are the Lonoir grapes, a black Spanish grape which grows wild in the area. The family immigrated from Italy in 1883, and you can see the family history on display in photographs on the walls. When you stop by, you can tour the small reserve area and taste the current selections. This is probably the most interesting and worthwhile stop on a wine connoisseur's tour.

The heavy limestone walls and imposing architecture of the **Val Verde County Courthouse**, *400 Pecan Street,* dominates the courthouse square. In the northeast corner of the square, the jail, built in 1885, is preserved. The Victorian building was built in 1887 by Italian masons. Just south of the courthouse, the **Sacred Heart Church**, *310 Mills Street,* still stands, but is closed to the public.

The **Whitehead Memorial Museum**, *1308 South Main Street, Tel. 830/774-7568; admission $3 adults, $2 children,* was once a store. Today the building houses historic memorabilia from the area. Outside stands a replica of the saloon where Judge Roy Bean held court in Langtry. The graves of the Judge and his son were moved to the museum in the 1960s. Another building on the museum grounds is a barn and livery. Although the displays do concern Del Rio's past, the museum is a hodgepodge of history borrowed from surrounding towns as well.

NIGHTLIFE & ENTERTAINMENT

The most entertaining way to spend an evening is to visit **Acuna, Mexico**; see *Excursions & Day Trips* below.

SPORTS & RECREATION

Enjoyed by both the United States and Mexico, **Lake Amistad National Recreation Area**, *Highway 90, Del Rio, Tel. 830/775-7491*, has 67,000 acres of water and has over 850 miles of shoreline. The lake, populated by bass, crappie, perch and drum, is very popular with fishermen. During certain times of the year, hunting of small game and birds is permitted. Three swimming beaches, picnic areas and campgrounds are located throughout the Amistad area are open to the public. Walking trails and boat launches are located throughout the park.

ECO-EDUCATIONAL TOURISM

*To thoroughly explore the archaeology of the region, contact the **Rock Art Foundation, Inc.**, 4833 Fredericksburg Road, San Antonio, Tel. 210/ 525-9907 or 888/525-9907. The group, which is primarily concerned with education and preservation, conducts tours of the area's many rock art sites. You can learn form members about the research and lore associated with the ancient Native American history. Regular tours are held on the first weekend of each month. Tours usually include one site in the area and last one day. Some strenuous hiking may be required.*

*Another group that conducts seminars about the Seminole Canyon and surrounding area is the **Big Bend Natural History Association**, P. O. Box 196, Big Bend, TX 79834, Tel. 915/477-2236. The topics of the seminars are diverse – from astronomy to photography – and are held at points of interest throughout west Texas. Former topics include edible and useful plants of the Amistad National Recreation Area, and Rock Art and Archaeology.*

A number of archaeological sites can be visited. **Seminole Canyon State Park**, *Highway 90, Comstock, Tel. 915/292-4464*, offers easily accessible and impressive cave paintings. The one mile guided tour offered daily at 10am and 3pm visits a site which was inhabited for thousands of years. The Native Americans who lived in the canyon left amazing pictographs of people, animals and mysterious symbols. The park has 30 campsites, most with full hook-ups, and eight miles of hiking trails. Mountain biking is allowed on the six mile canyon overlook trail. Seminole Canyon is 45 miles northwest of Del Rio.

EXCURSIONS & DAY TRIPS
ACUNA, MEXICO

Those who have seen the movie *El Mariachi* will recognize **Acuna, Mexico**. The colorful buildings and quiet streets are a pleasure for a casual stroll. The first eight blocks of the main street, Calle Miguel Hidalgo, is a pedestrian thoroughfare which leads to the border crossing. Neon signs advertising restaurants and bars hang over the street and buzz to life at dusk. The small shops along the street carry the usual arts and crafts, and a few have ceramics, hand-made furniture and sterling silver jewelry of high quality.

If you want to stay overnight and grab a meal, try:

HOTEL SAN ANTONIO, *300 Calle Hidalgo, Acuna, Mexico. Rates $45 to $60. Credit cards accepted.*

This Spanish-style hotel has clean, comfortable rooms with modern baths. Of the two wings, the old section is actually more comfortable and is just over the main building. The new wing, across the parking lot, has rooms that are slightly larger. The friendly staff speaks English and caters to American tourists. The restaurant on the premises serves good, inexpensive food. A Mexican breakfast costs about US$2. The parking lot is in the center of the hotel and is a safe place to leave your vehicle.

CROSBY'S, *Calles Hidalgo y Matamoros, Acuna, Mexico. Credit cards accepted.*

This is the most famous restaurant and bar in Acuna, and by far has the most personality of any of the bars on the border. The restaurant, with its white table cloths and attentive service, is excellent. You can order the standard enchiladas or try something different such as a steak or fresh fish fillet. A meal including dessert is under $20. Next door, the cozy bar gets absolutely rowdy on some weekends and the friendly crowd often contains faces from all over the world. The giant margaritas are the most requested drink, but the best on the menu is the Blue Hawaiian.

Across the street is the **Corona Club**, a large bar which stays open late for dancing if the crowd is large enough.

BRACKETTVILLE

If you simply drive through, **Brackettville** may look like a ghost town. Small white houses, many deserted, line the sleepy streets. And it may be hard to find an open store or gas station. But stop in Brackettville for history and you will not be disappointed. The town was settled by Black

Seminoles, former slaves who lived and migrated with the Seminole Indians.

The town grew up around **Fort Clark**, which was built in 1852 and remained an active military post for over 100 years. The fort stands on the southwestern frontier of Texas, about 20 miles from the Rio Grande. Here the military stood strong against Commanche raids on settlers and helped secure the Texas-Mexico border. Fort Clark was home to some of the famous Buffalo Soldiers, the African-American cavalrymen who served in western forts after the Civil War. Brackettville and Fort Clark are located on Highway 90, 32 miles east of Del Rio.

Today visitors to Fort Clark can learn history and enjoy recreational facilities. The **Fort Clark Springs Association**, *Box 345, Brackettville, Tel. 830/563-2493*, offers camp sites, two golf courses and a spring-fed pool. The Officers Club, built in 1939, has been renovated into a restaurant.

A total of 15 caves make up the **Kikapoo Caverns**, *Brackettville, Tel. 830/563-2342 or 800/792-1112*, an undeveloped state park area. Kikapoo Caverns are open to the public by tours guided by Texas State Park personnel. One of the largest caves, Green Cave, is a habitat for migrating Brazilian Freetail Bats throughout the summer months until October. Visitors can ride fourteen miles of rigorous mountain bike trails. **Kikapoo Caverns State Park** is near Brackettville, which is on Highway 90 west of San Antonio. When taking Highway 90 to Brackettville, take Ranch Road 674 north from Brackettville. Clock 22 miles, then look for a gate which is just past the Edwards County line. Be certain to make reservations for a guided tour. The park is closed to regular visitors and used as a hunting area in the fall.

If the real version of the Alamo in San Antonio is just not enough for you, there is the **Alamo Village**, *Ranch Road 674, Brackettville*, a movie set with a reproduction of the Alamo. The site does not keep regular hours.

UVALDE & LANGTRY

Further east, in **Uvalde**, you will find one of the best kept art secrets in the country. The **First State Bank**, *200 East Nopal Street, Uvalde, Tel. 830/278-6231*, has an amazing collection of art on display in the lobby. Most notable is an original Rembrandt, the centerpiece of the collection donated by Dolph Briscoe, a former state governor. You may view the collection during regular bank hours, 9am to 3pm on weekdays.

The **Uvalde Grand Opera House**, *104 West North Street, Uvalde, Tel. 830/278-4184*, built in 1891, is still used for occasional performances. Most of the building has been offices for decades, but part of the opera house is a museum and you can take a free tour of the frontier building.

Northwest of Del Rio, in the small town of **Langtry**, is the former site of the "Law West of the Pecos." The **Judge Roy Bean Visitor Center** is located on the site where the famous saloon that doubled as a court house stood. The saloon, The Jersey Lily, and the town were named after a famous actor of the time, Lily Langtry, who the Judge admired. A small museum has dioramas that show scenes from Langtry in the 1880's. A new, larger museum and visitors center is under construction.

PRACTICAL INFORMATION

The **Del Rio Chamber of Commerce**, *1915 Avenue F, Del Rio, Tel. 830/775-3551 or 800/889-8149*, publishes a number of informative brochures about area history and tourist information.

MIDLAND/ODESSA

Midland stands on the rocky Texas plains, halfway between El Paso and Dallas. The city is a vibrant, modern haven with an active cultural scene. Midland has weathered the roughest historic and economic storms. The city was in the thick of battles between Commanches and settlers. When the oil boom arrived, prosperity flooded the region. Consequently, when Texas oil went bad, the city faced rough times.

Midland and **Odessa** are practically twin cities, located ten miles apart on Interstate Highway 20.

ARRIVALS & DEPARTURES

Midland is served by Southwest Air, the commuter service of American and Continental Airlines. The **Midland International Airport** is between Midland and Odessa; from Interstate Highway 20, exit Highway 1788.

Greyhound Bus (*Tel. 800/231-2222 for reservations*), provides transportation through Midland, *1308 West Front Street, Tel. 915/682-2761*, and Odessa, *500 North Jackson Street, Tel. 915/332-5711*.

ORIENTATION

Both Midland and Odessa are on business loops of Interstate Highway 20. Odessa is the more western of the two cities.

In Midland, Highway 250 forms a loop around the north of the city. Highway 349, or Rankin Highway, bisects the city center from north to south. Loop 338 encircles Odessa, and Highway 385 becomes Grant Avenue, the main north-south street in the city center.

GETTING AROUND TOWN

Major auto rental agencies such as **Budget**, *Tel. 915/563-1352*, and **Enterprise** *Tel. 915/689-9500*, serve Midland. The local agency, **AA Auto Rentals**, *Tel. 915/694-8275*, can provide cars for local trips.

There is no public transportation service in Midland. Visitors must rely on their own transportation or use one of the area taxi services, such as **A1 Taxi**, *Tel. 915/ 697-2521,* or **Yellow Checker Cab**, *Tel. 915/682-1661.*

WHERE TO STAY

MIDLAND HILTON AND TOWERS, *117 West Wall Avenue, Midland, Texas 79701. Tel. 915/683-6131 or 800/774-1500, Fax 915/683-0985. Rates: $60 to $255. Credit cards accepted.*

You can walk downtown from the Hilton, although you will feel like you're in the heart of cosmopolitan Midland in this 11-story, 256 room hotel. You may see a genuine Texas oil man, since the concierge caters to guests of the local oil industry. Three restaurants in the hotel offer southwestern and traditional American cuisine. The local museums are only a few blocks away. The hotel offers a good fitness center.

MELLIE VAN HORN'S INN, *903 North Sam Houston Street, Midland. Tel. 915/337-3000. Rates: $69 to $99. Credit cards accepted.*

The inn was built in 1938 and used as dormitory-style accommodation for single teachers working in Midland schools. After the boarding house closed in 1975, the building was renovated into a bed and breakfast type inn. Each of the sixteen rooms has a private bath and is decorated with antique furnishings. Breakfast is included. The central location makes this an ideal place to stay if you want to get a feel for old-time Midland.

BEST WESTERN GARDEN OASIS, *110 West Interstate Highway 20, Odessa. Tel. 915/337-3006 or 800/528-1234, Fax 915/332-1956. Rates: $48 to $58. Credit cards accepted.*

This hotel strives to be an oasis in the desert with a large atrium and heated pool. The recreational facilities include a spa and sauna. Guests may take advantage of the free shuttle service to Midland International Airport.

MIDLAND DAYS INN, *4717 Highway 80, Midland. Tel. 915/699-7727, Fax 915/699-7813. Rates: $32 to $47. Credit cards accepted.*

The 90 room motel was recently remodeled and redecorated. Recreational facilities include an outdoor pool and use of a golf course. A barbershop and safe-deposit boxes are on the premises.

ODESSA DAYS INN, *3075 East Business Loop 20, Odessa. Tel. 915/335-8000 or 800/DAYS-INN, Fax 915/335-9562. Rates: $44 to $56. Credit cards accepted.*

The hotel has a lounge and an outdoor pool for guests. Extra perks include coffee at any time for guests, and coffee and donuts every morning. This is a simple motel convenient for those passing through the area on a road trip.

WHERE TO EAT

WALL STREET BAR AND GRILL, *115 East Wall Street, Midland. Tel. 915/684-8686. Credit cards accepted.*

You will be able to find many national chain restaurants in Midland, but this is the only place you will find truly excellent cuisine. When you walk into Wall Street Bar and Grill, it seems that the Old West comes alive again. The interior of this bar is straight out of a saloon scene in a movie. What makes the atmosphere incredible is that the decorations are all authentic antiques. The menu includes steaks and the city's freshest and best fish. The food is prepared with traditional recipes. Dinner costs under $20. On the weekends a brunch comes with fresh fruit and home-baked sweet rolls.

SEEING THE SIGHTS

The substance that put Odessa on the map is the focus of the **Petroleum Museum**, *1500 Interstate Highway 20 West, Midland, Tel. 915/683-4403, Monday to Saturday 9am to 5pm, Sunday 2pm to 5pm.* But this museum includes an entire history of the area, showing the role that oil production made in the development of Midland and Odessa.

The **Confederate Flight Museum**, *9600 Wright Drive, Midland, Tel. 915/563-1000, Monday to Saturday 9am to 5pm, Sunday noon to 5pm,* is all about aircraft, but has nothing to do with the Civil War. The museum houses an extensive collection of planes and military equipment from World War II. Every October the museum holds an air show that relives the combat flights of World War II. Explosions, fire and sirens are all part of the staged spectacle.

The office of the president of the United States is honored at the **Presidential Museum**, *622 North Lee Street, Odessa, Tel. 915/332-7123 or 800/862-7123, Tuesday to Saturday 10am to 5pm, closed Sunday and Monday, admission free.* Permanent exhibits include campaign posters (including "Pat Paulsen for President"), White House memorabilia and a library of over 3500 volumes. Temporary exhibits are featured throughout the year. The museum is located in downtown Odessa, just north of Highway 80.

Just six miles south of Odessa you will find a meteor crater so large that you can walk through a nature trail within its circumference. The **Odessa Meteor Crater**, *Interstate Highway 20 West, Odessa*, measures 500 feet in diameter. From Odessa, travel west on Interstate Highway 20, exit Farm Road 1936 and travel south for three and one-half miles.

SPORTS & RECREATION

The last week of August brings the **Permian Basin Open** to Odessa. The $200,000 purse attracts some of the best — but as yet not well known

— professional golfers. The **Club at Mission Dorado**, *Tel. 915/561-8811*, hosts the competition.

NIGHTLIFE & ENTERTAINMENT

THE GLOBE THEATER, *Odessa College, 2308 Shakespeare Road, Odessa. Tel. 915/332-1586.*

Odessa has an active arts scene and some of the best theater west of the Dallas-Fort Worth area. Although a western city may seem an unlikely place for Shakespeare, the Globe Theater presents Shakespeare's plays in a setting designed to replicate the original Globe Theater in England. The theater is also used for traditional country music performances. Every April, Odessa College presents the Shakespeare Festival. The theater and Shakespearean library are open daily from 9am to 5pm.

PERMIAN PLAYHOUSE, *310 West 42nd Street, Odessa. Tel. 915/362-2329.*

Odessa community theater presents dramatic, musical and youth productions throughout the year. This theater has received national recognition for the quality of its productions. Don't miss the chance to see excellent community theater when in the area.

EXCURSIONS & DAY TRIPS

The town of **Monahans** sprang up as a watering hole for the railroad, and grew with the oil industry of the early twentieth century. This is a rest stop for those weary of long miles of bland highway or thirsty for a taste of absurdity: the small town has an unusual museum, the **Million Barrel Museum**, *Highway 80, closed Monday, Tuesday to Saturday, 10am to 6pm, Sunday 2pm to 6pm; free admission.* What does a city do with a one-million barrel storage facility of oil when there is no need to fill it? Open a recreational park, of course. The tank is actually more of a man-made crater. One small corner has a 400 seat theater. The historic part of the park is a turn-of-the-century hotel, the old city jail house and some agricultural machinery. The Million Barrel Museum is just east of Monahans on Highway 80 — you cannot miss it.

You will not find an ocean in west Texas, but there sure are sand dunes. The **Monahans Sandhills State Park**, *Park Road 41, Monahans, Tel. 915/943-2092 or 800/792-1112*, has over 3800 acres of sand dunes, some reaching 70 feet in height. The park has picnic areas, camping facilities and trailer hook-ups. You'll find unusual flora and fauna that maintain the eco-system of the dunes. Over 600 acres are reserved for horseback riding. The Visitor's Center has exhibits explaining the natural phenomena of the desert dunes. Tours by four-wheel-drive vehicle are available. Visitors can take a short, self-guided walking tour. During the summer, park rangers host campfire lectures in the evening. From Interstate Highway 20, exit Park Road 41 (mile marker 86).

PRACTICAL INFORMATION

Tourism information is available from **The Midland Chamber Convention and Visitors Bureau**, *109 North Main, Midland, Tel. 915/683-3381 or 800/624-6435.*

The **Odessa Cultural Council**, *Tel. 915/337-1492*, provides information and schedules of upcoming cultural events at the Permian Playhouse, the Globe Theater and many other theater and music events in the city.

FORT STOCKTON

The area around **Fort Stockton** is an oasis in the brutal arid climate. In 1859, Fort Stockton was settled on what was then the Old San Antonio Road, a trade route linking San Antonio with El Paso. Today, as in the previous century, Fort Stockton is rest stop for weary travelers.

The downtown area retains the quiet charm of yeas past. The county courthouse is surrounded by historic buildings, such as the 1883 school house and the 1875 Catholic Church.

ARRIVALS & DEPARTURES

Fort Stockton is a popular rest stop for travelers heading toward Big Bend. The town is about 110 miles north of Big Bend, at the intersection of Interstate Highway 10 and Highway 290.

ORIENTATION

Main Street begins at Highway 290. At this intersection an 11-foot tall roadrunner statue, "Paisano Pete," greets visitors. Follow Main Street down to the center of the city. On the left of downtown stands old Fort Stockton, which has a short audio presentation that works at all times.

GETTING AROUND TOWN

Roadrunner Bus Tours, *open daily 11am to 6pm, Tel. 915/336-8052*, offers a tour of Fort Stockton, or you can purchase an audio cassette and drive yourself.

WHERE TO STAY

GLASS MOUNTAIN BED AND BREAKFAST, *Highway 385, Fort Stockton. Tel./Fax 915/395-2435 or 800/695-8249. Rates: $ 75. Credit cards accepted.*

Escape to the open west Texas country life. Only the stars provide light outdoor light at Glass Mountain Manor, and the sounds you hear will be cattle or horses. Guests stay in the small original ranch house which was built at the turn-of-the-century. The seclusion and privacy of the entire house are yours; only one set of guests is accommodated at a time and you have the run of the house. All the fixings for breakfast are left in the house. Glass Mountain Manor is located on Highway 385, 26 miles south from Fort Stockton.

BEST WESTERN SWISS CLOCK INN, *3201 West Dickinson, Fort Stockton. Tel. 915/336-8521 or 800/528-1234. Rates: $38 to $56. Credit cards accepted.*

This is a comfortable hotel with a homey atmosphere. A lounge and cafe are in the hotel, and there's an outdoor pool. The inn is about three miles from the center of town. From Interstate 10, take exit #256 south.

DAYS INN, *1408 North Highway 285, Fort Stockton. Tel. 915/336-7500 or 800/ DAYS-INN, Fax 915/336-7501. Rates: $39 to $59. Credit cards accepted.*

This 50 room motel has a hair salon and outdoor pool. There is plenty of parking space for recreational vehicles. Guests may bring their pets. Continental breakfast is included with all rooms.

LA QUINTA, *2601 Interstate Highway 10 West, Fort Stockton. Tel. 915/ 336-9781 or 800/531-5900, Fax 915/336-3634. Rates: $59 to $67. Credit cards accepted.*

La Quinta offers breakfast and airport shuttle service to guests. Both families and business travelers will find adequate facilities here. Phones have computer connections for modem use and dry cleaning service is available. Recreational facilities include an outdoor pool. The motel offers both a restaurant and room service. Children under the age of 18 stay free in parents' room.

KOA CAMPGROUND, *Interstate Highway 10 at exit 264, Fort Stockton. Tel. 915/395-2494. Rates: $17.50 per night.*

The KOA campground has all the facilities you need to make roughing it seem like a pleasure trip. The facilities for the 85 campsites include a restaurant, store and pool.

WHERE TO EAT

FORT STOCKTON BAKERY, *600 West Dickenson, Fort Stockton. Tel. 915/336-7232.*

This small bakery serves fresh, delicious pastry and cinnamon rolls. The Mexican specialties include huge cookies and cinnamon rolls. When you walk in, take a metal tray and pair of tongs and help yourself to the selections along the wall. For lunch you can have tortas, rolls with fillings of brisket, ham or hamburger baked in ($2.80).

SEEING THE SIGHTS

Fort Stockton, *300 East 3rd Street, Tel 915/336-2400, Monday to Saturday 10am to 1pm and 2pm to 5pm*, the military fort that gave its name to this town was in use for only 28 years, from 1858 to 1886. A number of the original 35 stone buildings remain, including the prison, barracks and officers' houses. The museum has a display of the gear and uniforms worn by the cavalry. Fort Stockton, like other Texas frontier forts, was the home of Buffalo Soldiers. The displays, especially the audio presentation in the jail building, gives insight into the difficult conditions the soldiers faced. You can walk around the historic buildings even when the fort complex is closed. As you walk up to the front porch of the old jail, a recorded story describes life in the frontier forts.

Anne Riggs was a hotelier from 1877 until 1931. The **Anne Riggs Memorial Museum**, *301 South Main Street, Tel. 915/336-2167, Monday to Saturday 10am to noon and 1:30pm to 5pm, Sunday 1:30 to 5pm; admission $1 adults, 50¢ children*, was once the city's hotel. The rooms hold displays about the history and culture of Fort Stockton. One room remains furnished as it would have been for hotel guests in 1905. The museum provides a unique glimpse into the frontier life of west Texas. During the summer months of June, July and August, the museum remains open until 8pm.

The town also has a modern landmark of interest. The **Ste. Genevieve Winery** produces inexpensive yet high quality table wine. The winery is a project of private winemakers and University of Texas researchers. The Domaine Corridor Vineyard and facility is in the Escondido Valley. A visit to the winery provides education about high-tech winemaking and a general course on wine tasting. The winery is just off Interstate Highway 10 at McKenzie Road, Exit 285.

SHOPPING

Beautiful hand-made pottery is sold at **In the Round**, *204 West 2nd Street, Tel. 915/336-3542, Monday to Saturday 9am to 6pm*. The pieces reflect the simplicity of the southwest and are designed for daily use.

PRACTICAL INFORMATION

The **Fort Stockton Visitor Center** is located in the historic city train station at the intersection of Business Highway 10 and Main Street.

FORT DAVIS

Fort Davis was founded in 1856 as a US military post. Ranchers began to tame the surrounding area in the late 1800's. The beautiful mountains and desert combine to make a stunning landscape. The area is popular with campers, hikers and hunters.

The altitude, clear skies and open ranges give the Davis Mountain region the best conditions for stargazing. And this is why the University of Texas chose Fort Davis as the site for the **McDonald Observatory**. The facility is open to the public for tours and sun and stargzing.

On the Saturday of Labor Day Weekend, the **Fort Davis Festival** is held on the grounds of the national park. History buffs will enjoy the participants who dress in period costume. For more information about these events, contact the Superintendent of Fort Davis National Historical Park, *P. O. Box 1456, Fort Davis 79734, Tel. 915/426-3224.*

ARRIVALS & DEPARTURES

Fort Davis is located at the intersection of Highways 118 and 17. From Interstate Highway 10, take Highway 17 south at Balmorhea; from Highway 90 take Highway 118 north from Alpine or Highway 17 north from Marfa. The town is very small; the hotels are located in the center of the city. The points of interest are just northwest of the city, on Highway 118.

WHERE TO STAY

THE DRUGSTORE AND OLD TEXAS INN, *Box 822 Main Street, Fort Davis. Tel. 915/426-3118 or 800/DAVIS-MT. Rates: $45 to $65. Credit cards accepted.*

The only place on the town square besides the Hotel Limpia to hang your hat for the night is the Old Texas Inn. The six rooms upstairs from the Drugstore are large and furnished with homey, old-western decor. The friendly atmosphere and comfortable decor make a welcoming environment. The central living area has a large television and comfortable couch. In the morning, have the best breakfast in west Texas style, downstairs at the Drugstore. The Drugstore sells western memorabilia, a selection of interesting books about Texana and souvenirs. On the weekends locals fill the restaurant, indulging in the hearty and inexpensive breakfast specials.

LIMPIA HOTEL, *Main Street on the Square, Fort Davis. Tel. 915/426-3237 or 800/662-5517, Fax 915/426-3983. Rates: $59 to $110. Credit cards accepted.*

The Limpia is far more than a hotel, it is an entire complex of lodgings which includes the historic 32 room hotel, a guest house and camping facilities. The hotel still has the fancy touches that made it a first-rate accommodation in 1912, decorative tin ceilings, moldings and period furniture. The hotel has 12 suites with kitchens and living areas. The sun porch overlooks the main square.

You cannot miss the Limpia; it is the largest building in town and dominates the main square. The Limpia has the only bar in the county, Sutler's Club. The casual yet refined western bar serves drinks and food. You must purchase a membership to the club for a nominal charge.

INDIAN LODGE, *Indian Lodge State Park, Park Road 3, Fort Davis. Tel. 915/426-3254. Rates: Credit cards accepted.*

The Indian Lodge is like a back-to-nature resort. The lodge was built in the style of the Pueblo Native American settlements. The beautiful white adobe walls stand out against the mountainous desert backdrop of the secluded setting. An outdoor pool and patios accent the different levels of the rambling building. The oldest section of the lodge, built in the 1930s, have cedar ceiling beams, fireplaces and original western-style furnishings. The 39 rooms have modern amenities such as telephones, televisions and central heat and air conditioning. You can pass your days hiking the park trails through the Davis Mountains and your evenings stargazing at the almost always clear skies. The Black Bear Restaurant serves excellent breakfast, lunch and dinner meals. Complimentary breakfast served to all guests.

PRUDE GUEST RANCH, *Highway 118, Fort Davis. Tel. 915/426-3202 or 800/458-6232, Fax 915/426-3502, Rates: $65 to $75. Credit cards accepted.*

This little dude ranch in the big mountains of west Texas offers a taste of Texas. The cowboy theme runs through the dining hall decoration. A rodeo area and a scattering of exotic animals provide the ranch feeling. The guest lodges are the better rooms, and are located some distance from the main entrance of the ranch. Family Bunk rooms offer dormitory style accommodations. The Ranch Bunkhouse can hold from 8 to 20 people per room and no sheet or towels are provided. Near the entrance you will find rows of campsites with full hook-ups. Meals can be purchased ($5.50 to $7.95). Take Highway 118 northwest from Fort Davis for six miles.

WHERE TO EAT

HOTEL LIMPIA DINING ROOM, *Main Street on the Square, Fort Davis. Tel. 915/426-3237. Credit cards accepted.*

The intimate country-style dining room at the Hotel Limpia serves the best food in west Texas. The bread is a source of pride for the restaurant, which makes all of its rolls on-site. The entrees include beef and pasta specialties, all have excellent sauces and are cooked to perfection. The Burgundy Marinated Roast Beef ($8.95) can best be described as succulent. Fried Beef Tenderloin is the gourmet version ($9.95) of chicken fried steak. The Adobe Spaghetti is made with a sassy southwestern style sauce and large chunky fresh vegetables. You may have seconds of most of the food, but that may ruin your appetite for dessert. All the pies and cakes are made in-house.

BLACK BEAR RESTAURANT, *Indian Lodge State Park, Park Road 3, Fort Davis. Tel. 915/426-3254.*

A meal in the Black Bear Restaurant is just what you need to be fortified for a day of hiking though the park's nature trails. The restaurant for the Indian Lodge makes excellent food, for very reasonable prices. The CCC Sandwich is a grilled chicken breast on a freshly baked roll ($4.25). Hamburgers come with a number of additions including jalapenos or green chilies ($3.75). Heartier appetites will enjoy the hearty Chicken Fried Steak ($6.95) or 14 ounce Ribeye Steak ($12.95). The menu includes home-made soup, daily vegetable selections and Tex-Mex food.

SEEING THE SIGHTS

The **Fort Davis National Historic Park**, *Highways 17 and 118, Tel. 915/426-3224, Fax 426-3122,* is only a few blocks from the center of town. When the fort was established by the United States government in 1861, it had already been in operation since 1854. Its mission was to protect travelers on the road that connected San Antonio to El Paso. The fort was intended to curb the threat of the outlaw raiders who plagued this no-man's-land. At the time, as a visitor can well imagine, there was little other settlement in the region. The dry desert and foreboding landscape stretched as far as the eye could see.

The entire national park encompasses about 460 acres. However, the visitor's center museum are small complexes. Visitor can take a self-guided tour through the restored enlisted men's barracks and four other buildings dating from the 1880's. Foundations of the military buildings remain uncovered from archaeological investigation and hiking trails are also accessible. Fort Davis is open daily from 8am to 6pm; during the winter months the closing time moves ahead to 5pm. Other historical programs and lectures are held during the year, especially in the summer months. Evening tours are conducted in the fall and winter. To reach Fort Davis, take Highway 17 south from Interstate Highway 10 for 39 miles. Admission to the museum is $2 per person; children and educational groups are admitted free.

The **Davis Mountains State Park** *Highway 118, Tel. 915/426-3254,* has over 18,000 acres of preserved land with hiking trails and camp sites. The Indian Lodge is located on the park grounds. During the summer months, park rangers host educational seminars in the park amphitheater and guided nature walks. The park is located six miles west of Fort Davis on Highway 118.

If you continue along Highway 118, then climb Spur 78, you will reach the highest point in the Davis Mountains, where you'll find the **University** of Texas McDonald Observatory, *Tel. 915/426-3640*. You can tour the large reflecting telescopes, which do not actually observe celestial objects but gather light and data. A new and larger telescope is under construction at the observatory. Visitors can watch an orientation film at the visitors center, then take a tour of one of the telescopes. Tours are given every day at 9:30am and 3:30pm (during the winter tours at 2pm only). After the tour a question and answer session is held.

On Friday and Saturday evenings, Star Parties are held, where visitors can learn about and observe the night sky with the resident astronomers. On weekends the sun can be viewed through a special telescope at 11am and 3:30pm (during the winter tours viewing at 11am only). The Star Parties and sun observation are free to the public. Visitors can look to the heavens through the largest telescope once per month. The fee is $20 per person and reservations are required. The observation sessions should be booked at least four months in advance.

EXCURSIONS & DAY TRIPS

Some of the mysteries of the desert are explained at the **Chihuahuan Desert Research Institute**, *Highway 118, open daily 1pm to 5pm*. This is the only desert research institute in the state. The visitors center gives information about the desert habitat and how man has used the native resources. The institute is located three and one-half miles south of Fort Davis.

The San Solomon Springs feed a warm, deep pool in **Balmorhea State Park**. The absolutely clear water is full of fish — some of which are endangered species — and is a favorite place for scuba divers and skin divers. The water remains a constant 70 degrees Fahrenheit, regardless of the winter cold or summer heat. You can camp in the state park, which has campsites with full hook-ups including cable television. A small motel with 18 units is available for rental. The state park is located four miles west of Balmorhea. From Interstate Highway 10, go south on Highway 17 to the park entrance.

PRACTICAL INFORMATION

The **Fort Davis Chamber of Commerce** is located in the Hotel Limpia lobby, *Main Street on the Square, Fort Davis, Tel. 915/426-3237*.

ALPINE

The city of **Alpine** has intellect, art and natural beauty. Area ranches raise mohair sheep and depended on Alpine as a center of commerce. Once a ranching town, Alpine now relies on art and tourism for its sustenance. You can see the mohair warehouses by the railroad station.

They are among the numerous historic buildings in the town. Alpine is the seat of the largest county in Texas, Brewster.

After the railroad tamed the frontier, Alpine became a whistle stop on the transcontinental line. Time and again the community was devastated by fires. In 1888, 1907, 1911 and 1946 fires destroyed major parts of the city. Many of the old buildings are now artists' studios and shops.

Sul Ross University casts a stately shadow upon the city. For over ten years the university has been the site of the **Texas Cowboy Poetry Gathering**. Local ranchers and cowhands share true stories in the form of poetry, song and narrative. The event lasts three days and usually is held on the first weekend of March.

ARRIVALS & DEPARTURES

The regional airport is served by **Dallas Express Airlines**, *Tel. 800/529-0925*, a small a commuter airline which flies into Dallas Love Field four times a week. The charter airline **Skies of Texas**, *Tel. 915/837-2290*, based in Alpine, offers flights by special arrangement.

You can step off the train at the **Amtrak Station**, *102 West Holland Street, Tel. 800/USA-RAIL*, right in the center of the historic downtown. This is a good point for a break in the long journey across west Texas.

By car, you can reach Alpine from Interstate Highway 10 by heading south on Highway 90.

ORIENTATION

Alpine is on the northern ridge of the Glass Mountains, on Highway 90. Highway 118 runs from Big Bend (Study Butte entrance) in the south through Fort Davis and the Davis Mountains in the north. Alpine is the only stop on the Amtrak train line between Del Rio and El Paso.

WHERE TO STAY

THE CORNER HOUSE, *801 East Avenue E, Alpine. Tel. 915/837-7161 or 800/585-7795. Rates: $40 to $65. Credit cards accepted.*

This beautiful home, built in 1937, is located a few blocks from Sul Ross University and a short distance from downtown. The accommodations include four guest rooms with private baths and unique decor, such as a mural, a fireplace and full bookshelves. You can enjoy the sumptuous food even if you are not a guest. The Corner House Cafe serves Scottish food from 11:30am to 2:30pm every day. The owner is an expert on the Big Bend region and enjoys sharing his knowledge about the area.

WHITE HOUSE INN, *2003 Fort Davis Highway, Alpine. Tel. 915/837-1401, Fax 837-2197. Rates: $75. Credit cards accepted.*

This stately southern home has six rooms for guests, each with a private bath. The traditional decor invites relaxation, as do the large porches that run the length of the house, and the beautiful tree-filled yard. Breakfast is included with each room, and lunch or dinner can be ordered for an additional charge.

WHERE TO EAT

REATA, *203 North 5th Street, Alpine. Tel. 915/837-9232. Credit cards accepted.*

The flavor of the west accents the excellent food at Reata. The cowboy bean dip is a zesty appetizer, and more pleasing to the palate than the jalapeno and cilantro soup. Reata takes chances, combining spicy Mexican chorizo sausage with tomatoes and caramelized onion for the penne pasta sauce. And the payoff is in the exciting flavors. The chicken fried steak and ribeye are good entrees, but far more tempting is the roast pork loin with bourbon sautéed apples or the bar-b-cue shrimp enchiladas. The menu is unusual enough to keep you coming back for at least three meals (even in a row!). Open Monday to Saturday 11:30 to 2pm and 5:30pm to 10pm. The bar remains open until midnight.

ALPINE BAKERY, 302 *East Holland, Alpine. Tel. 915/837-7297.*

The Alpine Bakery has a complete selection of breakfast pastries and muffins as well as fresh coffee. Lunch is served Monday to Saturday until 3pm. Baked potatoes, quiche and fresh sandwiches are featured.

SEEING THE SIGHTS

Many of the buildings still in use today are living history lessons. The **Holland Hotel** was built in 1928 and was the center of social activity in the town. The train station has been in continuous use since before the present building went up in 1946.

The span of history — from the first traces of Native Americans to the present towns — is documented at the **Museum of the Big Bend,** *Sul Ross University, Tel. 915/ 837-8143, Tuesday to Saturday 9am to 5pm, Sunday 1pm to 5pm; admission free.* Many of the exhibits showcase artistic depiction of life in the Big Bend area. From Highway 290, take Entrance #2 into the university. The museum is to the west of the entrance.

SHOPPING

Downtown, many artists exhibit and sell their crafts at the **Arts and Crafts Mall of the Big Bend,** *101 West Holland Avenue, Tel. 915/837-7486.* Clothing, jewelry and paintings are among the offerings. Nearby, **Front Street Books,** *121 Holland Avenue, Tel. 915/837-3360,* sells maps, books about Big Bend and west Texas, regional newspapers and an excellent selection of nature and history books.

EXCURSIONS & DAY TRIPS
MARFA

Marfa was put on the map in 1955, or rather the big screen, when the movie *Giant* was filmed in the city. The cast, including James Dean and Elizabeth Taylor, stayed in the El Paisano Hotel in the center of the city. The El Paisano was built in 1928. The Spanish-style architecture is unique to the area The movie *Come Back to the Five and Dime, Jimmy Dean, Jimmy Dean,* is a fictional account of the personal aftermath of the filming of *Giant,* and might be set in Marfa.

But today, the city is more famous for the **Marfa Lights**. The lights are unexplained globes of light that appear on the horizon shortly after sundown. The lights were first spotted by residents in the late 1800's. Speculation about the cause of the lights abounds. Many believe that phosphorus gases are the cause, some opt for the ghost light theory, while others are convinced that the only explanation is otherworldly intrigue. Science offers no solution.

Marfa sits high in the mountains at an altitude of over 4,000 feet. The **Marfa Municipal Golf Course** has only nine holes, but can call itself the highest golf course in Texas.

Most visitors come to see the Marfa Lights, which appear shortly after sundown on almost every clear night. The city has a parking area for viewing the lights. Take Highway 90 east of Marfa. Nine miles outside of the city you will see a small parking area and an historical marker. Probably there will be a number of cars as well. The lights appear throughout the night; many spectators spend hours watching the ghost lights. Marfa is 26 miles west of Alpine on Highway 90.

PRACTICAL INFORMATION

The **Alpine Chamber of Commerce**, *106 North Third Street, Tel. 915/ 837-2326*, provides tourist information for the city and the surrounding area.

The **Marfa Chamber of Commerce**, *Tel. 915/729-4942*, provides tourist information.

BIG BEND NATIONAL PARK

The **Big Bend National Park** covers 267,000 square acres and is home to more than 400 species of wildlife. The park has both mountains and desert regions. The bend in the Rio Grande for which the park is named curves through three canyons. The park hotel is located in the basin of the tall Chisos Mountains. Camping areas are located throughout the park and range from full hook-ups to primitive; reservations are not taken for campsites.

Some of the state's most spectacular scenery and wildlife is in this park. The park has 14 hiking trails, ranging in difficulty from very easy paved trails to difficult climbs. The longest trail is 20 miles and the shortest less than one-third mile. Roads run thorough all regions of the park; many are paved and some are back-country trails.

The towns outside the park – **Terlingua**, **Lajitas** and **Study Butte** – are small villages that cater to park visitors. Tour companies and hotels in these towns offer rafting, horseback riding and hiking guided tours. Terlingua and Study Butte were small mining towns in the late nineteenth century. Some visitors stay in Marathon, which is 78 miles north of Big Bend on Highway 385. The Gage Hotel, in Marathon, is a first-rate establishment, but the long drive does not allow the serious nature lover adequate time to enjoy the scenery of the park.

Every November the winter heats up with the **Terlingua Chili Cook-Off**. The event promises to be the largest chili competition in the world. The event draws over 5,000 chili fans from all over the globe.

Lajitas is the product of the vision of a developer who saw a dude-ranch sort of oasis in the desert. The town is a modern rendition of an Old West street. The hotels are part of a large conference center which has a variety of recreational activities including a nine hole golf course, a pool, and a saloon/dance hall.

ARRIVALS & DEPARTURES

From Interstate Highway 10, the main entrance to the park is on Highway 385, south of Marathon. You can reach the west entrance by taking Highway 118 south from Alpine and turning east on Highway 170. Maps of roads, campsites and trails are available from the any park ranger station. Paved roads lead to the major campsites and ranger stations.

GETTING AROUND THE PARK

Some of the auto-trails cross rugged terrain but do not require four-wheel-drive vehicles. All roads and auto trails are clearly marked.

RANGER STATIONS IN BIG BEND

A ranger station is located at the northernmost entrance to the park, at Persimmon Gap on Highway 385. The Park Headquarters is located in the center of the park at Panther Junction. The Chisos Basin, where the only hotel in the park is located, is just west of Panther Junction. Boquillas Canyon and nearby Rio Grande Village, which has picnic areas and campsites, are in the eastern end of the park. Castolon and the ranger station near Santa Elena Canyon are in the southwestern area.

WHERE TO STAY
In Big Bend
CHISOS MOUNTAIN LODGE, *Big Bend National Park. Tel. 915/ 477-2291, Fax 477-2352. Rates: $54 to $77. Credit cards accepted.*

This is the only hotel in Big Bend. It's in the basin of the Chisos Mountains and is by far the best place to stay in the area. The location of the hotel alone is worth a trip to Big Bend. The road that leads to the hotel offers some of the most spectacular views in the park. A small paved trail leads to the favorite sunset overlook in the park. The trails and canyons are easily accessible from the hotel, and a number of trails begin at the hotel itself.

The rooms are modern and comfortable with phones, but no television. Each room has a balcony and views of the mountains and forest. Stone cottages, which are secluded from the main hotel complex, are also available. The restaurant and coffee shop serve good meals during the day and are open to the public. Rooms A1 to A12 have balconies that overlook the spectacular sunset view. Make reservations well in advance of your stay; the hotel is often booked months ahead.

Outside Big Bend
To arrange the rental of a house in the Big Bend area, contact **Lajitas on the Rio Grande**, *Star Route 70, Box 400, Lajitas 79852, Tel. 915/424-3471 or 800/944-9907.*

BADLANDS HOTEL, *Star Route 70, Lajitas. Tel. 915/424-3452 or 800/944-9907. $30 to $110 Credit cards accepted.*

The main accommodations facility of Lajitas offers motel rooms, modern cabins and apartments. Guests may use the nine hole golf course and pool. A frontier fortress-style inn stands on the spot of a former cavalry fort. The single story motel has a Mexican adobe theme exterior. A dozen shops and restaurants on the main street offer entertainment nearby. If you come here in the off-season, it is best to travel to this resort with a large group of friends, otherwise you may feel like you are visiting a ghost town. The campground offers full hook-ups for tents or recreational vehicles. The hotel is 13 miles form Big Bend.

BIG BEND MOTOR INN, *Terlingua. Tel. 915/371-2218 or 800/848-BEND. Rates: $59.95 to $79.95 Credit cards accepted.*

This motel has simple rooms with microwave ovens and refrigerators. The accommodations are sparse and suited for the most economical of travelers. The location is convenient to Big Bend and the motel can arrange outdoor excursions in the park.

Marathon

THE GAGE HOTEL, *102 Highway 90 West, Marathon. Tel. 915/386-4205 or 800/884-GAGE, Fax 915/386-4510. Rates: $65 to 100. Credit cards accepted.*

The Gage Hotel was built in 1920, on the half-million acre ranch owned by Alfred Gage. The hotel has been renovated into a modern facility with a restaurant and outdoor pool. Adobe walls, Mexican furnishings and rough timber ceilings accent the 37 rooms. The southwestern decoration is a posh atmosphere for a respite in the badlands of west Texas. Many choose to stay here when visiting Big Bend, although the park is 78 miles to the south.

You can stroll around Marathon to visit some of the turn-of-the-century buildings occupying the five blocks north and south of the post office. The Gage Hotel pretty much constitutes the entire city of Marathon. So when the hotel and its adjoining cafe shut down for afternoon siesta, there is nothing to do but get gasoline and get out of town. The Cafe Cenizo has a menu that offers a bit of variety from the standard west Texas fare. The Croque Macho is served on French bread (croissants are not macho) and comes with a side of onion rings ($5.25). Big Ed's Chicken Fried Steak ($11.95) is large and comes with potato salad and cole slaw. Shirley makes four varieties of home-cooked pies. The cafe is closed from 2pm to 6pm daily.

SEEING THE SIGHTS

The tallest point in the park is known as **Solitario**. It is a dome of molten rock measuring almost eight miles across and reaches a height of 5,128 feet. This is one of the largest formations of its type in the world, and one of the few nearly symmetrical natural structures. Solitario is found in the northeastern area of the park.

A rich variety of animals inhabit the park, including black bears, mountain lions and over 400 species of birds. The park rangers offer weekend hikes for wildlife watching. Many of the hiking trails have self-guided nature information posted on the route or available at the ranger stations.

The mighty **Rio Grande** snakes and curves its way for 1,896 miles, second in size in the US to the Mississippi only. You can travel for over 100 miles along the river by canoe or raft. Of the three canyons in the Big Bend area — Santa Elena, Mariscal and Boquillas — **Santa Elena** is the most spectacular. Its rock walls rise to over 1,500 feet and narrow passages mark the curving water. The emotion of the river changes with the subtleties of the seasons, so hiring a guide is a wise idea. You can cross the Rio Grande by rowboat to visit the tiny Mexican villages along the way, and stop by the cantina for an icy cold cerveza.

SPORTS & RECREATION

Even if you are not a hearty outdoors person, Big Bend can be the adventure of a lifetime for those who want to see the real west Texas. **Lajitas Stables**, *Star Route 7, Terlingua, Tel. 915/424-3238 or 888/508-7667, arrange*s combination trips of horseback riding and river rafting. Overnight trips include horses, camping equipment and a guide; prices start at $100 per day. Hourly trail rides include lunch ($16 per hour); three-day trips into the borderlands of Mexico are a specialty of Lajitas Stables.

You can visit Big Bend on horseback with **Turquoise Trailriders**, *Big Bend Motor Inn, Terlingua, Tel. 915/371-2212. The t*our company offers a variety of riding experiences for the novice or expert rider. Overnight camp-outs, half or full day trips or even excursions by the hour will let you see west Texas the way the cowboys did – from atop a horse. The guides provide local insight to the history, folklore and nature of the area. Bicycle rentals and tours may also be arranged.

Desert Sports, *Highway 170, Terlingua, Tel. 915/371-2727 or 888/989-6900*, offers tours that include camping expeditions, trips down the Rio Grande and mountain bike adventures. You can experience the hidden beauty of the canyons and mountains of Big Bend with the experienced guides at Desert Sports. Desert Sports is located on Highway 170 four miles west of the intersection with Highway 118.

Other local tour companies in the area include:
- **San Carlos Excursions**, *Tel. 915/424-3221*, for easy day tours of Big Bend
- **Far Flung Adventures**, *Tel. 800/359-4138*, specializes in rafting trips down the Rio Grande
- **Big Bend Rivers Tours**, *Tel. 915/424-3234 or 800/545-4240*, to get far off the beaten path
- **Texas River Expeditions**, *Tel. 800/839-4138, or* **Rio Grande Adventures**, *Tel. 800/343-1640*. Both are located in Study Butte.

EXCURSIONS & DAY TRIPS

The **Warnock Environmental Education Center**, *Farm Road 170, Lajitas, Tel. 915/424-3327*, occasionally sponsors exhibits of relevance to the Big Bend area, such as photography.

One of the only ghost towns in the state is in **Terlingua**. The small adobe homes of miners stand abandoned on a hillside overlooking the cemetery. Nearby **Presidio** also has a ghost town which was once an adobe mining camp for the Presidio Mining Company. The town was abandoned in 1931 with the demise of the silver mines. Predsidio is 45 miles west of Terlingua on Highway 170.

Fort Leaton, *Ranch Road 170, Presidio, Tel 915/229-3613, open daily 8am to 4:30pm,* may be the only walled fort in the state. In fact, it may be the only nationally recognized fort that was not an army outpost. This was a private building occupied by the Texas Rangers for a short time.

PRACTICAL INFORMATION

For tourist information, contact **Big Bend National Park General Information,** *Tel. 915/477-2251.*

The **Big Bend Natural History Association,** *Tel. 915/424-3252,* sponsors workshops about bird watching..

The **Big Bend Touring Society,** *Tel. 915/371-2548,* plans tours designed to your specifications.

The **Fort Davis State Bank** has an ATM at The Big Bend Motor Inn.

EL PASO

El Paso, once known as the "northern pass" to the Spanish, sits at an elevation of over 3,700 feet high in the Franklin Mountains. **Juarez, Mexico**, El Paso's twin city, is connected to the United States by five international bridges connecting the two cities.

El Paso is in the Mountain time zone. When driving to El Paso on Interstate Highway 10, the time zone changes from Central to Mountain at Van Horn, about 40 miles east of El Paso.

The surrounding **Franklin Mountains** offer one of the most beautiful evening skylines you can imagine. The scenic hills overlook an expanse of city lights that stretch across the entire horizon. El Paso and neighboring Juarez seem to disregard the international borders in the light of day as well. The Mexican and US cultures are found on both sides of the border, making these two cities each unique in their own country.

El Paso is the fabled land of cowboys and frontiersman. Long before Pancho Villa or even Billy the Kid roamed the Chihuahuan desert near El Paso, the Spanish claimed the land.

The city claims the right of the first **Thanksgiving celebration** in North America. According to the legend, 400 Spanish settlers and missionaries arrived in El Paso after a treacherous five month journey through the Chihuahuan Desert, from the town of Santa Barbara, Mexico. Their destination was Santa Fe, but the waters of the Rio Grande provided a diversion and rest stop. The leader, Don Juan do Onate, claimed the land for the Spanish crown, then held a feast of thanks. The first Thanksgiving is celebrated in an annual festival sponsored by the city of El Paso.

Some of the first explorers and settlers traversed the lands of El Paso in their drives for conquest, riches and the spread of Christianity. The first

Spanish colony in El Paso was a seventeenth century missionary settlement occupied by the Tigua Indians. It was not until the railroads brought
Americans from the east and west that El Paso became and English-
speaking community. Today you are likely to hear either English or
Spanish on either side of the border.

The railroad is the element that reshaped the El Paso area. In 1881,
railroad developers brought together the Southern Pacific, Santa Fe and
the Texas and Pacific Rail Lines. The lines met at the El Paso Union
Station, and Americans began to flood the sleepy village of El Paso in the
quest to move goods between the east and west coasts. The city maintained its role as an international crossroads when the Mexican railway
extended a line to El Paso Union Station a few years later.

El Paso's Festivals

Every April El Paso celebrates the **First Thanksgiving** at the Chamizal
National Memorial. A recreation of the event with period costume is
followed by musical performances. The El Paso Mission Trail Association,
P. O. Box 3789, El Paso, 79923, Tel. 915/534-0630 or 800/351-6024
organizes the First Thanksgiving and provides information about the
event.

A number of other festivals throughout the year highlight different
aspects of life in El Paso. The **Southwestern Livestock Show and Rodeo**
is held in February at the El Paso County Coliseum, Tel. 915/532-1401.
Memorial Day Weekend is a time of music and festivity in El Paso. The **El
Paso Jazz Festival** and the **International Balloon Festival** both fall on this
long weekend. A celebration of Latino culture, the **Fiesta de las Flores**,
takes place in Washington Park on Labor Day Weekend. The **International Chamber Music Festival**, *ProMusica, P. O. Box 522561, El Paso
79952, Tel. 915/532-9139, Fax 915/532-9199*, highlights the talent of
young musicians from all over the world. The festival takes place in the
first weeks of January and has been featured on National Public Radio.

ARRIVALS & DEPARTURES

The **El Paso International Airport** is served by American Airlines,
America West, Continental, Delta, Southwest and United. The airport is
located just east of the center of the city. From Interstate Highway 10, take
the Airway Boulevard Exit.

The historic **El Paso Union Station** is the Amtrak station, 700 San
Francisco Street, *Tel. 800/872-7245*. This downtown depot was restored
in 1982. Trains traveling eastbound stop in El Paso on Monday, Wednes-
day and Saturday; trains traveling westbound stop in El Paso Tuesday,
Thursday and Sunday. Just around the corner is the **Greyhound Bus
Station**, *200 West San Antonio Street, Tel. 800/231-2222*.

ORIENTATION

El Paso is on Interstate Highway 10. Highway 54 runs north to Ruidoso, New Mexico, and Highways 62 and 180 go northeast to Carlsbad, New Mexico. Interstate Highway 25 runs north to Las Cruces, New Mexico. Just south of El Paso is Juarez, Mexico. The main international crossing points, The Santa Fe and Stanton Bridges, are downtown. They handle pedestrian and motor traffic.

One way to see the city while getting the inside story about points of interest and legends of gunfighters and the Old West is to take an audio cassette guided tour form **Father Hubbard's Adventures**, *Tel. 915/591-8255.* The audio tapes include written directions around the city and can be purchased in gift shops or by contacting Father Hubbard.

GETTING AROUND TOWN

The most convenient way for tourists to enjoy the attractions of El Paso is by taking the trolley tours offered by the **Sun Metro**, *El Paso Union Station, 700-A San Francisco Street, Tel. 915/533-3333.* The "trolleys" are motor-driven buses reminiscent of years past in design only. True trolleys served the cities of El Paso and Juarez from 1885 to 1960, which were mule-driven at the turn-of-the-century.

Trolley routes run north-south and east-west through the downtown and historic visitors' areas of the city. The fare for regular city routes is 25¢ one-way. The trolleys run every 15 minutes during the day; service halts in the evening.

Special tour routes are operated to Juarez, Mexico and along the El Paso Mission Trail. The "Border Jumper" to Juarez makes numerous stops in Juarez and leaves on the hour from the Civic Center. You can return at any time of the day; the fare is $11. Every Thursday during the summer months, "Trolley on a Mission" travels the Mission Trail and stops at the Tigua Reservation for lunch. During the Christmas season a two and one-half hour tour takes visitors through the city and shows the decorations that light up the city with holiday spirit.

The trolley office is located at the Civic Center. To reach the Civic Center, from Interstate Highway 10, exit Mesa and go south. Turn west onto Main, then go south on Santa Fe. The large Civic Center has a parking garage entrance on Santa Fe Street.

Taxi services in El Paso include:
- **Border Taxi**, *Tel. 915/533-4282*
- **Checker Cab**, *Tel. 915/532-2626*
- **El Paso Cab**, *Tel. 915/598-9702*
- **Sun City Cab**, *Tel. 915/544-2211*
- **United Independent Cab**, *Tel. 915/590-8294*
- **Yellow Cab**, *Tel. 915/533-3433*

WHERE TO STAY
Central
CAMINO REAL HOTEL EL PASO, *101 South El Paso Street, El Paso. Tel. 915/534-3000 or 800/769-4300, Fax 915/534-3024. Rates: $69 to $295. Credit cards accepted.*

One of the premier hoteliers of Mexico offers the city of El Paso's finest accommodations. The building of the beautiful Camino Real Hotel has long been the best place to stay when visiting El Paso. The 17-story red brick building is the most distinctive peak of the downtown skyline, and has stunning views of El Paso. The hotel has junior and luxury suites, providing luxury, simplicity and understated elegance. Built in 1912, the hotel has undergone extensive renovation and addition. A delicious brunch is served on Sunday. This hotel was previously operated by Westin; a new Westin is being constructed in El Paso and is expected to open in 1999.

TRAVELODGE CITY CENTER, *409 East Missouri Street, El Paso. Tel. 915/544-3333 or 800/578-7878, Fax 915/533-4109. Rates: $49 to $65. Credit cards accepted.*

This is the budget hotel located closest to the city center, nine miles from downtown. Parking is free for hotel guests. All rooms have in-room coffee and tea, cable television and weekday newspaper. This is an excellent place to stay for those who want an economic hotel between the mountains and downtown. The hotel offers free shuttle service to the airport From Interstate Highway 10, take Exit 19.

HOLIDAY INN PARK PLACE, *325 North Kansas, El Paso. Tel. 915/ 533-8241 or 800/HOLIDAY. Rates: $69.*

This 119 room hotel often caters to business travelers whose interests require they stay near the financial district. The exterior of the building is simple, hotel styling. And the interior is furnished in the conservative traditional fashion. The fact that the hotel is a small high-rise allows guests to enjoy the view of the mountains and skyline. All rooms come with complimentary newspaper and coffee.

INTERNATIONAL YOUTH HOSTEL, *311 East Franklin Avenue, El Paso. Tel. 915/532-3661, Fax 915/532-0302. Rates: $14.80 per person. Credit cards accepted.*

The El Paso International Hostel offers a low-budget alternative to hotel stays. The Garner Hotel, built in 1922, is renovated into a modern hostel. The hostel is a member of the Hostelling International Association and is located close to downtown El Paso and Juarez, Mexico. Either private rooms or dormitory style rooms are available. The hostel has a full kitchen, laundry facilities and no curfew. Discounted rates offered for AYH members and weekly stays. The hostel is in the center of downtown; from Interstate Highway 10, take exit 19; follow Franklin Street.

Airport Area

EL PASO AIRPORT HILTON, *2027 Airway Boulevard, El Paso. Tel. 915/778-4241 or 800/774-1500, Fax: 915/779-1276. Rates: $65 to $195. Credit cards accepted.*

This rambling Hilton with 271 rooms on two floors received a full, modern renovation in 1994. The hotel is right next to the airport, and only minutes by car from downtown. If you are in the mood for some pampering, request a suite with a private hot tub. The large outdoor pool is heated, although the water rarely needs more than the El Paso sun to keep the water warm. The featured on-site restaurant serves the cuisine of northern Italy. The lounge offers satellite television featuring sports events and serves food late into the night.

EL PASO MARRIOTT HOTEL, *1600 Airway Boulevard, El Paso. Tel. 915/779-3300 or 800/228-9290. Rates: $115 to $134. Credit cards accepted.*

The Marriott is only one-quarter mile from the airport. Two restaurants and a lounge offer a variety of food service at all times of the day. Sports facilities include an indoor/outdoor pool and sauna. The rooms are large and tastefully furnished. Shuttle service between the hotel and airport is complimentary. From Interstate Highway 10, exit Airway Boulevard and go north. The hotel is two miles from the highway.

EMBASSY SUITES HOTEL, *6100 Gateway East, El Paso. Tel. 915/779-6222 or 800/362-2779. Rates: $89 to $94.*

The eight story Embassy Suites Hotel features a large atrium and substantial conference area. Each room is like an apartment in miniature, with a small kitchen and sitting area. The indoor pool is the highlight of the athletic facilities. A breakfast buffet and cocktail hour are included. From Interstate Highway 10, take the Geronimo exit. You should see the hotel on the south side of the highway.

RADISSON SUITE INN, *1770 Airway Boulevard, El Paso. Tel. 915/772-3333 or 800/333-3333, Fax 915/779-3323. Rates: $99 to $125.*

The 151 room hotel is located minutes from the airport. Every room at this Radisson is a suite with a sitting area, refrigerator and coffee maker. Rates include breakfast. The Radisson has a lovely outdoor pool and indoor workout area. Services such as room service and shuttles to the airport are available.

HOLIDAY INN AIRPORT, *6655 Gateway Boulevard West, El Paso. Tel. 915/778-6411 or 800/HOLIDAY. Rates: $75 to $80. Credit cards accepted.*

The Holiday Inn has an airy lobby and southwestern decor. The fresh renovation of the 203 rooms included the indoor/outdoor pool and fitness room. Courtesy shuttles will take guests to the airport or nearby shopping centers. From Interstate Highway 10, exit Airway Boulevard.

CLARION HOTEL, *6789 Boeing Drive, El Paso. Tel. 915/778-6789 or 800/252-7466, Fax 915/778-2288. Rates: $ 55 to $94.*

The comfortable ranch-house style Clarion is one-quarter mile from the airport. Some rooms have fireplaces, and all offer in-room video games. The fitness area includes an outdoor pool. Airport shuttle service available and breakfast is included. From Interstate Highway 10, Exit 25 close to the airport.

BEST WESTERN AIRPORT, *7144 Gateway East, El Paso. Tel. 915/ 779-7700 or 800/528-1234. Credit cards accepted. Rates: $41 to $75.*

Large, modern Best Western has 175 rooms and a heated pool. The airport is two miles from the hotel, and a courtesy shuttle is available. To get to the hotel, exit Interstate Highway 10 at Hawkins Boulevard.

SUNSET HEIGHTS BED AND BREAKFAST INN, *717 Yandell Avenue, El Paso. Tel. 915/544-1743 or 800/767-8513, Fax 915/544-5119. Rates: $70 to $165. Credit cards accepted.*

This beautiful three-story red brick home provides elegant accommodations. The decor offers the romance of the Victorian era. The four guest rooms have private baths and are furnished with period antiques. Accents such as stained-glass windows, chandeliers and fireplaces make this home one to remember. You awaken to a large gourmet breakfast in the morning and later in the day are treated to afternoon refreshments. Sunset Heights is located near downtown and the University of Texas at El Paso (UTEP) campus. From Interstate Highway 10, exit to Porfirio Diaz street. Take a right on Yandell Street; continue until Randolph Street.

WHERE TO EAT

Central

ARDOVINO'S, *206 Cincinnati Avenue, El Paso. Tel. 915/532-9483. Credit cards accepted.*

This wonderful deli is the place to buy genuine Italian groceries that make a meal authentic. If you are ready to eat, but not to cook, Ardovino's makes terrific pizza. The fresh sandwiches made from the deli can be taken out or eaten in the cozy dining room. The shop is located near the University of Texas at El Paso (UTEP) campus, in the Kern Place shopping center.

CASA JUARDO, *226 Cincinnati Street, El Paso. Tel. 915/532-6429 or 4772 Doniphan Street, El Paso. Tel. 915/833-1151. Credit cards accepted.*

Excellent Mexican food served in elegant surroundings has been the hallmark of Casa Juardo for over one generation. Long a favorite of local diners, Casa Juardo offers a full range of specialties for all tastes. The restaurant is known for its half-dozen different types of enchiladas. Local artists exhibit their work. Open Tuesday to Saturday 11am to 8pm.

CAFE CENTRAL, *109 North Oregon Street, El Paso. Tel. 915/545-CAFE. Credit cards accepted.*

This is probably the trendiest restaurant in town. During dinner music from the baby grand piano sets the mood. And the food lives up to the decor. Each day the menu changes, variations of northern Italian recipes are highlighted by the chef. A variety of selections such as duck and lamb are grilled to perfection. You can choose from the extensive selection of wine can compliment your meal. The restaurant is located downtown, just across the street from the Camino Real Hotel.

AMIGOS RESTAURANT, *2900 Montana Avenue, El Paso. Tel. 915/533-0155. Credit cards accepted.*

The menu is a mix of American favorites and Mexican staple dishes. The food is fresh and delicious; the atmosphere is festive. The chilaquiles ($5.65), a casserole with chicken, tortillas and red or green sauce is outstanding. One of the light plates, entomadas, tortillas with beans and fresh vegetables, is an excellent choice. The Cool Rellenos ($6.20), green chiles stuffed with guacamole or tuna on a bed of lettuce, is a refreshing alternative to a normal salad. This is an excellent place to come if not everyone in your group wants to have Mexican food. The menu includes selections such as T-bone steak ($10.70), spaghetti with meat sauce and sandwiches. During the week a lunch special is featured from 11am to 2pm.

CRAWDADDY'S, *212 Cincinnati Avenue, El Paso. Tel. 915/546-9104.*

The zest of Louisiana cooking comes to life at Crawdaddy's. This informal restaurant serves crawfish in a number of ways, but the best by far is the crawfish etouffee. The boiled crawfish appetizer is not just steaming hot, but fiery spicy. This is a favorite of the UTEP college crowd, who wash down the Cajun fire with bottles of beer. Open daily 4pm to 10pm.

LA HACIENDA, *1720 Paisano Street, El Paso. Tel. 915/532-5094. Credit cards accepted.*

Today La Hacienda is near downtown, but the original site was once part of the King's Highway connecting Mexico City to San Antonio. You can sit on the large outdoor patio that overlooks Mexico and enjoy some of the finest Mexican cuisine north of the border. Seasonings from the Yucatan and central Mexico make this food delicious.

LEO'S MEXICAN FOOD, *8001 North Mesa, El Paso. Tel. 915/833-5367. Credit cards accepted.*

El Paso loves Leo's so much, that the restaurants have five locations throughout the town. For over 46 years the home-grown recipes of Leo's has set the standard for Tex-Mex food. The menu is huge, but a sure short-cut to a good meal is to try one of the daily specials. Toasty sopapillas, small sweetbread topped with honey, are a specialty of the house.

THE RIB HUT, *2612 Mesa, El Paso. Tel. 915/532-RIBS. Credit cards accepted.*

A favorite of college students, near the University of Texas at El Paso (UTEP) campus, this informal restaurant features (of course) ribs. Catfish and steaks are other favorites. The atmosphere is that of a well-frequented dive. Every Wednesday is dollar rib night.

MICHELINO'S, *3615 Rutherglen, El Paso. Tel. 915/592-1700.*

For over 23 years this restaurant has served some of the best Italian food in El Paso. The long menu includes classic dishes such as eggplant parmigiana, and more unusual specialties like Chicken Jerusalem. The baked manicotti is prepared with hand-made pasta and a delicious blend of cheese. You can't go wrong with the oven fired pizzas. Open Monday to Friday 11am to 2pm and 5pm to 10pm.

ACQUARELLO RISTORANTE, *7500 North Mesa Drive, El Paso. Tel. 915/587-5995. Credit cards accepted.*

The sumptuous food of northern Italy features pasta made right in Acquarello's own kitchen. The wood-burning oven bakes the pizza crust to crisp perfection. Antipasti courses include a succulent Insalata di Mare. Pasta is served as a first course here, in the Italian tradition. The Fettucini Salmone has a delicate flavor, while the Spaghetti Pescatore has a more robust sea-food sauce. The veal and lamb are both excellent dinner selections. Reservations are recommended.

Cafes

DOLCE VITA, *205 Cincinnati Street, El Paso. Tel 915/533-8482. Credit cards accepted.*

Art hangs on the wall, and in the back a bulletin board lists the latest happenings. Dolce Vita has all the components of a great cafe, including an entire array of coffee and coffee drinks, all of which can be ordered decaffeinated. All day this cafe is filled with students seeking a comfortable repose. In the evening the crowd becomes markedly trendier, as many prefer a quiet drink and dessert instead of a loud bar. Open daily 8am to midnight.

SOUJOURNS COFFEEHOUSE, *127 Pioneer Plaza, El Paso. Tel. 915/532-2817. Credit cards accepted.*

Sourjourns is a refreshing place to have a light breakfast or lunch, and is conveniently located in the Pioneer Plaza. The menu offers sandwiches and soups, which will not ruin your dessert, the highlight of the visit. Open Monday 7:30am to 3pm; Tuesday to Thursday, 7:30am to 10pm; Friday 7:30am to midnight; Saturday 10am to midnight; closed Sunday.

Near El Paso

BILLY CREW'S, *1200 Country Club Boulevard, Santa Teresa, New Mexico. Tel. 505/589-2071. Credit cards accepted*

This restaurant is not just out of town – it is in another state. The drive to New Mexico takes only a half-hour from the center of El Paso and is well worth the trip for true steak lovers. Billy Crew's opened its doors in 1956 and has been a favorite of El Pasoans since then. All steak lovers will find the right cut from the extensive selection of meat on the menu. Seafood and chicken are also featured. The adjoining piano bar lets you relax after your meal. From Interstate Highway 10, exit North Mesa Street and continue for three miles.

CATTLEMAN'S STEAKHOUSE, *Indian Cliff's Ranch, Fabens. Tel. 915/544-3200. Credit cards accepted.*

The Indian Cliff's Ranch is an unusual spot for an excellent restaurant. The ranch itself is a tourist attraction with exhibits of cattle, rattlesnakes, and party facilities. Yet even native El Pasoans averse to dude ranches vouch for the quality of the steaks at the Cattleman's. The secret to the barbecue is the mesquite smoking method. You can jump on the free hay rides that the ranch offers every Sunday. The ranch is about 20 miles east of El Paso. From Interstate Highway 10, travel east from downtown. Exit Fabens turn north; the ranch is five miles from the highway. Monday to Friday 4:30pm to 10pm; Saturday 4pm to 10pm; Sunday noon to 9pm

SEEING THE SIGHTS

Before El Paso had its name, a small settlement known as Magoffinville existed on the banks of the Rio Grande. The **Magoffin Homestead**, *1120 Magoffin Avenue, Tel. 915/533-5147, open daily 9am to 4pm*, stands as the historic landmark of that era. The Magoffin family played a major role in shaping west Texas. The original family house was destroyed in the 1868 flood of the Rio Grande. The present museum is a replica of that home and was built in 1875. The architectural features, such as thick adobe walls, rough timber and native materials represent the blending of the traditions of Mexico and the American west.

A sister community to Magoffinville was **Hart's Mill Settlement**, *1720 West Paisano Drive*. In the mid-nineteenth century, the mill served the small communities which would later grow into El Paso. The mill no longer remains, but the small home in which Hart raised his family still stands at the site of the mill. One of the first US military installations in the area, **Old Fort Bliss**, *1844 West Paisano*, stood across from Hart's Mill. Some of the original housing quarters remain.

Boot Hill, the final resting place of the folks that made El Paso part of the Old West, is found in **Concordia Cemetery**. You can visit the grave

---

EL PASO'S SCENIC DRIVES

The rolling hills of the El Paso area are the hallmark of the city, which lies nestled in a mountain pass. For a scenic tour of the area's urban beauty, starting in downtown El Paso, take Interstate Highway to the Mesa Drive exit. Follow Mesa to Rim Road and take a right. Rim Road winds along a hillside, then turns into Scenic Drive. There are parking areas on these roads, which are very popular as evening rendezvous spots.

Another scenic route, Transmountain Road, cuts through Franklin Mountain State Park and part of Fort Bliss. This road will show you the natural beauty of the area as it winds along the mountain pass known as Smuggler's Gap. To the east of the state park is Casner Range, a large land preserve which is part of Fort Bliss. To reach Transmountain road, take Interstate Highway 10 west, away from the city. Exit Loop 375.

---

of John Wesley Hardin, the famous outlaw, who is buried on Boot Hill. The cemetery is a piece of history and its five sections contain a wealth of information for the curious. To reach the cemetery from Interstate Highway 10, exit Copia Street. The cemetery is between Yandell Street and Gateway West.

The **Chamizal National Memorial**, *800 South Marcal Street*, commemorates the solution to border disputes between the United States and Mexico. The **Paisanos Gallery**, *Tel. 915/532-7273, open daily 8am to 5pm*, exhibits art of significance to the culture and history of the area. The amphitheater is the site of free concerts and festivals.

The Missions

The El Paso missions are some of the first colonial settlements in North America. The mission settlement here is the result of the disputes between the Spanish and Native American tribes in New Mexico. After being forced out of the lands that today are New Mexico, Spanish missionaries and Native Americans built three missions in Texas. The stories of the missions are full of natural disasters and struggle. The determination to maintain these religious settlements, after numerous reconstruction, is a tribute to the faith of the early settlers of west Texas. The missions, now in urban El Paso, are still in use, holding regular services and tours.

The **Mission Ysleta**, *9501 Socorro Road*, has transformed itself many times during its history. The site of the Corpus Christi de la Ysleta del Sur Mission was settled in 1680 as a temporary refugee camp for Native Americans fleeing conflict in northern New Mexico. After a decade of occupation, a Mission building was constructed. However, this would not

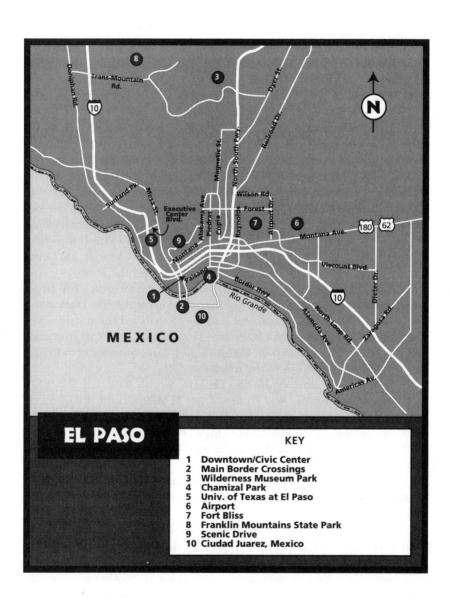

EL PASO

KEY

1 Downtown/Civic Center
2 Main Border Crossings
3 Wilderness Museum Park
4 Chamizal Park
5 Univ. of Texas at El Paso
6 Airport
7 Fort Bliss
8 Franklin Mountains State Park
9 Scenic Drive
10 Ciudad Juarez, Mexico

prove to be permanent, because flood waters from the Rio Grande destroyed the mission in 1742, then again in 1821. The mission was renamed the San Antonio de la Ysleta after the first reconstruction, then again renamed Our Lady of Mount Carmel. Despite the many changes in the appearance and name of Mission Ysleta, the occupation has been constant for centuries and parts of the mission grounds have been worked for over three centuries. Mission Ysleta is in an urban part of San Antonio. From Interstate Highway 10, take the Zaragoza Exit. Signs will indicate the way to Mission Ysleta, which is south from the highway, near the intersection of Zaragoza and Socorro Road.

Only one year after the Ysleta Mission, the **Nuestra Senora de la Limpia Conception de Socorro del Sur**, *Socorro Road, Tel. 915/859-7718,* was established. The name, which means "Our Lady of the Immaculate Conception of Socorro of the South," is usually shortened to simply "Socorro." The history of the mission is not less complicated than the name. The Socorro Mission moved from its original location to the present grounds because the Spanish feared the Native Americans living at the mission might revolt. Two floods, in 1692 and 1829, completely destroyed the mission. At different times the Socorro Mission has been administered by the Franciscans, secular leaders and the Jesuits.

Parts of the early structure are preserved in the mission. The large beams in the ceiling pre-date the building and exemplify the craftsmanship of the Native Americans who built and inhabited the mission. To reach Mission Socorro from Interstate Highway 10, exit Zaragoza and travel south on Zaragoza Street for four miles. Turn onto Socorro Road, signs will indicate the way to the mission.

The chapel of the **Presidio San Elizario**, *Socorro Road, Tel. 915/851-2333,* first stood on the San Elizario Fort, 37 miles to the south of its present location. The chapel was part of a fort built in 1777 that protected the Camino Real, the major road linking El Paso to San Antonio. During the United States war with Mexico the fort was demolished. The church was rebuilt in 1877 but fell victim to a fire in 1935, which destroyed the interior. The church remains true to the original architecture of the small adobe church. Presidio San Elizario is located six miles east of the Socorro Mission.

Daily tours of the missions depart from the El Paso Civic Center, *1 Civic Center Plaza, Tel. 915/544-0062, every* day at 10:30 am. From the comfort of an air conditioned trolley-style bus you can learn the history of the area and have free time to tour the mission complexes and shop in the gift shops. The tour lasts about four hours, and includes a stop for lunch.

The **Tigua Indian Reservation**, *305 Yaya Road, Tel. 915/859-5287, Tuesday to Sunday 8am to 4pm; closed Monday,* is the result of the settlements that established the missions in El Paso. During the weekend, visitors can watch scheduled dance performances by the Tigua.

The reservation's visitor center, the **Ysleta del Sur Pueblo**, has a museum and cafe. The museum documents the Tigua culture and visually chronicles the tribal history in Texas. The Cacique Cafe serves traditional Tigua food as well as regional fare. The Tigua Indian Reservation is on the Mission Trail. From Interstate Highway 10 east, exit Zaragoza and go south to Socorro Drive. Travel east on Socorro Drive to the intersection of Yaya Road.

Civic Center Area

The rich history and culture unique to the area is a source of pride for El Paso natives. The **Americana Museum**, *5 Civic Center Plaza, Tel. 915/542-0394, Tuesday to Saturday, 10am to 5pm; closed Sunday and Monday,* exhibits a collection of the artifacts and art of early Native Americans. The extensive collection includes pieces from Meso-American cultures. Painted murals depict the life of the Native Americans of nearby Hueco Tanks, which is now a state park. The museum provides an interesting educational experience; it is housed in the Performing Art Center in the Civic Center Plaza. To reach the Civic Center from Interstate Highway 10, exit Mesa and go south. Turn west onto Main, then go south on Santa Fe. The large Civic Center has a parking garage entrance on Santa Fe Street.

The centerpiece of the Arts District is the **El Paso Museum of Art**, *1211 Montana Street, Tel 915/541-4040, Tuesday to Saturday 10am to 5pm; Sunday 1pm to 5pm; closed Monday; admission free.* A variety of temporary exhibits grace the walls of the El Paso Art Museum. The museum's permanent exhibits includes the Kress Collection of Old European masterpieces, as well as American and Mexican paintings. The Mexican collection is one of the most extensive to be found anywhere and includes colonial art from the sixteenth century to modern works. The new art museum will open across from the Civic Center in 1998.

Museums

The **Bridge for Contemporary Arts**, *1112 East Yandell, Pioneer Plaza, Tel. 915/532-6707, Tuesday to Friday 11am to 6pm; Saturday 11am to 4pm; closed Sunday,* strives to promote local artists of all disciplines including painting, film, music and theater. The exhibits and performances vary greatly in content. Recent activities include poetry readings, the unveiling of a mural and a one-woman dramatic performance. Admission fees vary with events.

Insights, the El Paso Science Museum, *505 North Santa Fe Street, Tel. 915/542-2990, Tuesday to Saturday 9am to 5pm,* lets kids and grown-ups learn about science through hands-on participation. The 104 exhibits allow visitors to interact with science using every sense. The museum provides an overview of the technology that shapes our society and the future.

One of the most worthwhile museums in the state is the **Wilderness Museum**, *2000 Transmountain Road, Tel. 915/755-4332, Tuesday to Sunday 9am to 5pm; admission free*. The indoor/outdoor exhibits do not have much to do with wilderness. Instead the material culture of Native Americans is displayed in detail. Archaeological sites of Mexico and the United States southwest are brought into context with maps, artifacts and historic descriptions. Paintings depict the daily life of the tribes of west Texas. Visitors gain valuable insight to the petroglyphs and painted pottery and material culture of the area's first inhabitants.

The outdoor displays grant a unique glimpse into the life of the region before colonization. The nature trail stretches for one mile and has recreations of various houses including a pithouse, a partially under-ground structure with a twig roof, and a pueblo, an early agricultural settlement.

One of the most unusual collections traces the legacy of the officers who patrol the international border. The **Border Patrol Museum**, *4315 Transmountain, Tel. 915/759-6060*, is the only museum of its type in Texas. A collection of the memorabilia relating to the United States Border Patrol may at first seem to be a dry, even unenjoyable subject for a museum. However, the border between the US and Mexico was not always marked by fences, customs posts and bridges as it is today. The borderland was a nearly unexplored frontier, harsh and inhospitable. The story of the early lawmen in this area is a unique and insightful glimpse of part of the American story. The museum is located next to the Wilderness Museum.

The collection of the **El Paso Museum of History**, *Interstate Highway 10 east, exit Avenue of the Americas, Tel. 915/858-1928, Tuesday to Sunday 9am to 4:30pm, closed Monday; admission free*, traces the history of the El Paso area from the time of the Native Americans through the colonial conquest to the present day. The majority of exhibits portray the lives of the rugged frontiersmen who claimed and attempted to tame the land. The museum sponsors classes and lectures for all ages throughout the year. The museum is located at the intersection of Interstate Highway 10 and Avenue of the Americas.

Regional history is further explored at the **Centennial Museum**, *The University of Texas at El Paso (UTEP), Tel 915/747-5565, Tuesday to Saturday 10am to 4pm, closed Sunday and Monday*. The collection traces the history of the El Paso region through art, historical artifacts, and local geology. Temporary exhibits are featured.

The tranquil grounds of the **El Paso Holocaust Museum and Study Center**, *401 Wallenberg Drive, Tel. 915/833-5656*, give visitors the opportunity to reflect on the emotionally powerful exhibits. The collection includes a good deal of artifacts from the European Jewish ghettos and concentration camps of World War II. Visitors are educated about the Holocaust and reminded of the brutality of history. Tours are free for individuals and groups. Modern art adorns the museum and conveys the feelings of pain and perseverance of persecuted peoples. The Study Center sponsors speakers and provides resource materials for study of the Holocaust. To reach the museum from Interstate Highway 10, exit Executive Center and follow that road north. After 1.5 miles, turn Left on Mesa Drive; turn left onto Festival Street and then right onto Mardi Gras Street. This street will turn into Wallenberg Street.

The **El Paso Zoo**, *4001 Paisano, Tel. 915/541-4600, open daily, 9:30am to dusk; admission $3 adults, children 12 years and younger $1.50*, stretches across 18 acres and is the home of over 400 varieties of animals. The zoo is known for its outstanding collection of reptiles and the beautiful park-like atmosphere of the grounds. Endangered animals have a special home at the zoo, which is active in preservation of rare species. The aviary recreates a tropical South American environment with a variety of flora and fauna. The Grasslands Cafe serves lunch, snacks and ice cream during the normal hours of the zoo. From Interstate Highway 10, exit Paisano and travel south. The zoo is located at the intersection of Evergreen and Paisano streets. Signs will lead you to the zoo entrance.

Military Museums of Fort Bliss

El Paso has been important to the military since Texas entered the Union. The earliest military role was to protect settlers from attacks by Native American warriors and bandits. **Fort Bliss** was established in 1848 to fulfill this mission. In time, Fort Bliss gained importance as an air force training center. A number of museums at Fort Bliss provide insight into the role of the United States military in the El Paso region.

A number of museums at Fort Bliss give insight to the history of the American army on the western frontier. To reach the museums, take Airway Boulevard to the Robert E. Lee gate of Fort Bliss. The guard will give directions to the museums.

The **Artillery Museum**, *Mount Pleasanton Road, Building 5000, Fort Bliss, open daily 9am to 4:30pm*, documents the history of aviation defense in the Army. This is an appropriate topic for Fort Bliss, since it is one of the first and most significant air training grounds. Many of the displays are interactive.

The **Fort Bliss Museum**, *Pleasanton and Sheridan Roads, Fort Bliss, open daily 9am to 4:30pm*, is a recreation of what a frontier fort of the late 1800's would have looked like. The buildings are based on the plans of the Magoffinville fort, which was an early part of Fort Bliss. The Third Cavalry has been stationed near El Paso for nearly 150 years, and their history is documented at this museum.

Fort Bliss' tribute to the soldiers who have served the area is the **Museum of the Non-Commissioned Officer**, *Biggs Army Airfield, Building 11331, Fort Bliss, open Monday to Friday 9am to 4pm; Saturday to Sunday noon to 4pm*. The displays chronicle the large picture of military service; some of the artifacts pre-date the founding of the fort.

NIGHTLIFE & ENTERTAINMENT

The **El Paso Symphony**, *10 Civic Center Plaza, Tel. 915/532-3776*, presents concerts during the fall and spring. Performances are held at the **Performing Arts Center** at the Civic Center. **Music Ballet El Paso**, *Tel. 915/533-2200*, also uses this venue.

McKelligan Canyon Theater, *McKelligan Canyon, Tel. 915/532-3776*, *brings* music, ballet and theater to the beautiful outdoors. Throughout the year the canyon theater hosts a variety of performances, including the El Paso Symphony, the annual Shakespeare on the Rocks Festival, and Viva! El Paso.

Viva El Paso! is a musical extravaganza which tells the history of the settlement of the southwest. The musical runs during the summer months from June to August, and attracts over 60,000 attendees during that short season. Even the native El Pasoans turn out for the show. Performances begin at 8:30pm; a pre-show barbecue dinner is served at 7pm (reservations required).

Independence Day is celebrated with **Canyon Fest**, an all-day event featuring music, food and family activities. A new twist to the traditional fireworks is added with a laser show just after dark. The El Paso Association for the Performing Arts sponsors Canyon Fest every Fourth of July.

A completely different annual festival is **Ballet Under the Stars**, which is held at the McKelligon Canyon Amphitheater on Memorial Day weekend. The ballet performances are for three days only and tickets range in price fro $8 to $15, with discounts for students, children and senior citizens.

On Sunday nights from June through August, free concerts are held at the **Chamizal National Memorial Amphitheater**, *800 South San Marcial, Tel. 915/541-4481*. A wide variety of music is featured from reggae to classical to Latin. This annual series known as **Music Under the Stars** includes comedy and dance performances. The concerts are free of charge and sponsored by the city of El Paso.

The Tigua Indian Reservation operates the **Speaking Rock Casino and Entertainment Center**, *122 South Old Pueblo Road, Ysleta, Tel. 915/ 860-7777; credit cards accepted.* Blackjack, poker and low stakes baccarat are played at tables in the card room. The bingo room can seat 850 players, and the stakes can go as high as $50,000 per game. Wyngs Restaurant serves Tex-Mex food from 11am to 10:30pm with an adjoining bar open until 2am. The restaurant and bar are closed on Monday and Tuesday. From Interstate Highway 10, exit Zaragoza and go south. Turn east onto Alameda Street. Speaking Rock is located on Old Pueblo Road, just past the Ysleta Mission. The casino is open daily 1pm to 4am.

Bars & Clubs

JAXON'S BREWERY, *4799 North Mesa, El Paso. Tel. 915/542-0281; 1135 Airway, El Paso. Tel. 915/778-9696. Credit cards accepted.*

The two locations of this brewpub quickly became a tradition for El Paso's beer lovers. The six beers on tap were each made by Jaxon's brewmaster. The houseblend, Black Jack Stout, has a rich, full flavor. Other selections include Star Lite, Chihuahua Brown and Cactus Jack Pale Amber. There is always a special at Jaxon's. The grill cooks ups southwestern food, which is featured at Brewer Diners, set course events held throughout the year. The Mesa location is at the intersection of Mesa and Westside Streets.

CINCINNATI CLUB, *209 Cincinnati Street, El Paso.*

This bar brings the Old West theme of Cincinnati to the street of the same name. The dark wood interior is reminiscent of family room decoration in the 1970's. But the clientele come here for the extremely large margaritas and the relatively quiet atmosphere. Pub food such as fish and chips ($5.95) and hamburgers ($4.50) is served.

HEMINGWAY'S, *214 Cincinnati Street, El Paso. Tel. 915/532-7333. Credit cards accepted.*

This small college hangout is a favorite of the unpretentious set. Whether you wear a suit or a pair of shorts and tee-shirt, you will not be out of place here. The front room feels like someone's back-yard patio and often becomes standing-room-only crowded. The back area has larger tables and more breathing space. Hemingway's serves 132 types of bottled beer, and has twenty draft beer taps.

SPORTS & RECREATION

A hiker could spend weeks on the trails that lead through the mountains of the Chihuahuan Desert in the **Franklin Mountain State Park**, *Transmountain Road, Tel. 915/566-6441.* The park covers 24,000 acres of mountains and desert and is located in the city at the Woodrow

Bean and Transmountain Road. From Interstate Highway 10, exit Woodrow Bean Road, continue east and this will turn into Transmountain Road and cut through the park.

Golf Courses

The fact that El Paso generally experiences less than a week of cloudy days per year makes this area excellent for golfing. A few course for you to try are:

- **Ascarate Golf Course**, *Ascarate Park, El Paso. Tel 915/772-7381*
- **Desert East Driving Range**, *1351 Lee Trevino, El Paso. Tel. 915/591-4653*
- **Painted Dunes Golf Course**, *12,000 McCombs, El Paso. Tel. 915/533-4416*
- **Vista Hills Golf and Tennis Club**, *2210 Trawood, El Paso. Tel. 915/592-4558.*

Spectator Sports

The **Sun Bowl Stadium** hosts the annual college Sun Bowl Football championship. The University of Texas at El Paso football team plays here on weekends during the regular season. The large stadium occasionally has music and other performances. To reach the Sun Bowl from Interstate Highway 10, take the University of Texas at El Paso exit. Signs will guide you to the parking lots for the Sun Bowl. For more information, contact the **Sun Bowl Association**, *4100 Rio Bravo, Tel. 915/533-4416.*

SHOPPING

In the 1920's, the Paradise Hotel occupied the building that today is **Placita Santa Fe** shopping center. That the hotel was a house of ill repute is one of the less kept secrets in El Paso. A number of antique shops, import stores and art galleries fill the renovated historical building today. Some of the shops are open seven days a week.

Art Galleries

El Paso's vibrant art community is accessible to everyone at the many local galleries and shops. **Adair Margo Gallery**, *415 East Yandell Street, Tel. 915/533-0048, is one* of El Paso's finest galleries exhibiting modern art. The gallery is proud of its international stature; most of the talent featured is of local artists.

The objects at **Counterpoint**, *2626 North Stanton, Tel. 915/545-5073 or 888/CNT-POINT*, exemplify the latest and best designs. Decoration from Europe merges practical function with innovative style. Lights, candleholders and games are among the accent pieces offered. Open Monday to Saturday 11am to 6pm; closed Sunday.

The **Galeria Palacio**, *1716 Montana Avenue, Tel. 915/544-3589,* gives visitors insight into the regional art scene within the context of the international Latin movement. Featured artists include painters from throughout Latin America, and the focus of the gallery remains true to local artists. Serious collectors will enjoy the quality of the work displayed. Exhibits change often. Open Tuesday to Friday 11am to 6pm; Saturday noon to 5pm; closed Sunday and Monday.

Bright colors and humanistic themes highlight local artist Hal Marcus' paintings which adorn the University of Texas at El Paso and the El Paso Courthouse. Marcus showcases his work in his family home, the **Hal Marcus Gallery**, 2403 North Mesa Street, *Tel. 915/533-9090.* His work is well received throughout the world. Marcus works in stained glass and illustration also. All varieties of his art are available at the gallery. Open Tuesday to Saturday 10am to 6pm; closed Sunday and Monday.

One of the best places in the state to buy art, furniture and decorations from all over the world is **Galeria San Ysidro**, *801 Texas Avenue, Tel. 915/544-4444.* The gallery is really more like a department store because of the size — it occupies three floors of a former factory. The eclectic mix of art ranges from modern to antique. The stock changes almost daily, since new shipments are constantly arriving from all reaches of the globe. The prices are reasonable and the casual atmosphere makes shopping here a pleasure. From Interstate Highway 10, exit Mesa and go south to Texas. The store is near the intersection of Virginia and Texas Streets. Open Monday to Friday 9am to 5pm; Saturday 9am to 3pm; closed Sunday.

The **El Paso Chile Company**, *909 Texas Avenue, Tel. 915/544-3434,* lets you take the taste of Texas home. This store specializes in salsas, sauces and spices that will add zip to your next southern meal. Gift packages, clothes and cookbooks are also sold. Open Monday to Friday 10am to 5pm; Saturday 10am to 2pm; closed Sunday.

The largest mall in the El Paso area is **Cielo Vista Mall**, *Interstate Highway 10 East, Tel. 915/779-7070.* Four department stores, 140 shops and a number of informal restaurants are found in this shopping center. From Interstate 10, take the Hawkins Boulevard Exit.

Western Wear

The essential element of Texan fashion is a good pair of boots. Whether you want low-heeled lace-ups or the fanciest high-heeled snake-skin boots, you can find them at the large outlets in El Paso. The outlets sell discontinued and slightly defective boots for about 50 percent less than retail prices.

The oldest bootmaker in the area is Lucchese Boots at the **Lucchese Boot Outlet**, *6601 Montana, Tel. 915/778-8680.* Lucchese boots were worn by the Duke, John Wayne. The Lucchese Outlet is located near the airport.

The most recognizable name in bootmaking, **Tony Lama**, has no less than three outlet stores. The largest and easiest to find is just east of downtown on Interstate Highway 10 at the Mesa Exit, *Tel. 915/581-8192*. For custom-made boots go to **Champion Attitude**, *505 South Cotton Street, Tel. 915/534-7783*. The bootmaking process takes three days, but you will wind up with just the right details and comfort.

EXCURSIONS & DAY TRIPS

For centuries people have visited **Hueco Tanks**, giant granite outcroppings that form natural cisterns. To the Native Americans, the Hueco Tanks were an oasis in the west Texas desert. The area has many examples of rock art left by Native Americans over the centuries. Hikers can journey through the Hueco Tanks State Park. The extraordinary rock face is one of the best sites for rock climbing in the state. The **Hueco Tanks State Park**, *Tel. 915/857-1135, open daily 8am to 5pm*, is 22 miles northeast of El Paso; there are picnic facilities, 20 campsites and wildlife observation areas. To reach the park from El Paso, take Highway 62 north.

The lower end of the Guadalupe Mountains extends from New Mexico into northwestern Texas. The **Guadalupe Mountains National Park**, *Highways 62 and 189, Pine Springs, Tel. 915/828-3251*, covers over 86,000 acres, the majority of which is in New Mexico. The environment of the mountains is dramatically different than the surrounding land in west Texas. Many of the mountains reach heights of over 8000 feet, and pine forest covers the area. Elk, deer and forest animals inhabit the park, which has a cooler environment than the surrounding desert. Although this is a popular area for backpacking, there are no facilities in the park; all overnight visitors must stay at back-country campsites. Park Rangers present educational evening programs from April through September. Many tourists stop by the park on the way to Carlsbad Caverns, New Mexico, which is 55 miles north.

For adventurous travelers who want to journey south of the border, **Pan American Tours**, *P. O. Box 9401, El Paso, 79984, Tel. 800/876-3942 or 351-1612*, offers tours of Mexico's spectacular **Copper Canyon** and the **southern Baja Peninsula**. Most tours include travel on the famous Chihuahua/Pacific Railway, which cuts through the mountains of the northwest Mexican state of Chihuahua. Packages range in length from four to eight days.

PRACTICAL INFORMATION

For car assistance or information, contact the **American Automobile Association**, *1201 Airport Boulevard, Suite A1, El Paso, Tel 915/778-9521*.

The **Texas Department of Transportation** operates a large travel information center just outside El Paso. The information provided at the center deals with the entire state of Texas and is free. The travel information center is located on Interstate Highway 10 at the border of Texas and New Mexico.

JUAREZ, MEXICO

Juarez is not a typical Mexican city, especially for a border town. Much of the city looks like a city in the US, with traffic congestion, new shopping centers and office buildings. The city has a population of about 1.4 million, and some estimate the city's growth as much as 100,000 people per year.

ARRIVALS & DEPARTURES

Most people who travel between El Paso and Juarez go by car. Of course, tourists are not most people, and the traffic problems on the international bridges are reason enough to not take your car across. Unlike other towns on the Texas-Mexico border, walking across the border is not the simplest solution. Juarez is very spread out and you may want to visit a number of areas in the city.

The **El Paso-Juarez Trolley Company**, *One Civic Center Plaza, El Paso, Tel. 915/544-0061 or 800/259-6284*, is the best way to see the city and get around. Adult fare is $11, children four to twelve years old $8.50 and children under three ride free. The trolleys run hourly from April to October, Sunday to Tuesday 9am to 4pm, Wednesday to Saturday, 9am to 5pm. From November to March, daily 9am to 4pm.

ORIENTATION

The areas of interest to tourists are relatively small compared to the entire city, which stretches out from the border with rapidly expanding neighborhoods.

GETTING AROUND TOWN

The trolley crosses the international bridge close to downtown El Paso and continues across the Rio Grande, past Chamizal National Park (Mexico). During most times of the year, tourists prefer to take taxis and not walk around the city, because of the intense heat and noticeable automobile exhaust fumes. Use only taxis that are clearly marked and always negotiate the price for the ride before you get in, even if you are at a restaurant or hotel. Usually you can negotiate the price to half the original quote for the ride.

The **El Paso Juarez Trolley** makes 11 stops in Mexico and one in the United States, at El Paso's Civic Center. To reach the Civic Center from Interstate Highway 10, exit Mesa and go south. Turn west onto Main, then go south on Santa Fe. The large Civic Center has a parking garage entrance on Santa Fe Street.

The trolley stops at a number of shops and restaurants and the museum area of Juarez. The next-to-the-last stop in Juarez is the City Market, where you can find souvenirs galore.

WHERE TO STAY

HOTEL LUCERNA, *3976 Paseo Triunfo de la Republica, Juarez City, Chihuahua, Mexico. Tel. 91/800-66-300 (in Mexico) or 800/LUCERNA (in the United States). Rates: $77 to $82. Credit cards accepted.*

The large, modern hotel Lucerna has a five star rating. You can enjoy the style and flavor of Mexico in comfort here. The two restaurants and lobby bar offer good food and atmosphere. The pool is in the center of a traditional Mexican-style patio courtyard. All rooms have television and phones that are suitable for business travelers. This hotel is directly across the street from the Holiday Inn.

WHERE TO EAT

CHIHUAHUA CHARLIE'S, *2525 Plaza de la Republica, Juarez. Tel. 13-12-54.*

The Carlos n' Charlie's restaurants have managed to provide Juarez with the best food and most fun you will find on the border. You could easily ruin your appetite with the fresh margaritas and basket of hot-from-the-oven bread. But you would not want to miss the entrees. The Pollo Yucateco ($5) is chicken prepared with mild spices from the Yucatan region of Mexico. The Filete Reyes ($7), a beef filet with garlic and mild peppers prepared at your table, is entertainment as well as good food. The dessert line-up includes caramel or mango crepes, and cakes prepared on-site (each about $2). On the weekends the bar is hopping and live music fills the air. Breakfast is served all day, every day.

SEEING THE SIGHTS/NIGHTLIFE & ENTERTAINMENT

Juarez differs from other Mexican border towns in the newness of many of the shopping centers. You might think you're in the US in the crowded city streets and upscale strip malls. The trolley runs a circular route and covers the major points of interest.

The city **Cathedral**, *Plaza de Armas* (the main square) is worth a visit. The streets surrounding the plaza are closed to traffic and lined with vendors selling everything from household goods to curios.

The older **bars** are lined up along Avenida Juarez, a pedestrian street which begins at the international bridge and continues to the main square. This is where you will find the typical border-town diversions such as campy souvenirs and dusty bars that smell like tequila.

The **Juarez Racetrack**, *Avenida El Galgodromo, Tel 915/542-1942*, has greyhound racing all year long. The **Jockey Club** is a comfortable restaurant with a view of the track.

SHOPPING

The last stop on the trolley route in Juarez is the **City Market**, a new tourist market. In general prices are unnecessarily high, and much of the silver is not sterling. The shops just outside the market sell nice pottery, glassware and liquor for reasonable prices. *The City Market is on Avenida de 16 Septiembre, about one mile from the international bridge.*

If you are searching for high-end retail shopping, try the **Export Free Store**, *Avenida Juarez 114-A, Tel. 16/12-31-50. This duty free* store resembles those found in airports and caters to clientele shopping for liquor and tobacco; the store does not charge any Mexican tax. They clam to have the best prices on cigars, sunglasses and perfume. Of course, you are subject to the same alcohol and tobacco duties and restrictions when returning to the United States.

PRACTICAL INFORMATION

The **Juarez Tourist Bureau** can be reached by calling the office in Mexico, *Tel. 16/14-06-07 or 29-33-00*, or through the United States office, *Tel. 800/406-3491.*

INDEX

Abilene 24, 28, 174-176
Acuna (Mexico) 310, 314, 315
Airlines 53
Airports 53-54, see destination
    chapters
Alibates Flint Quarries National
    Monument 182
Alpine 327-330
Alamo 19, 37, 246, 258
Alamo (Texas) 294, 298
Allen's Landing (Houston) 201
Amarillo 13, 17, 22, 180-182
Anahuac National Wildlife Refuge
    67
Anderson 231
Angleton 218
Antiques 129, 211, 219
Aquarium Texas State, 280
Aransas Pass 283
Archaeology 17, 31, 236
Architecture 43, 159, 201-202,
    270-271
Armadillo 29
Astroworld 206
Athens (Texas) 26, 34, 238
Audobon Society 288
Austin 14, 16, 21, 24, 25, 33-34,
    88-111
    Arrivals & Departures 90
    Getting Around Town 90-91
    Nightlife & Entertainment 106-
        110
    Seeing the Sights 104-106
    Sports & Recreation 110
    Where to Eat 95-104
    Where to Stay 91-95
Austin, Stephen F. 37-38

Baffin Bay 284, 285
Baja Peninsula 354
Ballet
    Dallas 163
    Fort Worth 172
    Houston 207
Ballooning
    Festival 336
    National Scientific Facility 235
Balmorhea 327
Bandera 34, 142-144
Banking & Money 63
Barbecue 79
Baseball 70
Basketball 70, 267
Bats, Mexican Freetail 30, 107
Battleship Texas 44, 212
Beaches 67, 217, 277, 290-291
Bed & Breakfast 60-61
Baylor University 111
Baytown 195-196
Beaches 67, 217, 283, 290
Bears 29
Bean, Judge Roy 13, 316-317
Bible Belt 44
Big Bend National Park 20, 29, 314,
    330-335
Big Thicket 28, 218
Biking 66, 140, 210
Bird Watching 281, 288
Bison 30
Blanco 129
Bluebonnets 48
Bob cats 29
Bonnie and Clyde 45
Boomtowns 44
Boot Hill 343

Bowie, Jim 38
Bracketville 315-316
Brazoria 218
Brazos River 18
Brenham 18, 34, 222-225
Breweries 25, 84, 206, 221, 263, 274
Brownsville 20, 286-290
Bryan/College Station 229-231
Burton 226-227
Buffalo Gap 177
Bus Travel 54-55
Buffalo 179
Buffalo Soldiers 41-42
Butterflies, Monarch 30, 48

Cadillac Ranch 13, 181
Caddoan Mounds 31, 236
Calcutta (festival) 310
Caldwell 231-233
Camino Real 32, 37, 241, 246
Canton 165
Canyon Fest 350
Canyons
    Boquillas 331
    Caprock 28, 36, 179
    Copper (Mexico) 354
    Santa Elena 333
    Seminole 310, 314
Capitol, State 21, 105
Car Travel 55
Carnegie Libraries 43
Castroville 23, 32, 268-272
Cattle Drives 174
Caverns
    Kikapoo 316
    Longhorn 111
    Natural Bridge 125
Central Texas: see Hill Country
Chain Restaurants 81-82
Chamizal National Memorial 344
Chappell Hill 228-229
Chicanos 32
Chihuahuan Desert 20, 29, 327
Chihuahuan Desert Research
Institute 327
Chisholm Trail 42
Cinco de Mayo 32

Clear Lake Area 206
Climate 50
Columbus 218-220
Columbus Ships 280
Comfort 136-139
Conspiracy Museum 13
Copper Canyon, Mexico 20
Coronado, Francisco 36
Corpus Christi 19, 25, 275-283
Cost of Living and Travel 63
Courthouses, historical 43
Cowboys 32, 141, 263
Cowboy Gathering 304
Cowboy Poetry Gathering 328
Crockett, Davy 38
Cruises 54
Cypress Bayou 245

Dallas 13, 14, 18, 22, 145-166
    Arrivals & Departures 145-146
    Getting Around Town 148
    Nightlife & Entertainment
        163-164
    Seeing the Sights 159-163
    Shopping 165
    Sports & Recreation 164-165
    Where to Eat 152-159
    Where to Stay 149-152
Dallas Cowboys 70
Dallas Fort Worth International
    Airport 53, 145-146, 166
Davis Mountains 18, 326
Dealy Plaza 18, 160
Deep Ellum 18, 162
Del Rio 25, 310-315
Desert 20, 29
Devil's Backbone 117
Dinosaurs 35, 173
Diving, Scuba 281, 294
Dogwood Trails 233
Dublin, Texas 26

Easter Fires 130
Eco-Tourism 52, 314
El Paso 13, 14, 20, 23, 29, 335-355
    Arrivals & Departures 336
    Getting Around Town 337

Nightlife & Entertainment
350-351
Seeing the Sights 343-350
Shopping 352-354
Sports & Recreation 351-352
Where to Eat 340-343
Where to Stay 338-340
Enchanted Rock 16, 22, 134
Egypt, Texas 26
European Immigrants 32, 142, 221,
232, 269
Events, Major Annual 74-75

Ferries 57
First Thanksgiving 74, 335, 336, 336
Fisheries, Texas Freshwater Center
238
Fishing 69, 142, 268, 281, 285, 303,
314
Food Festivals 76-77
Football 70, 110, 352
Foreign Consulates 52-53
Forests 27
National 242
Fort Bliss 349
Fort Davis 324-327
Fort Sam Houston 264-265
Fort Stockton 321-323
Forts, US Frontier 42, 175, 288, 306,
316, 323, 324, 326, 335
Fort Worth 14, 24, 28, 166-174
Arrivals & Departures 166-167
Getting Around Town 167
Nightlife & Entertainment 172
Seeing the Sights 170
Sports & Recreation 173
Where to Eat 169-170
Where to Stay 167-169
Franklin Mountains 351
Fredericksburg 21, 130-135

Galleria, Dallas 165; Houston 211
Galveston 18, 22, 44, 214-218
Genealogy 49
Glen Rose 268
Goliad 274
Gonzales 274-275
Grapeland 236-237

Great Plains 28
Gruene 16, 125
Guadalupe Mountains 354
Guadalupe River 125
Guest Ranches 61
Gulf of Mexico 19, 70

Hardin, John Wesley 42
Harlingen 298
Health Concerns 64
Hell's Half-acre 17, 172
Hermann Park 71
Hickock, Wild Bill 42
Highways 56-57
Hiking 68
Hill Country 16, 35, 28, 87
Hill Country State Natural Area 67,
143
History 35-48
Holidays 64
Horseback Riding 67
Hotels and Motels 59
Houston 13, 14, 18, 22, 24-25,
184-214
Arrivals & Departures 186-187
Getting Around Town 188-190
Nightlife & Entertainment
206-208
Seeing the Sights 201-206
Shopping 211-212
Sports & Recreation 209-211
Where to Eat 196-201
Where to Stay 190-196
Houston Cotton Exchange 184
Houston, Sam 38, 40-41, 186
Hueco Tanks 31, 354
Hughes, Howard 44
Hunting 68, 309

Independence, Texas 227-228
Institute of Texas Cultures 263
Itineraries 24-26
Italy, Texas 26

Jacksonville 34, 236
Jefferson 243-245
Johnson, President Lyndon Baines
46, 64, 127

Johnson City 127-130
Juarez, Mexico 20, 355-357
Junction 307-301
Juneteenth 64

Kennedy, President John, F. 13
Kerrville 16, 139-142
Kerrville Folk Festival 75, 139
Kids, traveling with 71-73
Kimball Art Museum 171
Kingsville 20, 25, 284-286
King Ranch 20, 25, 284, 285, 286
King William District, San Antonio
    254, 261

LBJ Ranch 128
La Grange 220-222
Laguna Atacosta National Wildlife
    Refuge 289
Laguna Gloria Museum 106
Lajitas 331
Lake, Amistad 310, 314; Meredith
    182
Langtry 316-317
Laredo 23, 299-301
Latinos 32
Laughlin Air Force Base 310
Laws 65
Lexington, USS 280
Liberty 212
Lighthouse, Port Isabel 290
Llano 133
Llano Estacado Plain 28
London,Texas 26
Longhorn Steer 29
Los Ebanos 298
Lubbock 17, 177-180
Luckenbach 135
Lumberton 218

Major Events 74
Malls, Outlet 117, 127
Mardi Gras 215
Marfa Lights 13, 330
Market Square, Houston 184
Matamoros, Mexico 20, 25, 289, 294
McAllen 294-299

McDonald Observatory 20, 24, 304,
    324, 326-327
Mexico, travel to 52, 58-59
Mesquite 145
Meteor Crater, Odessa 319
Midland/Odessa 317-321
Mission 294-297
Missionaries 36, 310
Missions 20, 37
    El Paso 20, 344-347
    Grapeland 236-237
    San Antonio 19, 37, 246, 258,
        260-261
    San Augustine 242
Monahans Sandhills 320
Moody Gardens 217
Mount Alberta 120
Mountain Lions, 29
Movies 33
Museums 72
Music 32, 34
Musicals, outdoor 75, 350
Mustang Island 67, 283

NASA 46, 206
Nada, Texas 26
National Park, Lyndon Baines
    Johnson 128
National Forests: see Forests
National Seashore: see Padre Island
Native Americans 14, 19, 30-31,
    35-36, 179, 182, 346
New Braunfels 16, 28, 121-127
New Mexico 337, 354
New York, Texas 26
Nuevo Laredo, Mexico 299, 302-303

Odessa: see Midland
Old San Antonio Road (OSR): see
    Camino Real
Opera
    Dallas 163
    Fort Worth 172
    Houston 207
Opossum 30

Padre Island 277-278
National Seashore 67, 283
South Padre Island 20, 290-294
Palestine, Texas 233-237
Palo Duro Canyon 17, 28, 145
Pan Handle 28, 145
Panna Maria 274
Park Systems 61, 66-67, see State
Parks
Parks, Amusement 71, 116, 126,
206-207
Paris, Texas 26
Petroglyphs 306, 314
Planning Your Trip 50-62
Plano 145
Plantation, Twin Oaks 245
Population 14
Port Aransas 283
Port Isabel 290
Porter, William Sidney (O. Henry)
263
Prehistory 35
Presidio 334

Rattle Snakes 29
Rembrandt 316
Republic of the Rio Grande 39, 301
Republic of Texas 39-40, 218
Reynosa, Mexico 296-297
Rio Grande 27, 29, 304, 333
Rio Grande City 298
Rio Grande Valley 29, 286-303
Rio Hondo 289
River Walk, San Antonio 19, 247,
254-256, 260, 265-266
Rivers 27, 29, 125, 304
Road Runners 29
Rodeos 143, 172, 174, 186, 209, 247,
310, 336
Route 66 13, 17, 180, 183
Running 69
Rusk 237

San Angelo 304-307
San Angelo State University 304
San Antonio 19, 23-25, 246-268
Arrivals & Departures 247-248
Getting Around Town 248-249

Nightlife & Entertainment
265-266
Seeing the Sights 258
Sports & Recreation 267
Where to Eat 254-258
Where to Stay 249-254
San Augustine 241-243
San Augustine Plaza, Laredo 301
San Jacinto Battle 39
San Jacinto Day 64
San Jacinto Monument 212
San Marcos 114-118
San Ygnacio 303
Santa Ana National Wildlife Refuge
298
Santa Anna, Gen. 39
Scorpions 20
Sea World 71, 266
Seguin 272-275
Seminole Canyon 28, 67
Sisterdale 139
Six Flags of Texas 47
Six Flags Over Texas Amusement
Parks, Dallas 71 ;San Antonio 266
Solitario 333
Sonora 28
South by Southwest Festival (SXSW)
88
South Padre Island 290-294
Southern Cooking 78
Southern Pacific Railroad 42
Southfork Ranch 166
Southwest Texas State University 114
Spanish Conquest 36
Spanish in Texas 32, 36, 47, 301, 310
Spectator Sports 70
Spindletop 43
Sports 66-70; see destination
chapters
State Fair 75
State Natural Area, Hill Country 268
State Parks
Abilene 176
Balmorhea 327
Caddoan Mounds 31, 236
Caprock Canyon 179
Cedar Hill 67
Davis Mountains 326

Dinosaur Valley 173
Falcon 303
Galveston Island 217
Kreische Brewery 221
Lyndon Baines Johnson 128
Lubbock Lake 31
McKinney Falls 66
Mission Tejas 237
Mustang Island 67, 283
Pedernales Falls 128
San Jacinto 212
San Angelo 304
Seminole Canyon 67, 314
Texas State Railroad 236
Tyler 67, 241
Village Creek 218
Washington-on-the-Brazos 225, 228
State Symbols 48
Stockyards 170
Stonewall 34
Study Butte 331
Sul Ross University 328
Sundance Square 172
Symphony
   Dallas 163
   Fort Worth 172
   Houston 207

Tarantulas 30
Taxes 65
Telegrams 65
Temple 34
Terlingua 331, 334
Tex-Mex food 80
Texas A & M 70, 229, 230
Texas Department of Health 64
Texas Department of Transportation 50
Texas Instruments 46
Texas Medical Center 202
Texas Original 300 38, 227
Texas Parks and Wildlife Department 52, 62, 68, 69
Texas Rangers 38, 262, 335
Texas Rangers Musuem 113
Texas Tech University 35, 177

Thanksgiving Square 159
Theme Parks 71
Tigua Indian Reservation 346
Time 65
Timeline 41
Tours, Adventure 334; Historic 189, 219, 244, 275, 287, 321; Mexico, 354; see also destination chapters
Train travel 54
Treaty of Guadalupe Hidalgo 39
Trains (steam) 110, 236
Travel Specialists 51
Tubing 125
Tyler 238-241

University of Texas, at Austin 16, 70, 110; at Brownsville 289
Utopia, Texas 26
Uvalde 316

Waco 111-113
Washington-on-the-Brazos 72, 225, 228
Water Sports 70
Weather 50-51
Weimar, Texas, 26
Whooping Cranes 30
Wild Flower Loop 135
Wildcatters 44
Wildlife 29-30
Wildlife Refuges 30, 67, 173, 180, 268, 288, 289, 298
Wimberly 118-121
Wineries 25, 84, 139, 180, 225, 230, 313, 323
Witte Museum, San Antonio 262
Woodlands 27

XIT Ranch 17, 88

Youth Hostels 61

Zoos
   Brownsville 162, 288
   Dallas 162
   El Paso 349
   Fort Worth 171
   Houston 204

THINGS CHANGE!

Phone numbers, prices, addresses, quality of food, etc, all change. If you come across any new information, we'd appreciate hearing from you. No item is too small! Drop us an e-mail note at: Jopenroad@aol.com, or write us at:

Texas Guide
Open Road Publishing, P.O. Box 284
Cold Spring Harbor, NY 11724

TRAVEL NOTES

TRAVEL NOTES

TRAVEL NOTES